Garth Ennis   Darick Robertson

The BOYS ™

volume three: GOOD FOR THE SOUL

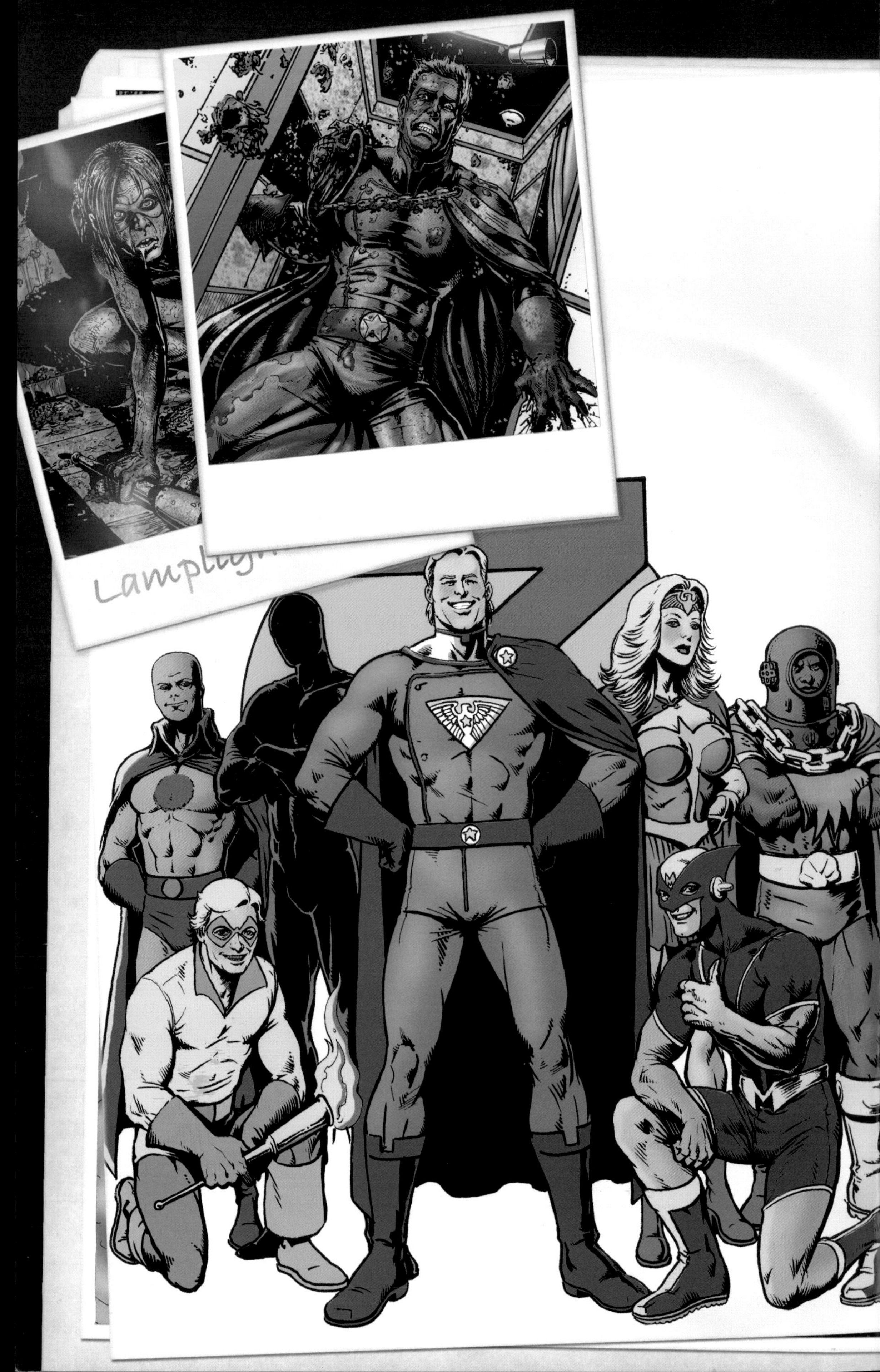
Lamplig

The BOYS ™

volume three: GOOD FOR THE SOUL

Written by:
GARTH ENNIS

Lettered by:
SIMON BOWLAND

Illustrated by:
DARICK ROBERTSON

Colored by:
TONY AVIÑA

Additional inks by:
MATT JACOBS

Covers by:
DARICK ROBERTSON
& TONY AVIÑA

The Boys created by:
GARTH ENNIS & DARICK ROBERTSON

Collects issues fifteen through twenty-two of The Boys,
originally published by Dynamite Entertainment.

Trade Design By: JASON ULLMEYER

THE BOYS™ VOLUME 3: GOOD FOR THE SOUL
ISBN: 9781848562738

Published by Titan Books, a division of Titan Publishing Group Ltd., 144 Southwark Street, London SE1 0UP. Contains materials originally published in The Boys™ #15-22. Copyright © 2008 Spitfire Productions Ltd. and Darick Robertson. All Rights Reserved. THE BOYS, all characters, the distinctive likenesses thereof and all related elements are trademarks of Spitfire Productions, Ltd. and Darick Robertson. DYNAMITE, DYNAMITE ENTERTAINMENT and its logo are ® & © 2008 DFI. All names, characters, events, and locales in this publication are entirely fictional. Any resemblance to actual persons (living or dead), events or places, without satiric intent, is coincidental. No portion of this book may be reproduced by any means (digital or print) without the written permission of the copyright holders except for review purposes. A CIP catalogue record for this book is available from the British Library.

Printed in Spain.

First published: April 2009
2 4 6 8 10 9 7 5 3 1

What did you think of this book? We love to hear from our readers. Please email us at readerfeedback@titanemail.com, or write to us at the above address.

To receive advance information, news, competitions and exclusive Titan offers online, please register as a member by clicking the "sign up" button at our website:
www.titanbooks.com

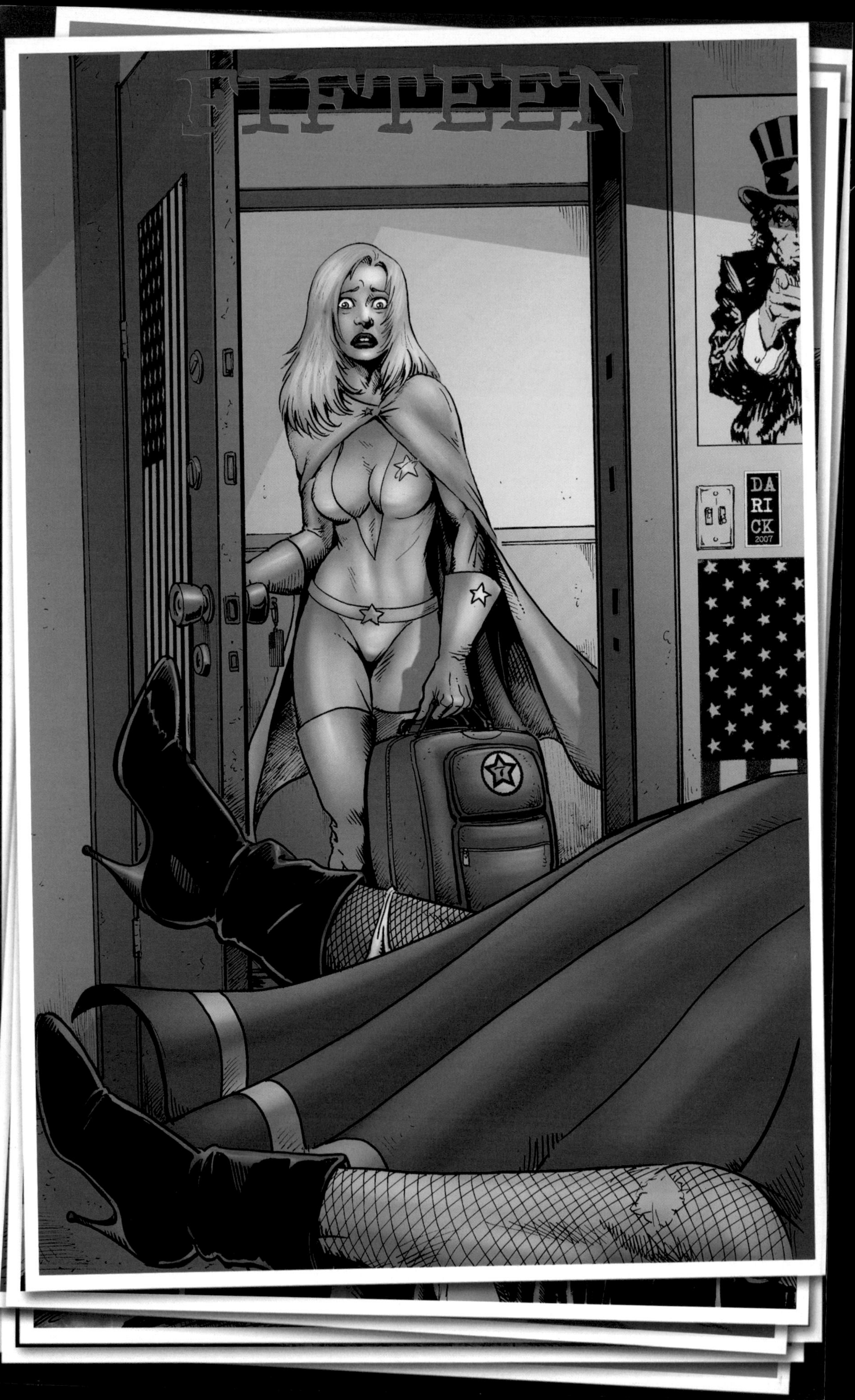
FIFTEEN
DARICK 2007

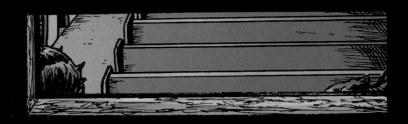

GOOD FOR THE SOUL
part one

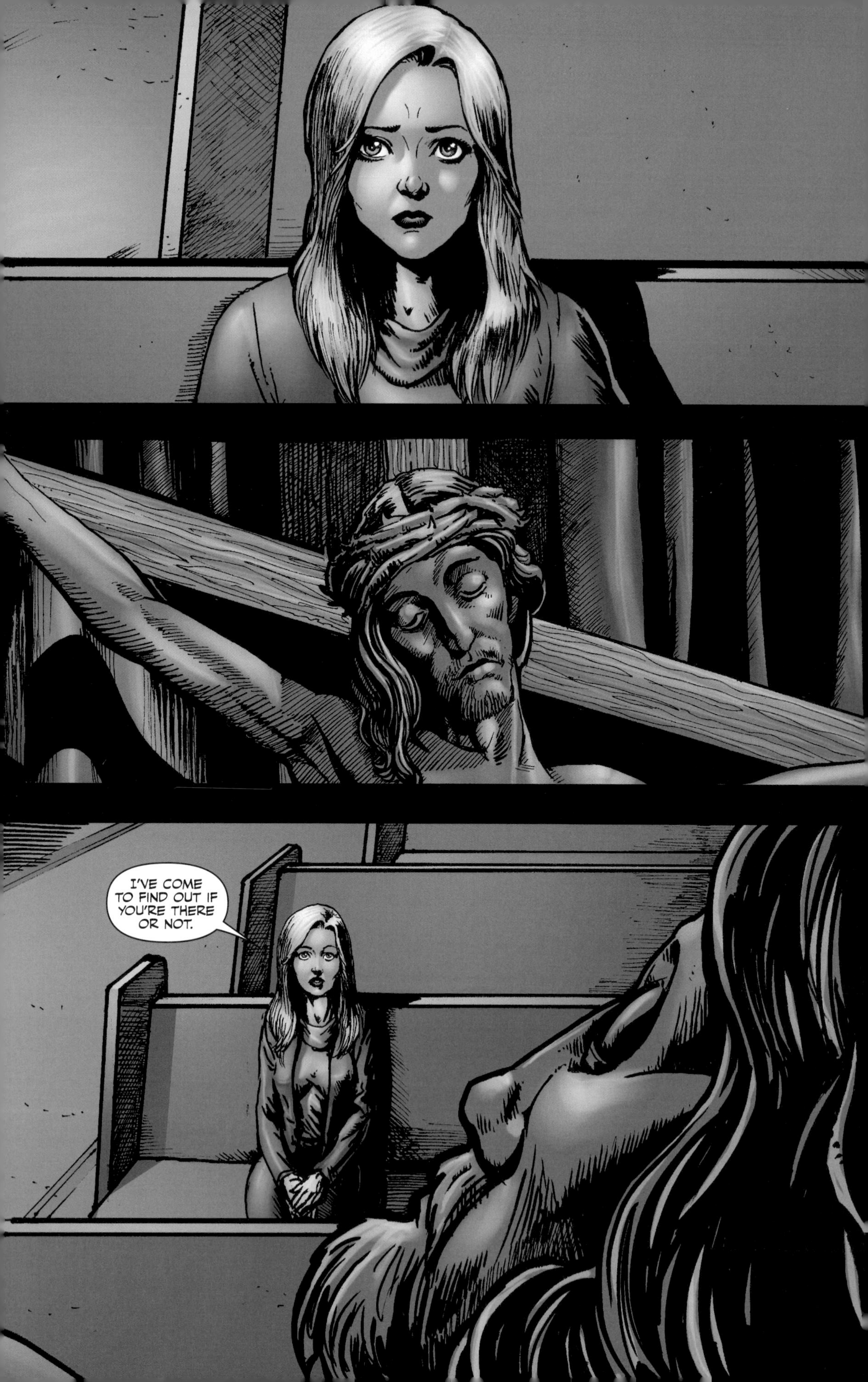
I'VE COME TO FIND OUT IF YOU'RE THERE OR NOT.

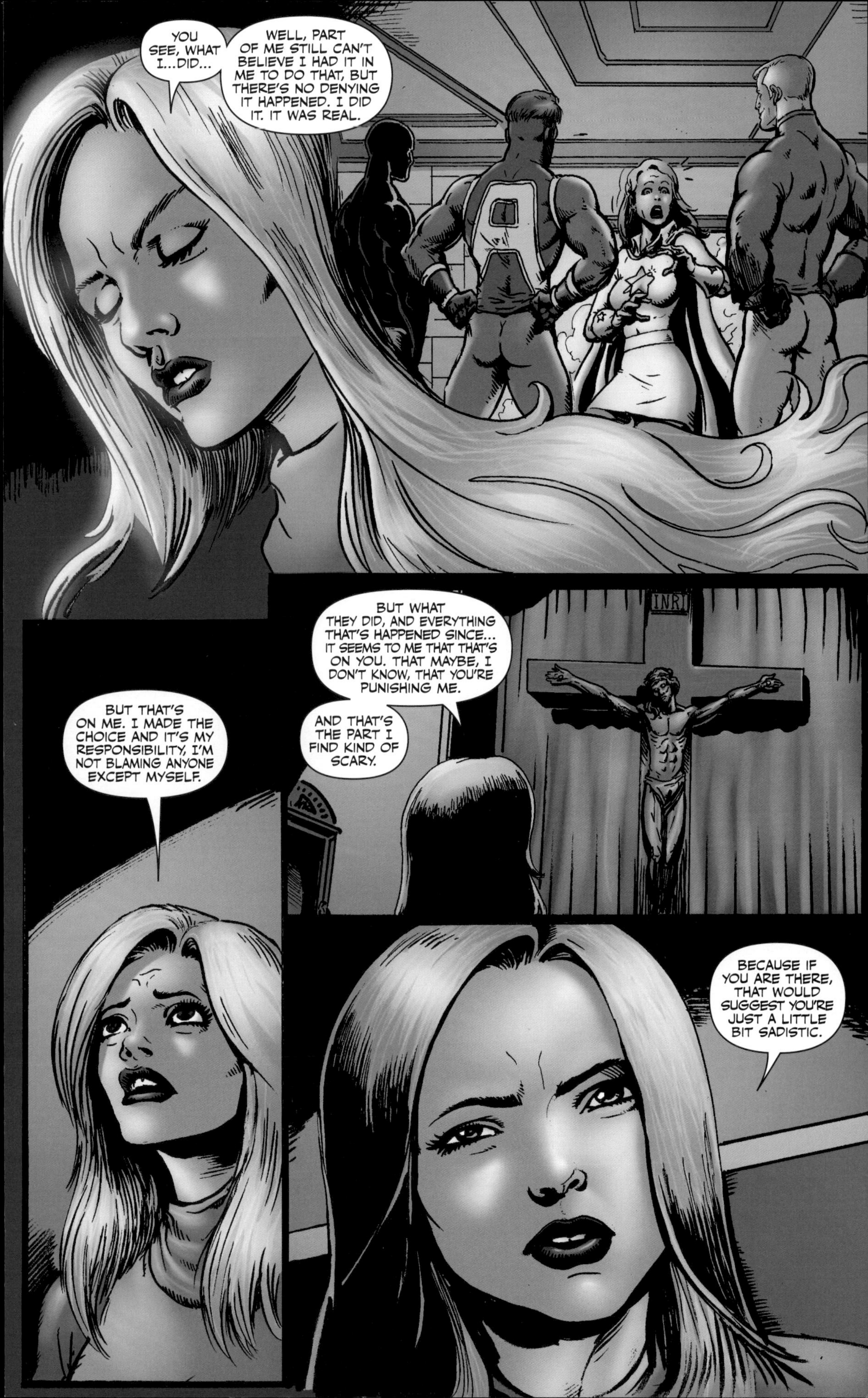
YOU SEE, WHAT I...DID...
WELL, PART OF ME STILL CAN'T BELIEVE I HAD IT IN ME TO DO THAT, BUT THERE'S NO DENYING IT HAPPENED. I DID IT. IT WAS REAL.
BUT THAT'S ON ME. I MADE THE CHOICE AND IT'S MY RESPONSIBILITY, I'M NOT BLAMING ANYONE EXCEPT MYSELF.
BUT WHAT THEY DID, AND EVERYTHING THAT'S HAPPENED SINCE... IT SEEMS TO ME THAT THAT'S ON YOU. THAT MAYBE, I DON'T KNOW, THAT YOU'RE PUNISHING ME.
AND THAT'S THE PART I FIND KIND OF SCARY.
INRI
BECAUSE IF YOU ARE THERE, THAT WOULD SUGGEST YOU'RE JUST A LITTLE BIT SADISTIC.

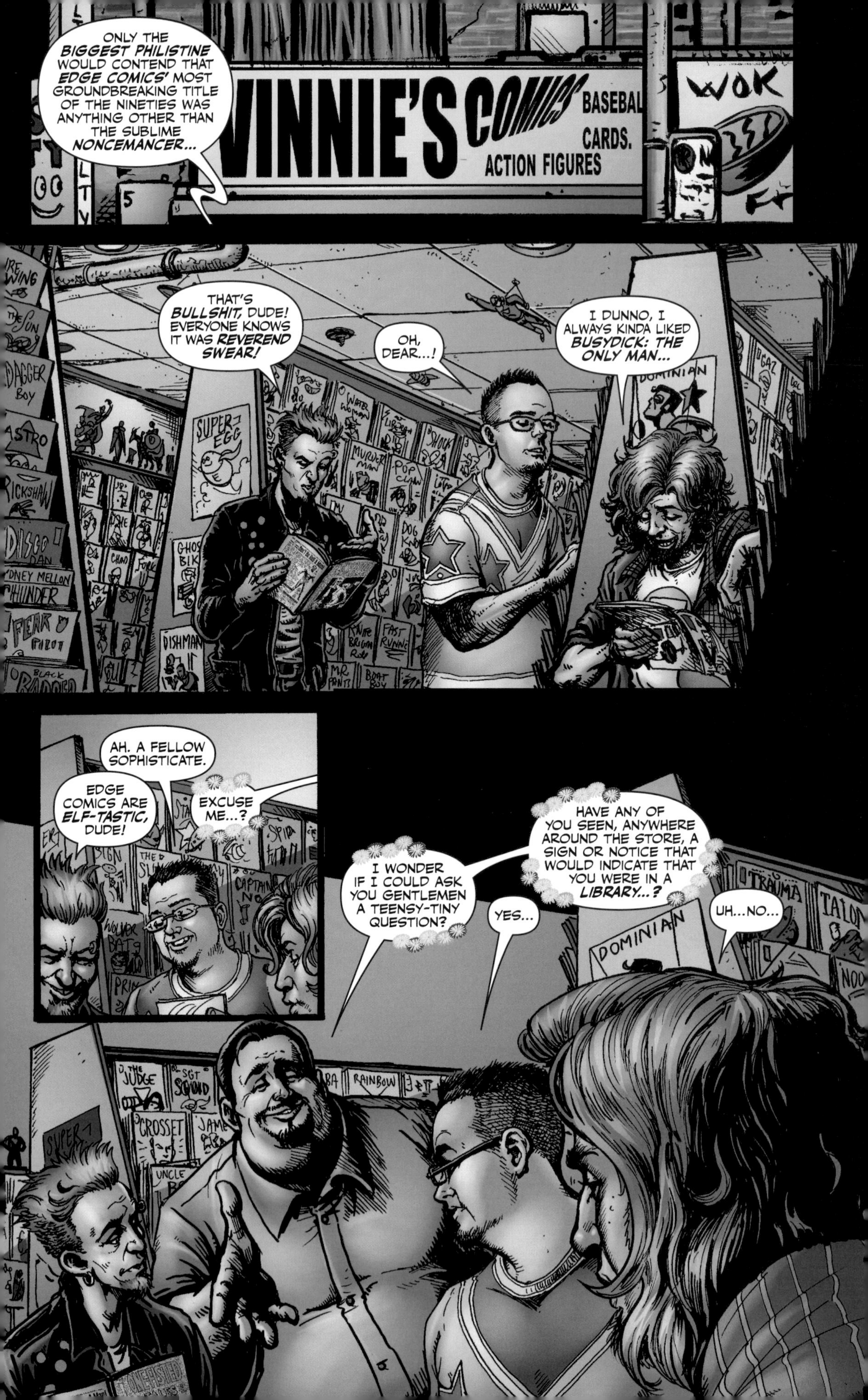
ONLY THE BIGGEST PHILISTINE WOULD CONTEND THAT EDGE COMICS' MOST GROUNDBREAKING TITLE OF THE NINETIES WAS ANYTHING OTHER THAN THE SUBLIME NONCEMANCER...
VINNIE'S COMICS
BASEBALL CARDS.
ACTION FIGURES
WOK
THAT'S BULLSHIT, DUDE! EVERYONE KNOWS IT WAS REVEREND SWEAR!
OH, DEAR...!
I DUNNO, I ALWAYS KINDA LIKED BUSYDICK: THE ONLY MAN...
AH. A FELLOW SOPHISTICATE.
EDGE COMICS ARE ELF-TASTIC, DUDE!
EXCUSE ME...?
I WONDER IF I COULD ASK YOU GENTLEMEN A TEENSY-TINY QUESTION?
YES...
HAVE ANY OF YOU SEEN, ANYWHERE AROUND THE STORE, A SIGN OR NOTICE THAT WOULD INDICATE THAT YOU WERE IN A LIBRARY...?
UH...NO...

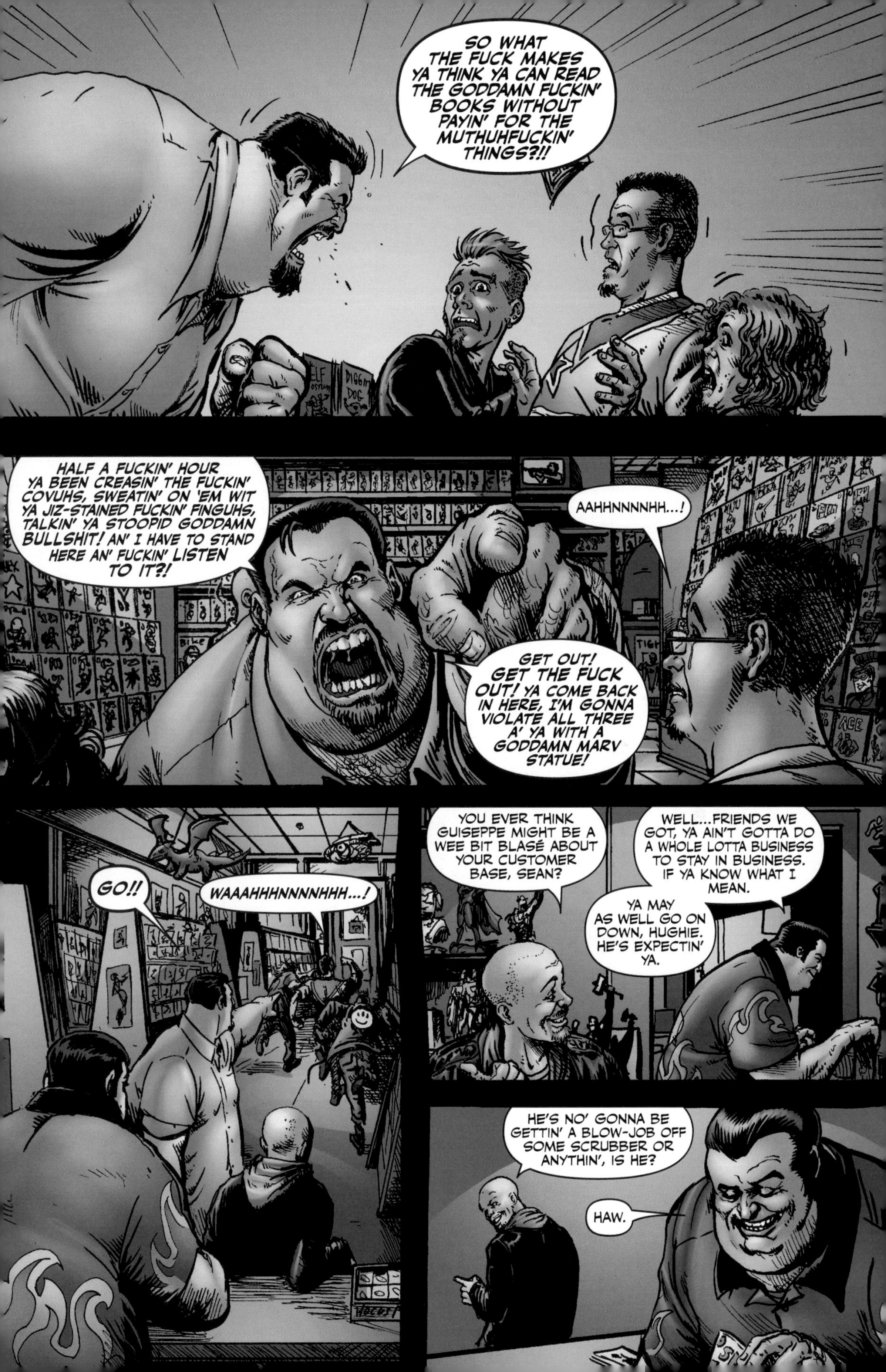
SO WHAT THE FUCK MAKES YA THINK YA CAN READ THE GODDAMN FUCKIN' BOOKS WITHOUT PAYIN' FOR THE MUTHUHFUCKIN' THINGS?!!
HALF A FUCKIN' HOUR YA BEEN CREASIN' THE FUCKIN' COVUHS, SWEATIN' ON 'EM WIT YA JIZ-STAINED FUCKIN' FINGUHS, TALKIN' YA STOOPID GODDAMN BULLSHIT! AN' I HAVE TO STAND HERE AN' FUCKIN' LISTEN TO IT?!
AAHHNNNNHH...!
GET OUT! GET THE FUCK OUT! YA COME BACK IN HERE, I'M GONNA VIOLATE ALL THREE A' YA WITH A GODDAMN MARV STATUE!
GO!!
WAAAHHHNNNNHHH...!
YOU EVER THINK GUISEPPE MIGHT BE A WEE BIT BLASÉ ABOUT YOUR CUSTOMER BASE, SEAN?
WELL...FRIENDS WE GOT, YA AIN'T GOTTA DO A WHOLE LOTTA BUSINESS TO STAY IN BUSINESS. IF YA KNOW WHAT I MEAN.
YA MAY AS WELL GO ON DOWN, HUGHIE. HE'S EXPECTIN' YA.
HE'S NO' GONNA BE GETTIN' A BLOW-JOB OFF SOME SCRUBBER OR ANYTHIN', IS HE?
HAW.

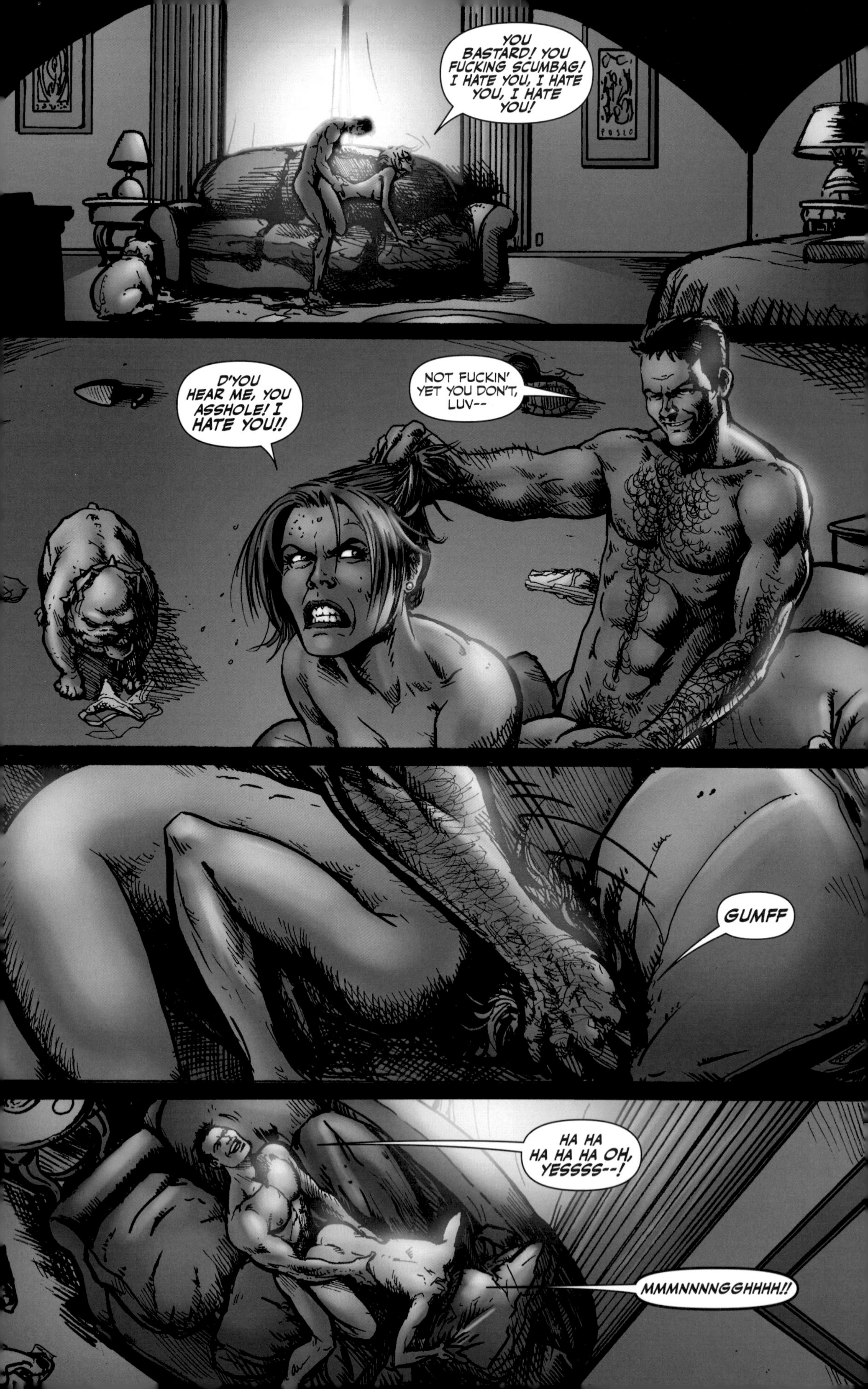
YOU BASTARD! YOU FUCKING SCUMBAG! I HATE YOU, I HATE YOU, I HATE YOU!
D'YOU HEAR ME, YOU ASSHOLE! I HATE YOU!!
NOT FUCKIN' YET YOU DON'T, LUV--
GUMFF
HA HA HA HA HA OH, YESSSS--!
MMMNNNNGGHHHH!!

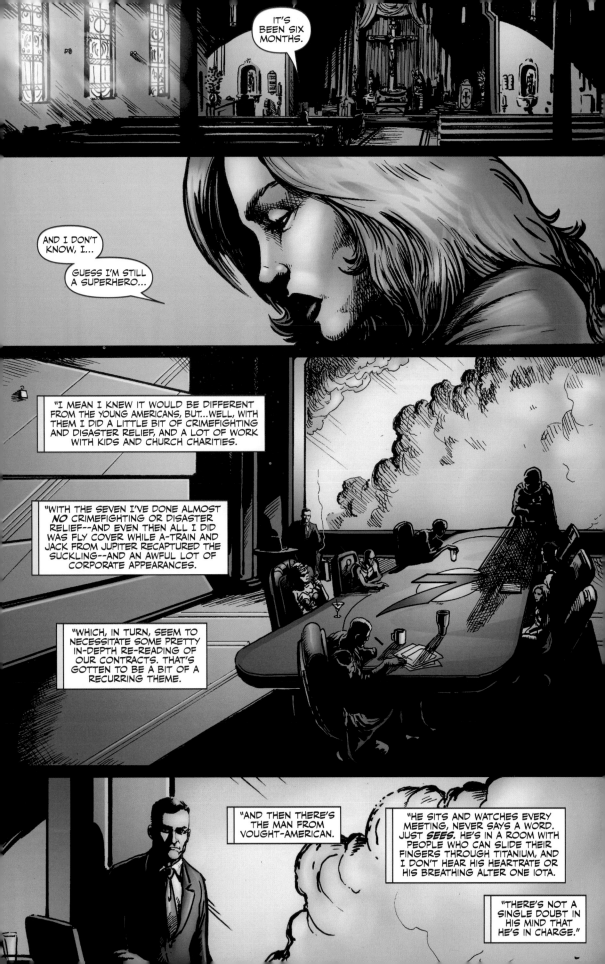

IT'S BEEN SIX MONTHS.

AND I DON'T KNOW, I...

GUESS I'M STILL A SUPERHERO...

"I MEAN I KNEW IT WOULD BE DIFFERENT FROM THE YOUNG AMERICANS, BUT...WELL, WITH THEM I DID A LITTLE BIT OF CRIMEFIGHTING AND DISASTER RELIEF, AND A LOT OF WORK WITH KIDS AND CHURCH CHARITIES."

"WITH THE SEVEN I'VE DONE ALMOST *NO* CRIMEFIGHTING OR DISASTER RELIEF--AND EVEN THEN ALL I DID WAS FLY COVER WHILE A-TRAIN AND JACK FROM JUPITER RECAPTURED THE SUCKLING--AND AN AWFUL LOT OF CORPORATE APPEARANCES."

"WHICH, IN TURN, SEEM TO NECESSITATE SOME PRETTY IN-DEPTH RE-READING OF OUR CONTRACTS. THAT'S GOTTEN TO BE A BIT OF A RECURRING THEME."

"AND THEN THERE'S THE MAN FROM VOUGHT-AMERICAN."

"HE SITS AND WATCHES EVERY MEETING, NEVER SAYS A WORD. JUST *SEES*. HE'S IN A ROOM WITH PEOPLE WHO CAN SLIDE THEIR FINGERS THROUGH TITANIUM, AND I DON'T HEAR HIS HEARTRATE OR HIS BREATHING ALTER ONE IOTA."

"THERE'S NOT A SINGLE DOUBT IN HIS MIND THAT HE'S IN CHARGE."

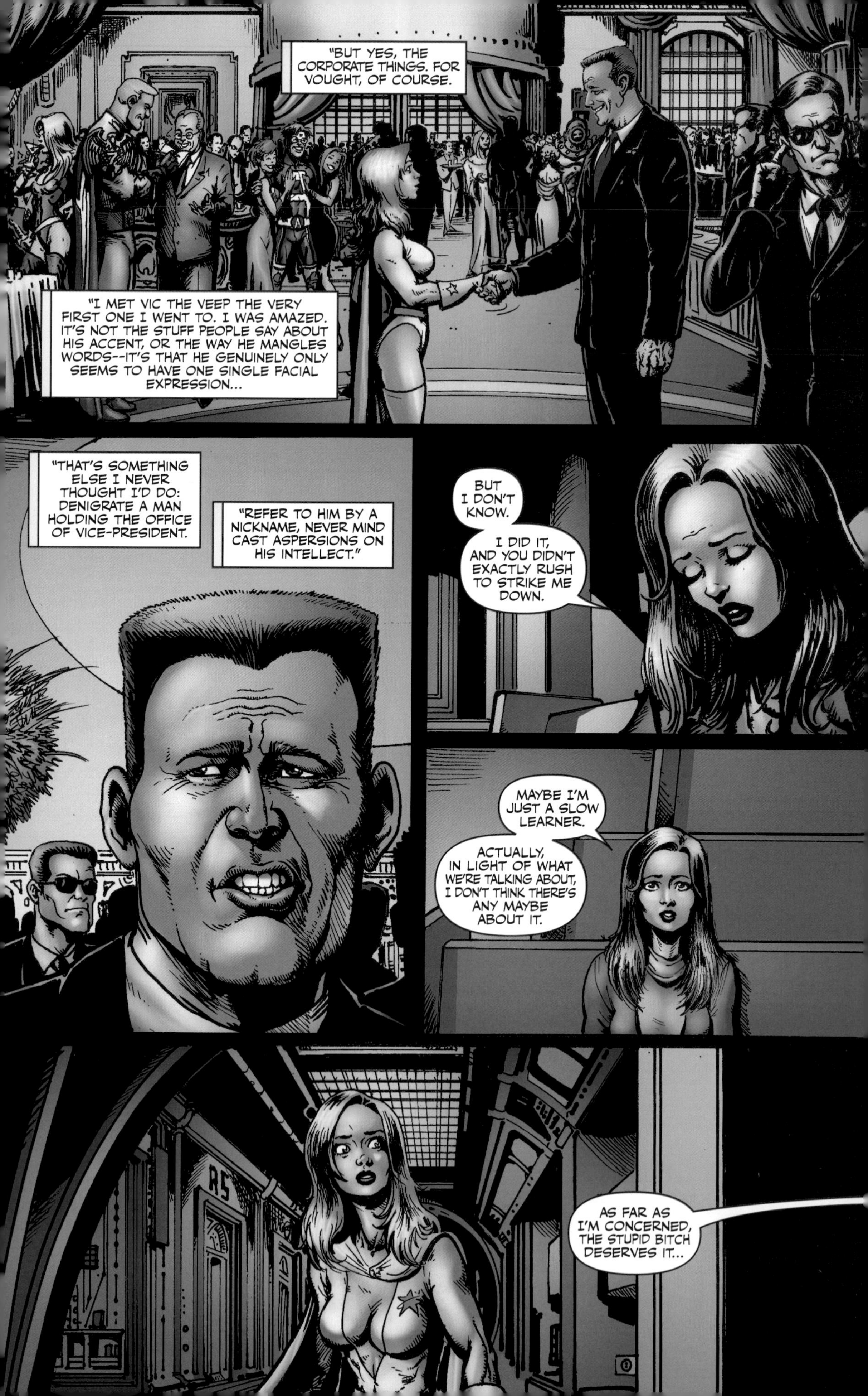
"BUT YES, THE CORPORATE THINGS. FOR VOUGHT, OF COURSE.
"I MET VIC THE VEEP THE VERY FIRST ONE I WENT TO. I WAS AMAZED. IT'S NOT THE STUFF PEOPLE SAY ABOUT HIS ACCENT, OR THE WAY HE MANGLES WORDS--IT'S THAT HE GENUINELY ONLY SEEMS TO HAVE ONE SINGLE FACIAL EXPRESSION...
"THAT'S SOMETHING ELSE I NEVER THOUGHT I'D DO: DENIGRATE A MAN HOLDING THE OFFICE OF VICE-PRESIDENT.
"REFER TO HIM BY A NICKNAME, NEVER MIND CAST ASPERSIONS ON HIS INTELLECT."
BUT I DON'T KNOW.
I DID IT, AND YOU DIDN'T EXACTLY RUSH TO STRIKE ME DOWN.
MAYBE I'M JUST A SLOW LEARNER.
ACTUALLY, IN LIGHT OF WHAT WE'RE TALKING ABOUT, I DON'T THINK THERE'S ANY MAYBE ABOUT IT.
AS FAR AS I'M CONCERNED, THE STUPID BITCH DESERVES IT...

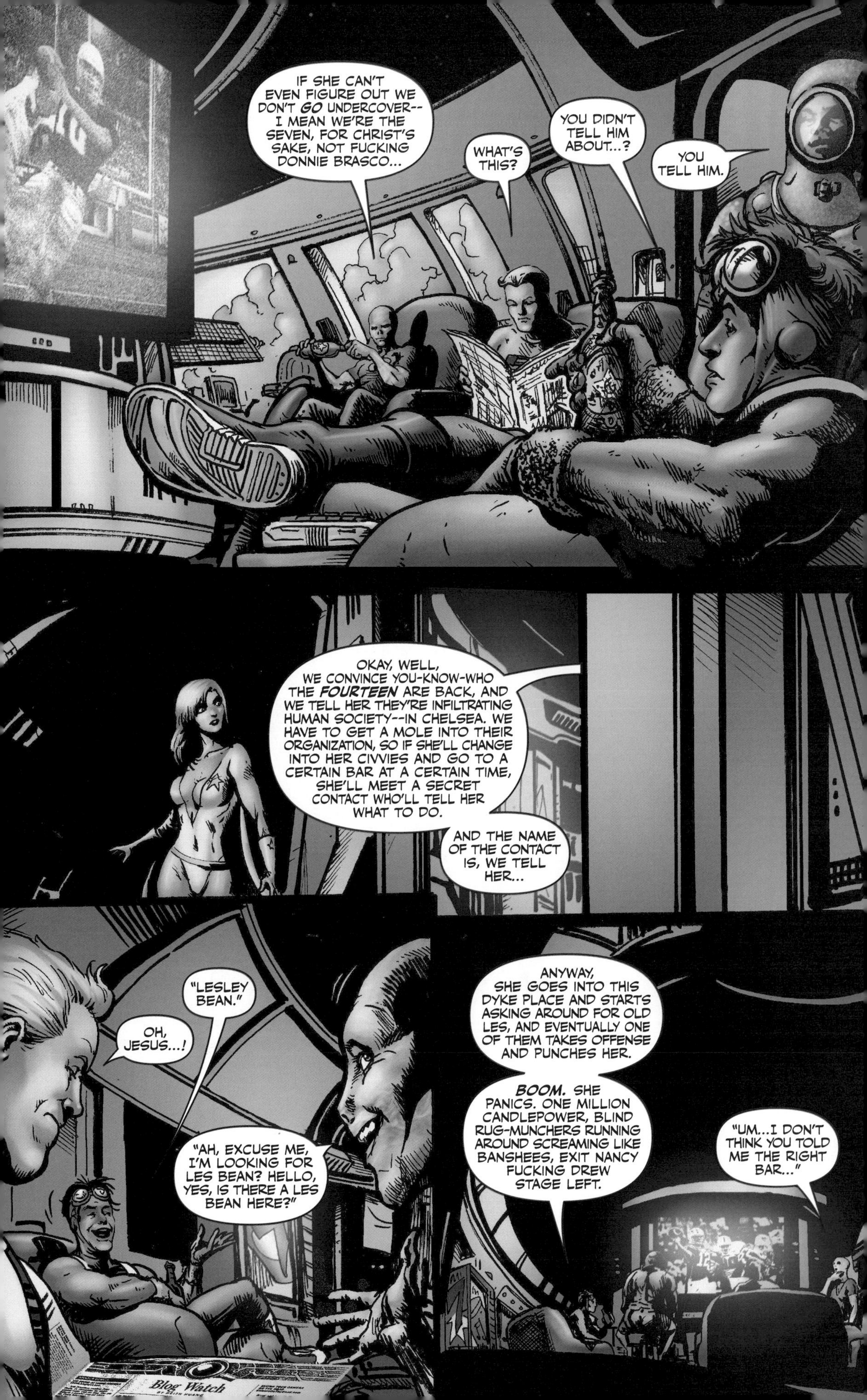
IF SHE CAN'T EVEN FIGURE OUT WE DON'T GO UNDERCOVER-- I MEAN WE'RE THE SEVEN, FOR CHRIST'S SAKE, NOT FUCKING DONNIE BRASCO...
WHAT'S THIS?
YOU DIDN'T TELL HIM ABOUT...?
YOU TELL HIM.
OKAY, WELL, WE CONVINCE YOU-KNOW-WHO THE FOURTEEN ARE BACK, AND WE TELL HER THEY'RE INFILTRATING HUMAN SOCIETY--IN CHELSEA. WE HAVE TO GET A MOLE INTO THEIR ORGANIZATION, SO IF SHE'LL CHANGE INTO HER CIVVIES AND GO TO A CERTAIN BAR AT A CERTAIN TIME, SHE'LL MEET A SECRET CONTACT WHO'LL TELL HER WHAT TO DO.
AND THE NAME OF THE CONTACT IS, WE TELL HER...
"LESLEY BEAN."
OH, JESUS...!
"AH, EXCUSE ME, I'M LOOKING FOR LES BEAN? HELLO, YES, IS THERE A LES BEAN HERE?"
ANYWAY, SHE GOES INTO THIS DYKE PLACE AND STARTS ASKING AROUND FOR OLD LES, AND EVENTUALLY ONE OF THEM TAKES OFFENSE AND PUNCHES HER.
BOOM. SHE PANICS. ONE MILLION CANDLEPOWER, BLIND RUG-MUNCHERS RUNNING AROUND SCREAMING LIKE BANSHEES, EXIT NANCY FUCKING DREW STAGE LEFT.
"UM...I DON'T THINK YOU TOLD ME THE RIGHT BAR..."
Blog Watch

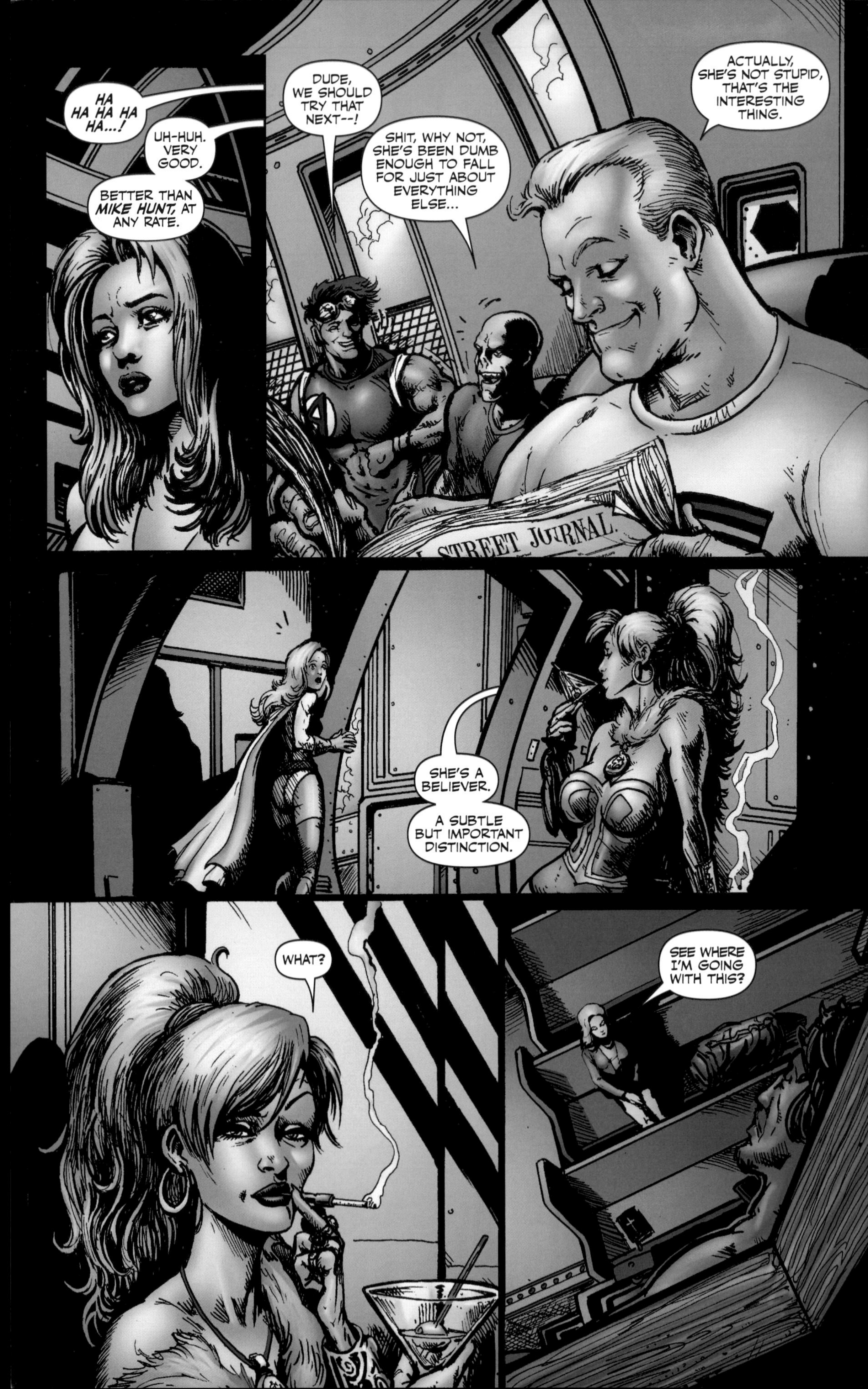
HA HA HA HA HA...!
UH-HUH. VERY GOOD.
BETTER THAN *MIKE HUNT,* AT ANY RATE.
DUDE, WE SHOULD TRY THAT NEXT--!
SHIT, WHY NOT, SHE'S BEEN DUMB ENOUGH TO FALL FOR JUST ABOUT EVERYTHING ELSE...
ACTUALLY, SHE'S NOT STUPID, THAT'S THE INTERESTING THING.
STREET JOURNAL
SHE'S A BELIEVER.
A SUBTLE BUT IMPORTANT DISTINCTION.
WHAT?
SEE WHERE I'M GOING WITH THIS?

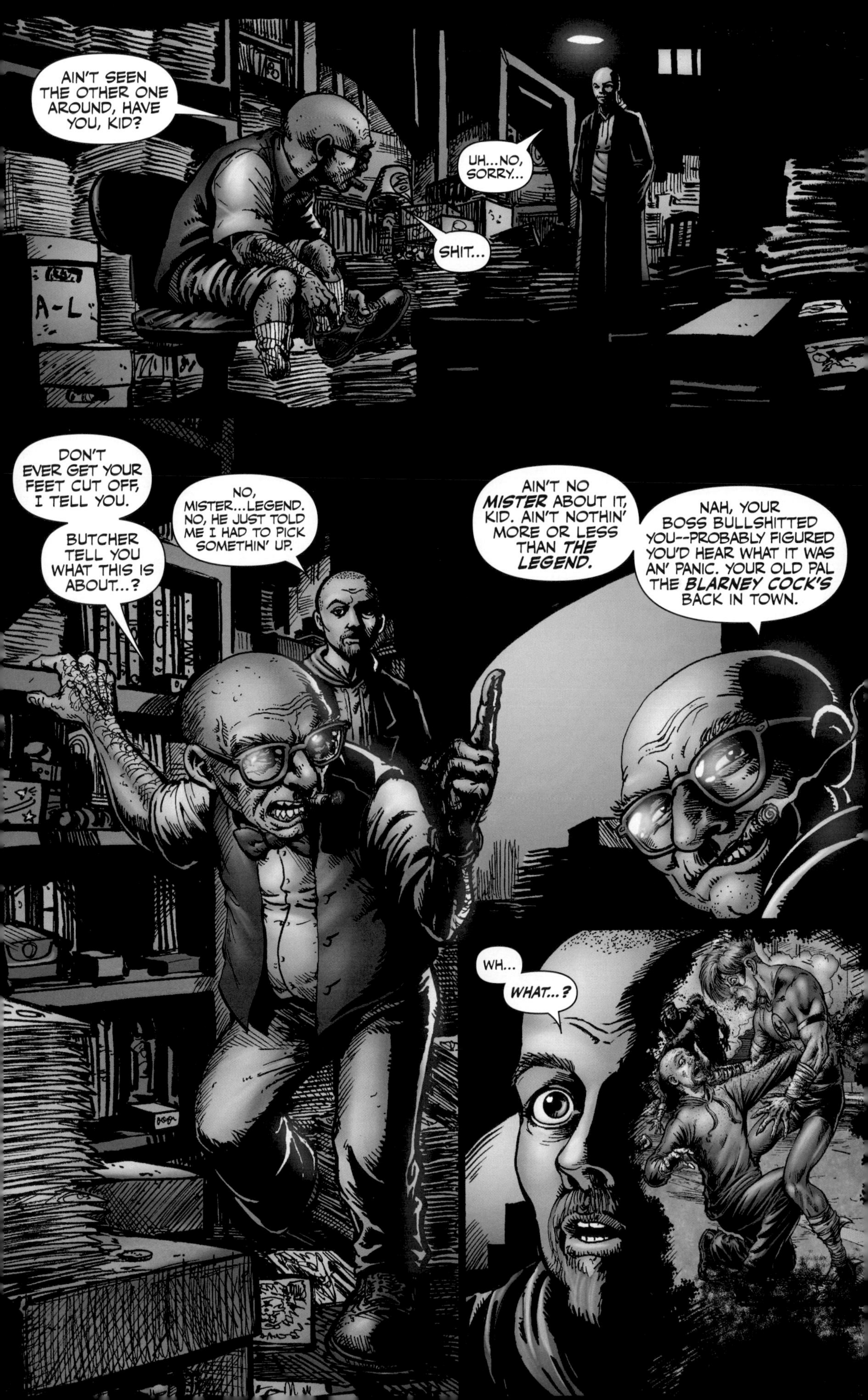
AIN'T SEEN THE OTHER ONE AROUND, HAVE YOU, KID?
UH...NO, SORRY...
SHIT...
DON'T EVER GET YOUR FEET CUT OFF, I TELL YOU.
BUTCHER TELL YOU WHAT THIS IS ABOUT...?
NO, MISTER...LEGEND. NO, HE JUST TOLD ME I HAD TO PICK SOMETHIN' UP.
AIN'T NO MISTER ABOUT IT, KID. AIN'T NOTHIN' MORE OR LESS THAN THE LEGEND.
NAH, YOUR BOSS BULLSHITTED YOU--PROBABLY FIGURED YOU'D HEAR WHAT IT WAS AN' PANIC. YOUR OLD PAL THE BLARNEY COCK'S BACK IN TOWN.
WH...
WHAT...?

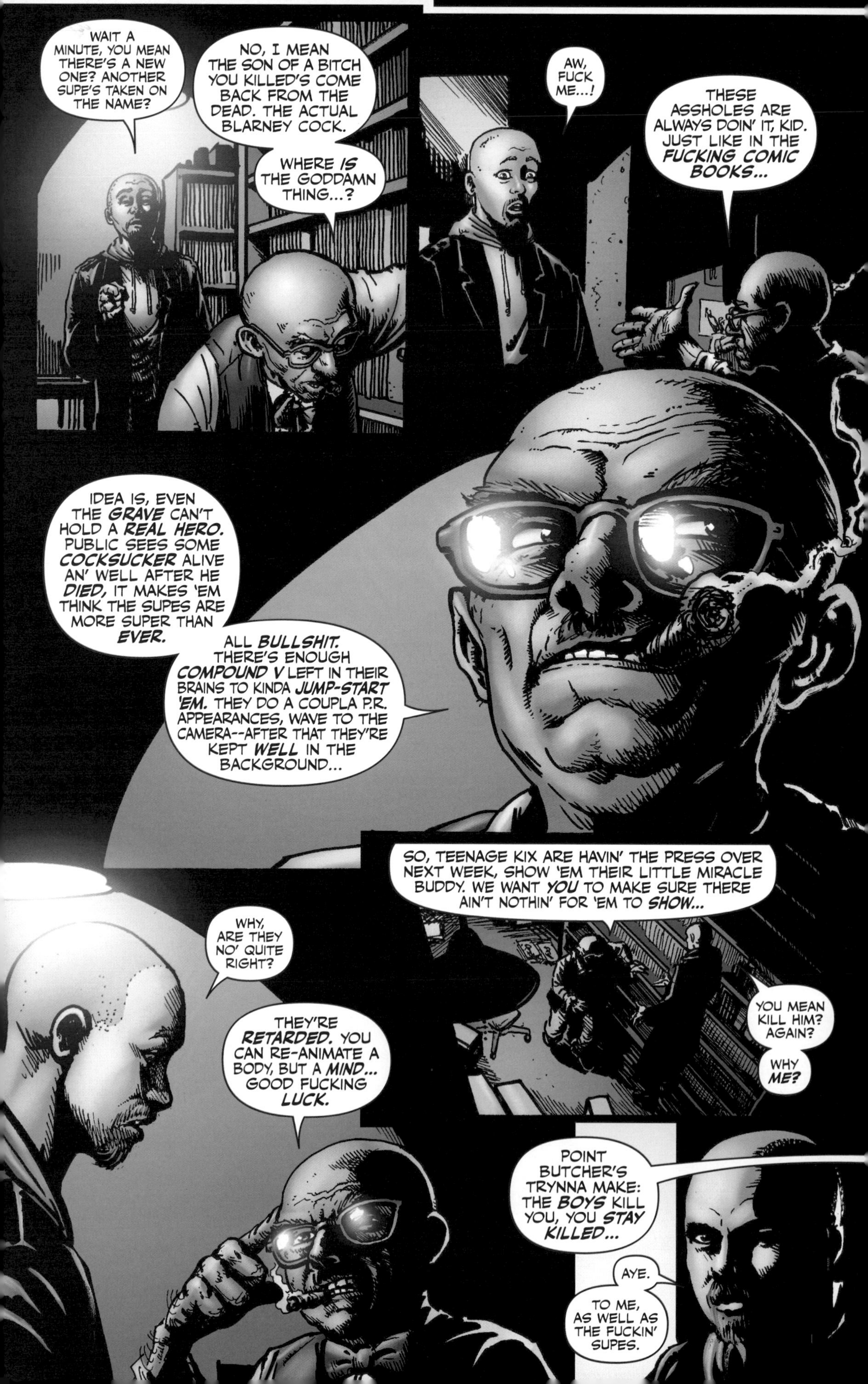
WAIT A MINUTE, YOU MEAN THERE'S A NEW ONE? ANOTHER SUPE'S TAKEN ON THE NAME?
NO, I MEAN THE SON OF A BITCH YOU KILLED'S COME BACK FROM THE DEAD. THE ACTUAL BLARNEY COCK.
WHERE IS THE GODDAMN THING...?
AW, FUCK ME...!
THESE ASSHOLES ARE ALWAYS DOIN' IT, KID. JUST LIKE IN THE FUCKING COMIC BOOKS...
IDEA IS, EVEN THE GRAVE CAN'T HOLD A REAL HERO. PUBLIC SEES SOME COCKSUCKER ALIVE AN' WELL AFTER HE DIED, IT MAKES 'EM THINK THE SUPES ARE MORE SUPER THAN EVER.
ALL BULLSHIT. THERE'S ENOUGH COMPOUND V LEFT IN THEIR BRAINS TO KINDA JUMP-START 'EM. THEY DO A COUPLA P.R. APPEARANCES, WAVE TO THE CAMERA--AFTER THAT THEY'RE KEPT WELL IN THE BACKGROUND...
SO, TEENAGE KIX ARE HAVIN' THE PRESS OVER NEXT WEEK, SHOW 'EM THEIR LITTLE MIRACLE BUDDY. WE WANT YOU TO MAKE SURE THERE AIN'T NOTHIN' FOR 'EM TO SHOW...
YOU MEAN KILL HIM? AGAIN?
WHY ME?
WHY, ARE THEY NO' QUITE RIGHT?
THEY'RE RETARDED. YOU CAN RE-ANIMATE A BODY, BUT A MIND... GOOD FUCKING LUCK.
POINT BUTCHER'S TRYNNA MAKE: THE BOYS KILL YOU, YOU STAY KILLED...
AYE.
TO ME, AS WELL AS THE FUCKIN' SUPES.

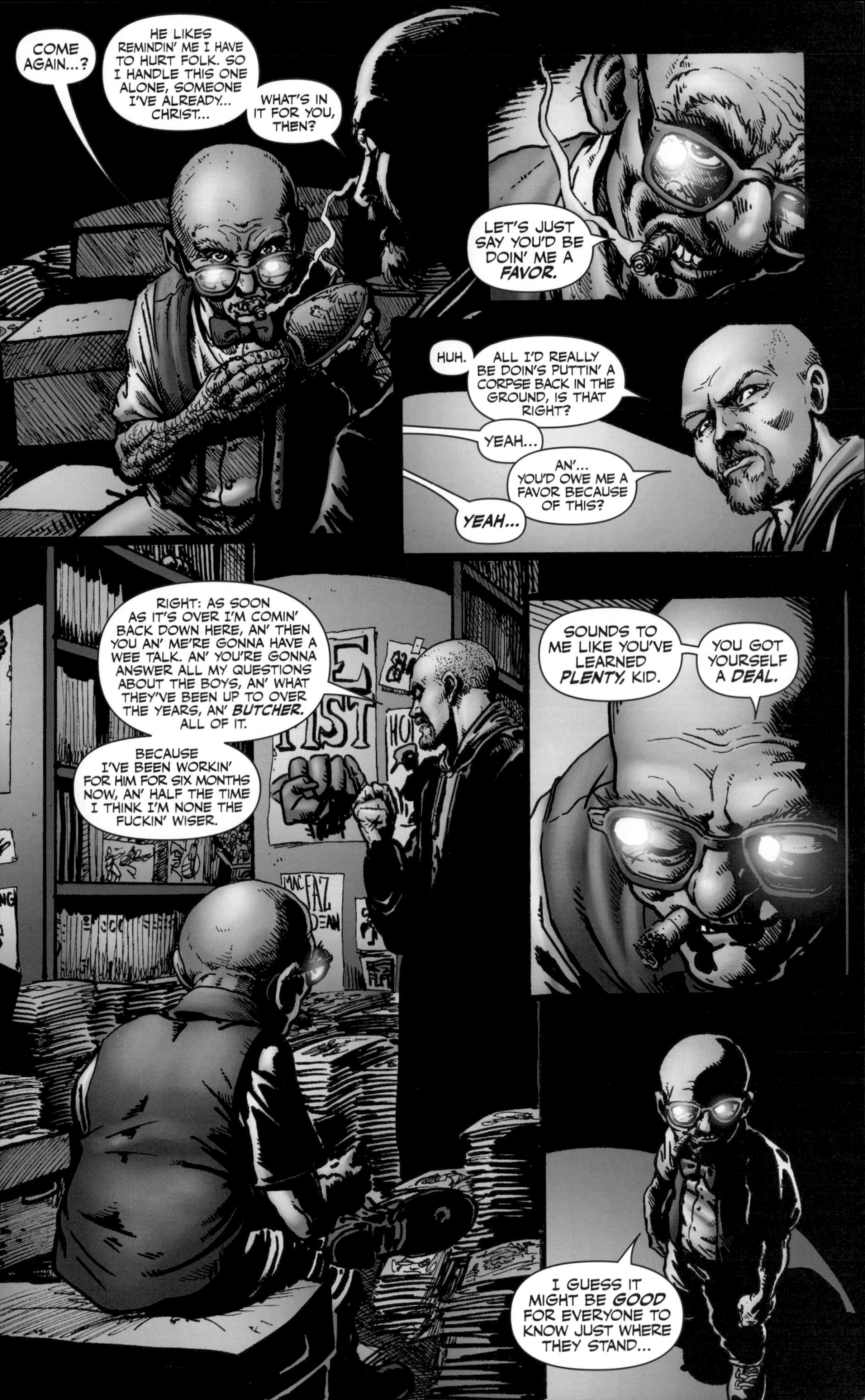
COME AGAIN...?
HE LIKES REMINDIN' ME I HAVE TO HURT FOLK. SO I HANDLE THIS ONE ALONE, SOMEONE I'VE ALREADY... CHRIST...
WHAT'S IN IT FOR YOU, THEN?
LET'S JUST SAY YOU'D BE DOIN' ME A FAVOR.
HUH.
ALL I'D REALLY BE DOIN'S PUTTIN' A CORPSE BACK IN THE GROUND, IS THAT RIGHT?
YEAH...
AN'... YOU'D OWE ME A FAVOR BECAUSE OF THIS?
YEAH...
RIGHT: AS SOON AS IT'S OVER I'M COMIN' BACK DOWN HERE, AN' THEN YOU AN' ME'RE GONNA HAVE A WEE TALK. AN' YOU'RE GONNA ANSWER ALL MY QUESTIONS ABOUT THE BOYS, AN' WHAT THEY'VE BEEN UP TO OVER THE YEARS, AN' BUTCHER. ALL OF IT.
BECAUSE I'VE BEEN WORKIN' FOR HIM FOR SIX MONTHS NOW, AN' HALF THE TIME I THINK I'M NONE THE FUCKIN' WISER.
SOUNDS TO ME LIKE YOU'VE LEARNED PLENTY, KID.
YOU GOT YOURSELF A DEAL.
I GUESS IT MIGHT BE GOOD FOR EVERYONE TO KNOW JUST WHERE THEY STAND...

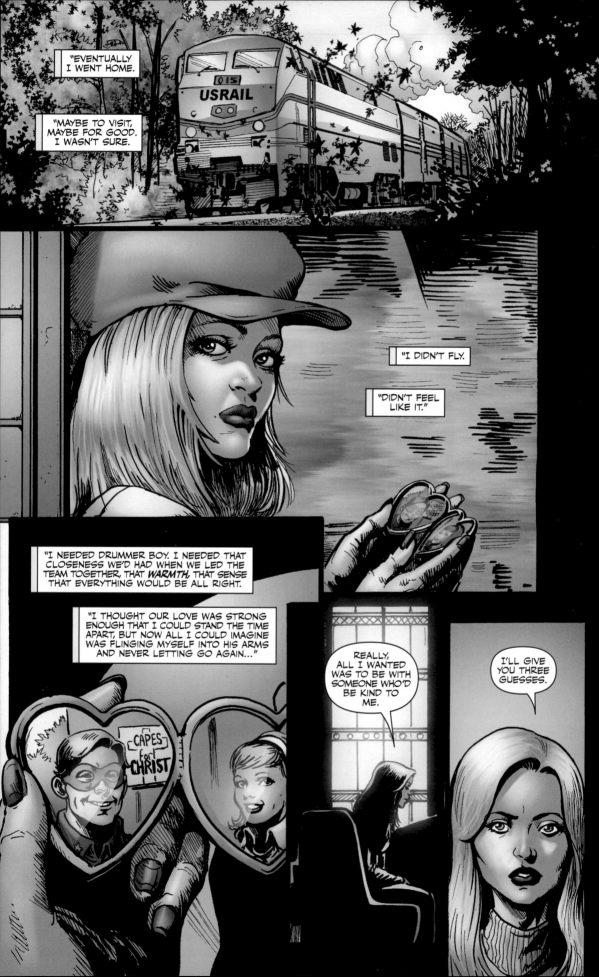

"EVENTUALLY I WENT HOME."

"MAYBE TO VISIT, MAYBE FOR GOOD. I WASN'T SURE."

USRAIL
015

"I DIDN'T FLY."

"DIDN'T FEEL LIKE IT."

"I NEEDED DRUMMER BOY. I NEEDED THAT CLOSENESS WE'D HAD WHEN WE LED THE TEAM TOGETHER, THAT *WARMTH*, THAT SENSE THAT EVERYTHING WOULD BE ALL RIGHT."

"I THOUGHT OUR LOVE WAS STRONG ENOUGH THAT I COULD STAND THE TIME APART, BUT NOW ALL I COULD IMAGINE WAS FLINGING MYSELF INTO HIS ARMS AND NEVER LETTING GO AGAIN..."

CAPES for CHRIST

REALLY, ALL I WANTED WAS TO BE WITH SOMEONE WHO'D BE KIND TO ME.

I'LL GIVE YOU THREE GUESSES.

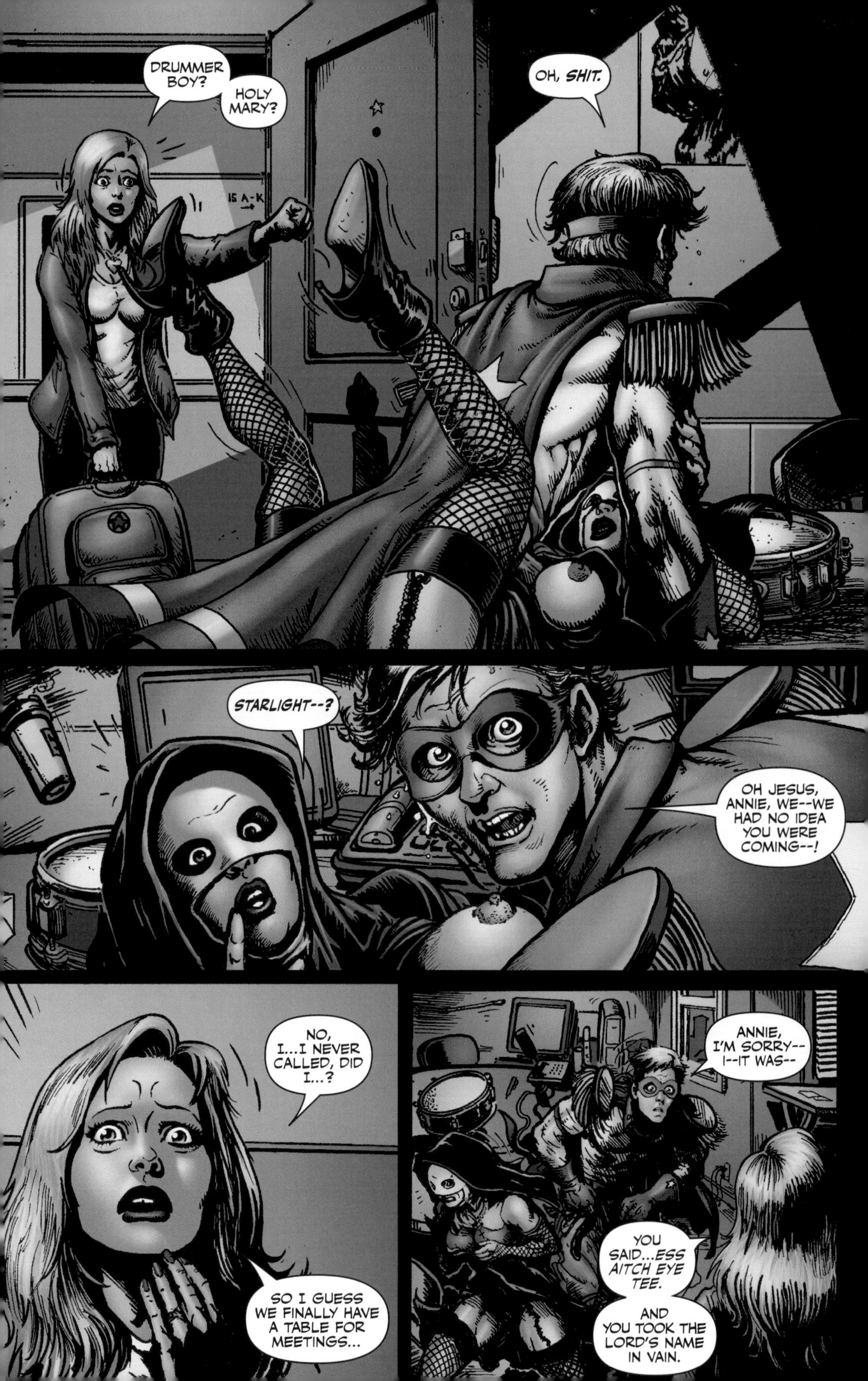
DRUMMER BOY?
HOLY MARY?
OH, SHIT.
15 A-K
STARLIGHT--?
OH JESUS, ANNIE, WE--WE HAD NO IDEA YOU WERE COMING--!
NO, I...I NEVER CALLED, DID I...?
SO I GUESS WE FINALLY HAVE A TABLE FOR MEETINGS...
ANNIE, I'M SORRY-- I--IT WAS--
YOU SAID...ESS AITCH EYE TEE.
AND YOU TOOK THE LORD'S NAME IN VAIN.

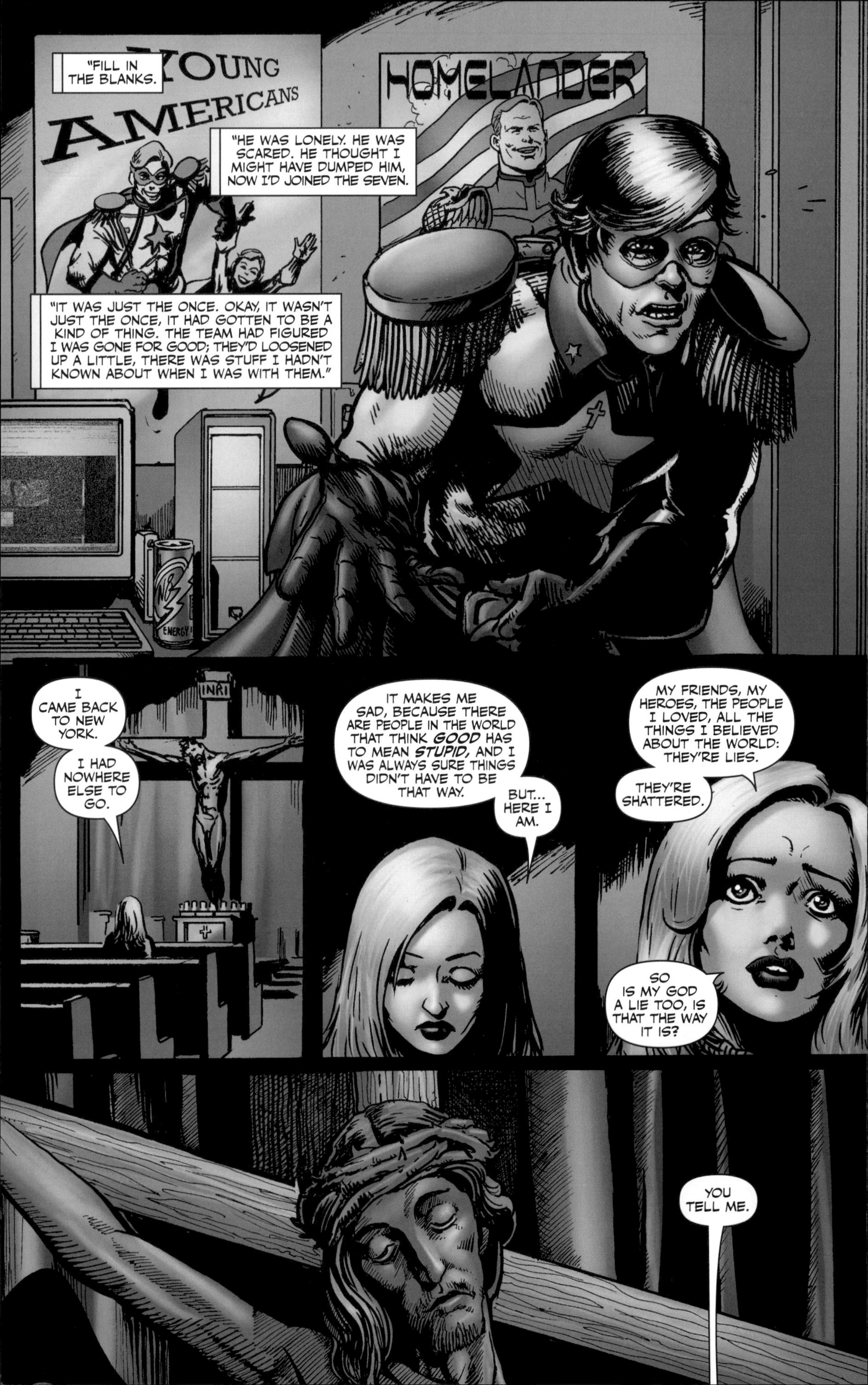
"FILL IN THE BLANKS.
YOUNG AMERICANS
HOMELANDER
"HE WAS LONELY. HE WAS SCARED. HE THOUGHT I MIGHT HAVE DUMPED HIM, NOW I'D JOINED THE SEVEN.
"IT WAS JUST THE ONCE. OKAY, IT WASN'T JUST THE ONCE, IT HAD GOTTEN TO BE A KIND OF THING. THE TEAM HAD FIGURED I WAS GONE FOR GOOD; THEY'D LOOSENED UP A LITTLE, THERE WAS STUFF I HADN'T KNOWN ABOUT WHEN I WAS WITH THEM."
ENERGY
INRI
I CAME BACK TO NEW YORK.
I HAD NOWHERE ELSE TO GO.
IT MAKES ME SAD, BECAUSE THERE ARE PEOPLE IN THE WORLD THAT THINK GOOD HAS TO MEAN STUPID, AND I WAS ALWAYS SURE THINGS DIDN'T HAVE TO BE THAT WAY.
BUT... HERE I AM.
MY FRIENDS, MY HEROES, THE PEOPLE I LOVED, ALL THE THINGS I BELIEVED ABOUT THE WORLD: THEY'RE LIES.
THEY'RE SHATTERED.
SO IS MY GOD A LIE TOO, IS THAT THE WAY IT IS?
YOU TELL ME.

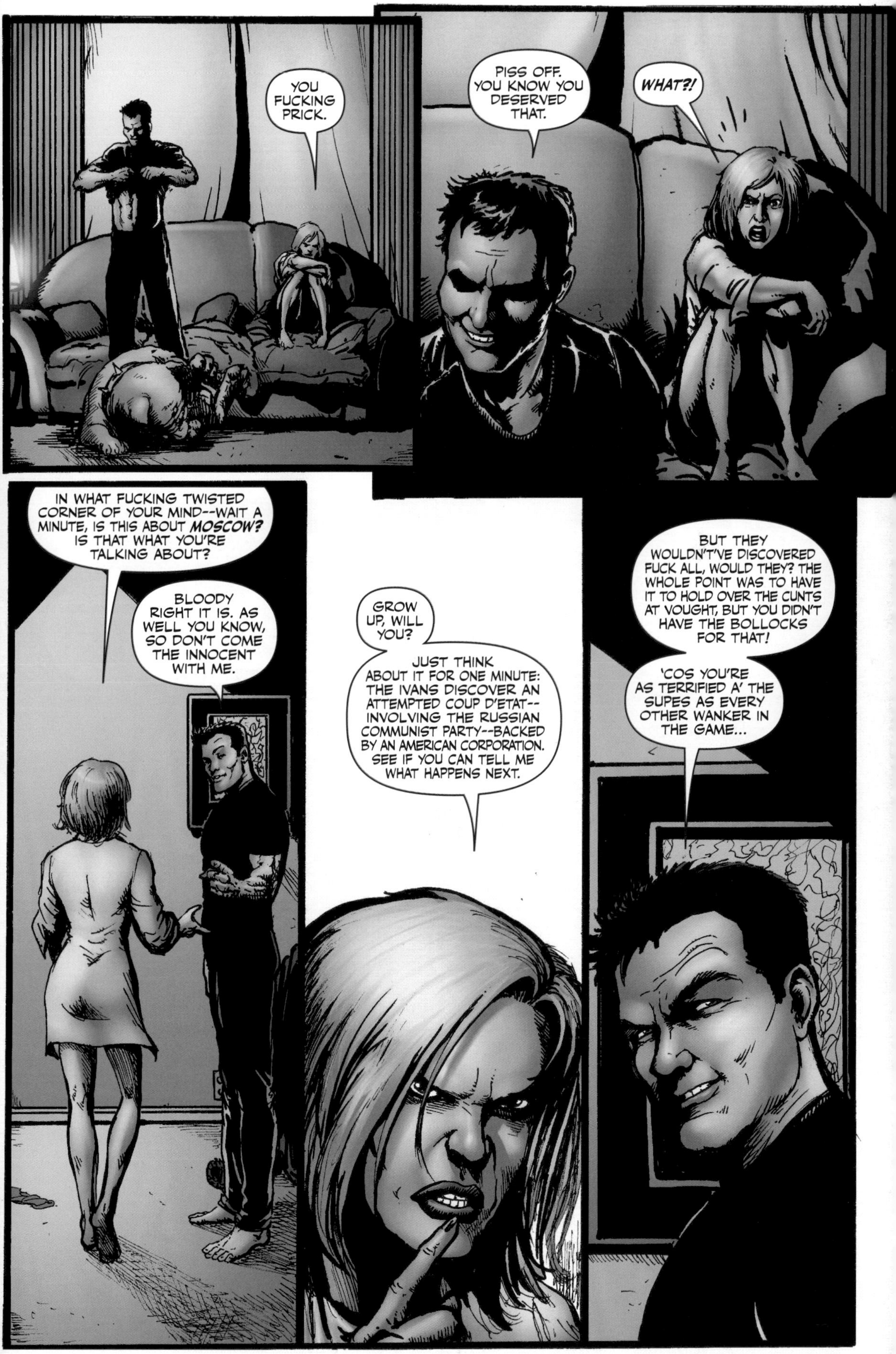
YOU FUCKING PRICK.
PISS OFF. YOU KNOW YOU DESERVED THAT.
WHAT?!
IN WHAT FUCKING TWISTED CORNER OF YOUR MIND--WAIT A MINUTE, IS THIS ABOUT *MOSCOW?* IS THAT WHAT YOU'RE TALKING ABOUT?
BLOODY RIGHT IT IS. AS WELL YOU KNOW, SO DON'T COME THE INNOCENT WITH ME.
GROW UP, WILL YOU?
JUST THINK ABOUT IT FOR ONE MINUTE: THE IVANS DISCOVER AN ATTEMPTED COUP D'ETAT--INVOLVING THE RUSSIAN COMMUNIST PARTY--BACKED BY AN AMERICAN CORPORATION. SEE IF YOU CAN TELL ME WHAT HAPPENS NEXT.
BUT THEY WOULDN'T'VE DISCOVERED FUCK ALL, WOULD THEY? THE WHOLE POINT WAS TO HAVE IT TO HOLD OVER THE CUNTS AT VOUGHT, BUT YOU DIDN'T HAVE THE BOLLOCKS FOR THAT!
'COS YOU'RE AS TERRIFIED A' THE SUPES AS EVERY OTHER WANKER IN THE GAME...

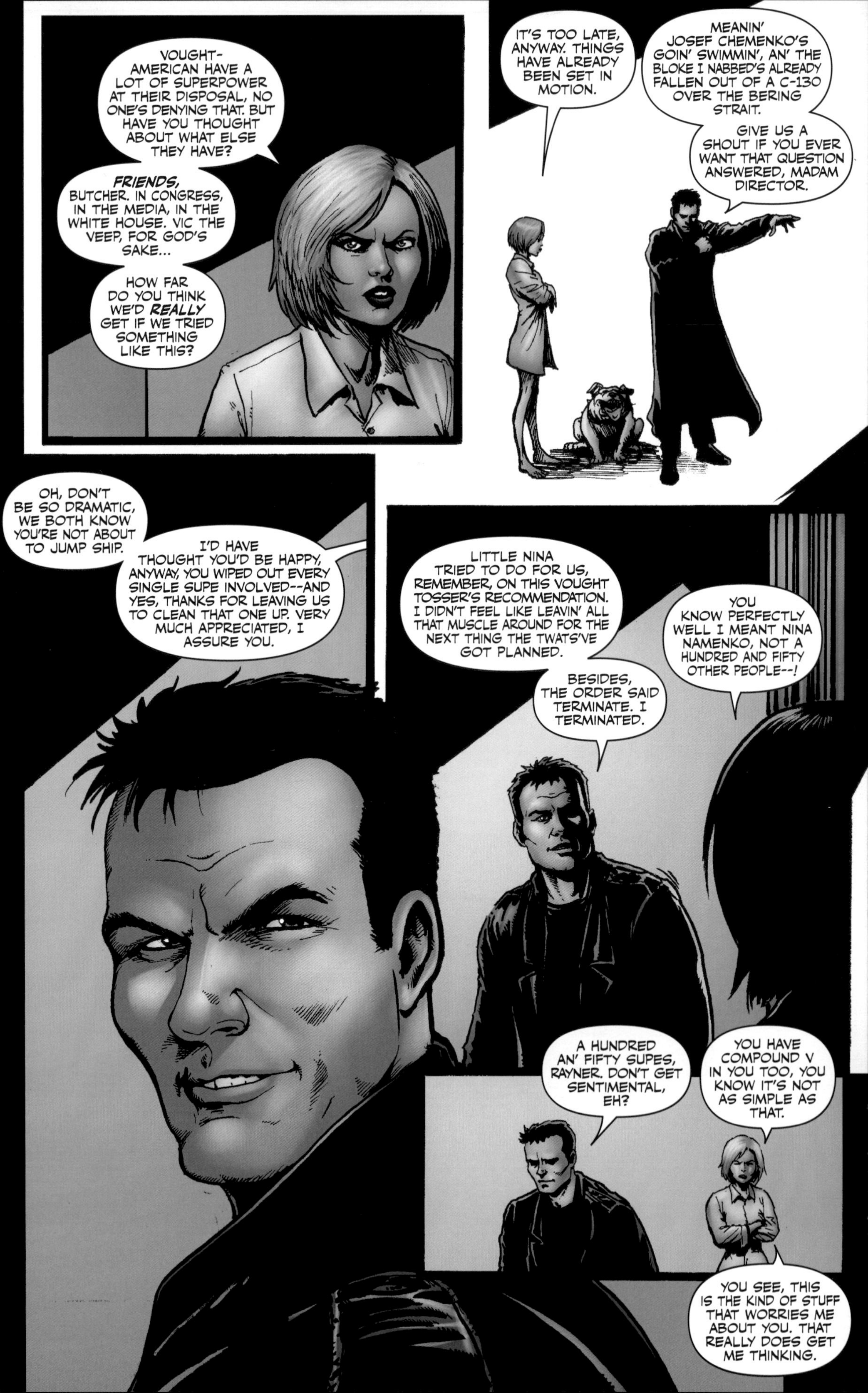
VOUGHT-AMERICAN HAVE A LOT OF SUPERPOWER AT THEIR DISPOSAL, NO ONE'S DENYING THAT. BUT HAVE YOU THOUGHT ABOUT WHAT ELSE THEY HAVE?
FRIENDS, BUTCHER. IN CONGRESS, IN THE MEDIA, IN THE WHITE HOUSE. VIC THE VEEP, FOR GOD'S SAKE...
HOW FAR DO YOU THINK WE'D *REALLY* GET IF WE TRIED SOMETHING LIKE THIS?
IT'S TOO LATE, ANYWAY. THINGS HAVE ALREADY BEEN SET IN MOTION.
MEANIN' JOSEF CHEMENKO'S GOIN' SWIMMIN', AN' THE BLOKE I NABBED'S ALREADY FALLEN OUT OF A C-130 OVER THE BERING STRAIT.
GIVE US A SHOUT IF YOU EVER WANT THAT QUESTION ANSWERED, MADAM DIRECTOR.
OH, DON'T BE SO DRAMATIC, WE BOTH KNOW YOU'RE NOT ABOUT TO JUMP SHIP.
I'D HAVE THOUGHT YOU'D BE HAPPY, ANYWAY, YOU WIPED OUT EVERY SINGLE SUPE INVOLVED--AND YES, THANKS FOR LEAVING US TO CLEAN THAT ONE UP. VERY MUCH APPRECIATED, I ASSURE YOU.
LITTLE NINA TRIED TO DO FOR US, REMEMBER, ON THIS VOUGHT TOSSER'S RECOMMENDATION. I DIDN'T FEEL LIKE LEAVIN' ALL THAT MUSCLE AROUND FOR THE NEXT THING THE TWATS'VE GOT PLANNED.
BESIDES, THE ORDER SAID TERMINATE. I TERMINATED.
YOU KNOW PERFECTLY WELL I MEANT NINA NAMENKO, NOT A HUNDRED AND FIFTY OTHER PEOPLE--!
A HUNDRED AN' FIFTY SUPES, RAYNER. DON'T GET SENTIMENTAL, EH?
YOU HAVE COMPOUND V IN YOU TOO, YOU KNOW IT'S NOT AS SIMPLE AS THAT.
YOU SEE, THIS IS THE KIND OF STUFF THAT WORRIES ME ABOUT YOU. THAT REALLY DOES GET ME THINKING.

WELL IF I EVER STICK A CAPE ON AN' START USIN' ORDINARY HUMAN BEIN'S TO WIPE ME ARSE WITH, YOU'LL KNOW YOU WERE RIGHT TO WORRY, WON'T YOU?

LOOK... I DIDN'T MEAN...

YOU REMEMBER THE DAY WE MET?

WHAT?

NOVEMBER OH-ONE. CHRIST, THE FUCKIN' GLEAM YOU HAD IN YOUR EYE.

BE NICE TO PUT IT DOWN TO ME WINNIN' CHARM, BUT THAT WEREN'T IT. DAKOTA BOB HAD JUST GONE INTO PAKISTAN.

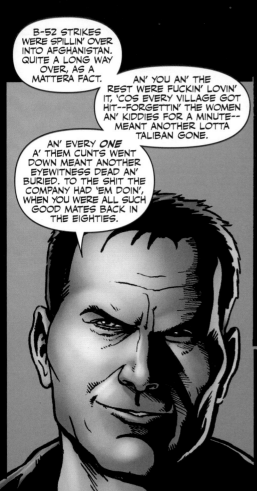

B-52 STRIKES WERE SPILLIN' OVER INTO AFGHANISTAN. QUITE A LONG WAY OVER, AS A MATTERA FACT.

AN' YOU AN' THE REST WERE FUCKIN' LOVIN' IT, 'COS EVERY VILLAGE GOT HIT--FORGETTIN' THE WOMEN AN' KIDDIES FOR A MINUTE-- MEANT ANOTHER LOTTA TALIBAN GONE.

AN' EVERY ONE A' THEM CUNTS WENT DOWN MEANT ANOTHER EYEWITNESS DEAD AN' BURIED. TO THE SHIT THE COMPANY HAD 'EM DOIN', WHEN YOU WERE ALL SUCH GOOD MATES BACK IN THE EIGHTIES.

RUNNIN' GUNS TO PEOPLE YOU SHOULDN'T. WETWORK IN FRIENDLY COUNTRIES. HEROIN.

NO WRITTEN ORDERS FOR ANY A' THEM STRIKES. BUT IF THERE WAS, I WONDER WHOSE NAME WOULDA BEEN ON THEM?

WE DESERVE EACH OTHER, YOU AN' ME.

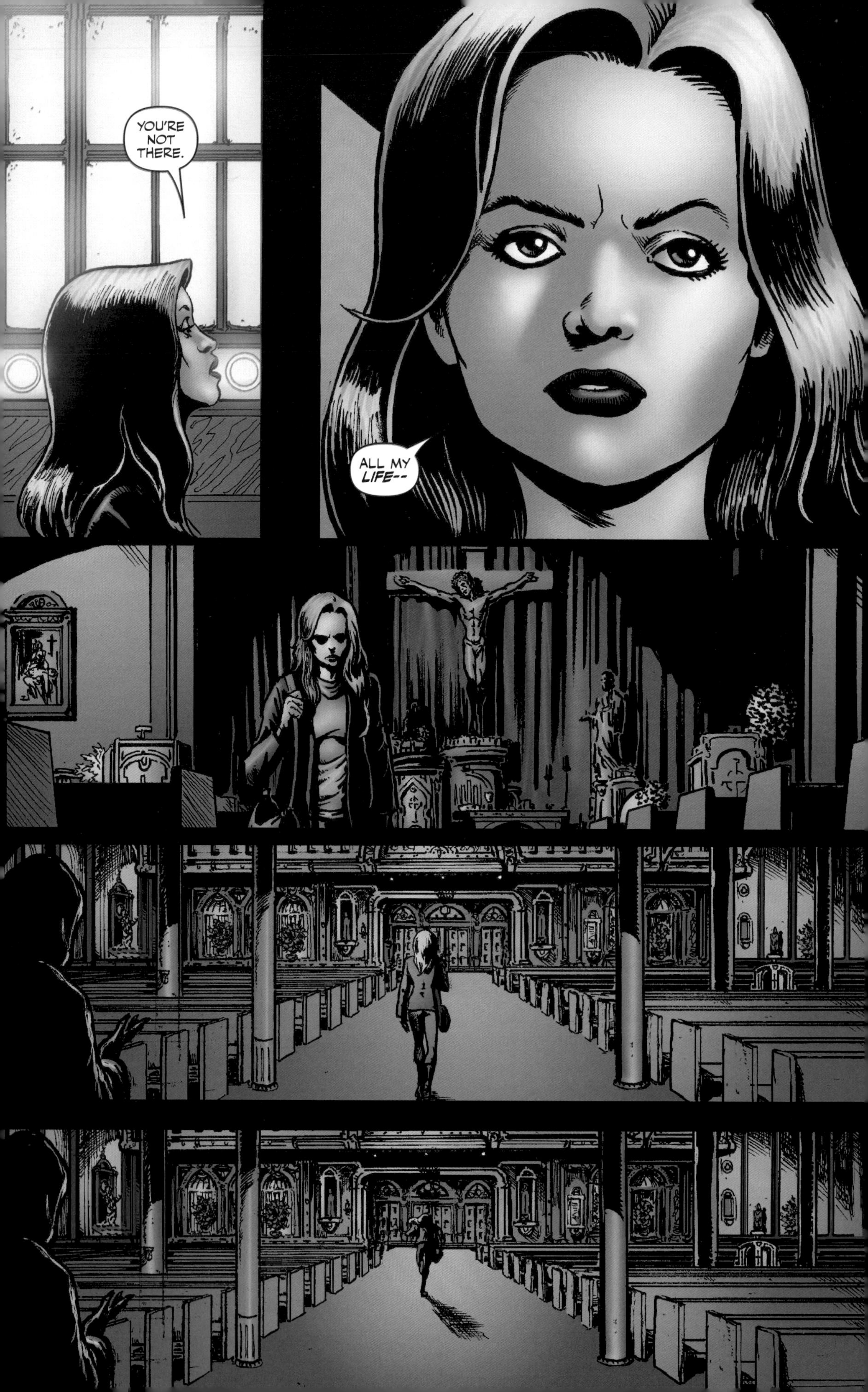
YOU'RE NOT THERE.
ALL MY LIFE--

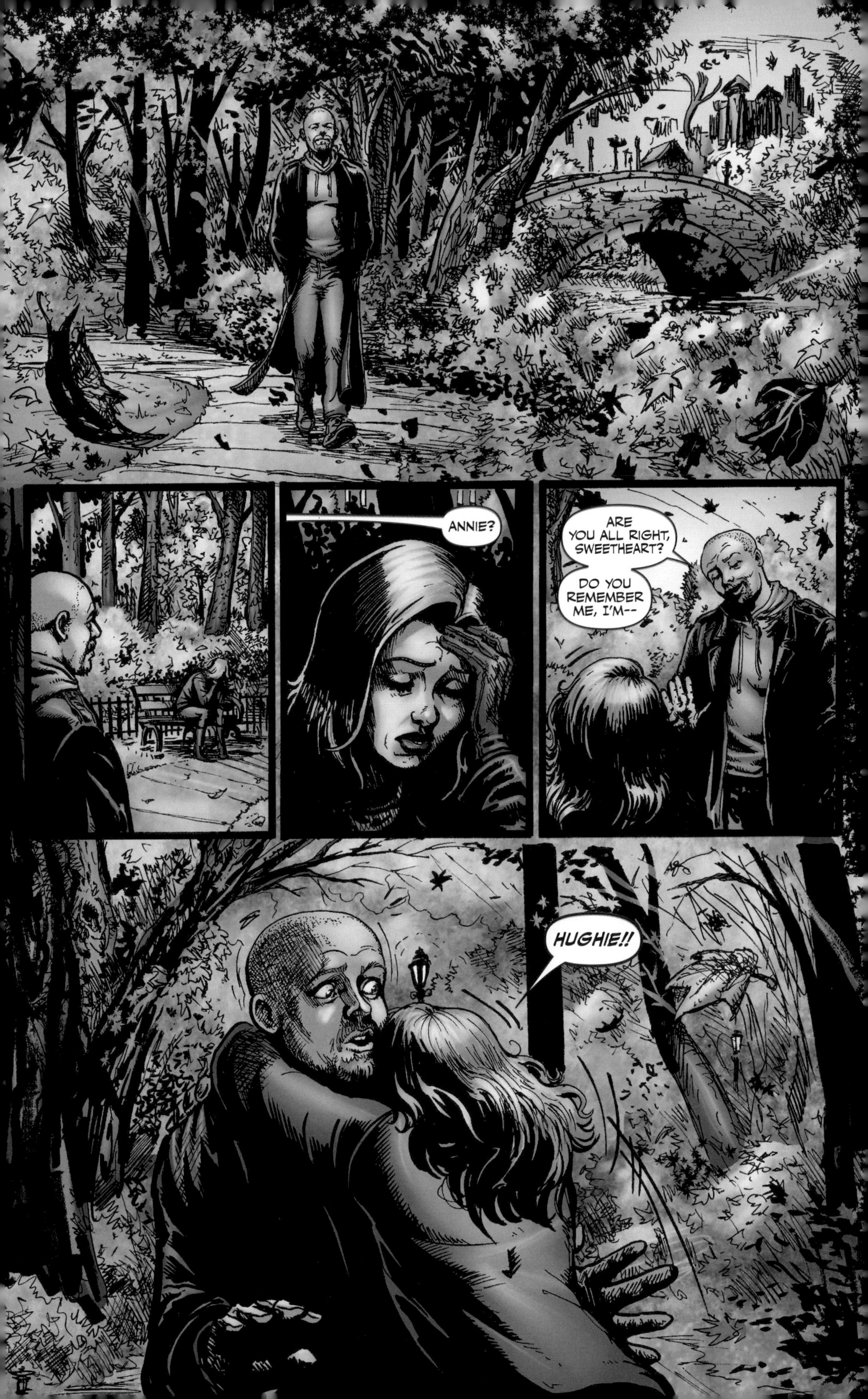
ANNIE?
ARE YOU ALL RIGHT, SWEETHEART?
DO YOU REMEMBER ME, I'M--
HUGHIE!!

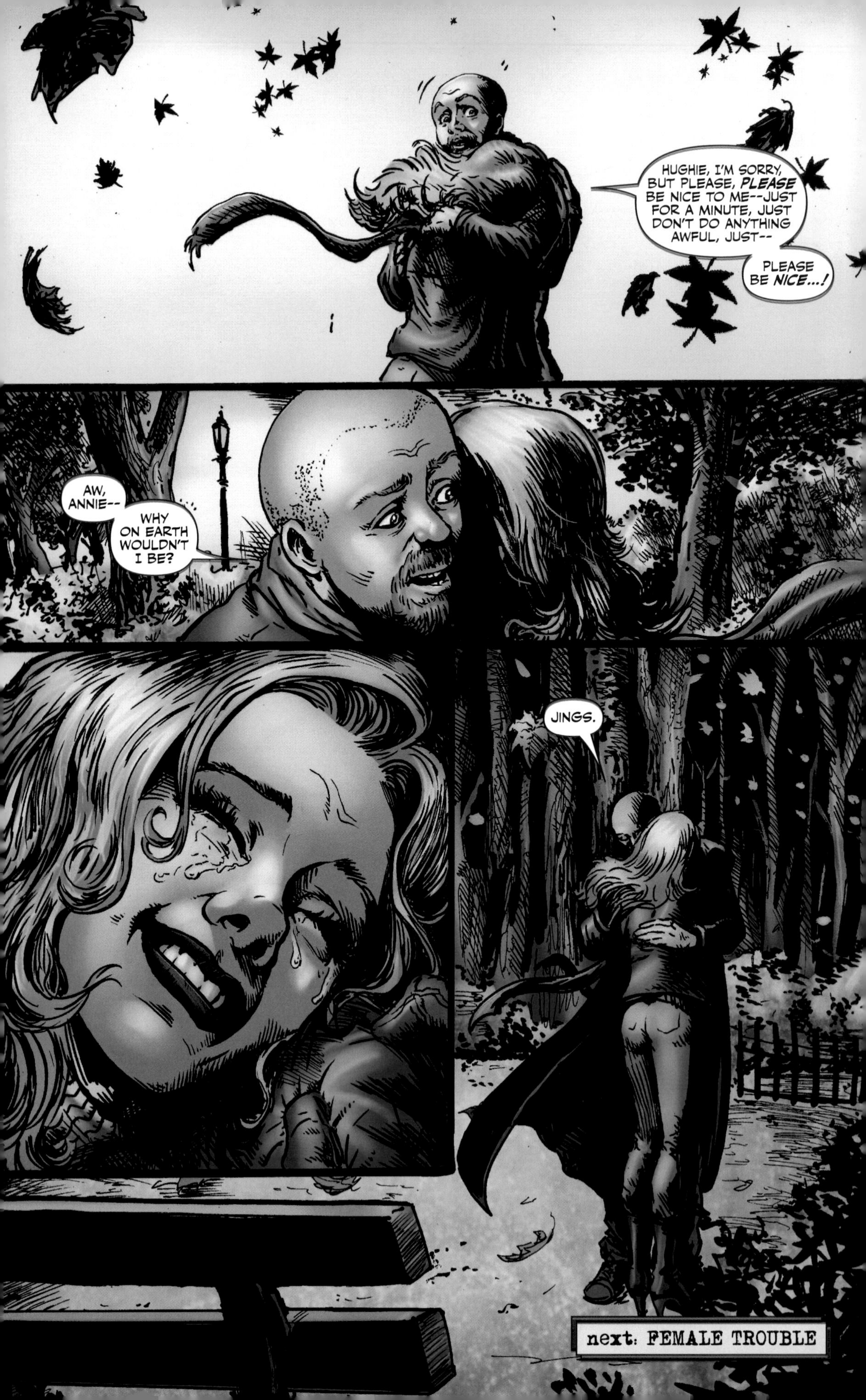
HUGHIE, I'M SORRY, BUT PLEASE, *PLEASE* BE NICE TO ME--JUST FOR A MINUTE, JUST DON'T DO ANYTHING AWFUL, JUST--
PLEASE BE *NICE*...!
AW, ANNIE--
WHY ON EARTH WOULDN'T I BE?
JINGS.
next: FEMALE TROUBLE

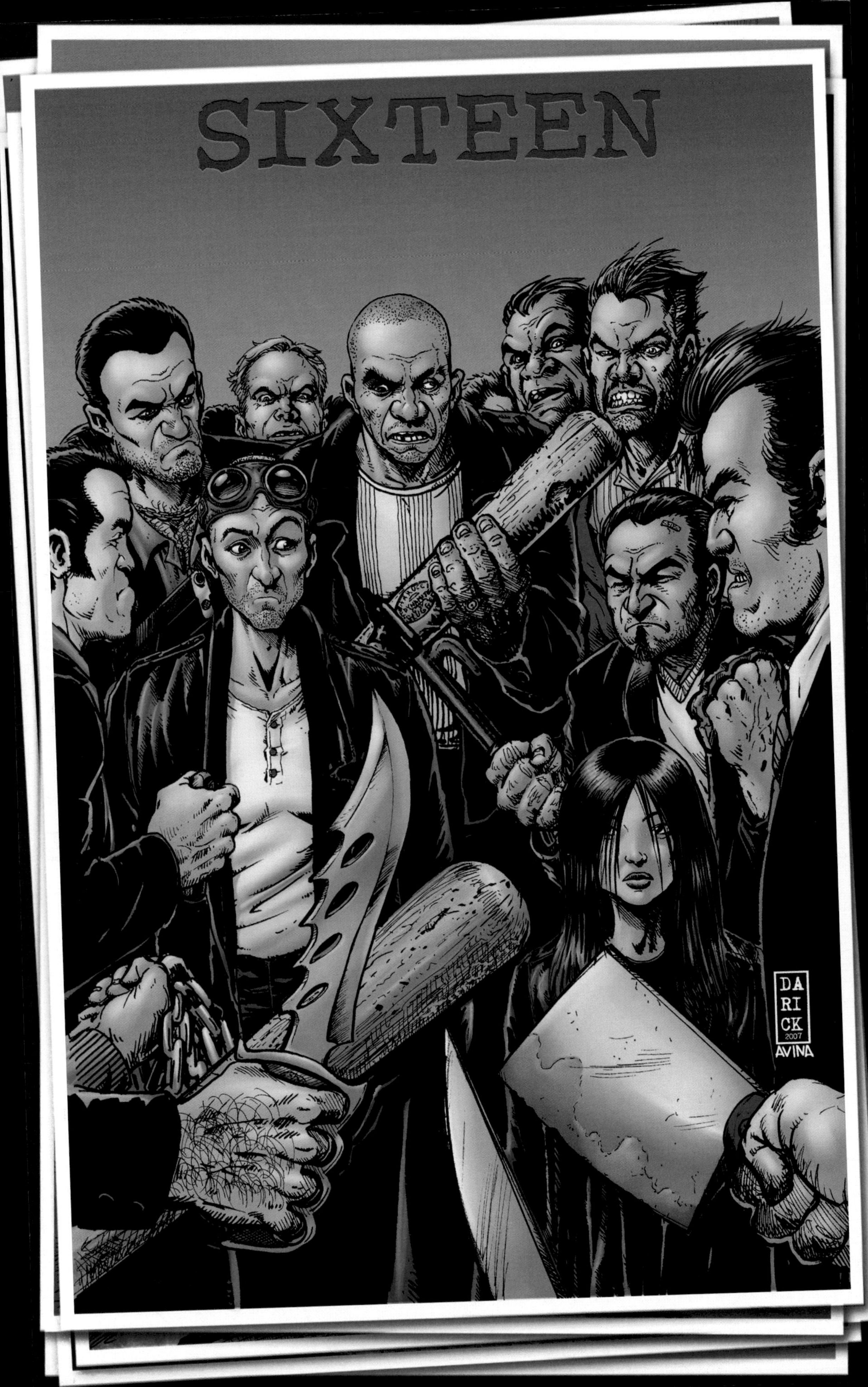
SIXTEEN
DA
RI
CK
2007
AVINA

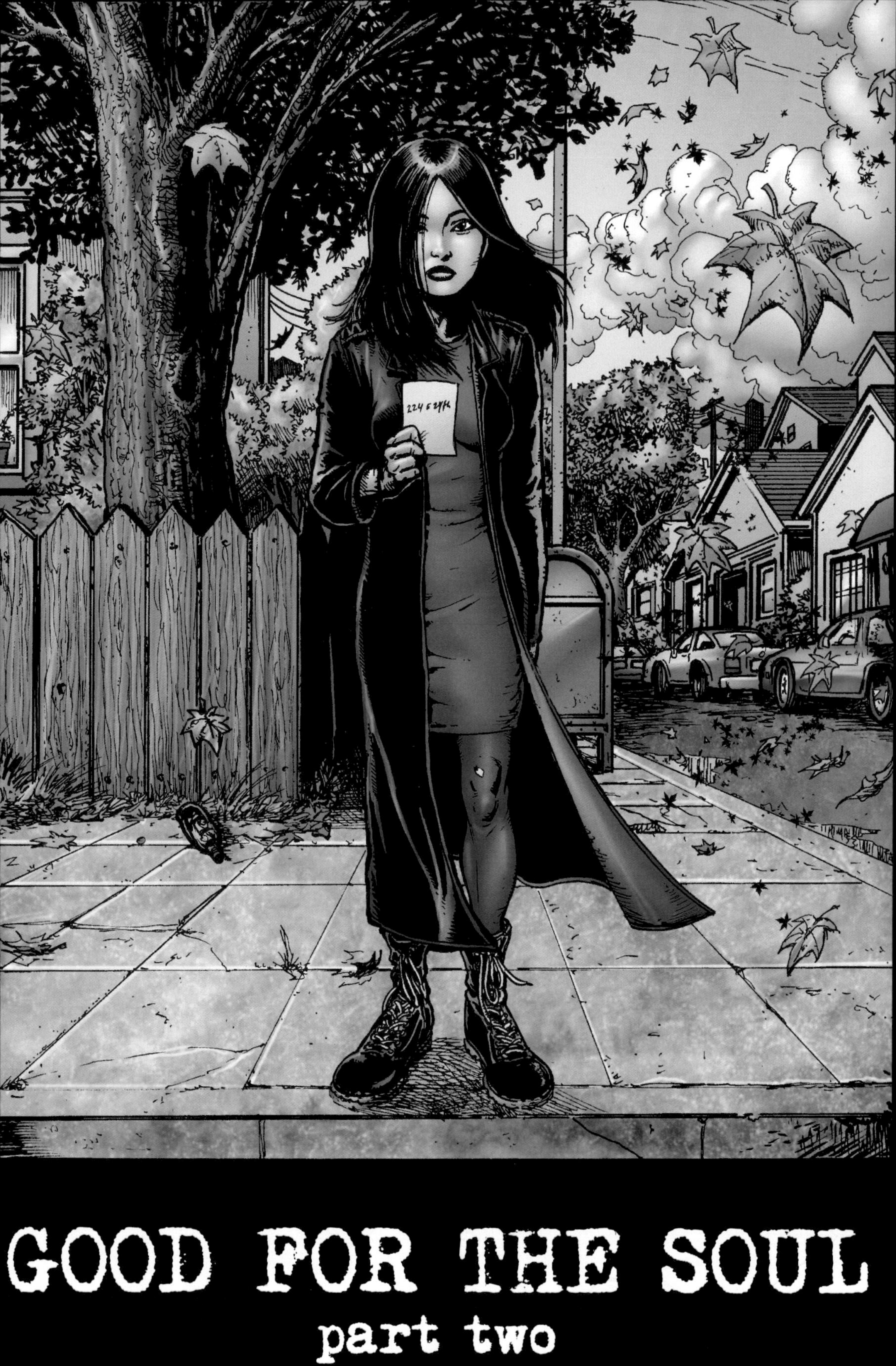

GOOD FOR THE SOUL
part two

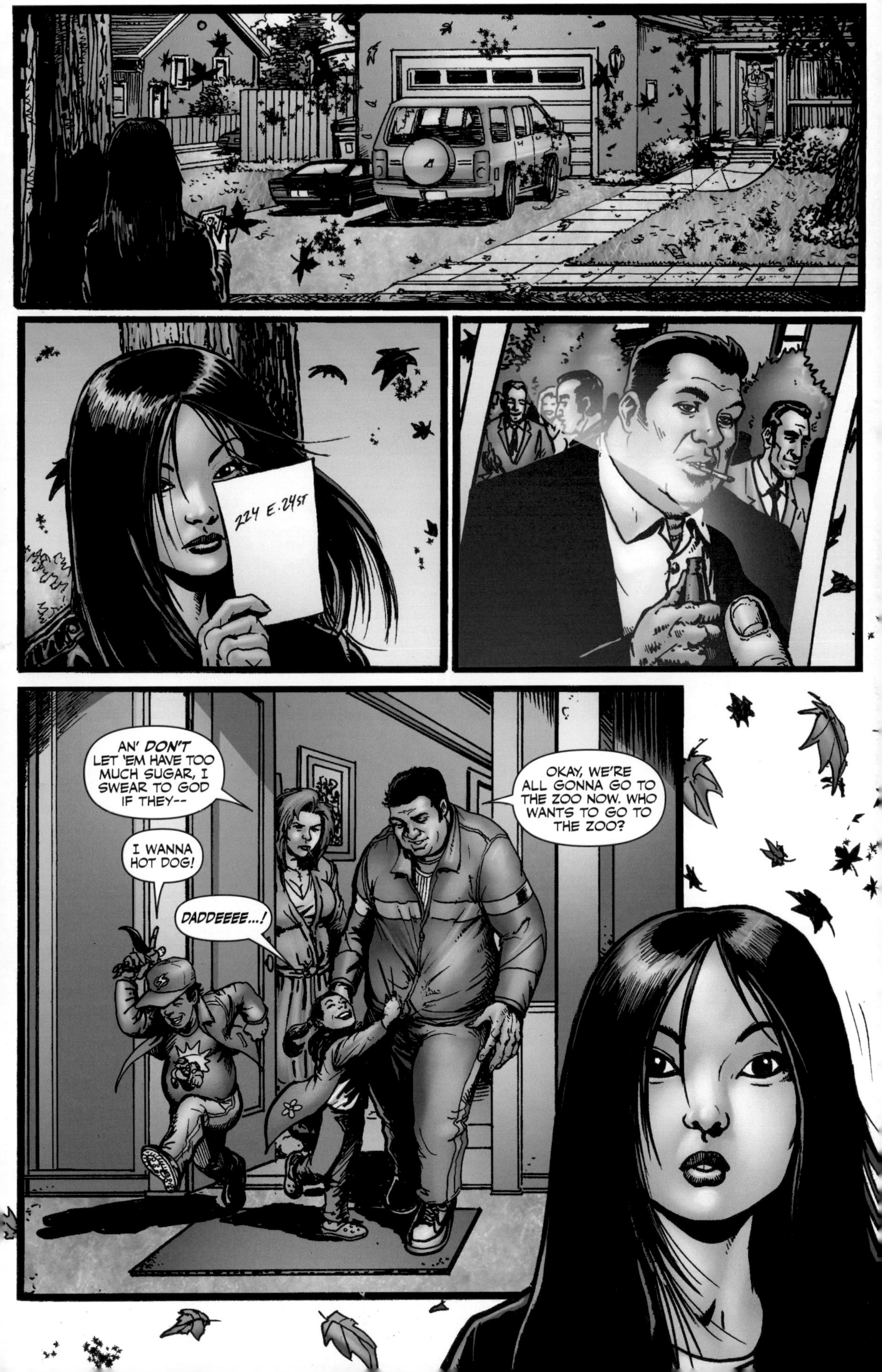
224 E. 24ST
AN' DON'T LET 'EM HAVE TOO MUCH SUGAR, I SWEAR TO GOD IF THEY--
OKAY, WE'RE ALL GONNA GO TO THE ZOO NOW. WHO WANTS TO GO TO THE ZOO?
I WANNA HOT DOG!
DADDEEEE...!

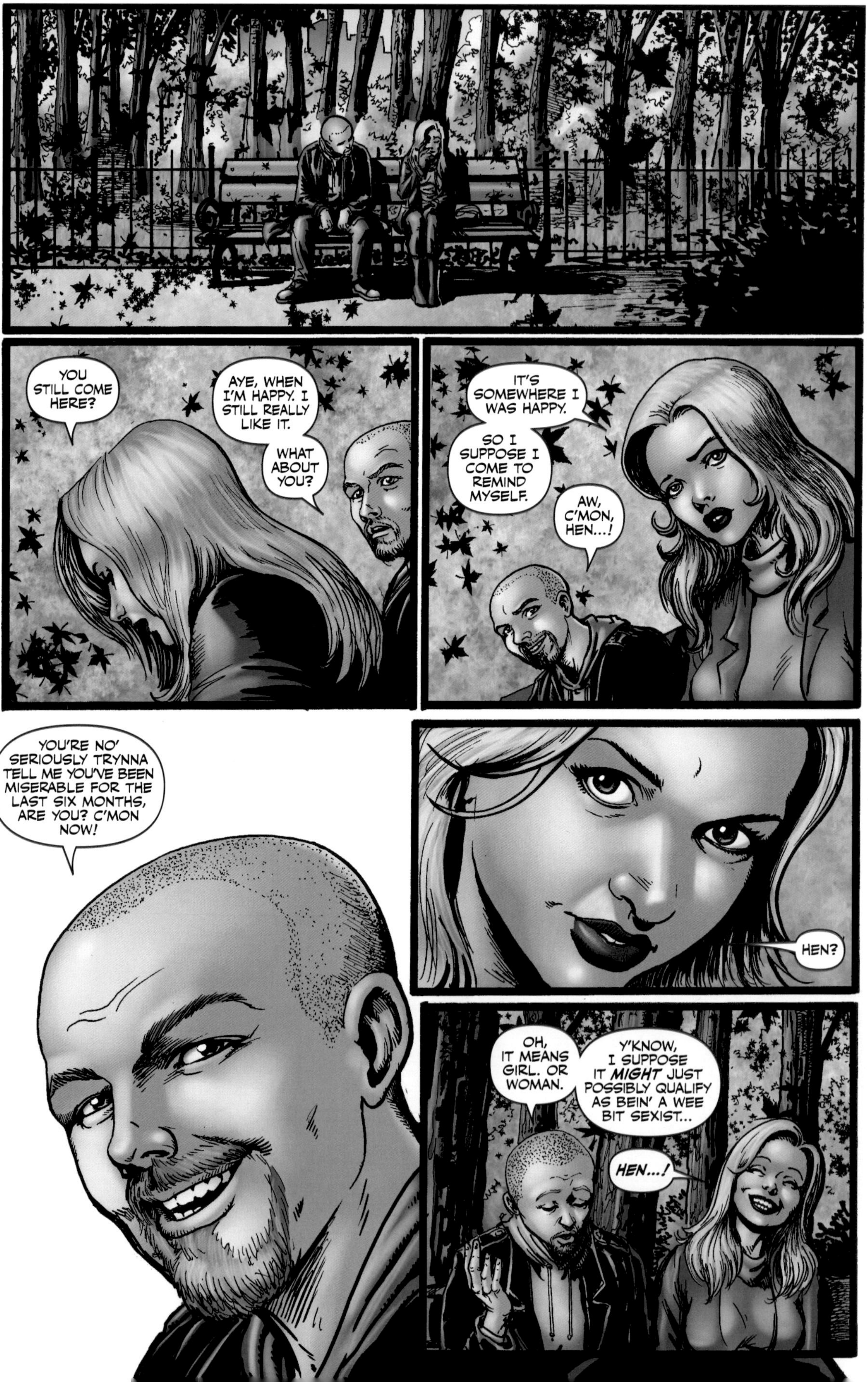
YOU STILL COME HERE?
AYE, WHEN I'M HAPPY. I STILL REALLY LIKE IT.
WHAT ABOUT YOU?
IT'S SOMEWHERE I WAS HAPPY.
SO I SUPPOSE I COME TO REMIND MYSELF.
AW, C'MON, HEN...!
YOU'RE NO' SERIOUSLY TRYNNA TELL ME YOU'VE BEEN MISERABLE FOR THE LAST SIX MONTHS, ARE YOU? C'MON NOW!
HEN?
OH, IT MEANS GIRL. OR WOMAN.
Y'KNOW, I SUPPOSE IT MIGHT JUST POSSIBLY QUALIFY AS BEIN' A WEE BIT SEXIST...
HEN...!

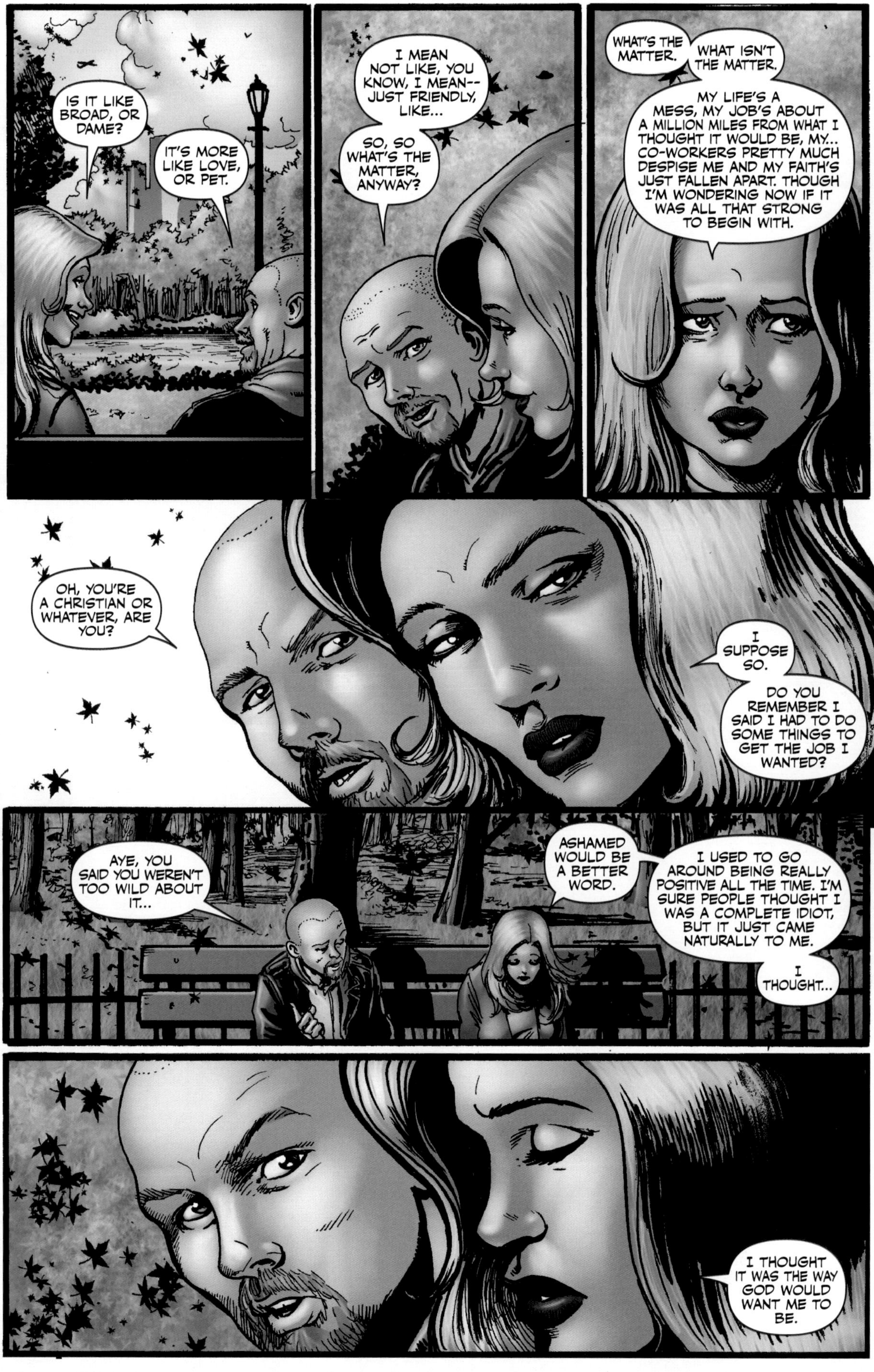

IS IT LIKE BROAD, OR DAME?
IT'S MORE LIKE LOVE, OR PET.
I MEAN NOT LIKE, YOU KNOW, I MEAN-- JUST FRIENDLY, LIKE...
SO, SO WHAT'S THE MATTER, ANYWAY?
WHAT'S THE MATTER.
WHAT ISN'T THE MATTER.
MY LIFE'S A MESS, MY JOB'S ABOUT A MILLION MILES FROM WHAT I THOUGHT IT WOULD BE, MY... CO-WORKERS PRETTY MUCH DESPISE ME AND MY FAITH'S JUST FALLEN APART. THOUGH I'M WONDERING NOW IF IT WAS ALL THAT STRONG TO BEGIN WITH.
OH, YOU'RE A CHRISTIAN OR WHATEVER, ARE YOU?
I SUPPOSE SO.
DO YOU REMEMBER I SAID I HAD TO DO SOME THINGS TO GET THE JOB I WANTED?
AYE, YOU SAID YOU WEREN'T TOO WILD ABOUT IT...
ASHAMED WOULD BE A BETTER WORD.
I USED TO GO AROUND BEING REALLY POSITIVE ALL THE TIME. I'M SURE PEOPLE THOUGHT I WAS A COMPLETE IDIOT, BUT IT JUST CAME NATURALLY TO ME.
I THOUGHT...
I THOUGHT IT WAS THE WAY GOD WOULD WANT ME TO BE.

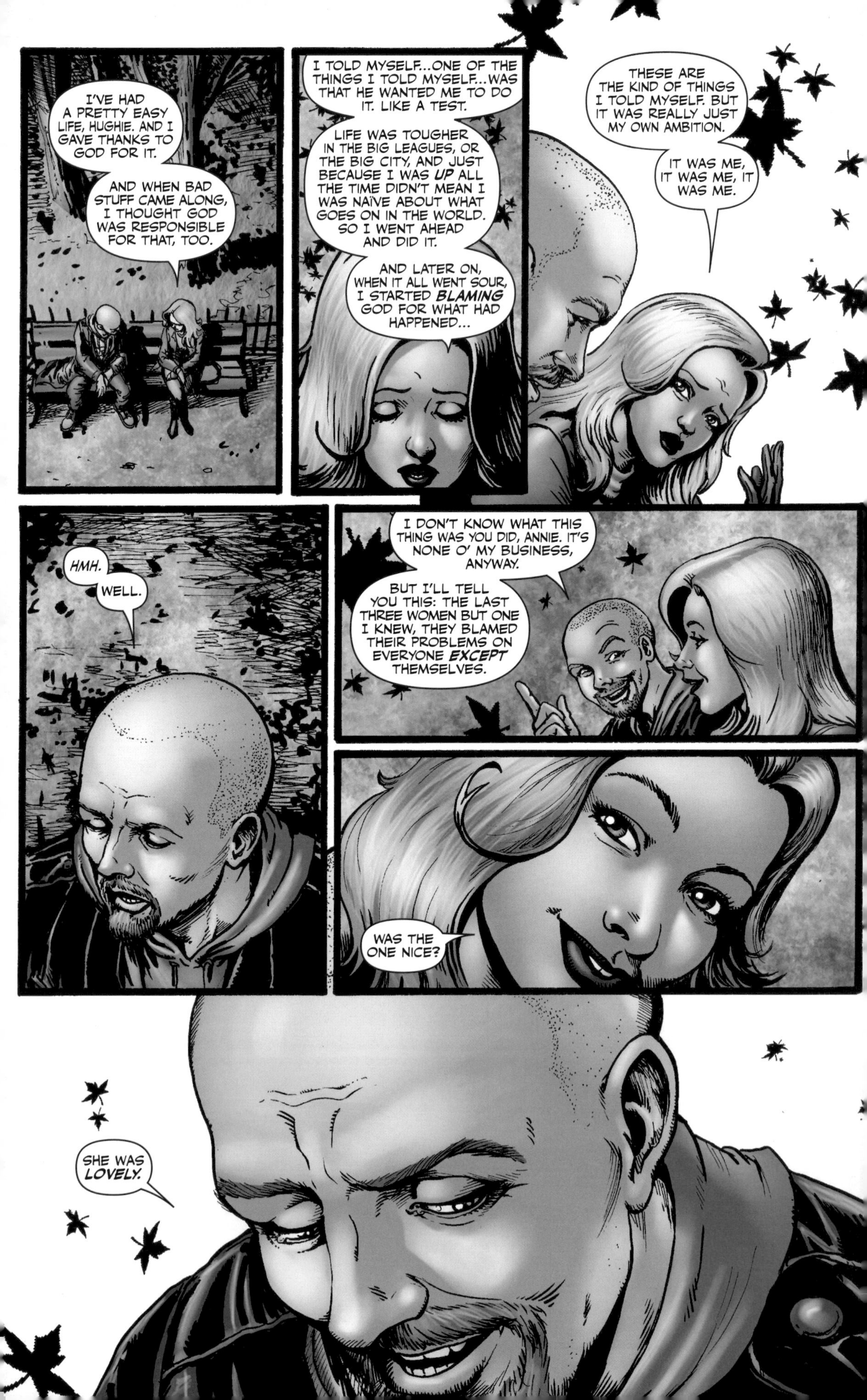

I'VE HAD A PRETTY EASY LIFE, HUGHIE. AND I GAVE THANKS TO GOD FOR IT.
AND WHEN BAD STUFF CAME ALONG, I THOUGHT GOD WAS RESPONSIBLE FOR THAT, TOO.
I TOLD MYSELF...ONE OF THE THINGS I TOLD MYSELF...WAS THAT HE WANTED ME TO DO IT. LIKE A TEST.
LIFE WAS TOUGHER IN THE BIG LEAGUES, OR THE BIG CITY, AND JUST BECAUSE I WAS *UP* ALL THE TIME DIDN'T MEAN I WAS NAÏVE ABOUT WHAT GOES ON IN THE WORLD. SO I WENT AHEAD AND DID IT.
AND LATER ON, WHEN IT ALL WENT SOUR, I STARTED *BLAMING* GOD FOR WHAT HAD HAPPENED...
THESE ARE THE KIND OF THINGS I TOLD MYSELF. BUT IT WAS REALLY JUST MY OWN AMBITION.
IT WAS ME, IT WAS ME, IT WAS ME.
HMH.
WELL.
I DON'T KNOW WHAT THIS THING WAS YOU DID, ANNIE. IT'S NONE O' MY BUSINESS, ANYWAY.
BUT I'LL TELL YOU THIS: THE LAST THREE WOMEN BUT ONE I KNEW, THEY BLAMED THEIR PROBLEMS ON EVERYONE *EXCEPT* THEMSELVES.
WAS THE ONE NICE?
SHE WAS *LOVELY.*

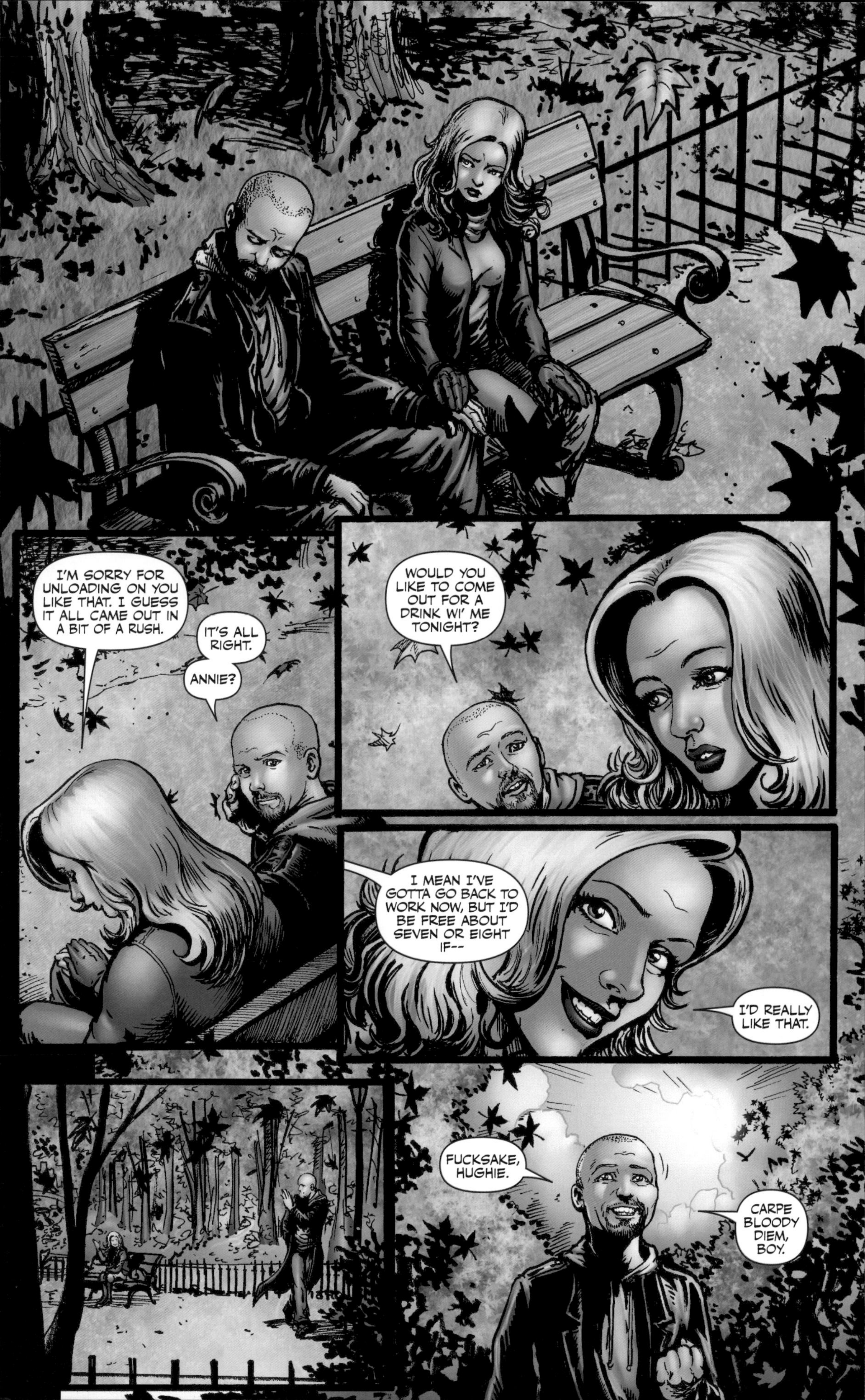
I'M SORRY FOR UNLOADING ON YOU LIKE THAT. I GUESS IT ALL CAME OUT IN A BIT OF A RUSH.
IT'S ALL RIGHT.
ANNIE?
WOULD YOU LIKE TO COME OUT FOR A DRINK WI' ME TONIGHT?
I MEAN I'VE GOTTA GO BACK TO WORK NOW, BUT I'D BE FREE ABOUT SEVEN OR EIGHT IF--
I'D REALLY LIKE THAT.
FUCKSAKE, HUGHIE.
CARPE BLOODY DIEM, BOY.

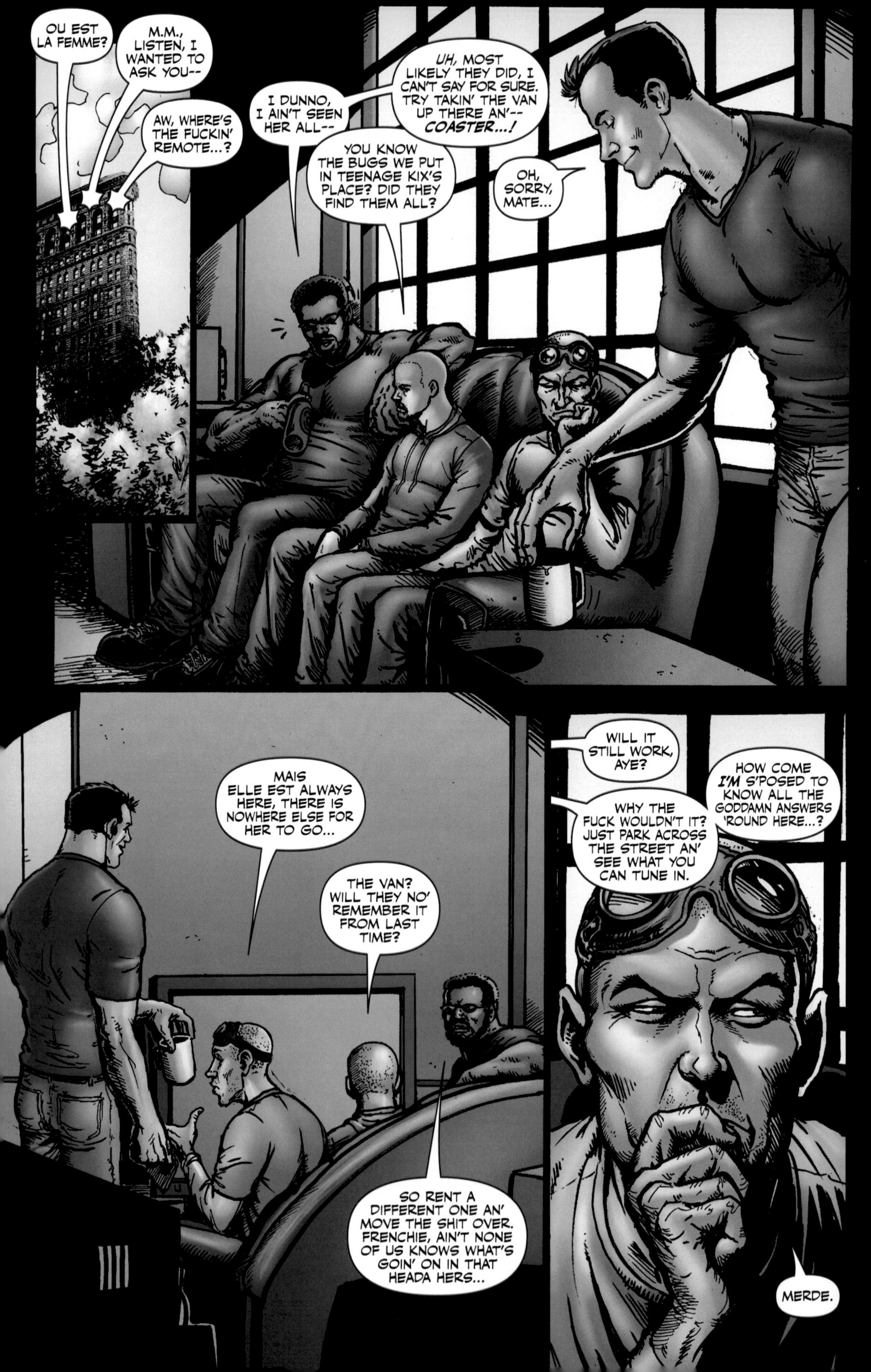
OU EST LA FEMME?
M.M., LISTEN, I WANTED TO ASK YOU--
AW, WHERE'S THE FUCKIN' REMOTE...?
I DUNNO, I AIN'T SEEN HER ALL--
UH, MOST LIKELY THEY DID, I CAN'T SAY FOR SURE. TRY TAKIN' THE VAN UP THERE AN'-- COASTER...!
YOU KNOW THE BUGS WE PUT IN TEENAGE KIX'S PLACE? DID THEY FIND THEM ALL?
OH, SORRY, MATE...
MAIS ELLE EST ALWAYS HERE, THERE IS NOWHERE ELSE FOR HER TO GO...
THE VAN? WILL THEY NO' REMEMBER IT FROM LAST TIME?
SO RENT A DIFFERENT ONE AN' MOVE THE SHIT OVER. FRENCHIE, AIN'T NONE OF US KNOWS WHAT'S GOIN' ON IN THAT HEADA HERS...
WILL IT STILL WORK, AYE?
WHY THE FUCK WOULDN'T IT? JUST PARK ACROSS THE STREET AN' SEE WHAT YOU CAN TUNE IN.
HOW COME I'M S'POSED TO KNOW ALL THE GODDAMN ANSWERS 'ROUND HERE...?
MERDE.

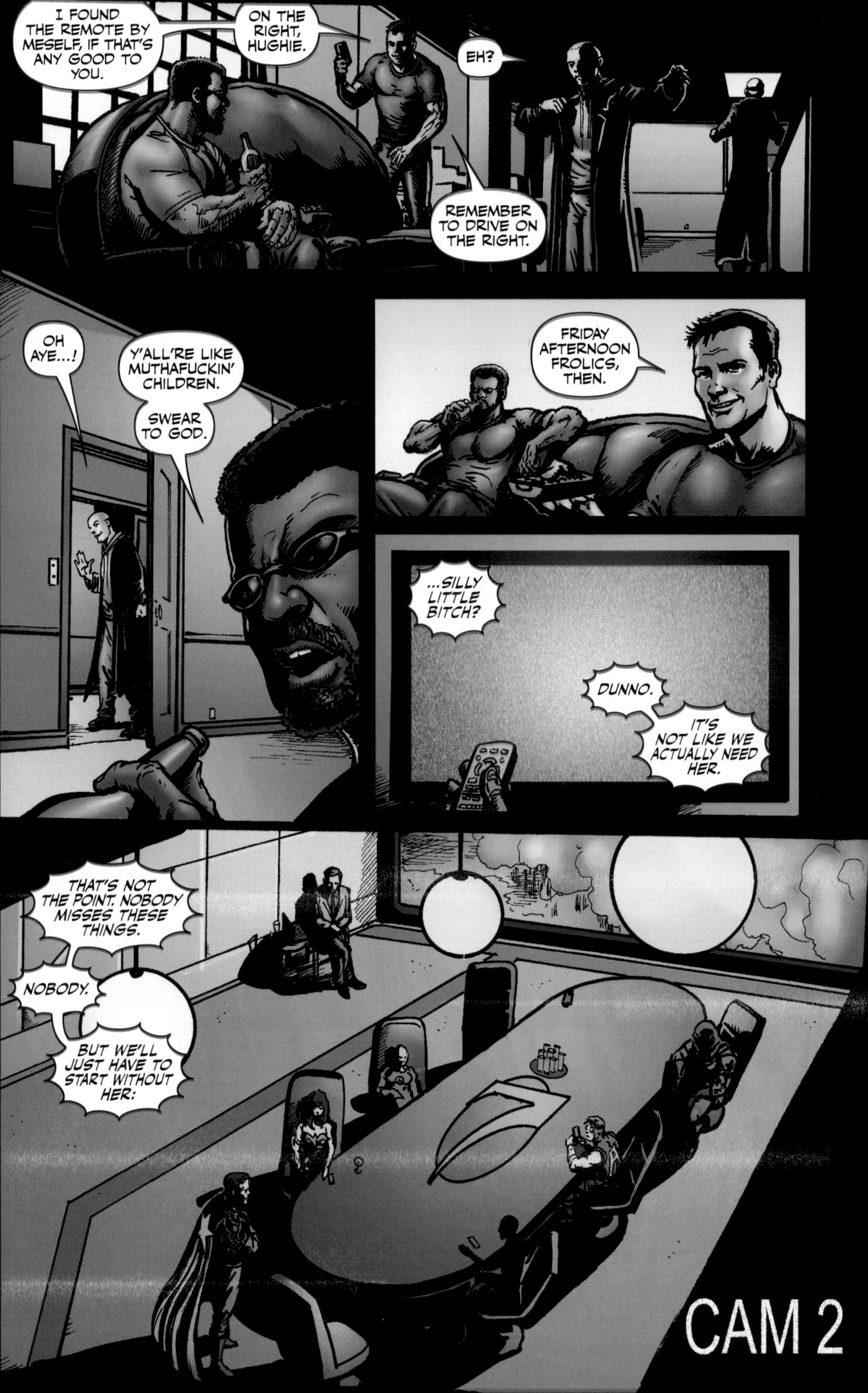
I FOUND THE REMOTE BY MESELF, IF THAT'S ANY GOOD TO YOU.
ON THE RIGHT, HUGHIE.
EH?
REMEMBER TO DRIVE ON THE RIGHT.
OH AYE...!
Y'ALL'RE LIKE MUTHAFUCKIN' CHILDREN.
SWEAR TO GOD.
FRIDAY AFTERNOON FROLICS, THEN.
...SILLY LITTLE BITCH?
DUNNO.
IT'S NOT LIKE WE ACTUALLY NEED HER.
THAT'S NOT THE POINT. NOBODY MISSES THESE THINGS.
NOBODY.
BUT WE'LL JUST HAVE TO START WITHOUT HER:
CAM 2

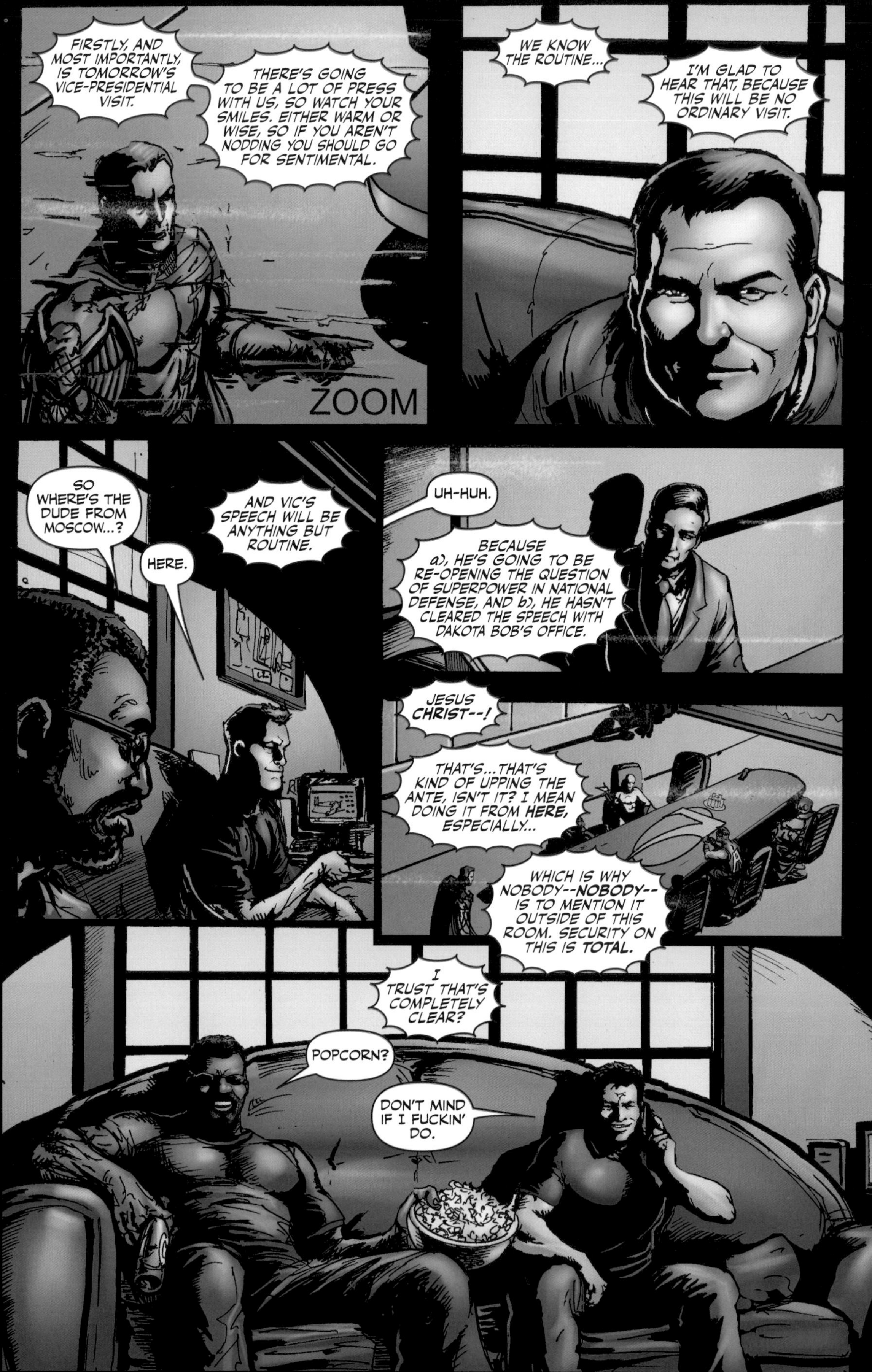
FIRSTLY, AND MOST IMPORTANTLY, IS TOMORROW'S VICE-PRESIDENTIAL VISIT.
THERE'S GOING TO BE A LOT OF PRESS WITH US, SO WATCH YOUR SMILES. EITHER WARM OR WISE, SO IF YOU AREN'T NODDING YOU SHOULD GO FOR SENTIMENTAL.
ZOOM
WE KNOW THE ROUTINE...
I'M GLAD TO HEAR THAT, BECAUSE THIS WILL BE NO ORDINARY VISIT.
SO WHERE'S THE DUDE FROM MOSCOW...?
AND VIC'S SPEECH WILL BE ANYTHING BUT ROUTINE.
HERE.
UH-HUH.
BECAUSE a), HE'S GOING TO BE RE-OPENING THE QUESTION OF SUPERPOWER IN NATIONAL DEFENSE, AND b), HE HASN'T CLEARED THE SPEECH WITH DAKOTA BOB'S OFFICE.
JESUS **CHRIST**--!
THAT'S...THAT'S KIND OF UPPING THE ANTE, ISN'T IT? I MEAN DOING IT FROM **HERE,** ESPECIALLY...
WHICH IS WHY NOBODY--**NOBODY**--IS TO MENTION IT OUTSIDE OF THIS ROOM. SECURITY ON THIS IS **TOTAL.**
I TRUST THAT'S COMPLETELY CLEAR?
POPCORN?
DON'T MIND IF I FUCKIN' DO.

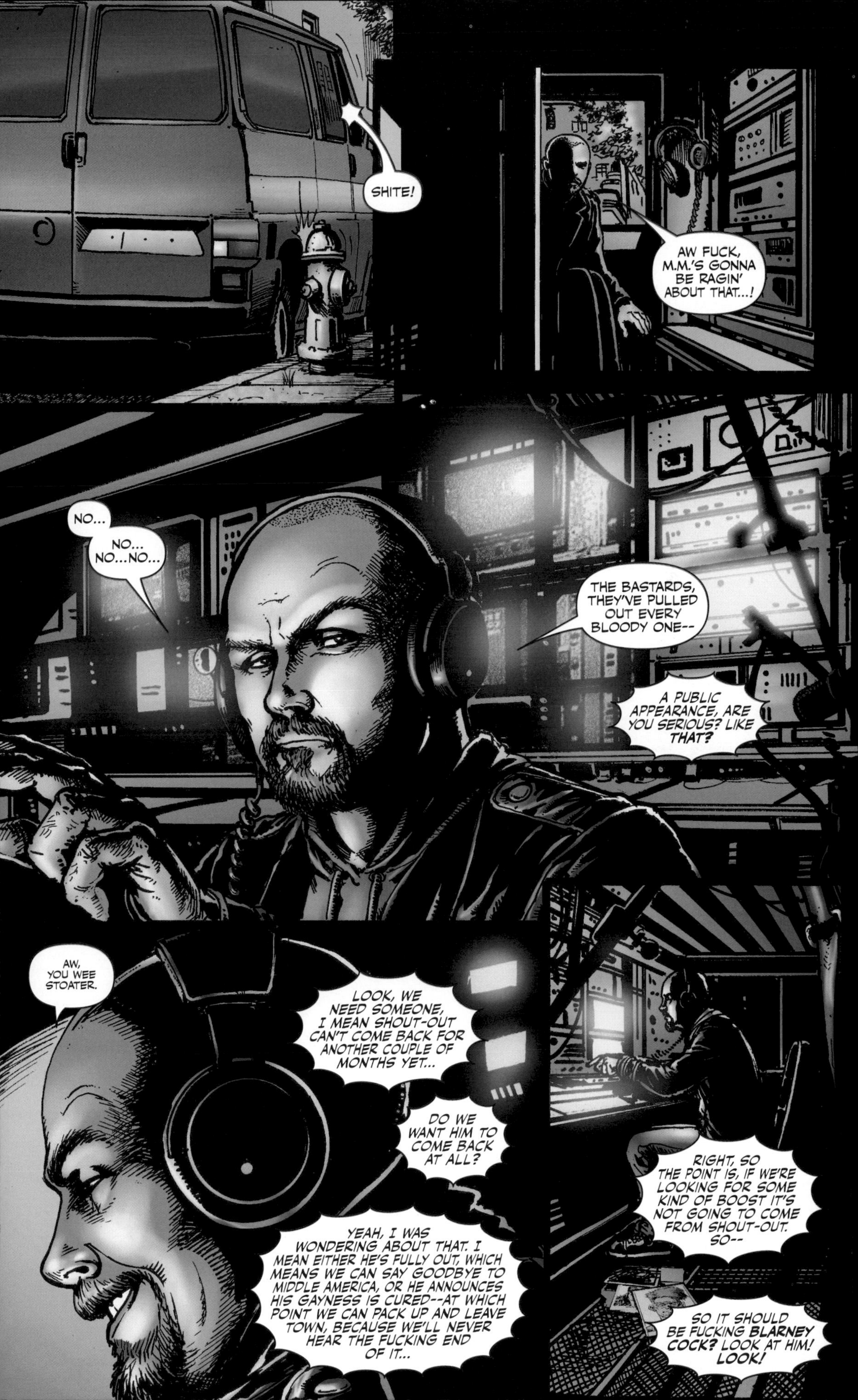
SHITE!
AW FUCK, M.M.'S GONNA BE RAGIN' ABOUT THAT...!
NO...
NO... NO...NO...
THE BASTARDS, THEY'VE PULLED OUT EVERY BLOODY ONE--
A PUBLIC APPEARANCE, ARE YOU SERIOUS? LIKE ***THAT?***
AW, YOU WEE STOATER.
LOOK, WE NEED SOMEONE, I MEAN SHOUT-OUT CAN'T COME BACK FOR ANOTHER COUPLE OF MONTHS YET...
DO WE WANT HIM TO COME BACK AT ALL?
YEAH, I WAS WONDERING ABOUT THAT. I MEAN EITHER HE'S FULLY OUT, WHICH MEANS WE CAN SAY GOODBYE TO MIDDLE AMERICA, OR HE ANNOUNCES HIS GAYNESS IS CURED--AT WHICH POINT WE CAN PACK UP AND LEAVE TOWN, BECAUSE WE'LL NEVER HEAR THE FUCKING END OF IT...
RIGHT, SO THE POINT IS, IF WE'RE LOOKING FOR SOME KIND OF BOOST IT'S NOT GOING TO COME FROM SHOUT-OUT. SO--
*SO IT SHOULD BE FUCKING **BLARNEY COCK?** LOOK AT HIM! **LOOK!***

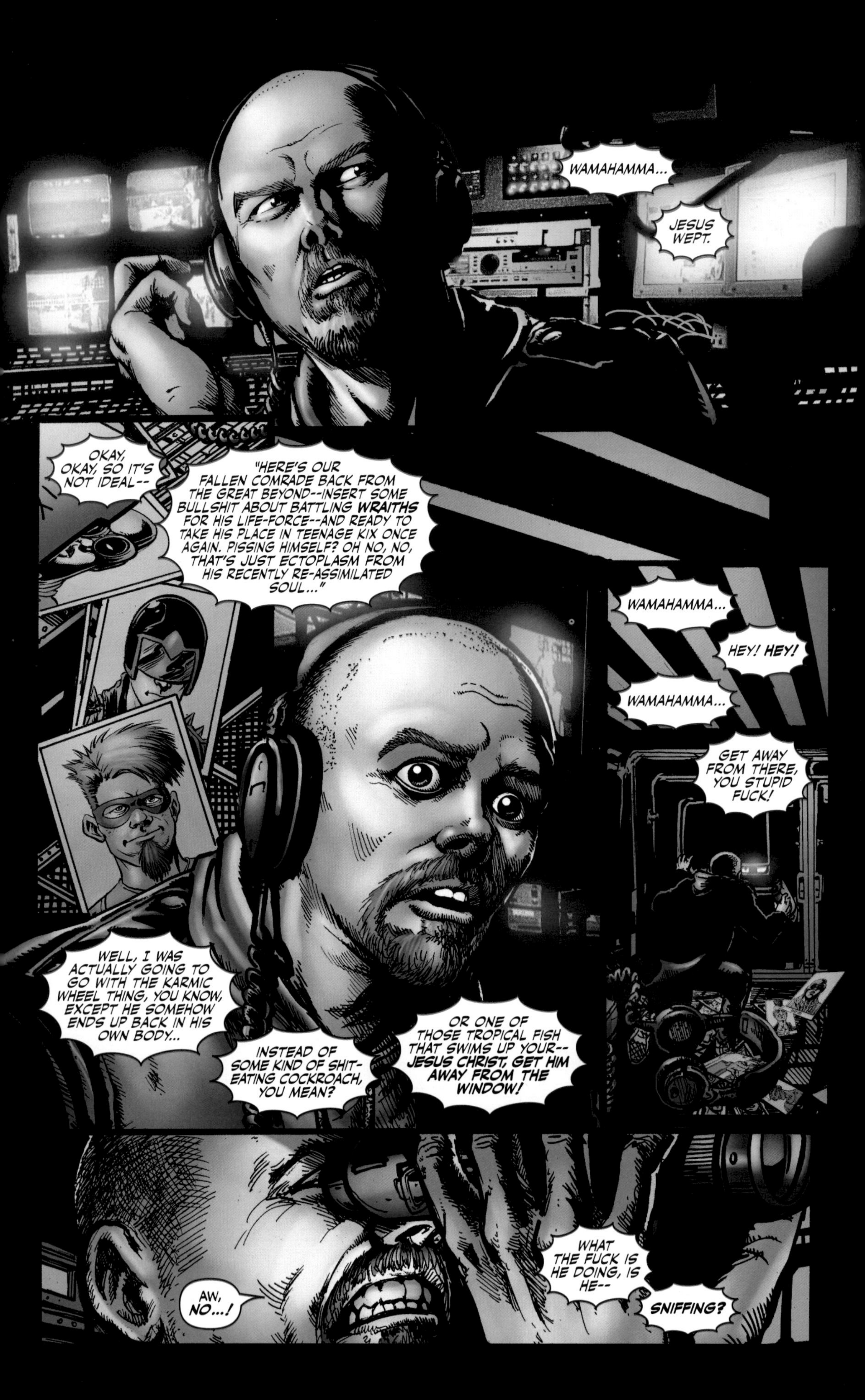
WAMAHAMMA...
JESUS WEPT.
OKAY, OKAY, SO IT'S NOT IDEAL--
"HERE'S OUR FALLEN COMRADE BACK FROM THE GREAT BEYOND--INSERT SOME BULLSHIT ABOUT BATTLING WRAITHS FOR HIS LIFE-FORCE--AND READY TO TAKE HIS PLACE IN TEENAGE KIX ONCE AGAIN. PISSING HIMSELF? OH NO, NO, THAT'S JUST ECTOPLASM FROM HIS RECENTLY RE-ASSIMILATED SOUL..."
WELL, I WAS ACTUALLY GOING TO GO WITH THE KARMIC WHEEL THING, YOU KNOW, EXCEPT HE SOMEHOW ENDS UP BACK IN HIS OWN BODY...
INSTEAD OF SOME KIND OF SHIT-EATING COCKROACH, YOU MEAN?
OR ONE OF THOSE TROPICAL FISH THAT SWIMS UP YOUR-- JESUS CHRIST, GET HIM AWAY FROM THE WINDOW!
WAMAHAMMA...
HEY! HEY!
WAMAHAMMA...
GET AWAY FROM THERE, YOU STUPID FUCK!
AW, NO...!
WHAT THE FUCK IS HE DOING, IS HE--
SNIFFING?

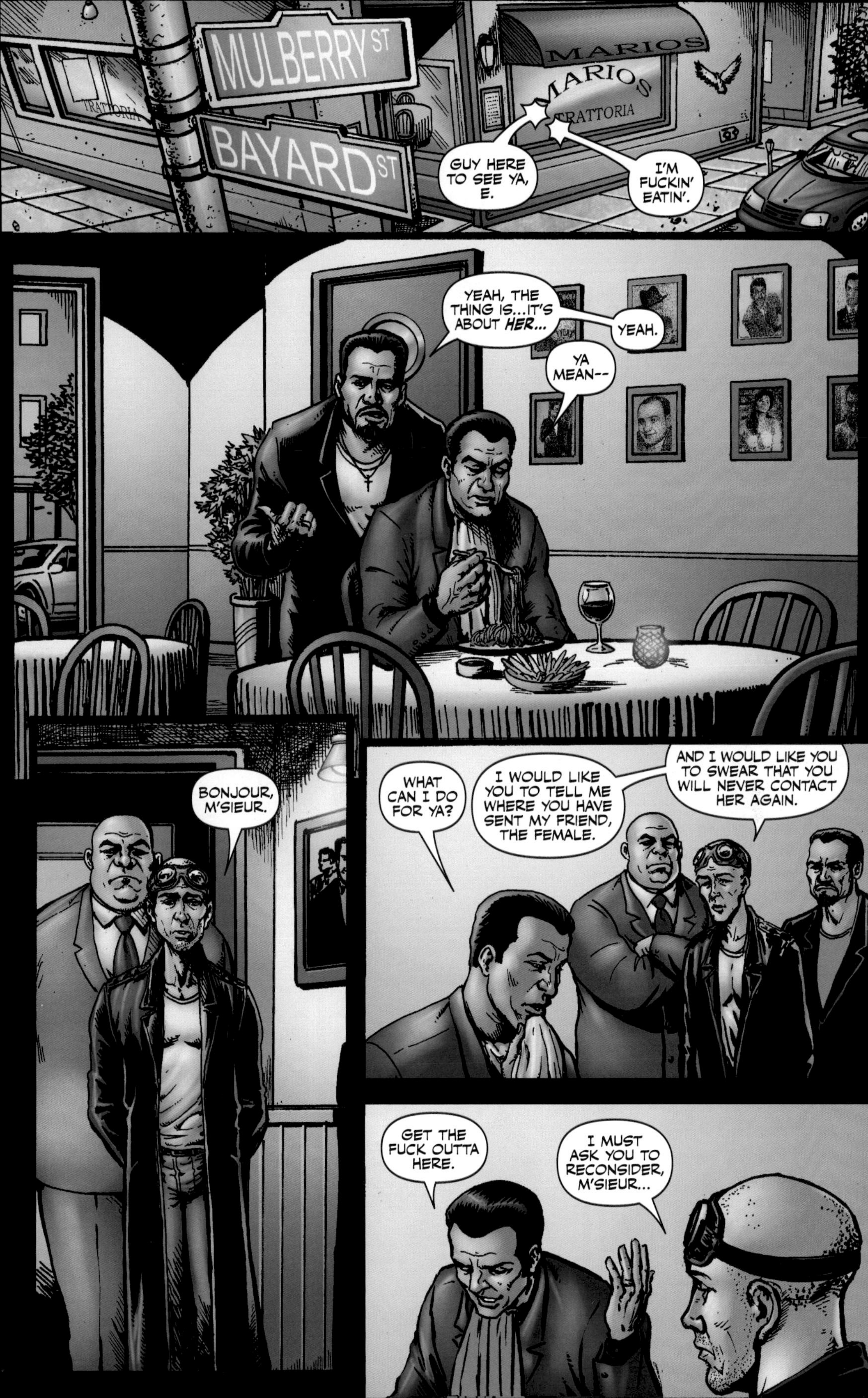
MULBERRY ST
BAYARD ST
MARIOS
MARIOS TRATTORIA
TRATTORIA
GUY HERE TO SEE YA, E.
I'M FUCKIN' EATIN'.
YEAH, THE THING IS...IT'S ABOUT HER...
YA MEAN--
YEAH.
BONJOUR, M'SIEUR.
WHAT CAN I DO FOR YA?
I WOULD LIKE YOU TO TELL ME WHERE YOU HAVE SENT MY FRIEND, THE FEMALE.
AND I WOULD LIKE YOU TO SWEAR THAT YOU WILL NEVER CONTACT HER AGAIN.
GET THE FUCK OUTTA HERE.
I MUST ASK YOU TO RECONSIDER, M'SIEUR...

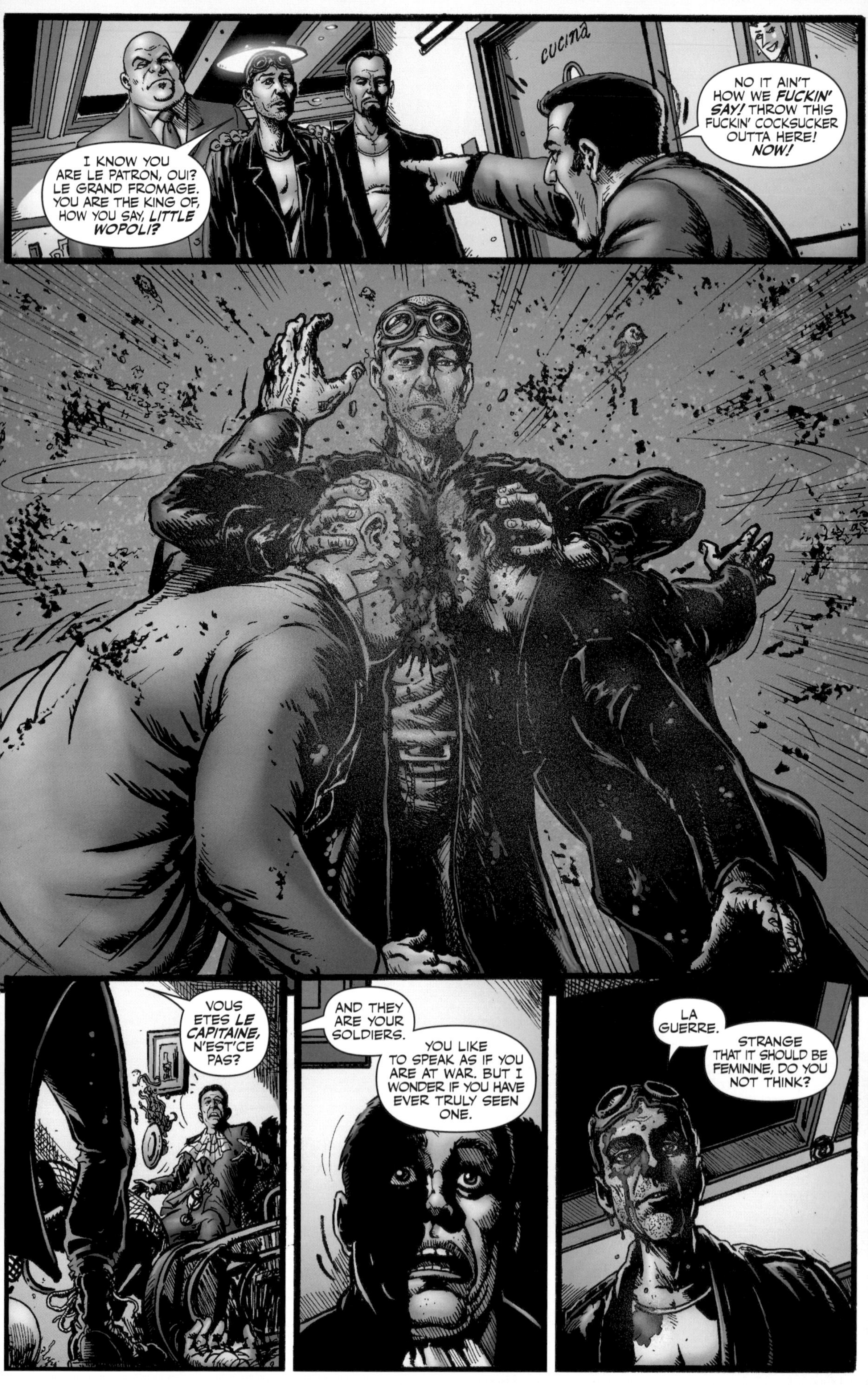

I KNOW YOU ARE LE PATRON, OUI? LE GRAND FROMAGE. YOU ARE THE KING OF, HOW YOU SAY, *LITTLE WOPOLI?*
NO IT AIN'T HOW WE *FUCKIN' SAY!* THROW THIS FUCKIN' COCKSUCKER OUTTA HERE! *NOW!*
VOUS ETES *LE CAPITAINE,* N'EST'CE PAS?
AND THEY ARE YOUR SOLDIERS.
YOU LIKE TO SPEAK AS IF YOU ARE AT WAR. BUT I WONDER IF YOU HAVE EVER TRULY SEEN ONE.
LA GUERRE.
STRANGE THAT IT SHOULD BE FEMININE, DO YOU NOT THINK?

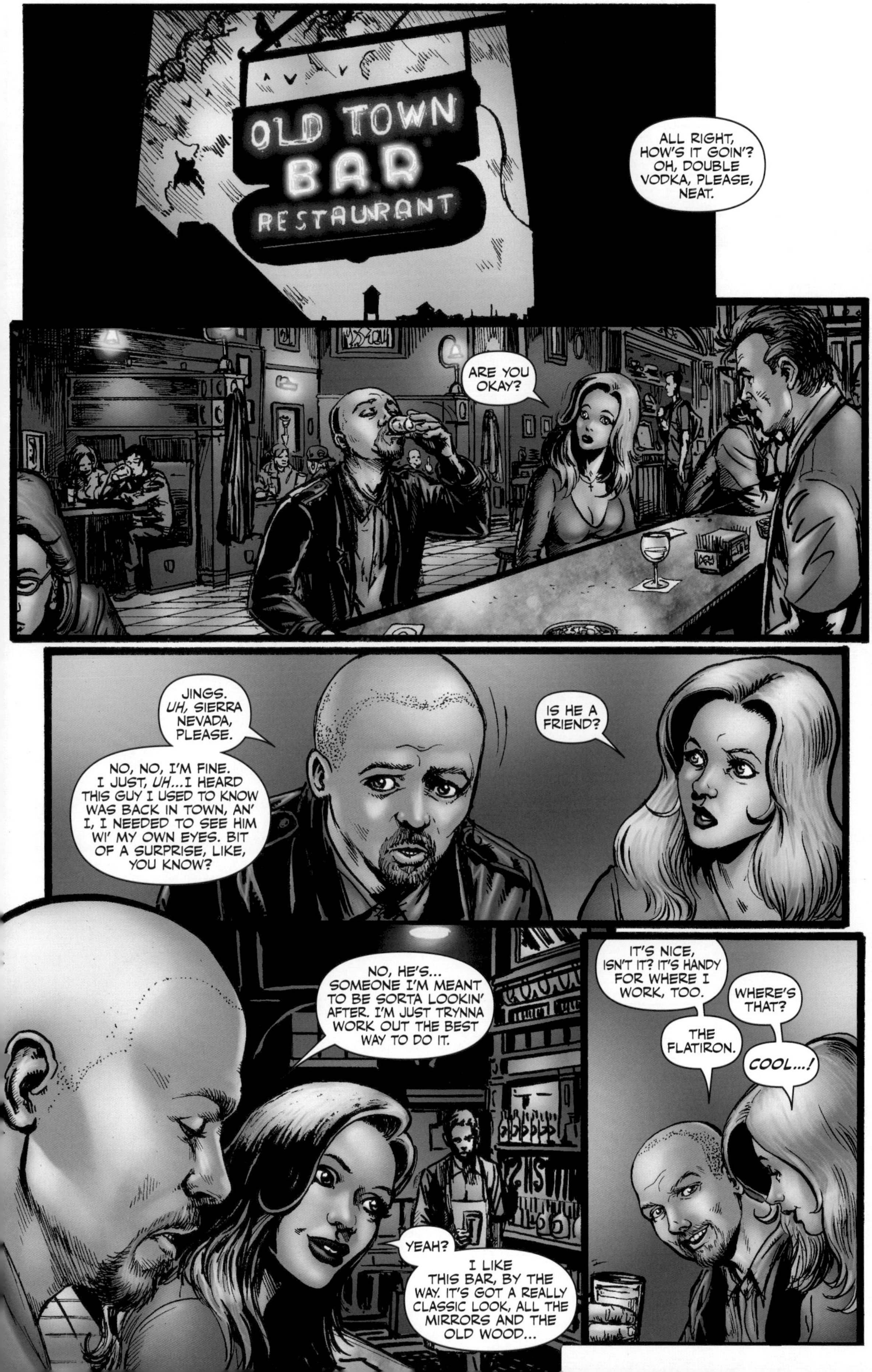
OLD TOWN BAR RESTAURANT
ALL RIGHT, HOW'S IT GOIN'? OH, DOUBLE VODKA, PLEASE, NEAT.
ARE YOU OKAY?
JINGS. *UH,* SIERRA NEVADA, PLEASE.
NO, NO, I'M FINE. I JUST, *UH*...I HEARD THIS GUY I USED TO KNOW WAS BACK IN TOWN, AN' I, I NEEDED TO SEE HIM WI' MY OWN EYES. BIT OF A SURPRISE, LIKE, YOU KNOW?
IS HE A FRIEND?
NO, HE'S... SOMEONE I'M MEANT TO BE SORTA LOOKIN' AFTER. I'M JUST TRYNNA WORK OUT THE BEST WAY TO DO IT.
YEAH?
I LIKE THIS BAR, BY THE WAY. IT'S GOT A REALLY CLASSIC LOOK, ALL THE MIRRORS AND THE OLD WOOD...
IT'S NICE, ISN'T IT? IT'S HANDY FOR WHERE I WORK, TOO.
WHERE'S THAT?
THE FLATIRON.
COOL...!

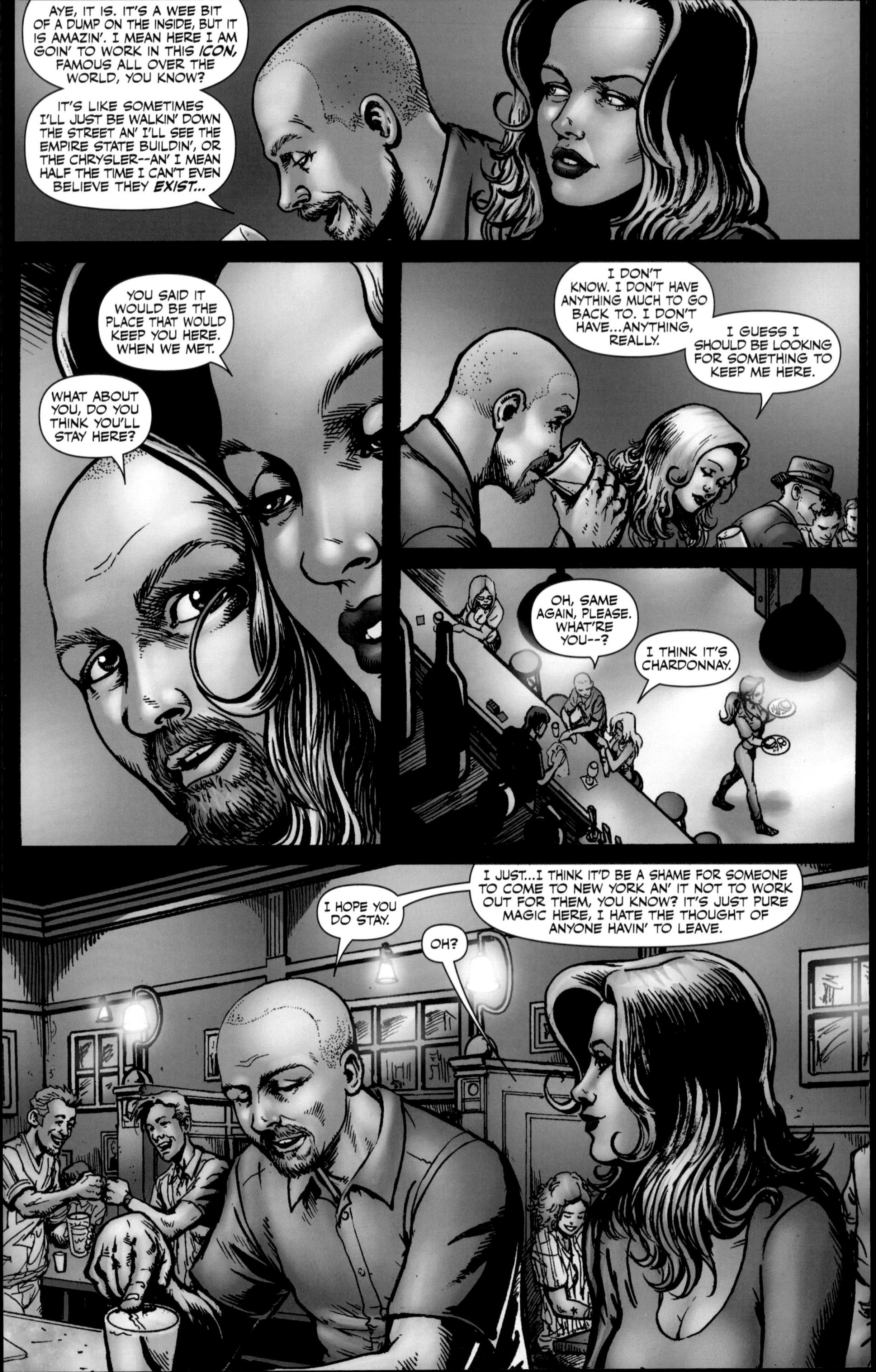
AYE, IT IS. IT'S A WEE BIT OF A DUMP ON THE INSIDE, BUT IT IS AMAZIN'. I MEAN HERE I AM GOIN' TO WORK IN THIS *ICON,* FAMOUS ALL OVER THE WORLD, YOU KNOW?
IT'S LIKE SOMETIMES I'LL JUST BE WALKIN' DOWN THE STREET AN' I'LL SEE THE EMPIRE STATE BUILDIN', OR THE CHRYSLER--AN' I MEAN HALF THE TIME I CAN'T EVEN BELIEVE THEY ***EXIST...***
YOU SAID IT WOULD BE THE PLACE THAT WOULD KEEP YOU HERE. WHEN WE MET.
WHAT ABOUT YOU, DO YOU THINK YOU'LL STAY HERE?
I DON'T KNOW. I DON'T HAVE ANYTHING MUCH TO GO BACK TO. I DON'T HAVE...ANYTHING, REALLY.
I GUESS I SHOULD BE LOOKING FOR SOMETHING TO KEEP ME HERE.
OH, SAME AGAIN, PLEASE. WHAT'RE YOU--?
I THINK IT'S CHARDONNAY.
I HOPE YOU DO STAY.
I JUST...I THINK IT'D BE A SHAME FOR SOMEONE TO COME TO NEW YORK AN' IT NOT TO WORK OUT FOR THEM, YOU KNOW? IT'S JUST PURE MAGIC HERE, I HATE THE THOUGHT OF ANYONE HAVIN' TO LEAVE.
OH?

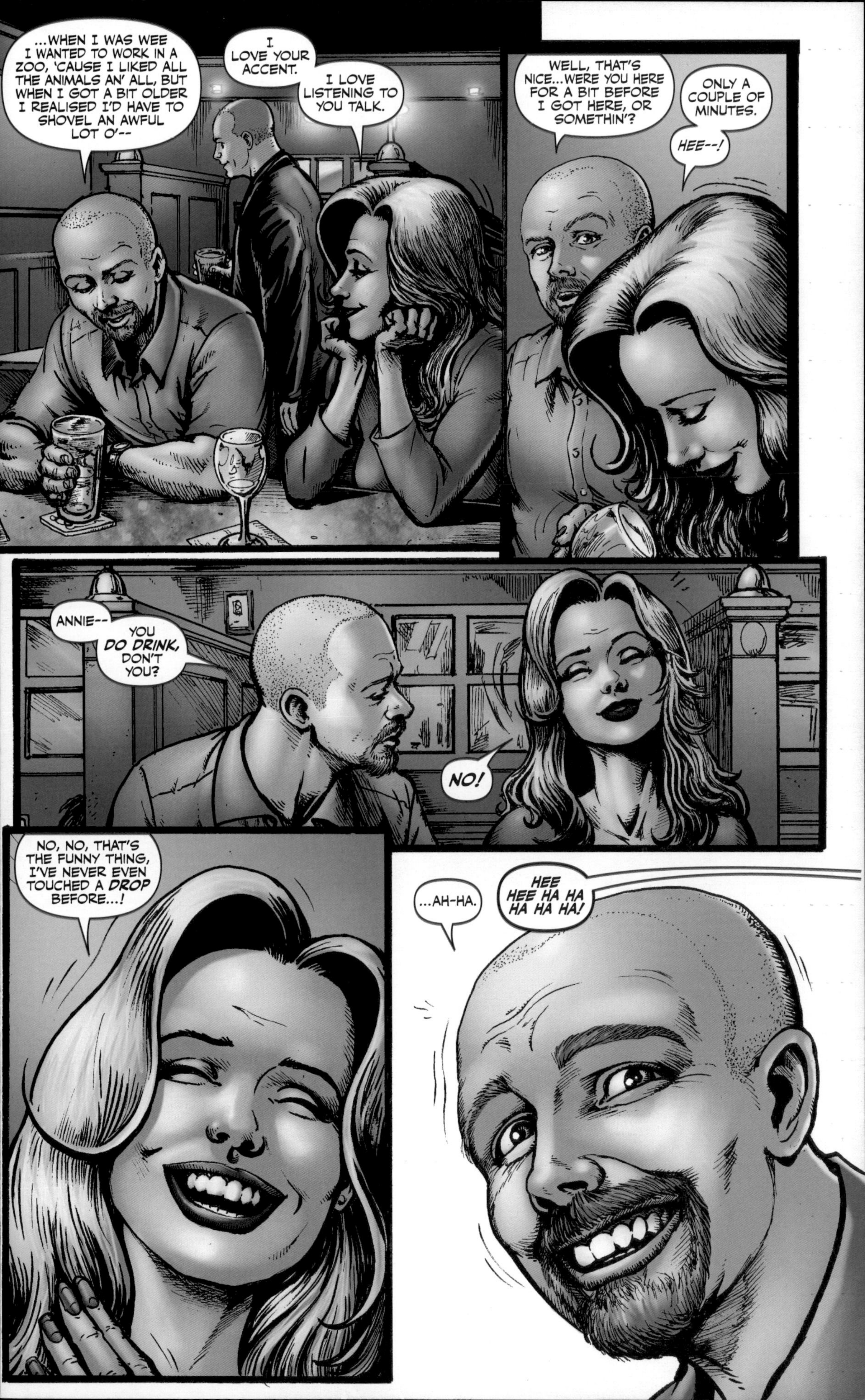
...WHEN I WAS WEE I WANTED TO WORK IN A ZOO, 'CAUSE I LIKED ALL THE ANIMALS AN' ALL, BUT WHEN I GOT A BIT OLDER I REALISED I'D HAVE TO SHOVEL AN AWFUL LOT O'--
I LOVE YOUR ACCENT.
I LOVE LISTENING TO YOU TALK.
WELL, THAT'S NICE...WERE YOU HERE FOR A BIT BEFORE I GOT HERE, OR SOMETHIN'?
ONLY A COUPLE OF MINUTES.
HEE--!
ANNIE--
YOU DO DRINK, DON'T YOU?
NO!
NO, NO, THAT'S THE FUNNY THING, I'VE NEVER EVEN TOUCHED A DROP BEFORE...!
...AH-HA.
HEE HEE HA HA HA HA HA!

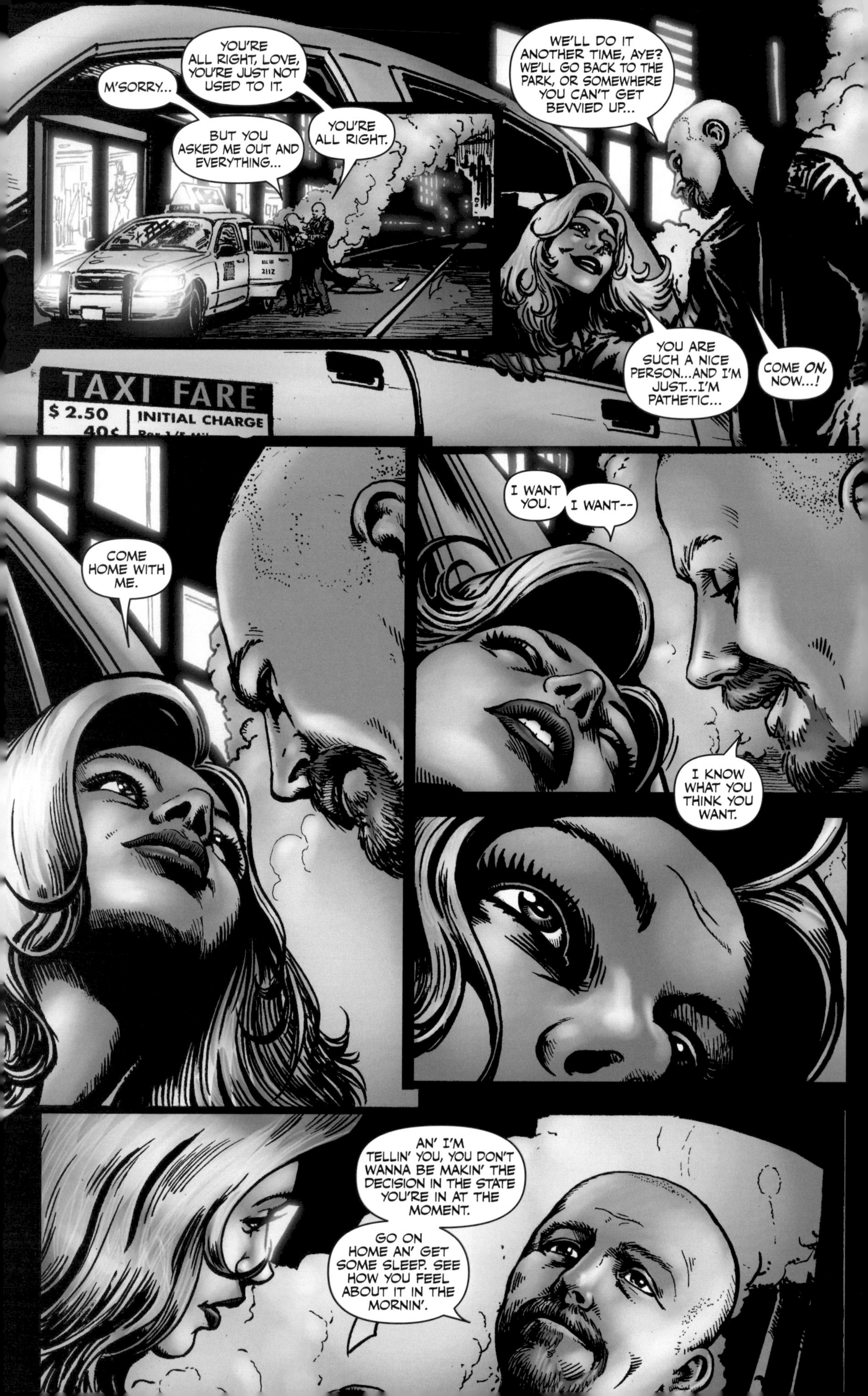
M'SORRY...
YOU'RE ALL RIGHT, LOVE, YOU'RE JUST NOT USED TO IT.
BUT YOU ASKED ME OUT AND EVERYTHING...
YOU'RE ALL RIGHT.
WE'LL DO IT ANOTHER TIME, AYE? WE'LL GO BACK TO THE PARK, OR SOMEWHERE YOU CAN'T GET BEVVIED UP...
YOU ARE SUCH A NICE PERSON...AND I'M JUST...I'M PATHETIC...
COME ON, NOW...!
TAXI FARE
$ 2.50 INITIAL CHARGE
40¢
COME HOME WITH ME.
I WANT YOU.
I WANT--
I KNOW WHAT YOU THINK YOU WANT.
AN' I'M TELLIN' YOU, YOU DON'T WANNA BE MAKIN' THE DECISION IN THE STATE YOU'RE IN AT THE MOMENT.
GO ON HOME AN' GET SOME SLEEP. SEE HOW YOU FEEL ABOUT IT IN THE MORNIN'.

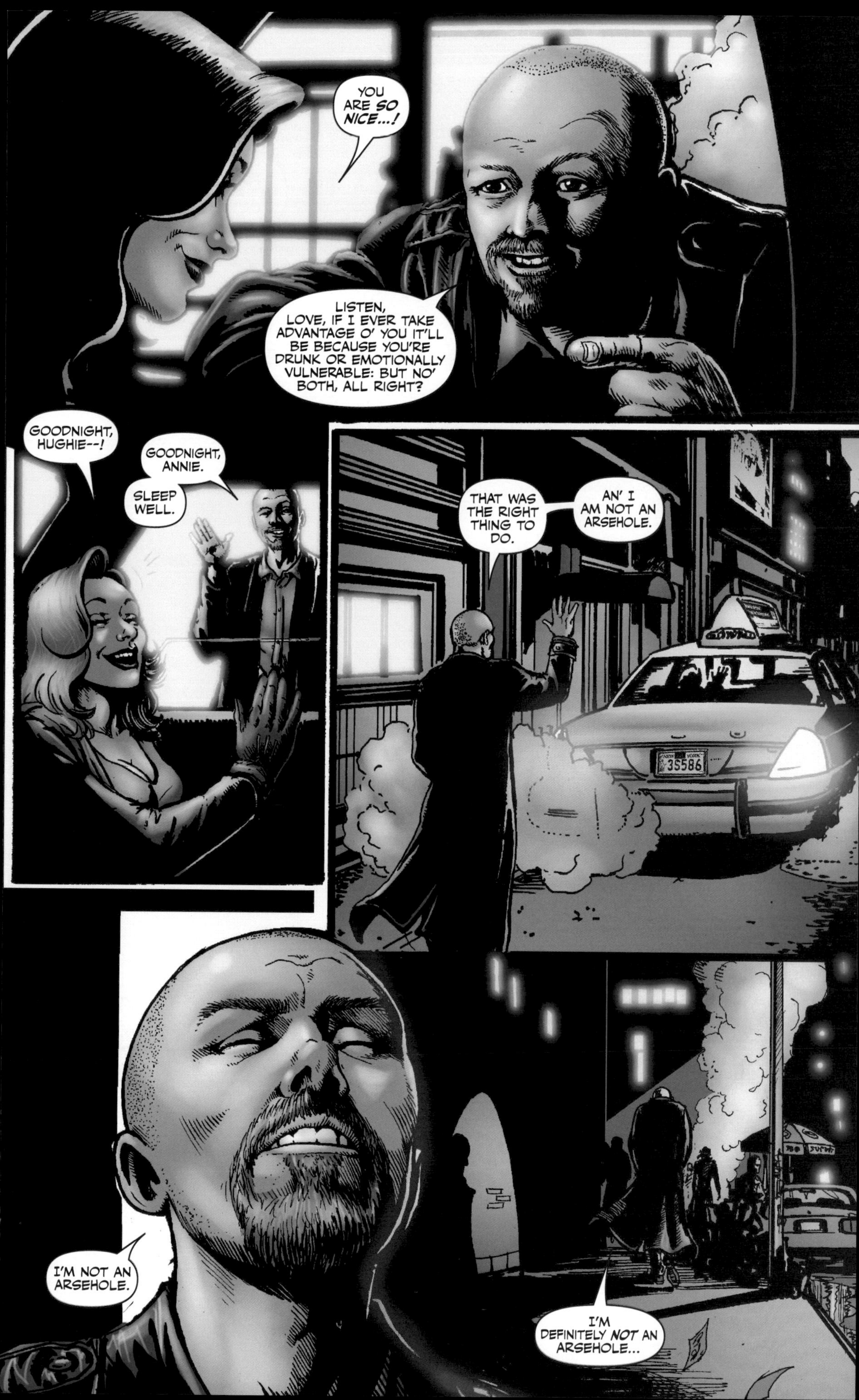
YOU ARE SO NICE...!
LISTEN, LOVE, IF I EVER TAKE ADVANTAGE O' YOU IT'LL BE BECAUSE YOU'RE DRUNK OR EMOTIONALLY VULNERABLE: BUT NO' BOTH, ALL RIGHT?
GOODNIGHT, HUGHIE--!
GOODNIGHT, ANNIE.
SLEEP WELL.
THAT WAS THE RIGHT THING TO DO.
AN' I AM NOT AN ARSEHOLE.
I'M NOT AN ARSEHOLE.
I'M DEFINITELY NOT AN ARSEHOLE...

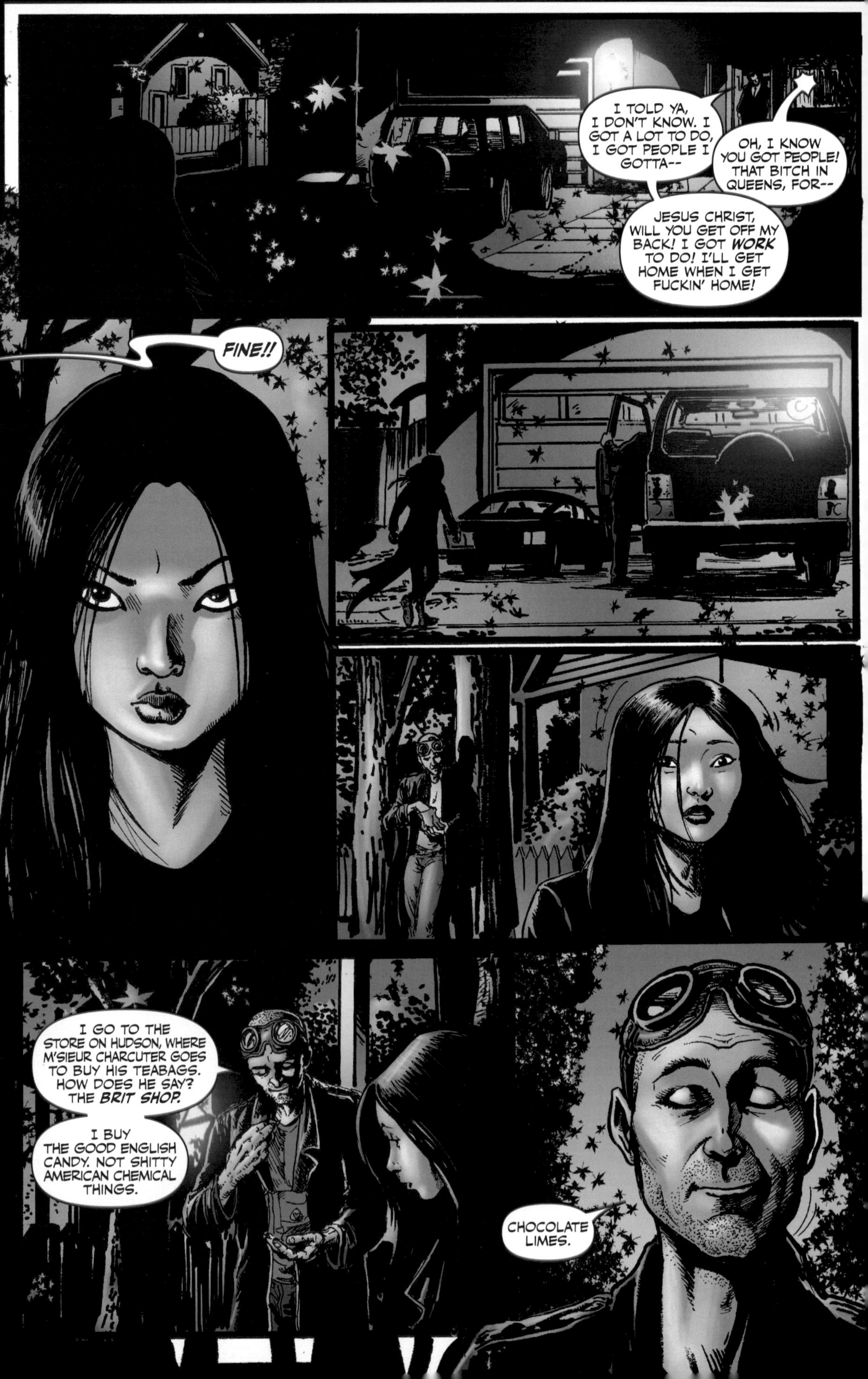
I TOLD YA, I DON'T KNOW. I GOT A LOT TO DO, I GOT PEOPLE I GOTTA--
OH, I KNOW YOU GOT PEOPLE! THAT BITCH IN QUEENS, FOR--
JESUS CHRIST, WILL YOU GET OFF MY BACK! I GOT WORK TO DO! I'LL GET HOME WHEN I GET FUCKIN' HOME!
FINE!!
I GO TO THE STORE ON HUDSON, WHERE M'SIEUR CHARCUTER GOES TO BUY HIS TEABAGS. HOW DOES HE SAY? THE BRIT SHOP.
I BUY THE GOOD ENGLISH CANDY. NOT SHITTY AMERICAN CHEMICAL THINGS.
CHOCOLATE LIMES.

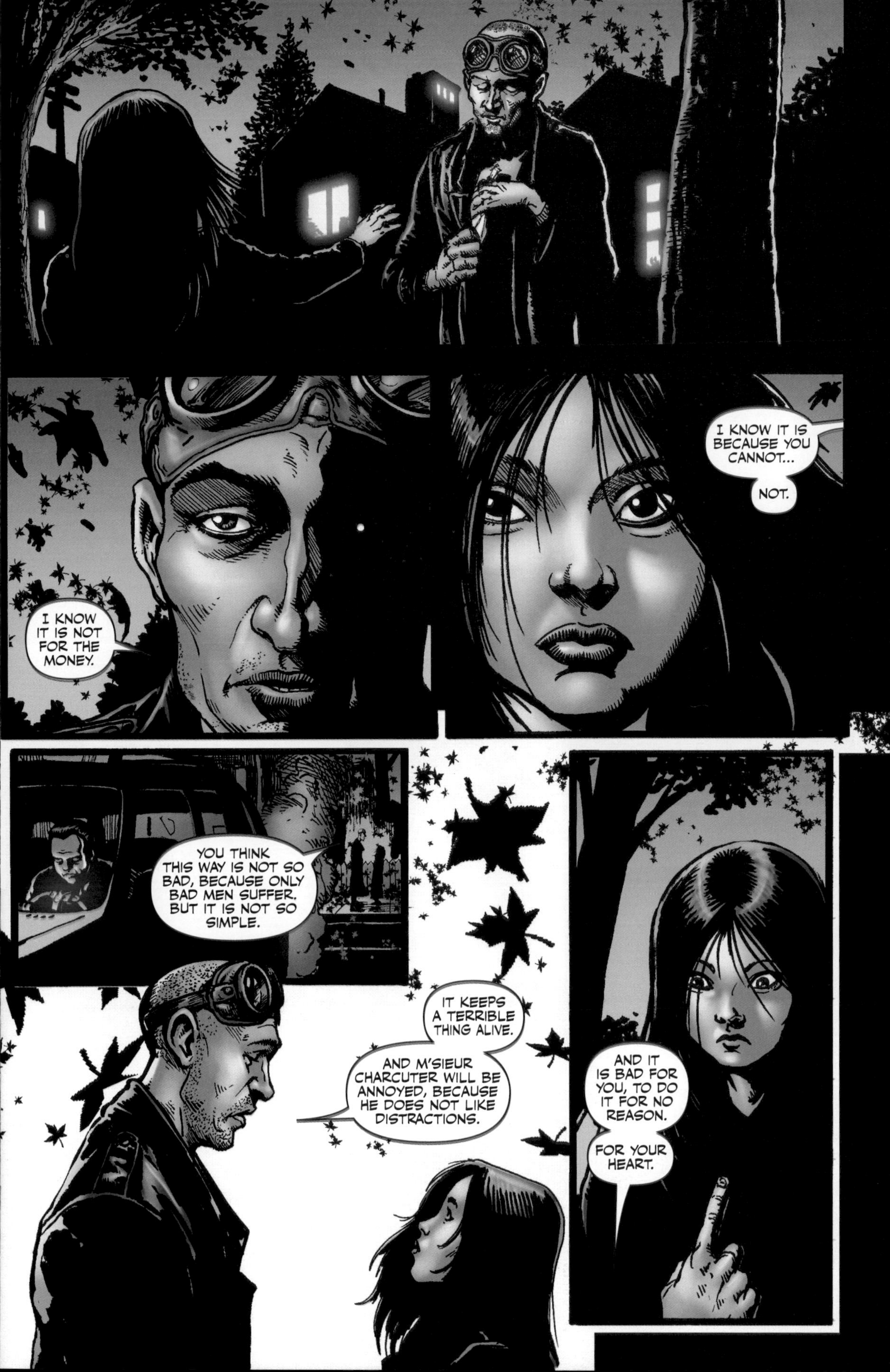
I KNOW IT IS NOT FOR THE MONEY.
I KNOW IT IS BECAUSE YOU CANNOT...
NOT.
YOU THINK THIS WAY IS NOT SO BAD, BECAUSE ONLY BAD MEN SUFFER. BUT IT IS NOT SO SIMPLE.
IT KEEPS A TERRIBLE THING ALIVE.
AND M'SIEUR CHARCUTER WILL BE ANNOYED, BECAUSE HE DOES NOT LIKE DISTRACTIONS.
AND IT IS BAD FOR YOU, TO DO IT FOR NO REASON.
FOR YOUR HEART.

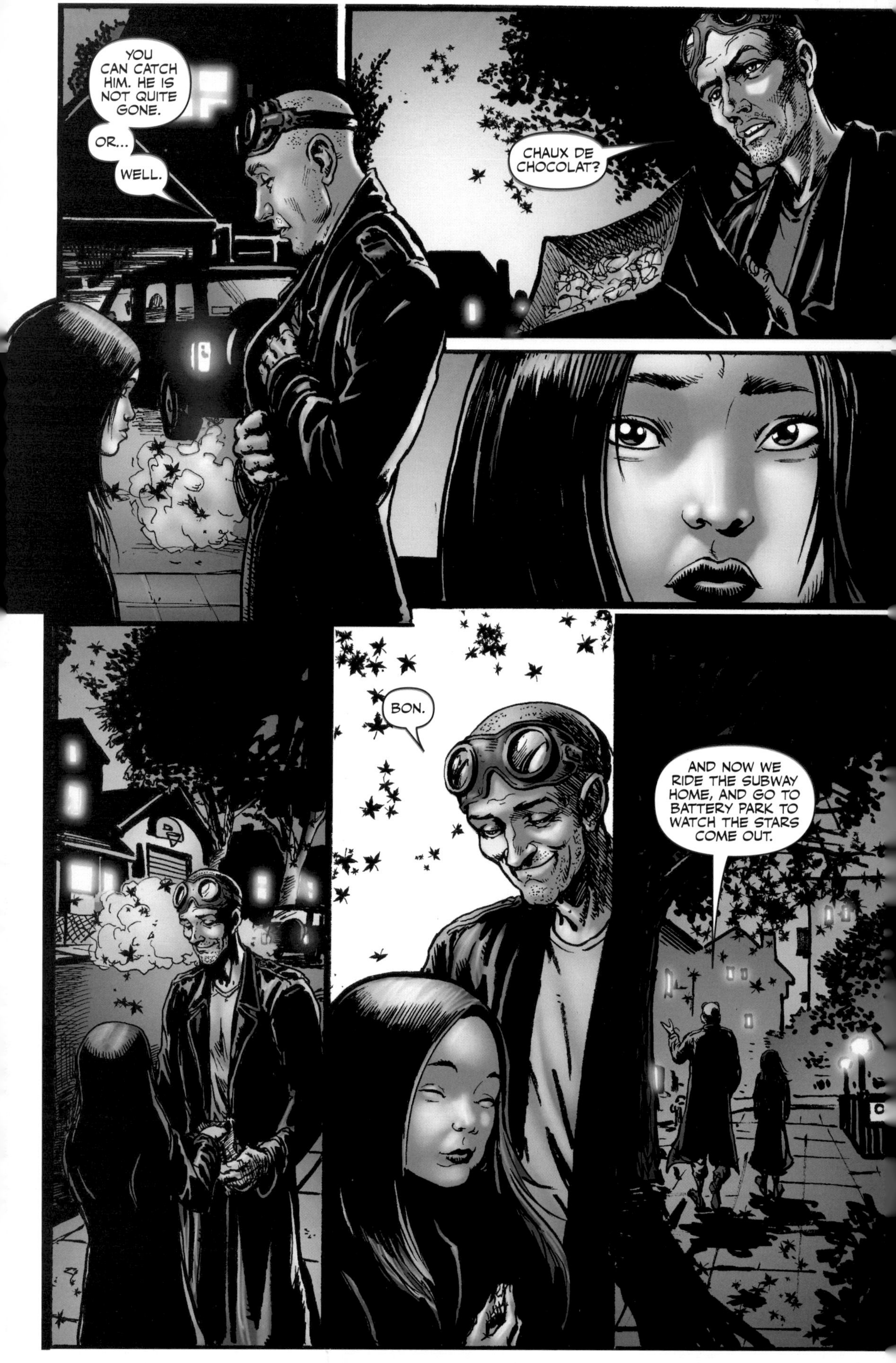
YOU CAN CATCH HIM. HE IS NOT QUITE GONE.
OR...
WELL.
CHAUX DE CHOCOLAT?
BON.
AND NOW WE RIDE THE SUBWAY HOME, AND GO TO BATTERY PARK TO WATCH THE STARS COME OUT.

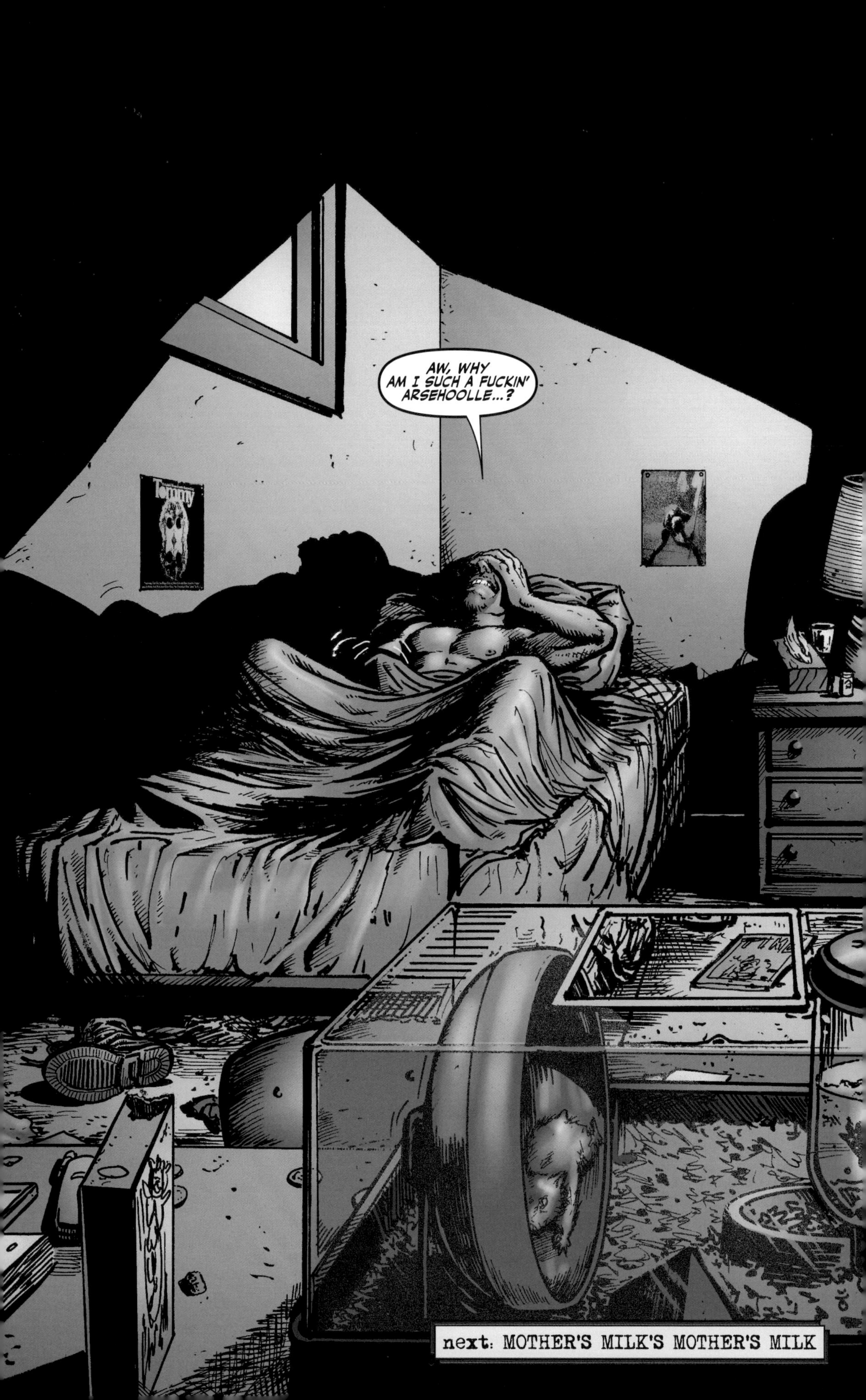
AW, WHY AM I SUCH A FUCKIN' ARSEHOOLLE...?
next: MOTHER'S MILK'S MOTHER'S MILK

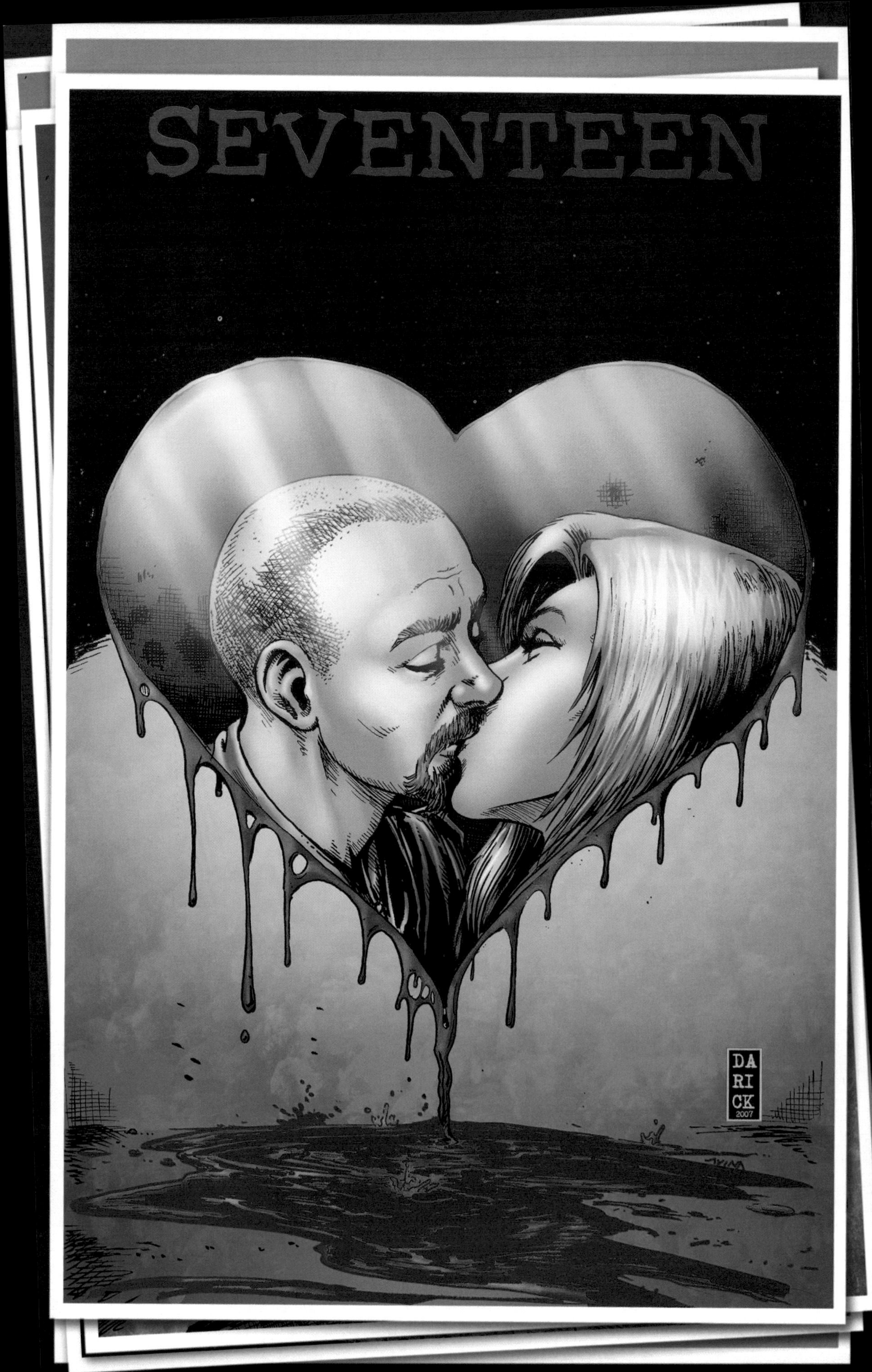
SEVENTEEN
DA
RI
CK
2007

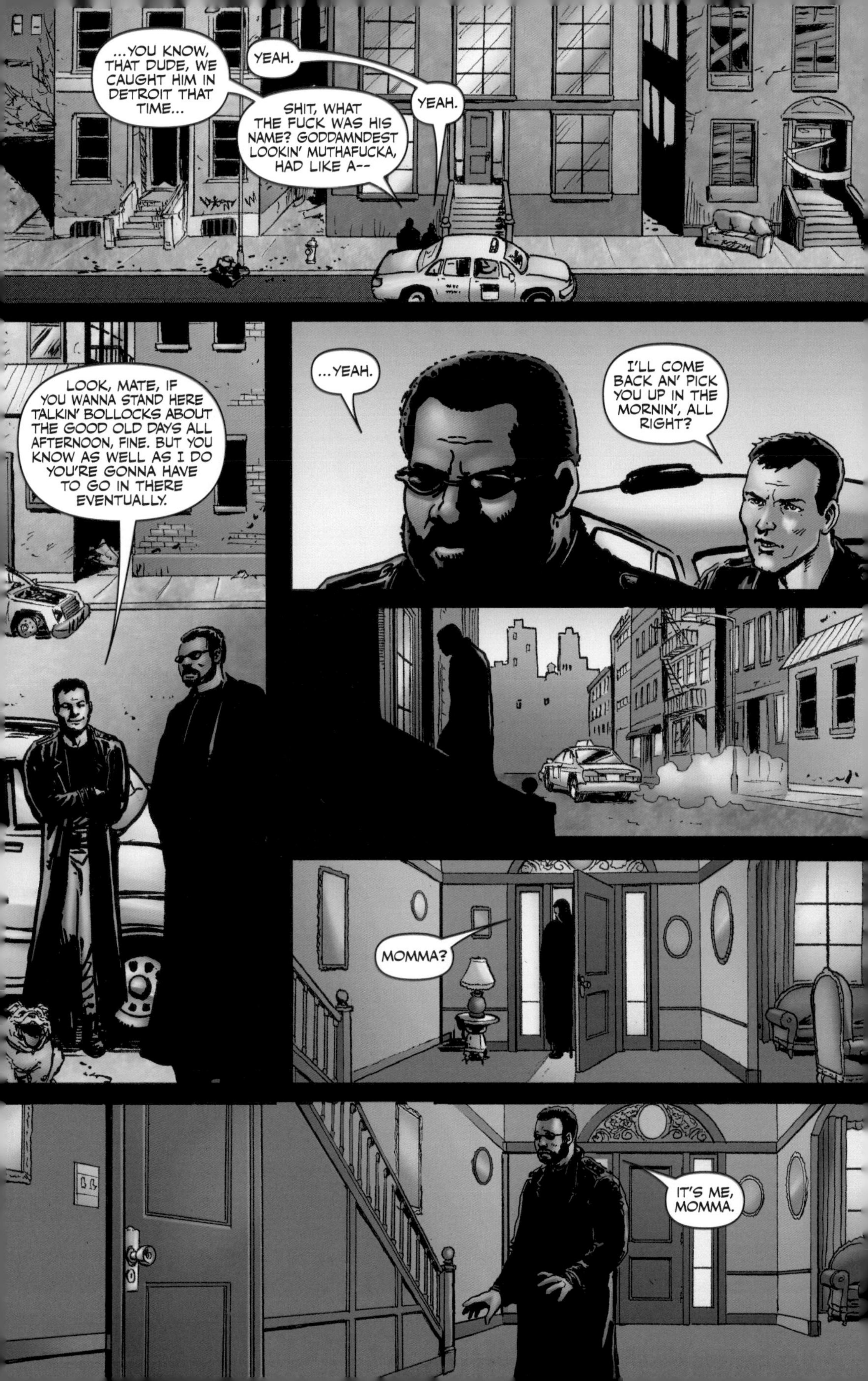
...YOU KNOW, THAT DUDE, WE CAUGHT HIM IN DETROIT THAT TIME...
YEAH.
SHIT, WHAT THE FUCK WAS HIS NAME? GODDAMNDEST LOOKIN' MUTHAFUCKA, HAD LIKE A--
YEAH.
LOOK, MATE, IF YOU WANNA STAND HERE TALKIN' BOLLOCKS ABOUT THE GOOD OLD DAYS ALL AFTERNOON, FINE. BUT YOU KNOW AS WELL AS I DO YOU'RE GONNA HAVE TO GO IN THERE EVENTUALLY.
...YEAH.
I'LL COME BACK AN' PICK YOU UP IN THE MORNIN', ALL RIGHT?
MOMMA?
IT'S ME, MOMMA.

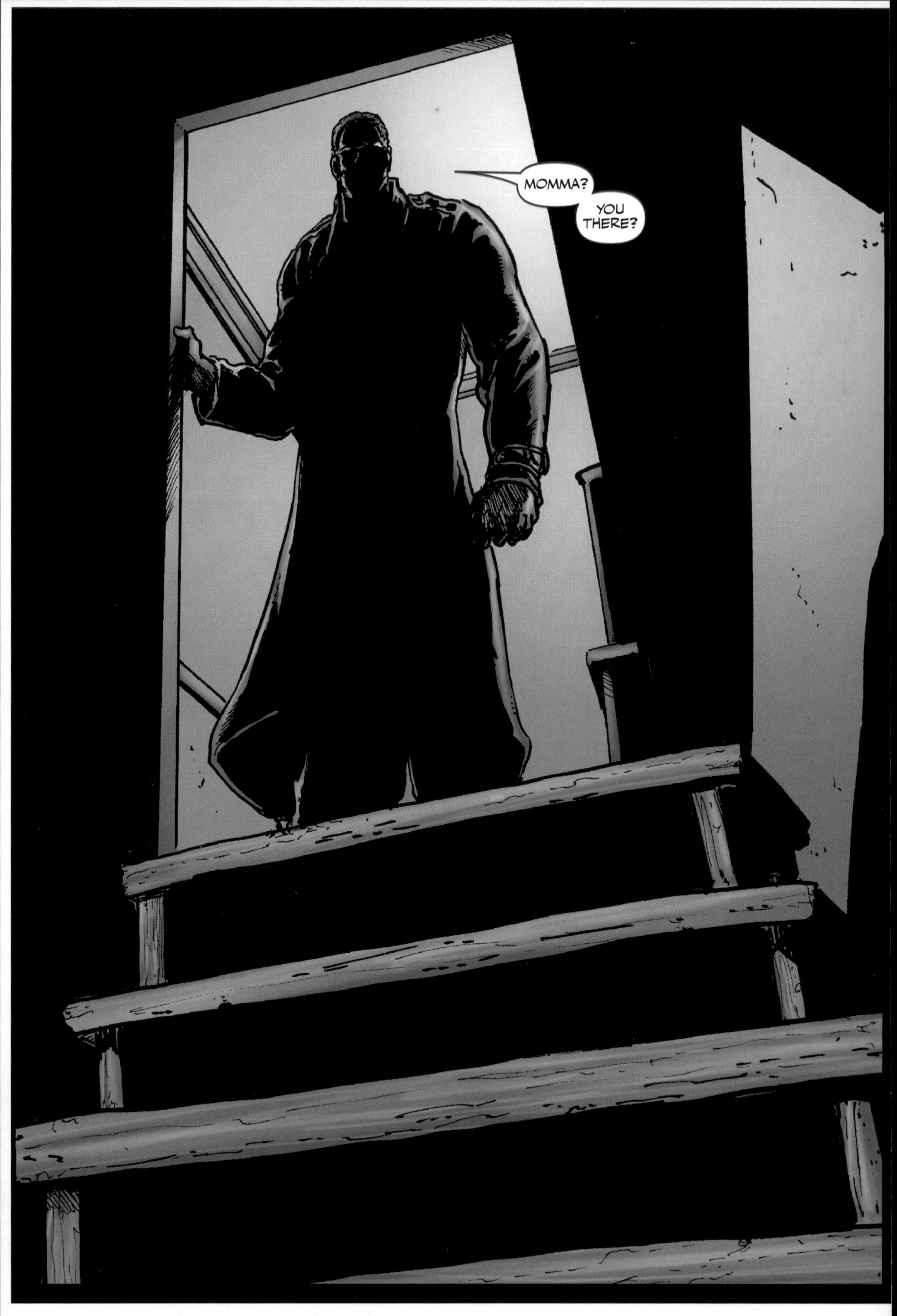
MOMMA?
YOU THERE?

GOOD FOR THE SOUL part three

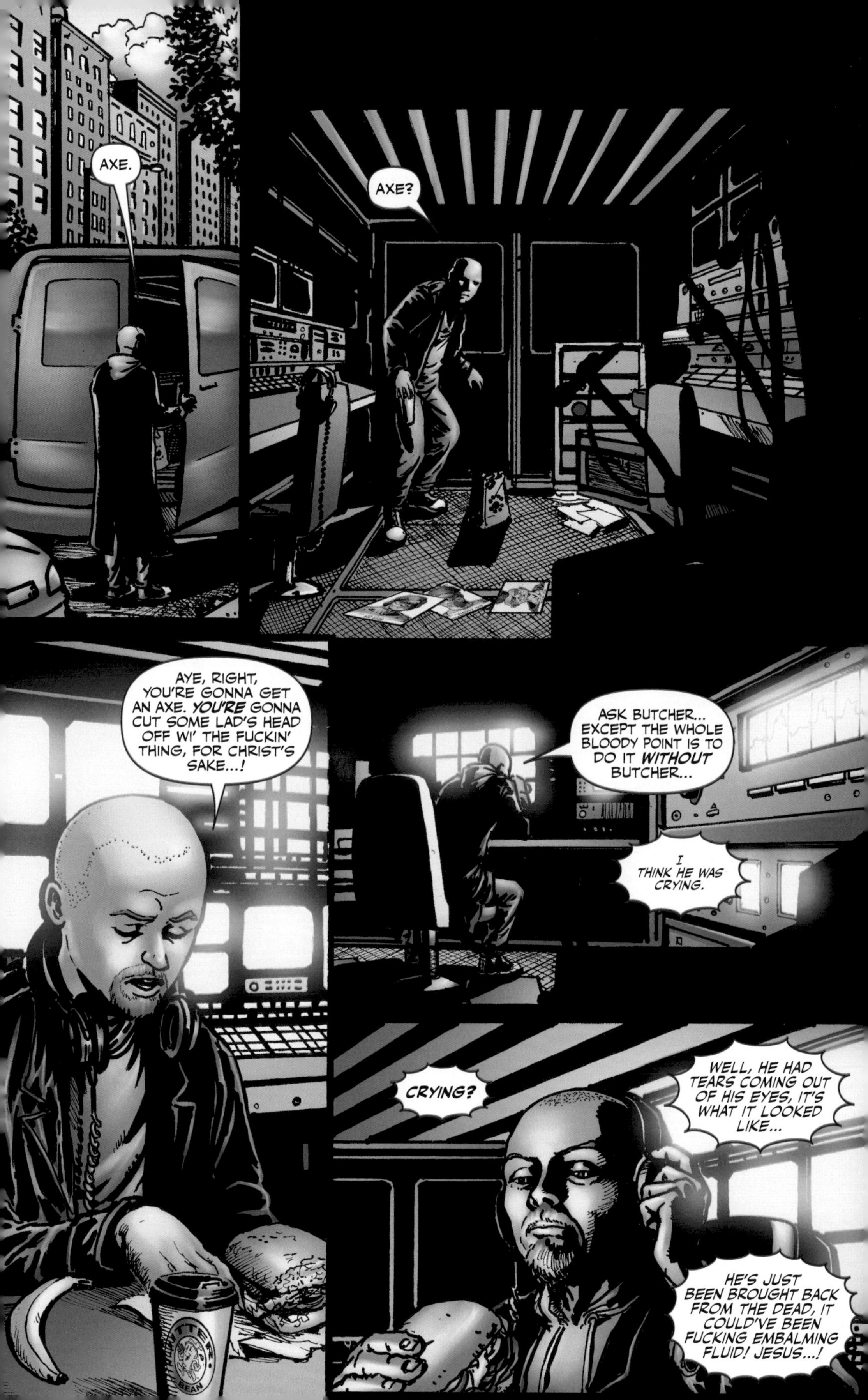
AXE.
AXE?
AYE, RIGHT, YOU'RE GONNA GET AN AXE. YOU'RE GONNA CUT SOME LAD'S HEAD OFF WI' THE FUCKIN' THING, FOR CHRIST'S SAKE...!
ASK BUTCHER... EXCEPT THE WHOLE BLOODY POINT IS TO DO IT WITHOUT BUTCHER...
I THINK HE WAS CRYING.
CRYING?
WELL, HE HAD TEARS COMING OUT OF HIS EYES, IT'S WHAT IT LOOKED LIKE...
HE'S JUST BEEN BROUGHT BACK FROM THE DEAD, IT COULD'VE BEEN FUCKING EMBALMING FLUID! JESUS...!

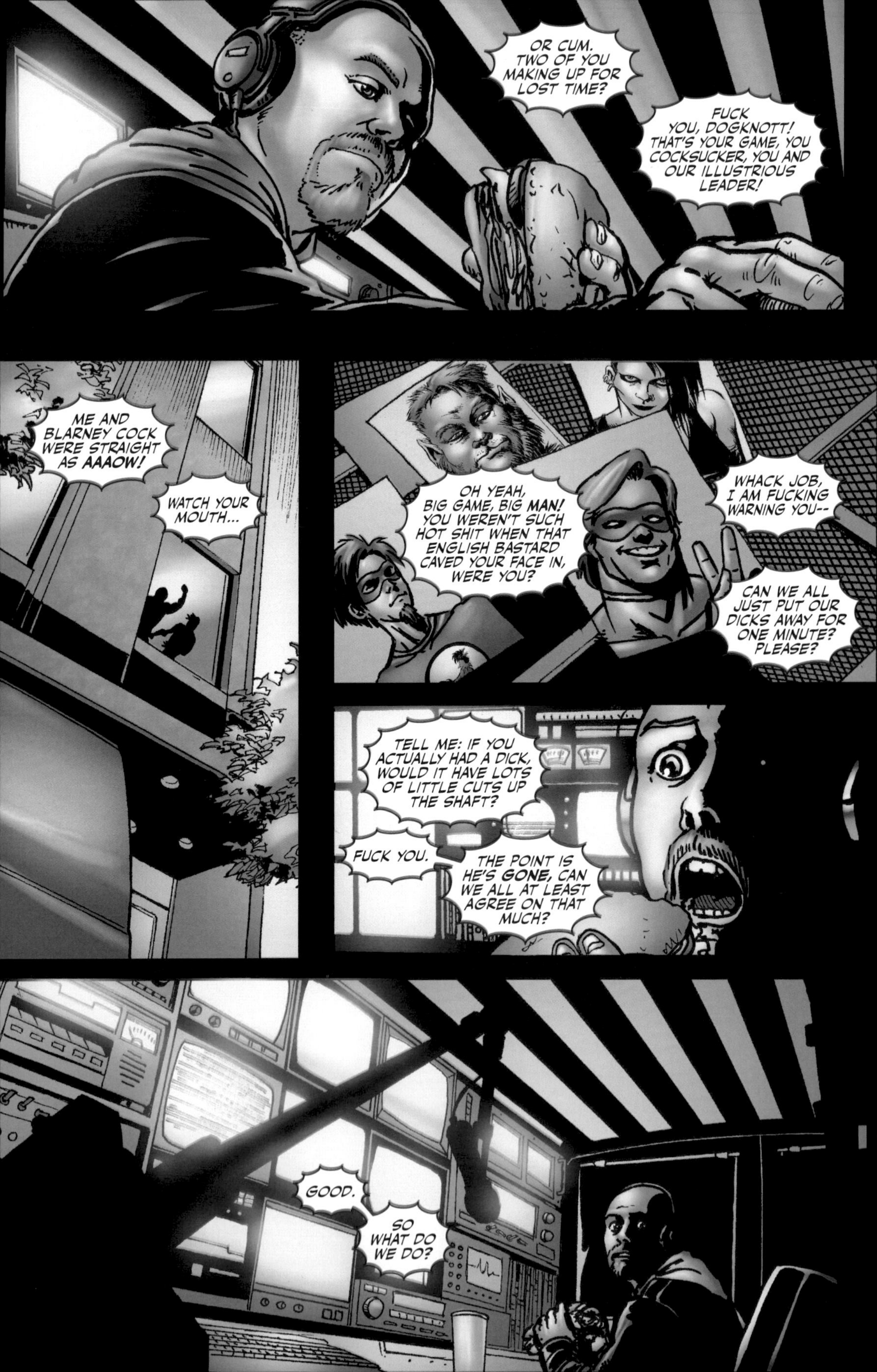
OR CUM. TWO OF YOU MAKING UP FOR LOST TIME?
FUCK YOU, DOGKNOTT! THAT'S YOUR GAME, YOU COCKSUCKER, YOU AND OUR ILLUSTRIOUS LEADER!
ME AND BLARNEY COCK WERE STRAIGHT AS AAAOW!
WATCH YOUR MOUTH...
OH YEAH, BIG GAME, BIG MAN! YOU WEREN'T SUCH HOT SHIT WHEN THAT ENGLISH BASTARD CAVED YOUR FACE IN, WERE YOU?
WHACK JOB, I AM FUCKING WARNING YOU--
CAN WE ALL JUST PUT OUR DICKS AWAY FOR ONE MINUTE? PLEASE?
TELL ME: IF YOU ACTUALLY HAD A DICK, WOULD IT HAVE LOTS OF LITTLE CUTS UP THE SHAFT?
FUCK YOU.
THE POINT IS HE'S GONE, CAN WE ALL AT LEAST AGREE ON THAT MUCH?
GOOD.
SO WHAT DO WE DO?

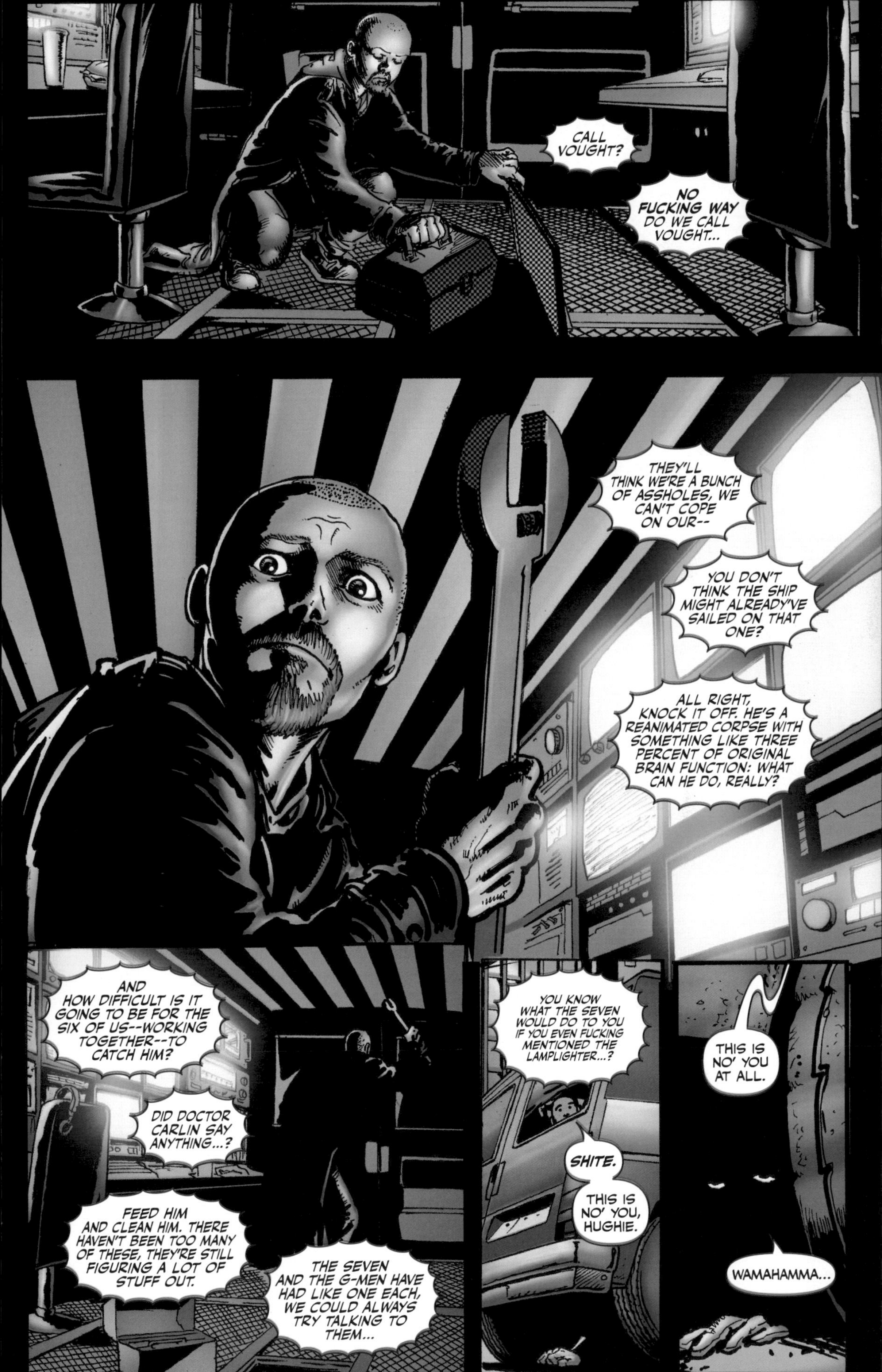

CALL VOUGHT?
NO FUCKING WAY DO WE CALL VOUGHT...
THEY'LL THINK WE'RE A BUNCH OF ASSHOLES, WE CAN'T COPE ON OUR--
YOU DON'T THINK THE SHIP MIGHT ALREADY'VE SAILED ON THAT ONE?
ALL RIGHT, KNOCK IT OFF. HE'S A REANIMATED CORPSE WITH SOMETHING LIKE THREE PERCENT OF ORIGINAL BRAIN FUNCTION: WHAT CAN HE DO, REALLY?
AND HOW DIFFICULT IS IT GOING TO BE FOR THE SIX OF US--WORKING TOGETHER--TO CATCH HIM?
DID DOCTOR CARLIN SAY ANYTHING...?
FEED HIM AND CLEAN HIM. THERE HAVEN'T BEEN TOO MANY OF THESE, THEY'RE STILL FIGURING A LOT OF STUFF OUT.
THE SEVEN AND THE G-MEN HAVE HAD LIKE ONE EACH, WE COULD ALWAYS TRY TALKING TO THEM...
YOU KNOW WHAT THE SEVEN WOULD DO TO YOU IF YOU EVEN FUCKING MENTIONED THE LAMPLIGHTER...?
SHITE.
THIS IS NO' YOU, HUGHIE.
THIS IS NO' YOU AT ALL.
WAMAHAMMA...

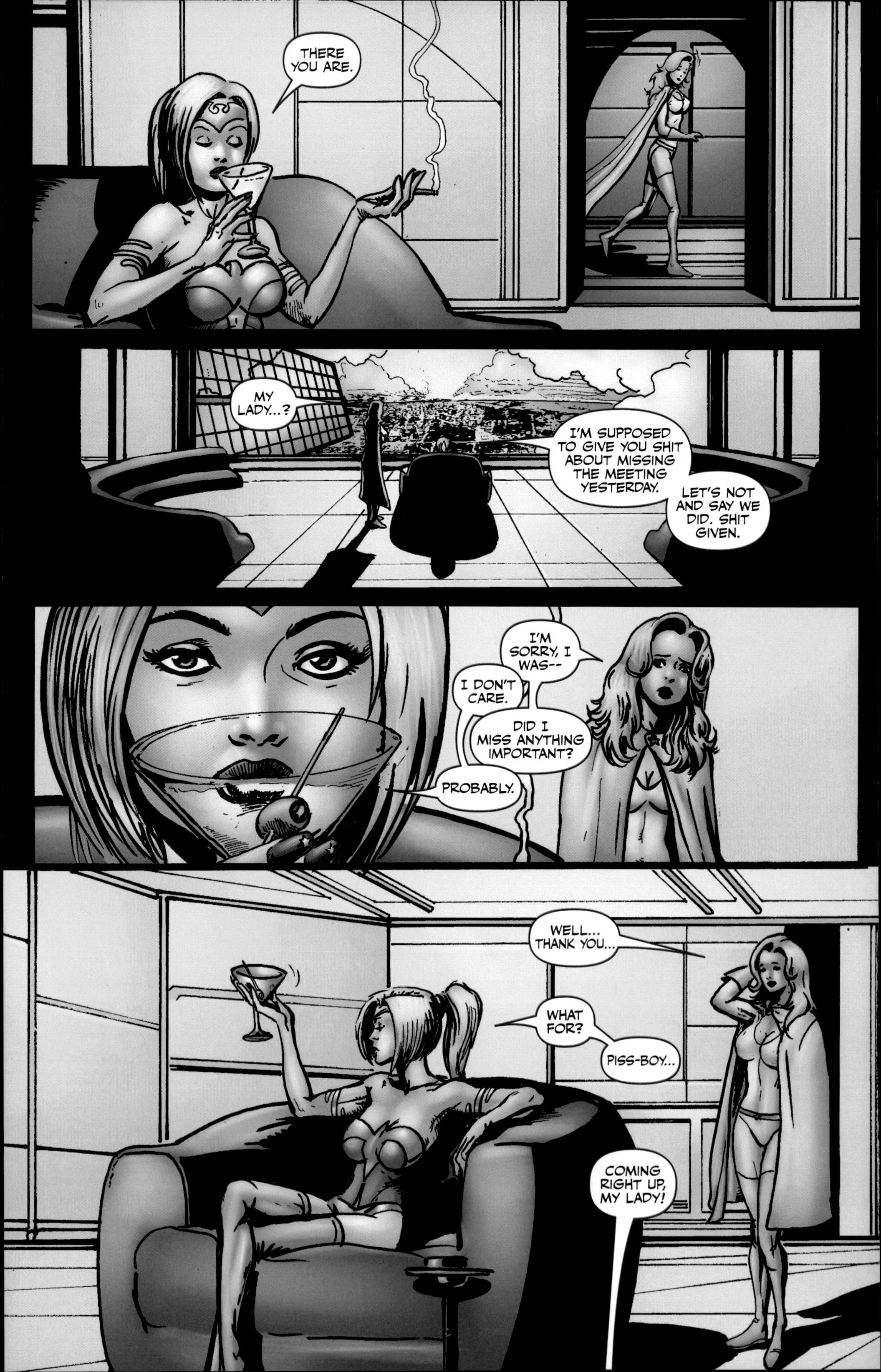
THERE YOU ARE.
MY LADY...?
I'M SUPPOSED TO GIVE YOU SHIT ABOUT MISSING THE MEETING YESTERDAY.
LET'S NOT AND SAY WE DID. SHIT GIVEN.
I'M SORRY, I WAS--
I DON'T CARE.
DID I MISS ANYTHING IMPORTANT?
PROBABLY.
WELL... THANK YOU...
WHAT FOR?
PISS-BOY...
COMING RIGHT UP, MY LADY!

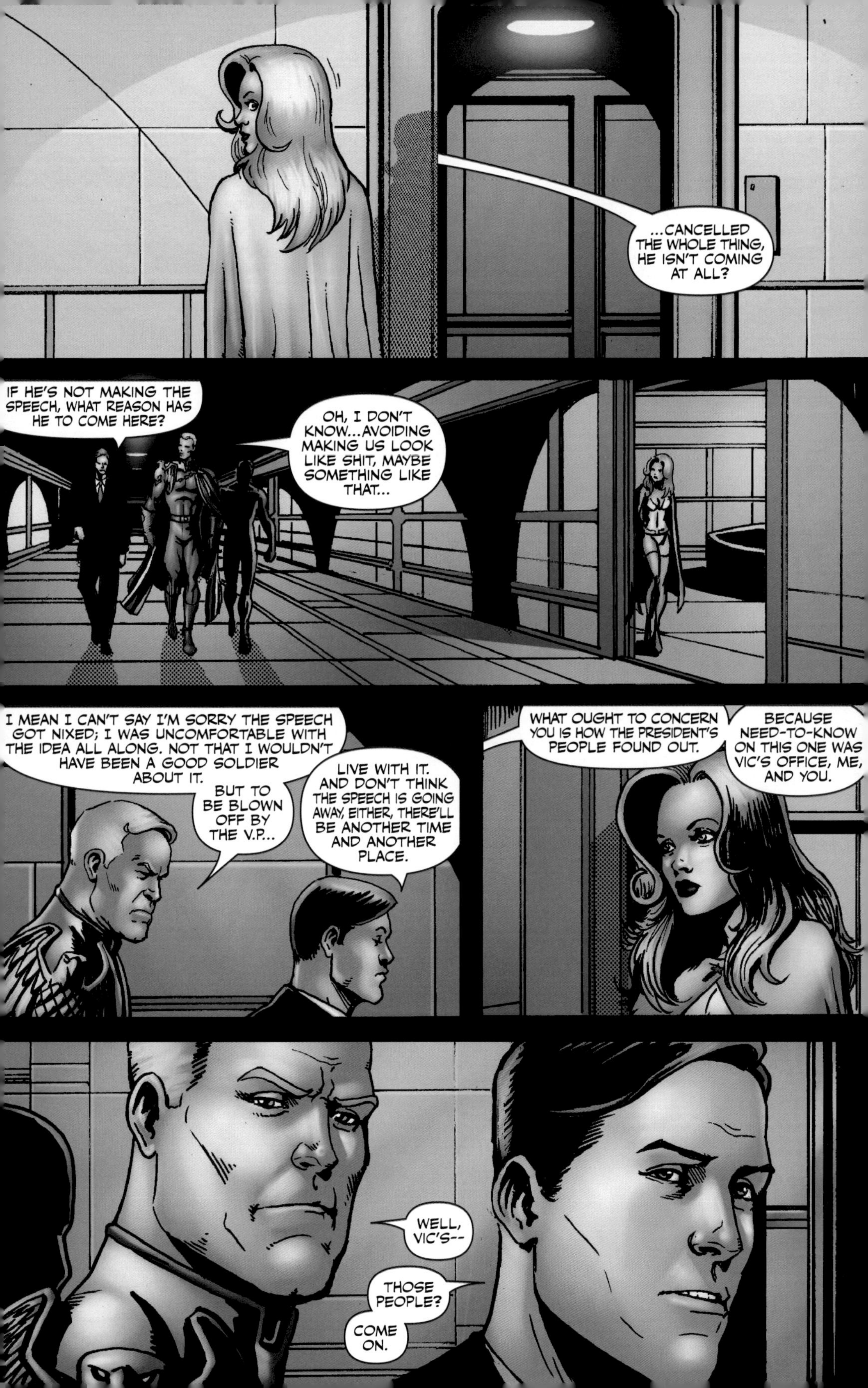
...CANCELLED THE WHOLE THING, HE ISN'T COMING AT ALL?
IF HE'S NOT MAKING THE SPEECH, WHAT REASON HAS HE TO COME HERE?
OH, I DON'T KNOW...AVOIDING MAKING US LOOK LIKE SHIT, MAYBE SOMETHING LIKE THAT...
I MEAN I CAN'T SAY I'M SORRY THE SPEECH GOT NIXED; I WAS UNCOMFORTABLE WITH THE IDEA ALL ALONG. NOT THAT I WOULDN'T HAVE BEEN A GOOD SOLDIER ABOUT IT.
BUT TO BE BLOWN OFF BY THE V.P...
LIVE WITH IT. AND DON'T THINK THE SPEECH IS GOING AWAY, EITHER. THERE'LL BE ANOTHER TIME AND ANOTHER PLACE.
WHAT OUGHT TO CONCERN YOU IS HOW THE PRESIDENT'S PEOPLE FOUND OUT.
BECAUSE NEED-TO-KNOW ON THIS ONE WAS VIC'S OFFICE, ME, AND YOU.
WELL, VIC'S--
THOSE PEOPLE?
COME ON.

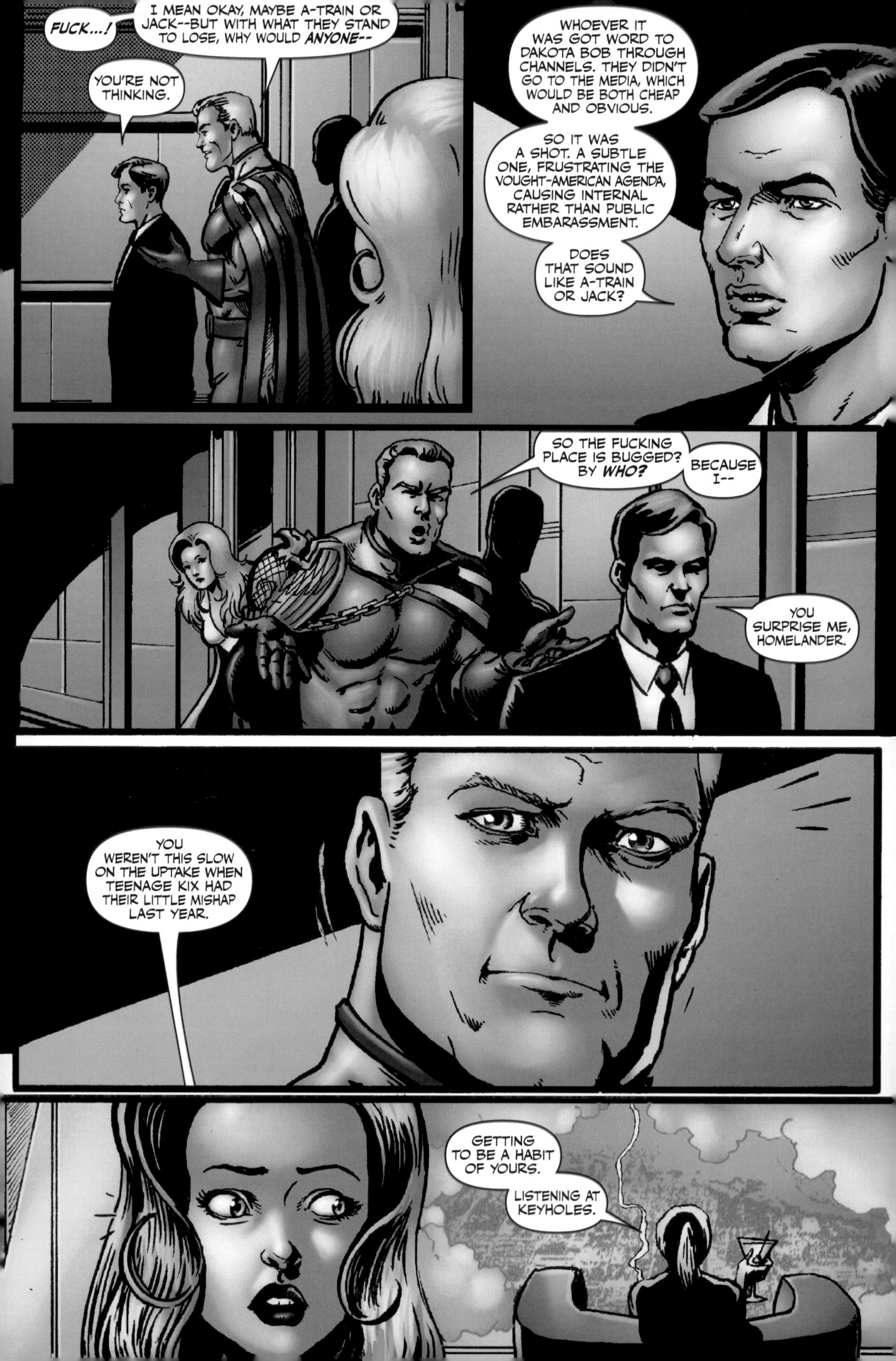

FUCK...!
I MEAN OKAY, MAYBE A-TRAIN OR JACK--BUT WITH WHAT THEY STAND TO LOSE, WHY WOULD *ANYONE*--
YOU'RE NOT THINKING.
WHOEVER IT WAS GOT WORD TO DAKOTA BOB THROUGH CHANNELS. THEY DIDN'T GO TO THE MEDIA, WHICH WOULD BE BOTH CHEAP AND OBVIOUS.
SO IT WAS A SHOT. A SUBTLE ONE, FRUSTRATING THE VOUGHT-AMERICAN AGENDA, CAUSING INTERNAL RATHER THAN PUBLIC EMBARASSMENT.
DOES THAT SOUND LIKE A-TRAIN OR JACK?
SO THE FUCKING PLACE IS BUGGED? BY *WHO?*
BECAUSE I--
YOU SURPRISE ME, HOMELANDER.
YOU WEREN'T THIS SLOW ON THE UPTAKE WHEN TEENAGE KIX HAD THEIR LITTLE MISHAP LAST YEAR.
GETTING TO BE A HABIT OF YOURS.
LISTENING AT KEYHOLES.

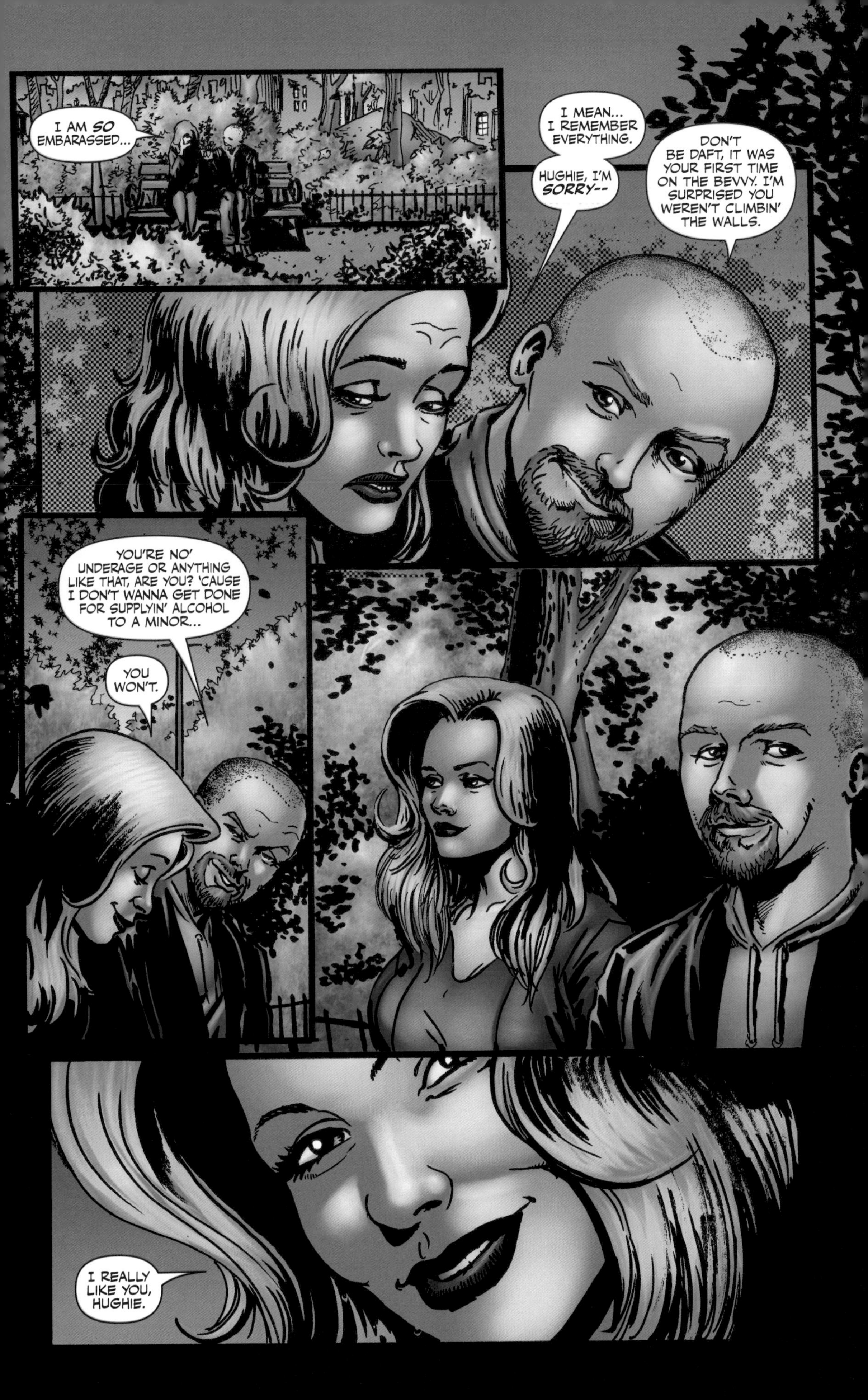
I AM *SO* EMBARASSED...
I MEAN... I REMEMBER EVERYTHING.
HUGHIE, I'M *SORRY--*
DON'T BE DAFT, IT WAS YOUR FIRST TIME ON THE BEVVY. I'M SURPRISED YOU WEREN'T CLIMBIN' THE WALLS.
YOU'RE NO' UNDERAGE OR ANYTHING LIKE THAT, ARE YOU? 'CAUSE I DON'T WANNA GET DONE FOR SUPPLYIN' ALCOHOL TO A MINOR...
YOU WON'T.
I REALLY LIKE YOU, HUGHIE.

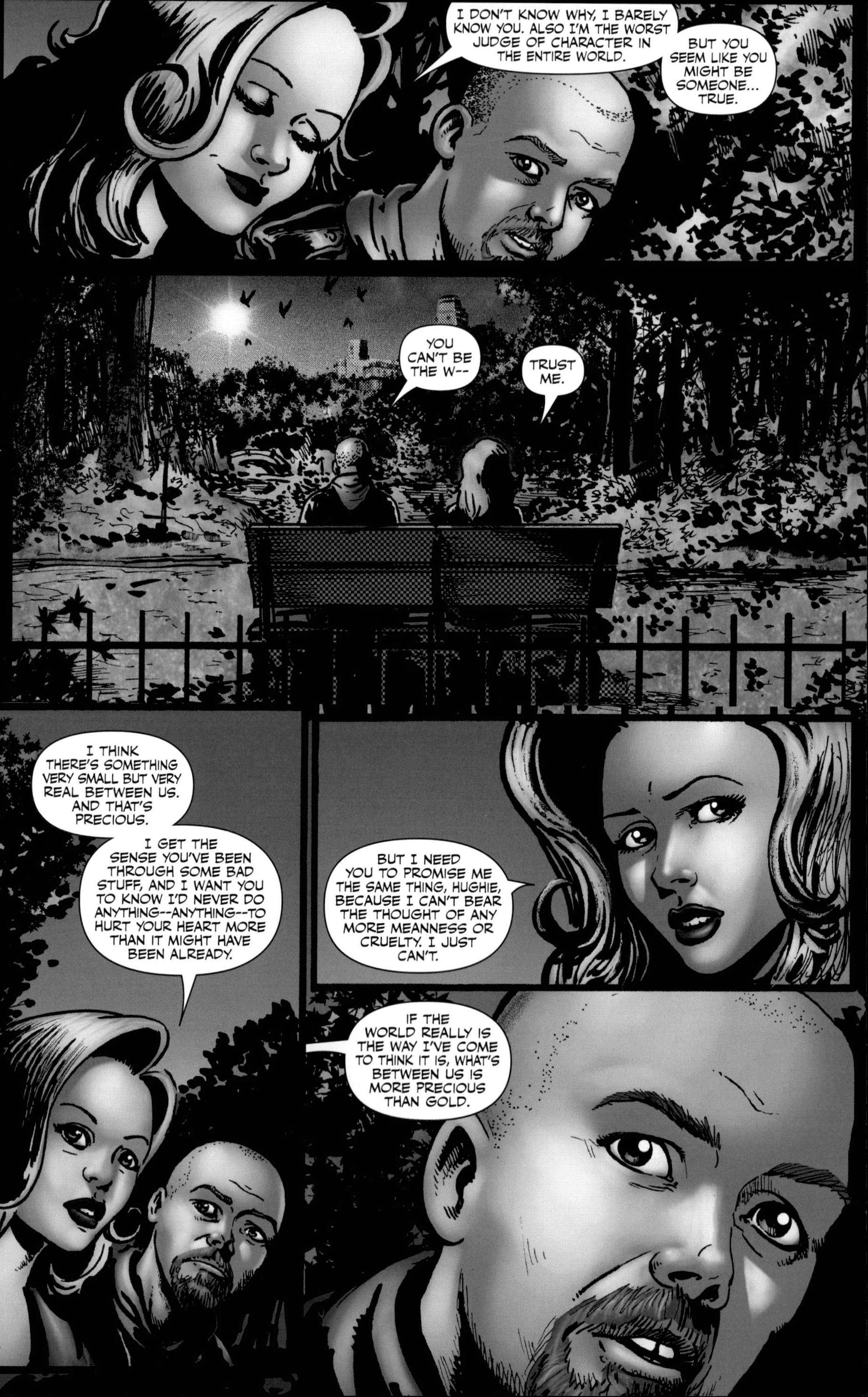
I DON'T KNOW WHY, I BARELY KNOW YOU. ALSO I'M THE WORST JUDGE OF CHARACTER IN THE ENTIRE WORLD.
BUT YOU SEEM LIKE YOU MIGHT BE SOMEONE... TRUE.
YOU CAN'T BE THE W--
TRUST ME.
I THINK THERE'S SOMETHING VERY SMALL BUT VERY REAL BETWEEN US. AND THAT'S PRECIOUS.
I GET THE SENSE YOU'VE BEEN THROUGH SOME BAD STUFF, AND I WANT YOU TO KNOW I'D NEVER DO ANYTHING--ANYTHING--TO HURT YOUR HEART MORE THAN IT MIGHT HAVE BEEN ALREADY.
BUT I NEED YOU TO PROMISE ME THE SAME THING, HUGHIE, BECAUSE I CAN'T BEAR THE THOUGHT OF ANY MORE MEANNESS OR CRUELTY. I JUST CAN'T.
IF THE WORLD REALLY IS THE WAY I'VE COME TO THINK IT IS, WHAT'S BETWEEN US IS MORE PRECIOUS THAN GOLD.

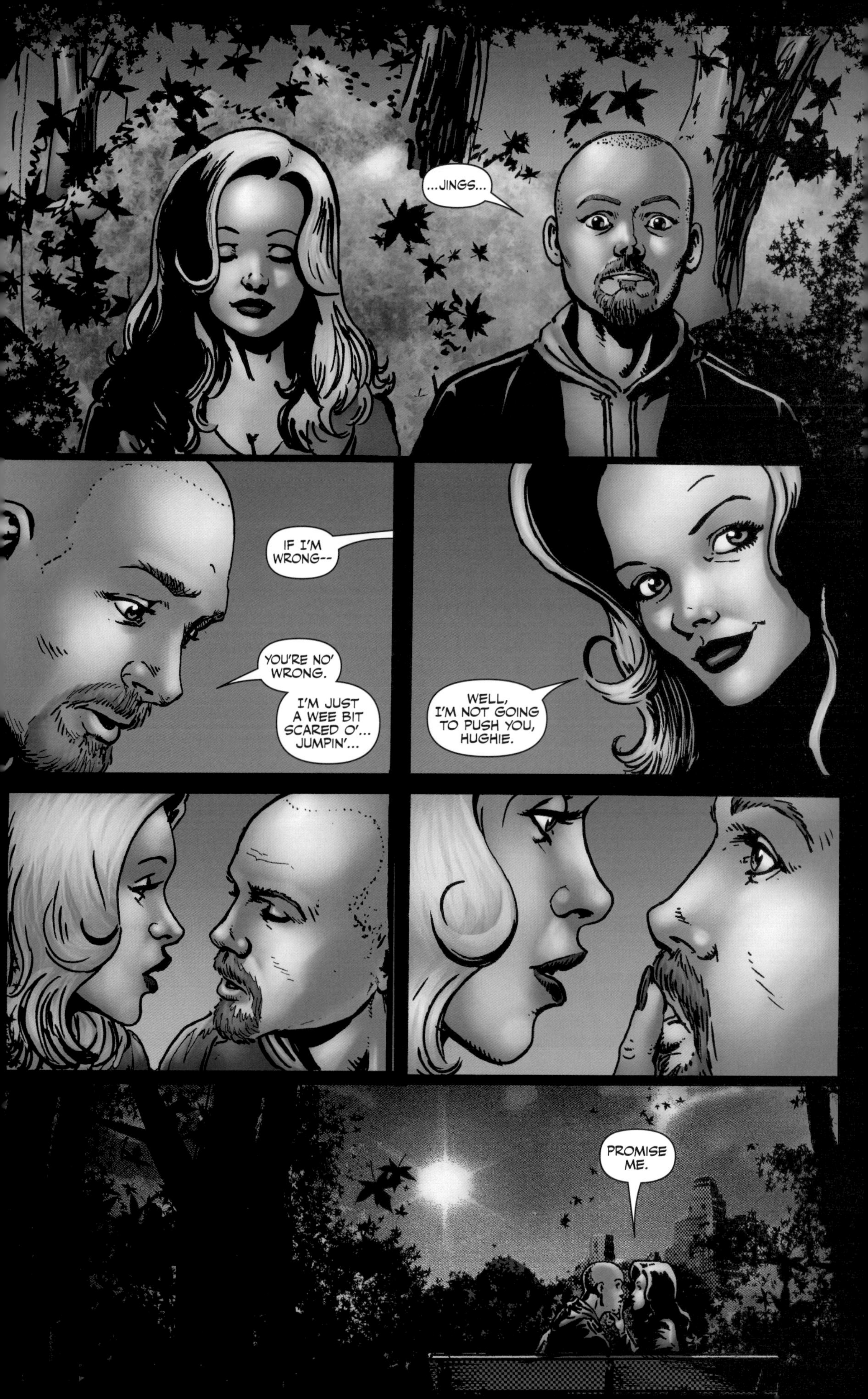
...JINGS...
IF I'M WRONG--
YOU'RE NO' WRONG.
I'M JUST A WEE BIT SCARED O'... JUMPIN'...
WELL, I'M NOT GOING TO PUSH YOU, HUGHIE.
PROMISE ME.

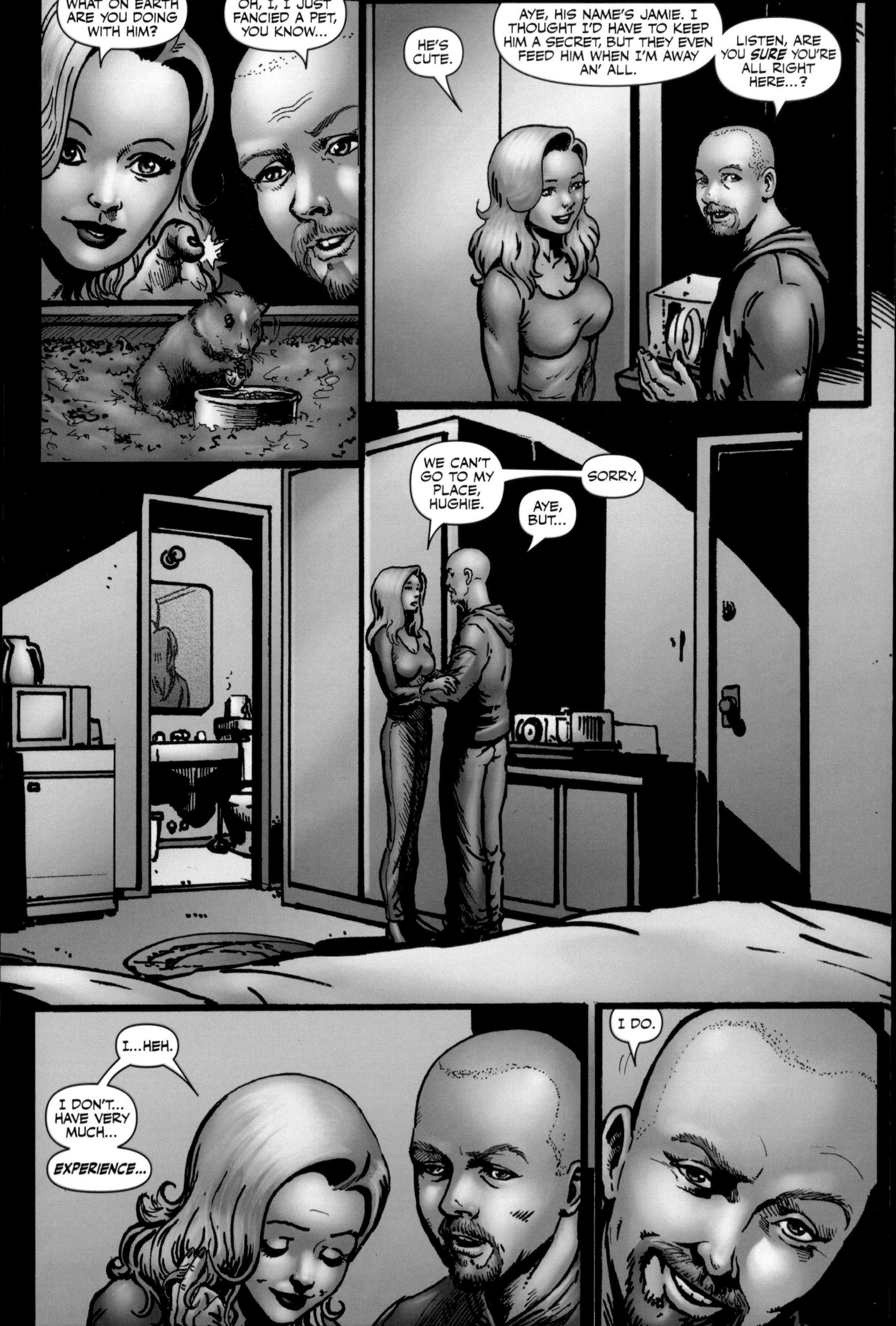
WHAT ON EARTH ARE YOU DOING WITH HIM?
OH, I, I JUST FANCIED A PET, YOU KNOW...
HE'S CUTE.
AYE, HIS NAME'S JAMIE. I THOUGHT I'D HAVE TO KEEP HIM A SECRET, BUT THEY EVEN FEED HIM WHEN I'M AWAY AN' ALL.
LISTEN, ARE YOU *SURE* YOU'RE ALL RIGHT HERE...?
WE CAN'T GO TO MY PLACE, HUGHIE.
SORRY.
AYE, BUT...
I...HEH.
I DON'T... HAVE VERY MUCH...
EXPERIENCE...
I DO.

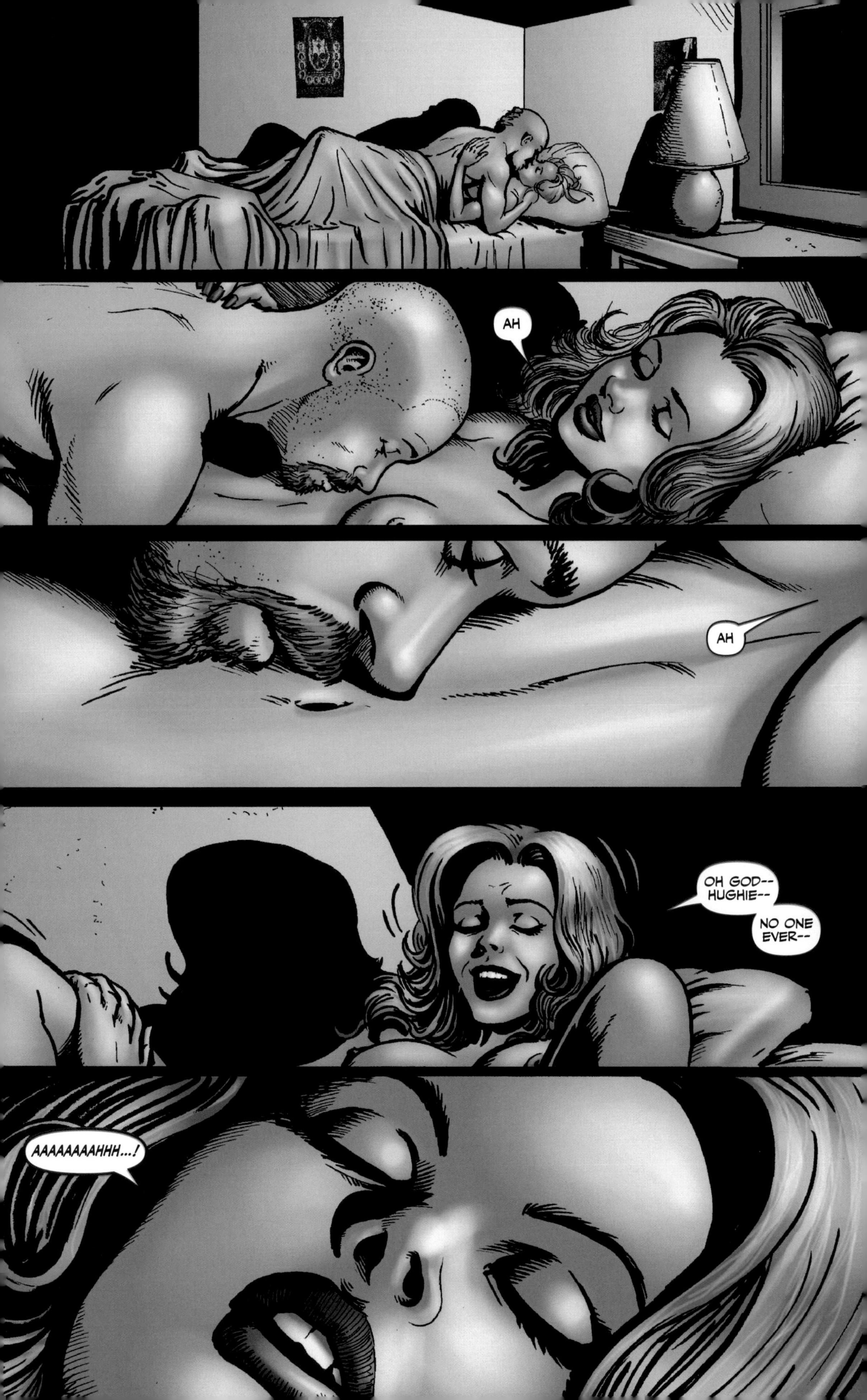
AH
AH
OH GOD--
HUGHIE--
NO ONE
EVER--
AAAAAAAAAHHH...!

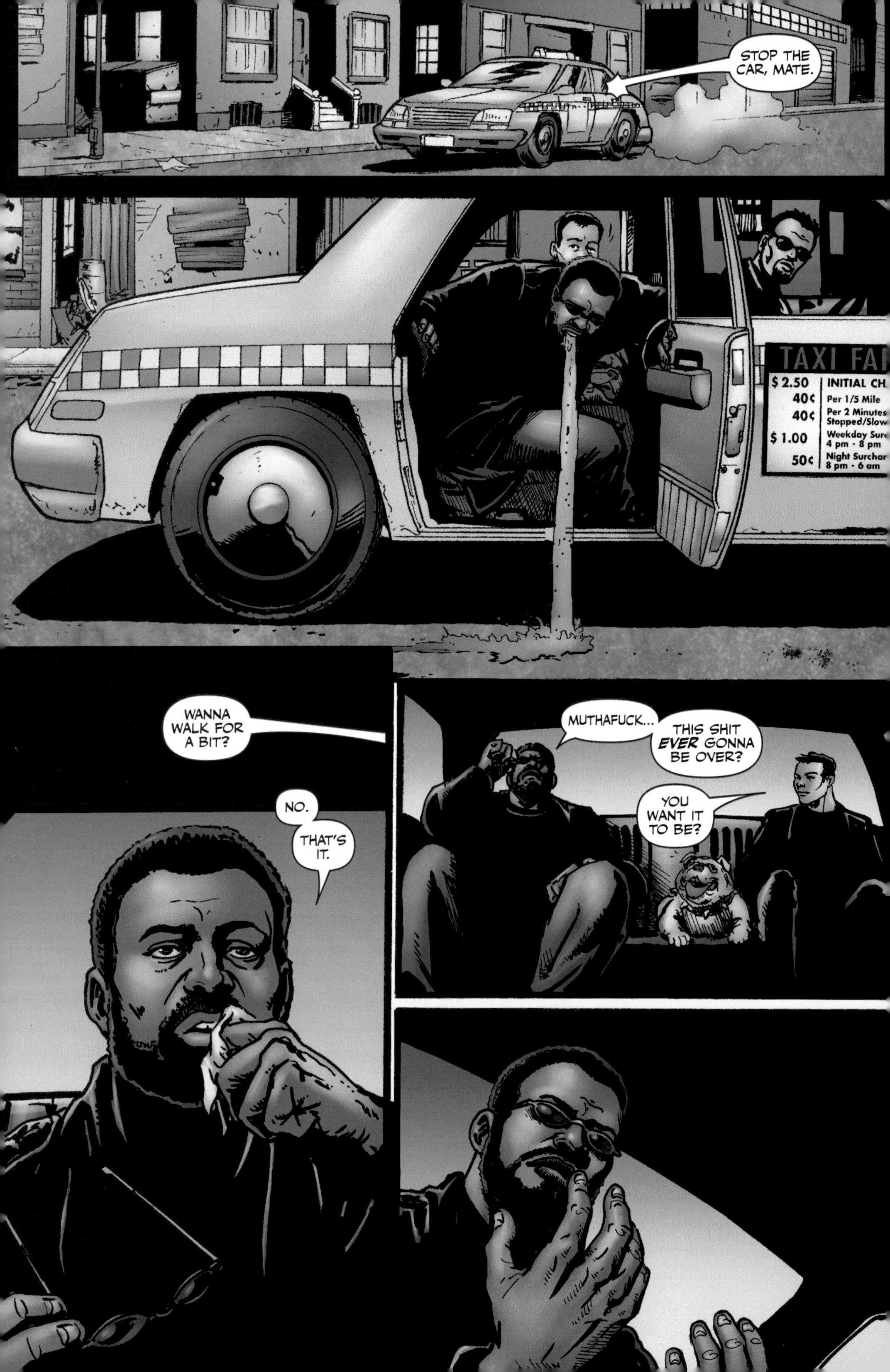
STOP THE CAR, MATE.
TAXI FA
$ 2.50 INITIAL CH
40¢ Per 1/5 Mile
40¢ Per 2 Minutes Stopped/Slow
$ 1.00 Weekday Sur 4 pm - 8 pm
50¢ Night Surchar 8 pm - 6 am
WANNA WALK FOR A BIT?
NO.
THAT'S IT.
MUTHAFUCK...
THIS SHIT *EVER* GONNA BE OVER?
YOU WANT IT TO BE?

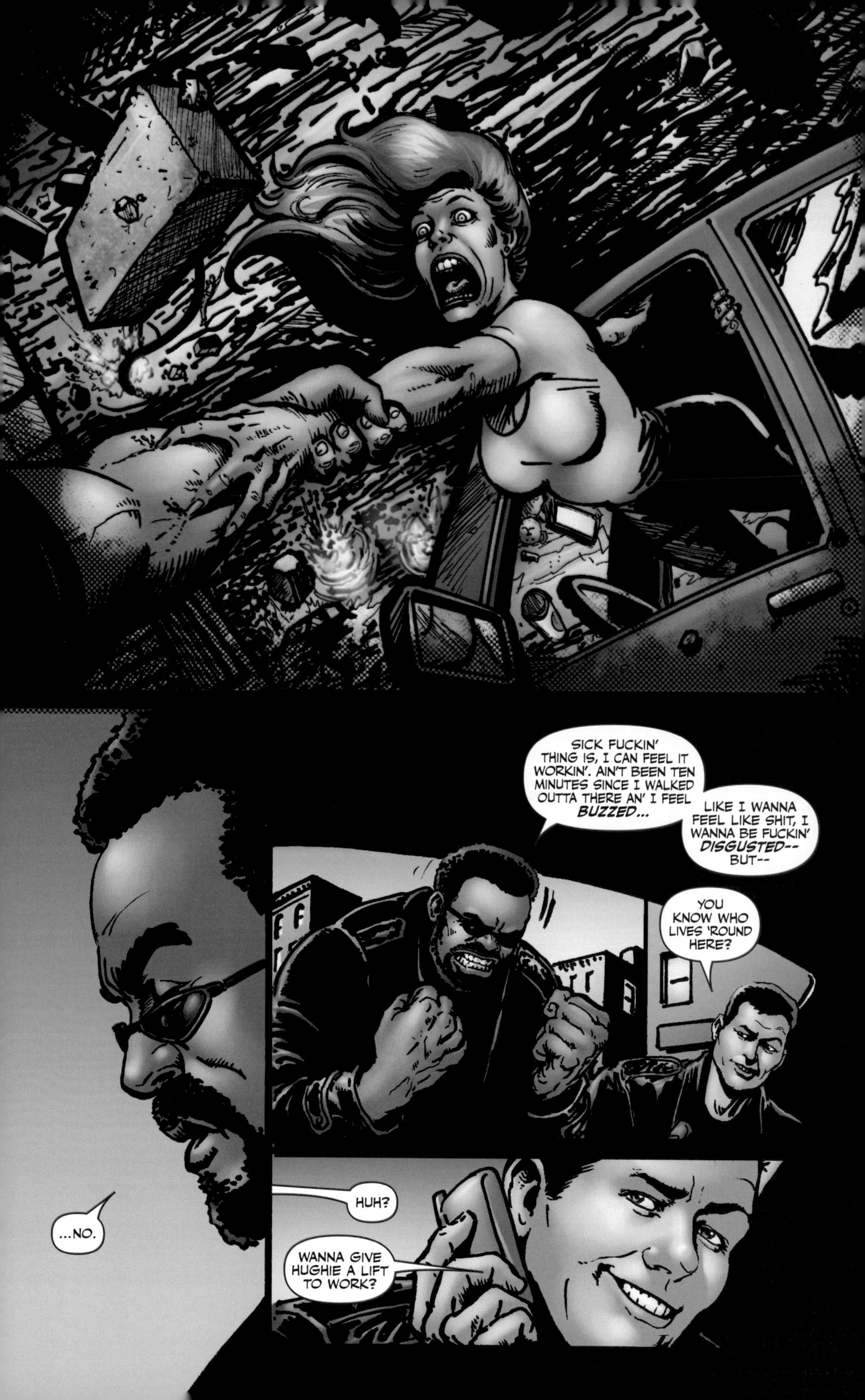
SICK FUCKIN' THING IS, I CAN FEEL IT WORKIN'. AIN'T BEEN TEN MINUTES SINCE I WALKED OUTTA THERE AN' I FEEL *BUZZED...*
LIKE I WANNA FEEL LIKE SHIT, I WANNA BE FUCKIN' *DISGUSTED--* BUT--
YOU KNOW WHO LIVES 'ROUND HERE?
...NO.
HUH?
WANNA GIVE HUGHIE A LIFT TO WORK?

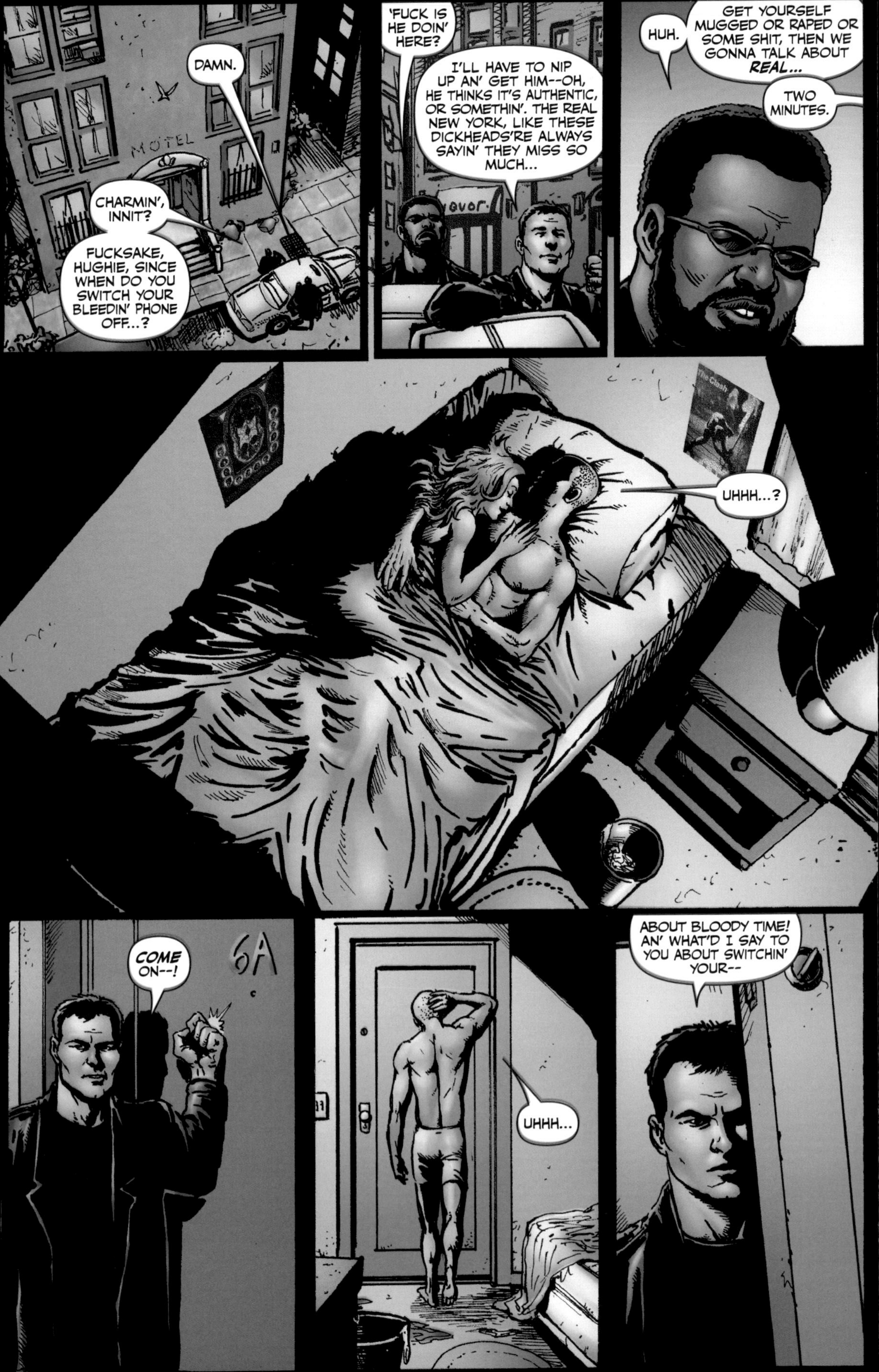
DAMN.
CHARMIN', INNIT?
FUCKSAKE, HUGHIE, SINCE WHEN DO YOU SWITCH YOUR BLEEDIN' PHONE OFF...?
'FUCK IS HE DOIN' HERE?
I'LL HAVE TO NIP UP AN' GET HIM--OH, HE THINKS IT'S AUTHENTIC, OR SOMETHIN'. THE REAL NEW YORK, LIKE THESE DICKHEADS'RE ALWAYS SAYIN' THEY MISS SO MUCH...
HUH.
GET YOURSELF MUGGED OR RAPED OR SOME SHIT, THEN WE GONNA TALK ABOUT *REAL*...
TWO MINUTES.
MOTEL
The Clash
UHHH...?
6A
COME ON--!
UHHH...
ABOUT BLOODY TIME! AN' WHAT'D I SAY TO YOU ABOUT SWITCHIN' YOUR--

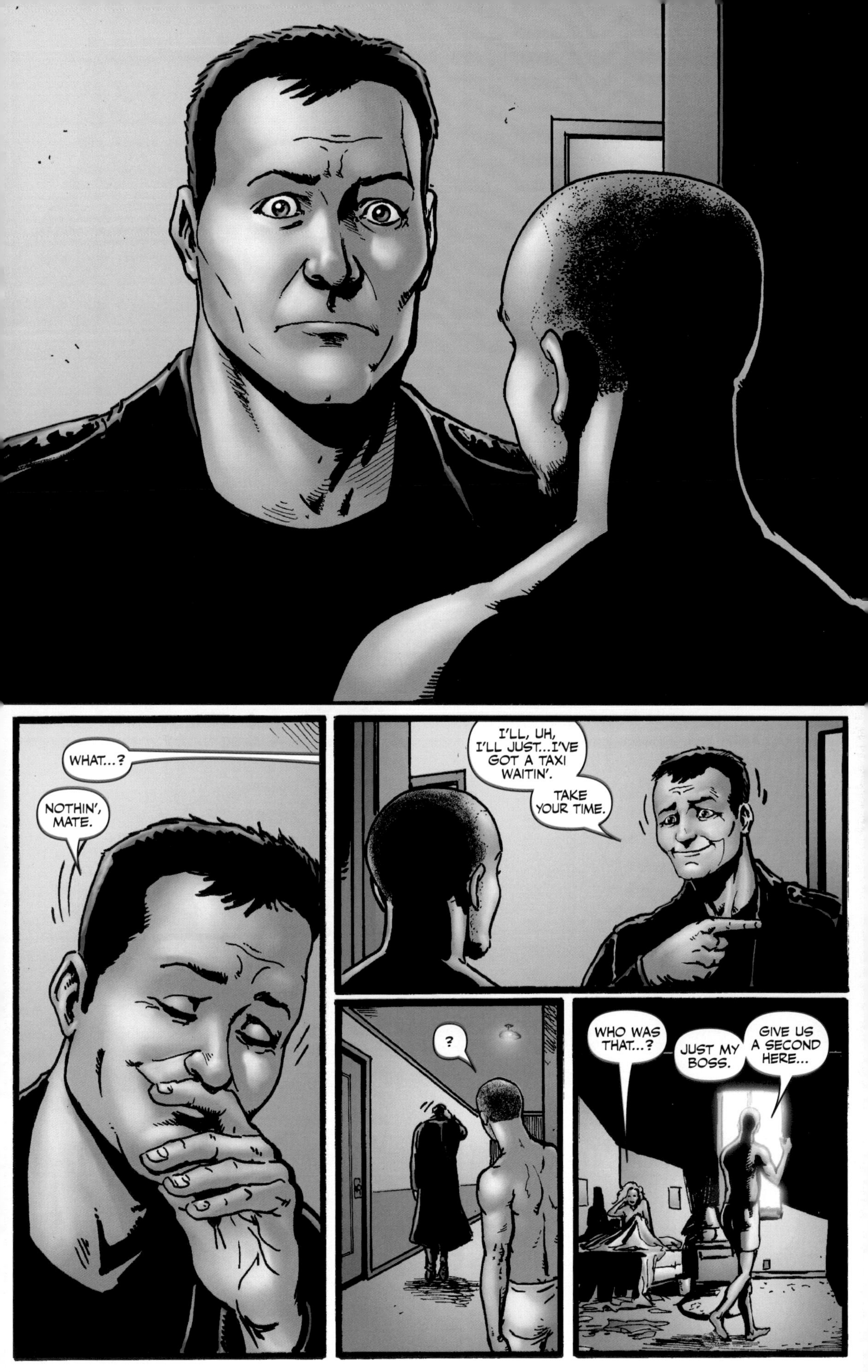
WHAT...?
NOTHIN', MATE.
I'LL, UH, I'LL JUST...I'VE GOT A TAXI WAITIN'.
TAKE YOUR TIME.
?
WHO WAS THAT...?
JUST MY BOSS.
GIVE US A SECOND HERE...

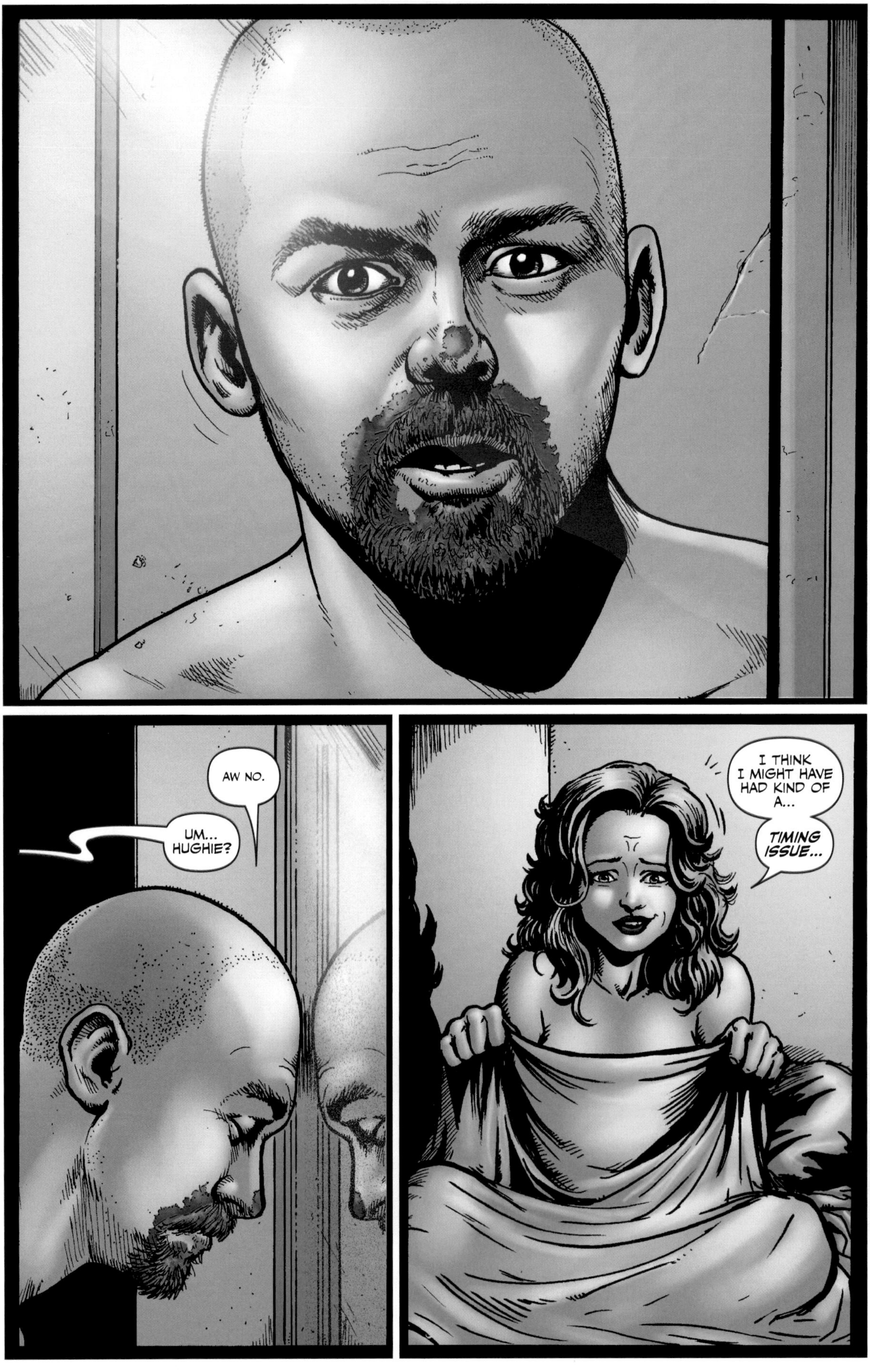
AW NO.
UM... HUGHIE?
I THINK I MIGHT HAVE HAD KIND OF A...
TIMING ISSUE...

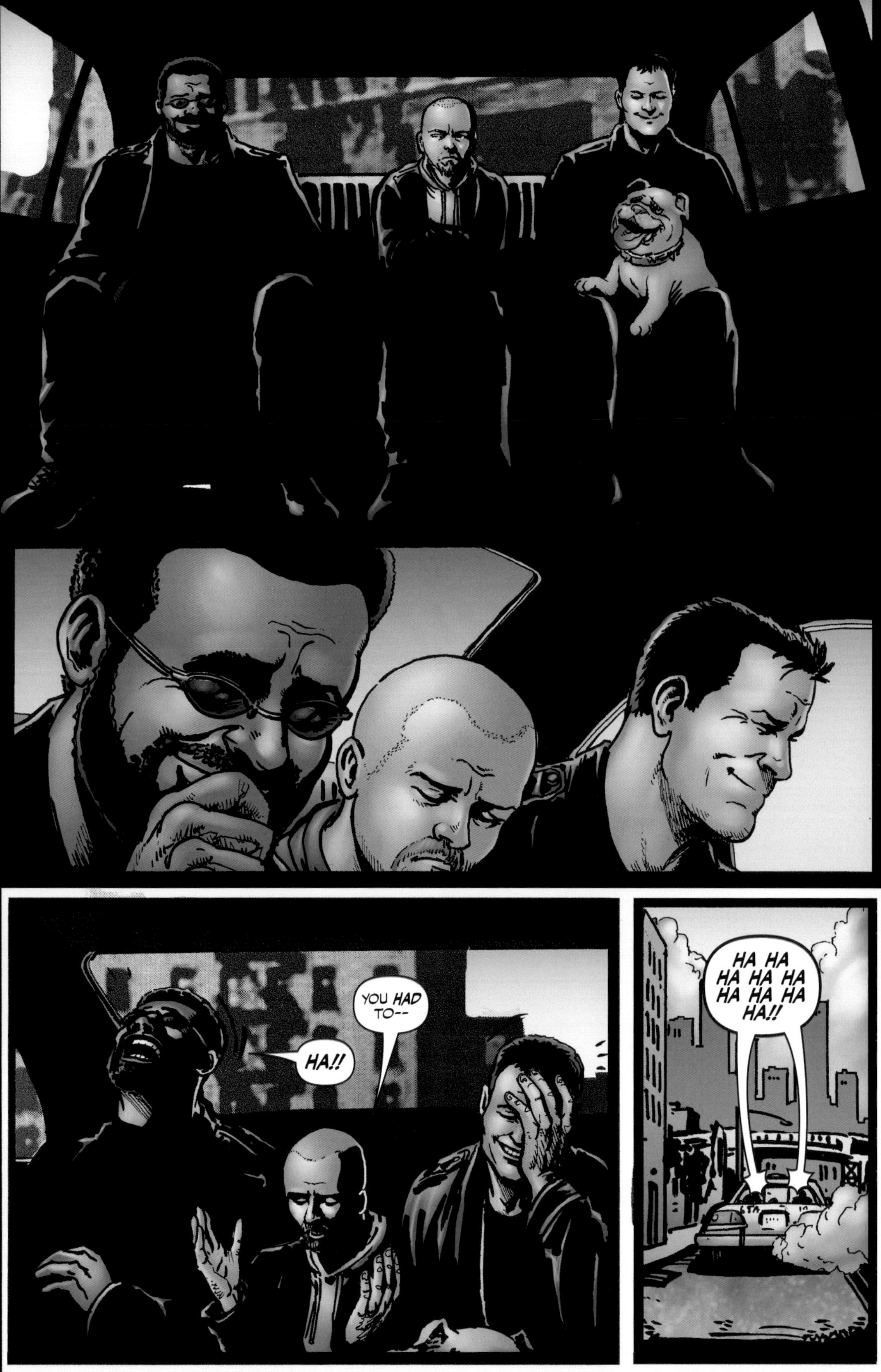
YOU HAD TO--
HA!!
HA HA HA HA HA HA HA HA HA!!

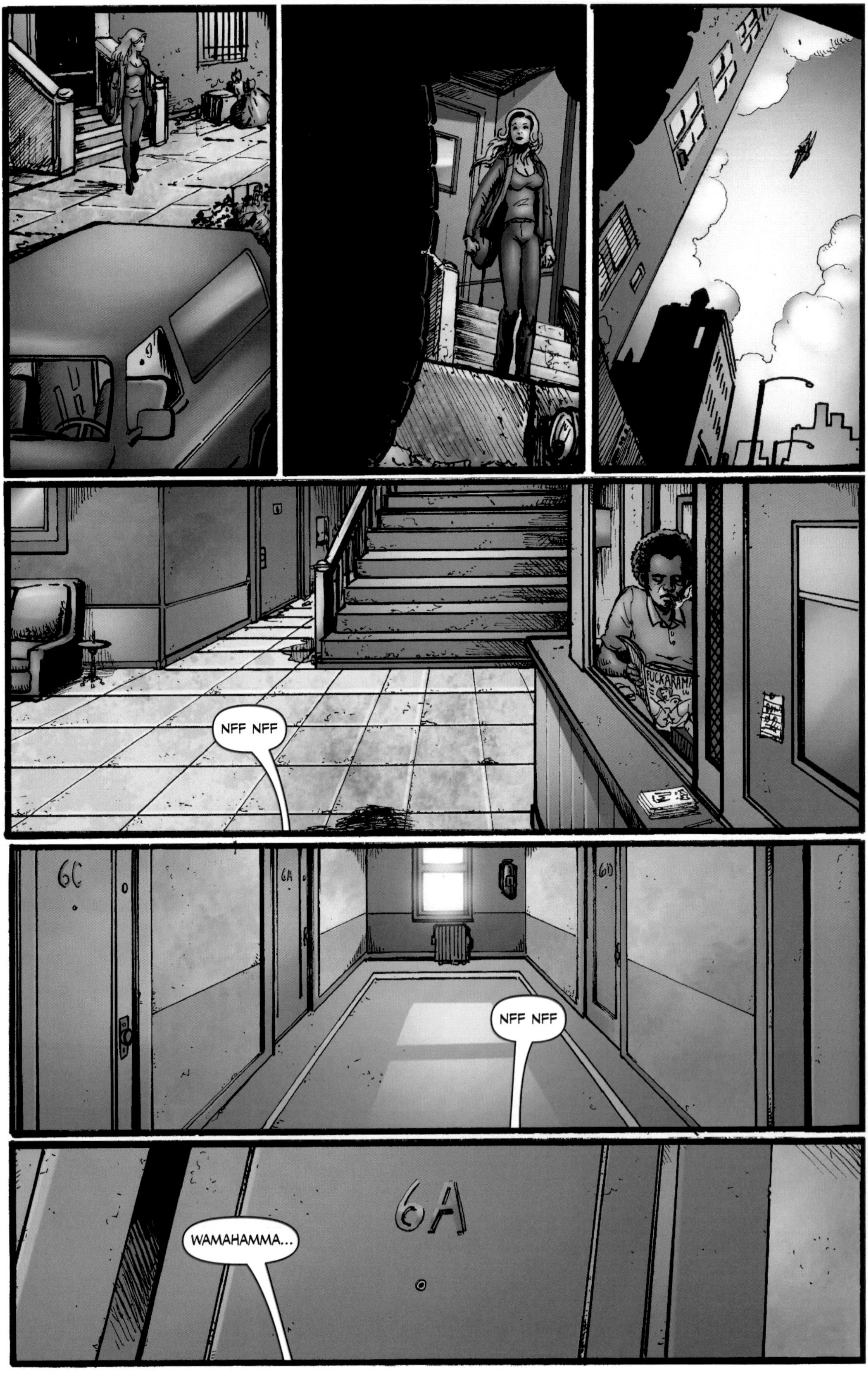

FUCKARAMA
NFF NFF
6C
6A
NFF NFF
6A
WAMAHAMMA...

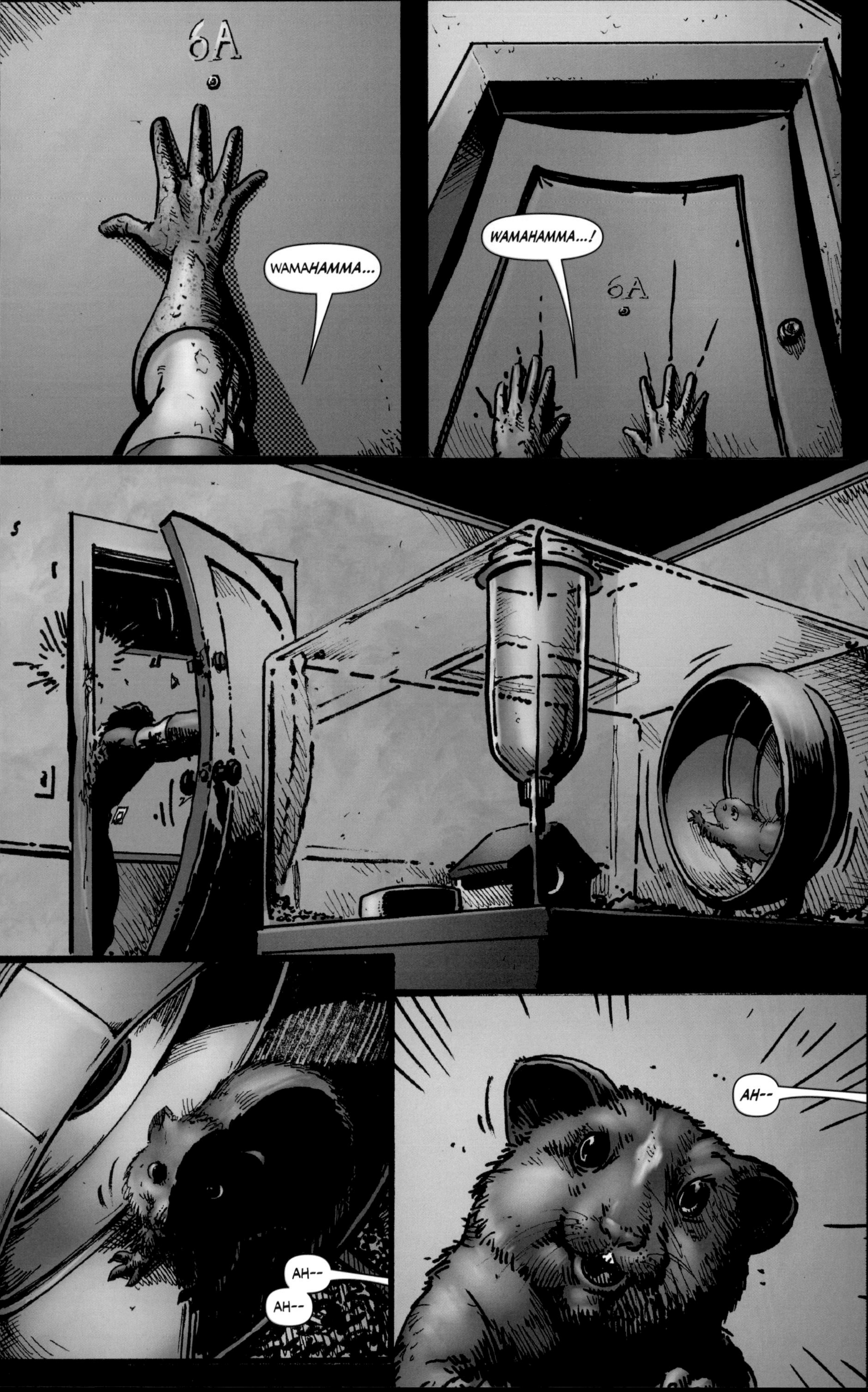
WAMAHAMMA...
WAMAHAMMA...!
6A
AH--
AH--
AH--

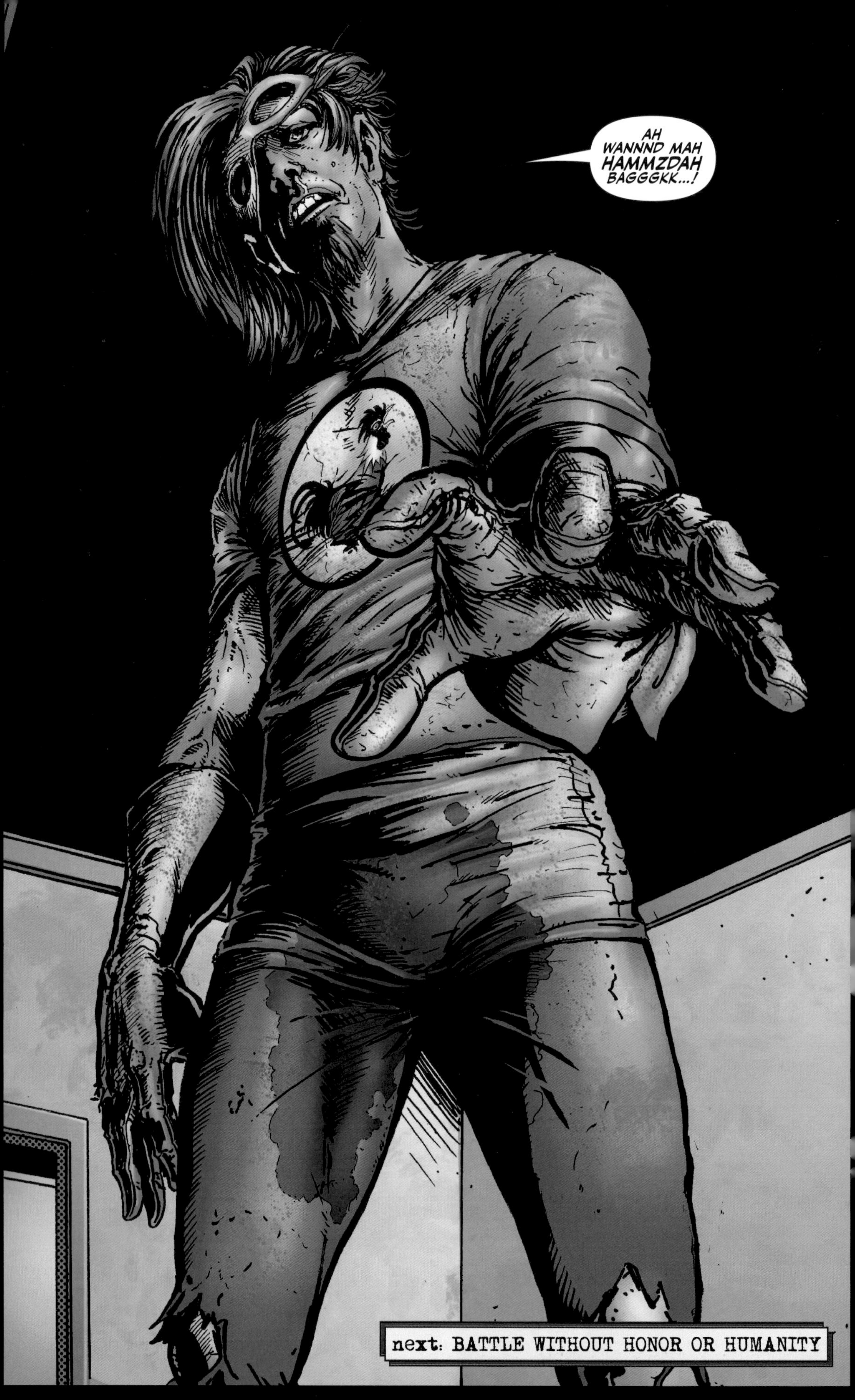
AH WANNND MAH HAMMZDAH BAGGGKK...!
next: BATTLE WITHOUT HONOR OR HUMANITY

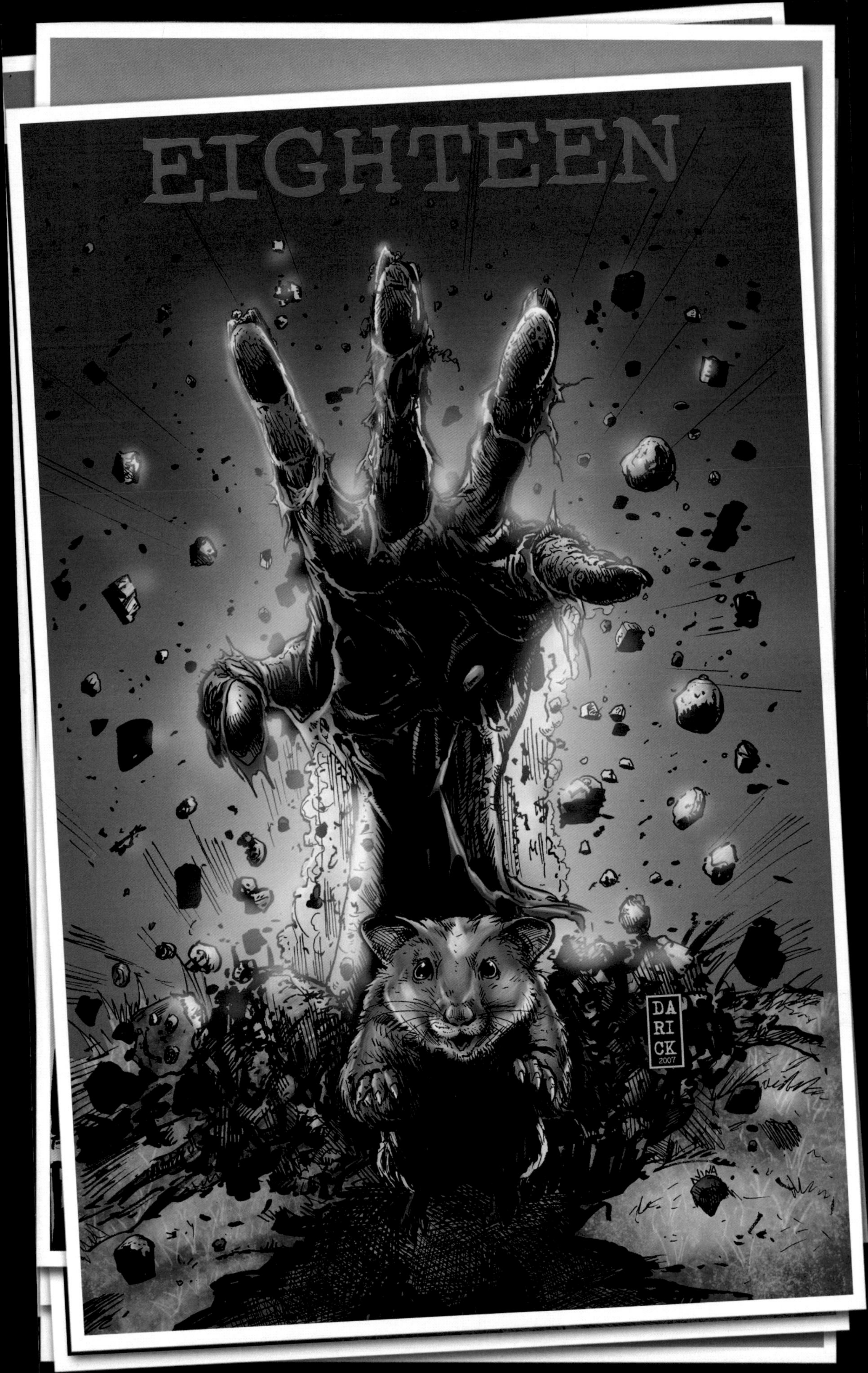
EIGHTEEN
DA
RI
CK
2007

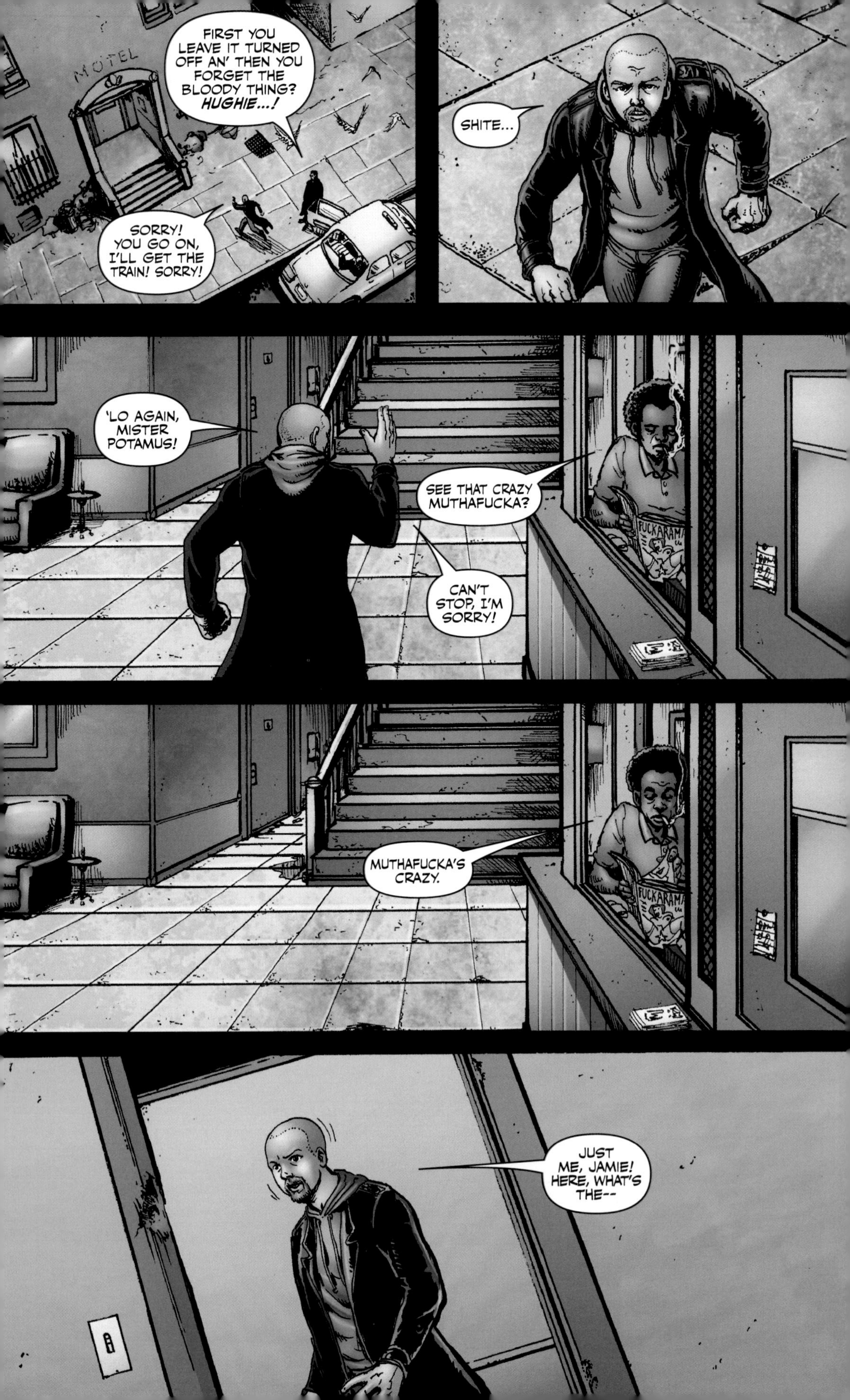
MOTEL
FIRST YOU LEAVE IT TURNED OFF AN' THEN YOU FORGET THE BLOODY THING? HUGHIE...!
SORRY! YOU GO ON, I'LL GET THE TRAIN! SORRY!
SHITE...
'LO AGAIN, MISTER POTAMUS!
SEE THAT CRAZY MUTHAFUCKA?
CAN'T STOP, I'M SORRY!
FUCKARAMA
MUTHAFUCKA'S CRAZY.
FUCKARAMA
JUST ME, JAMIE! HERE, WHAT'S THE--

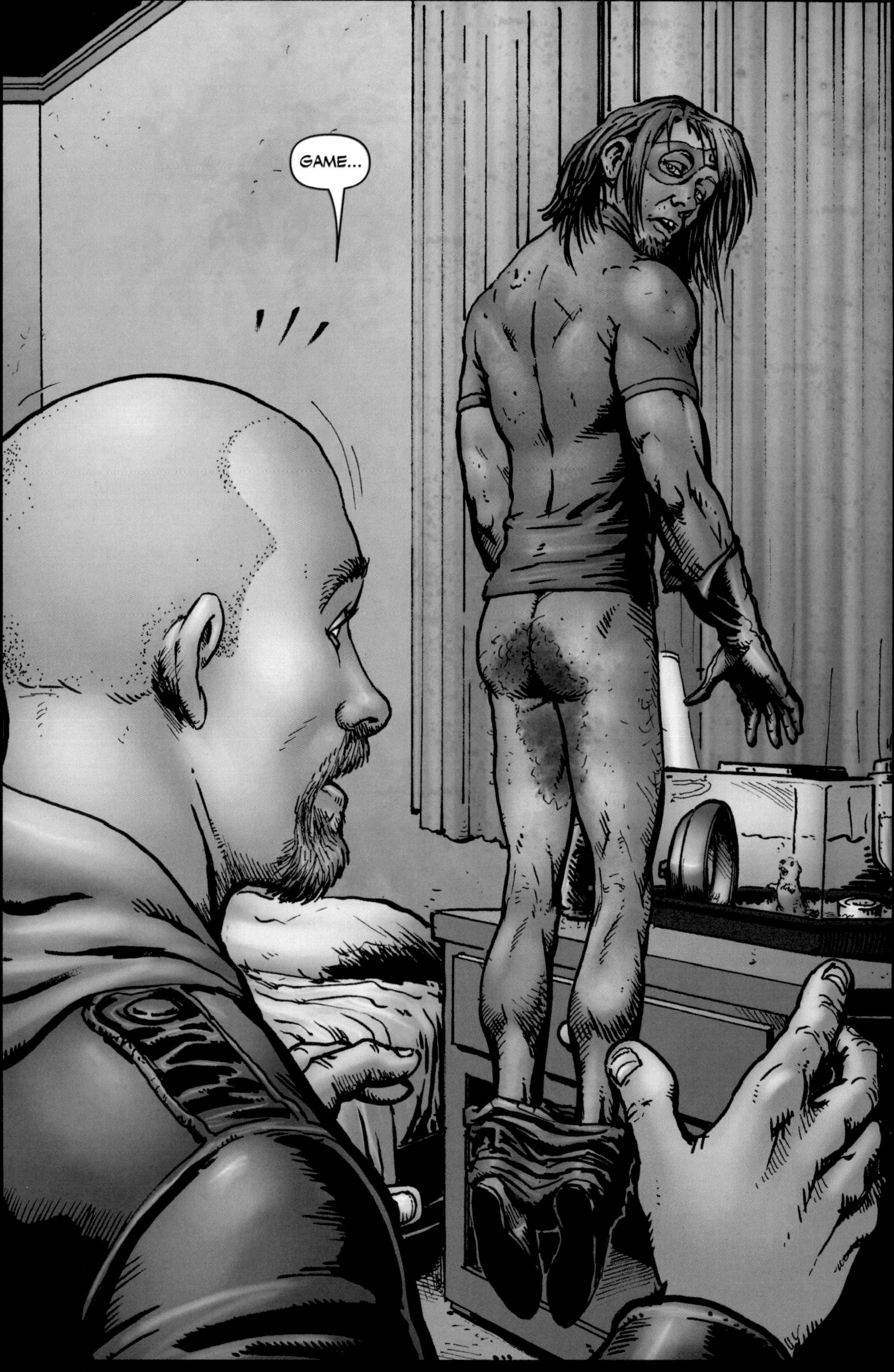
GAME...

GOOD FOR THE SOUL

conclusion

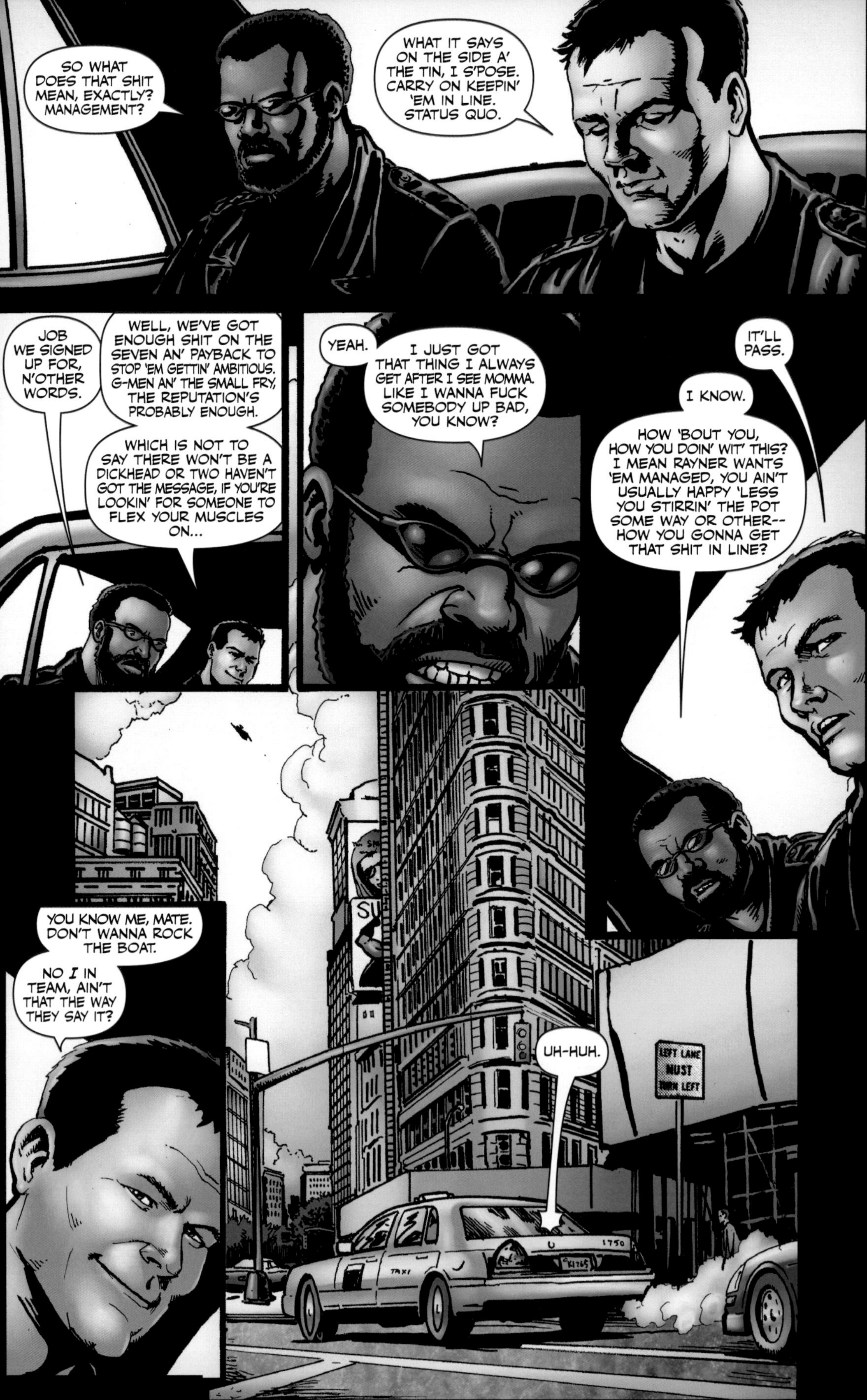
SO WHAT DOES THAT SHIT MEAN, EXACTLY? MANAGEMENT?
WHAT IT SAYS ON THE SIDE A' THE TIN, I S'POSE. CARRY ON KEEPIN' 'EM IN LINE. STATUS QUO.
JOB WE SIGNED UP FOR, N'OTHER WORDS.
WELL, WE'VE GOT ENOUGH SHIT ON THE SEVEN AN' PAYBACK TO STOP 'EM GETTIN' AMBITIOUS. G-MEN AN' THE SMALL FRY, THE REPUTATION'S PROBABLY ENOUGH.
WHICH IS NOT TO SAY THERE WON'T BE A DICKHEAD OR TWO HAVEN'T GOT THE MESSAGE, IF YOU'RE LOOKIN' FOR SOMEONE TO FLEX YOUR MUSCLES ON...
YEAH.
I JUST GOT THAT THING I ALWAYS GET AFTER I SEE MOMMA. LIKE I WANNA FUCK SOMEBODY UP BAD, YOU KNOW?
IT'LL PASS.
I KNOW.
HOW 'BOUT YOU, HOW YOU DOIN' WIT' THIS? I MEAN RAYNER WANTS 'EM MANAGED, YOU AIN'T USUALLY HAPPY 'LESS YOU STIRRIN' THE POT SOME WAY OR OTHER-- HOW YOU GONNA GET THAT SHIT IN LINE?
YOU KNOW ME, MATE. DON'T WANNA ROCK THE BOAT.
NO *I* IN TEAM, AIN'T THAT THE WAY THEY SAY IT?
UH-HUH.
LEFT LANE MUST TURN LEFT
TAXI
1750

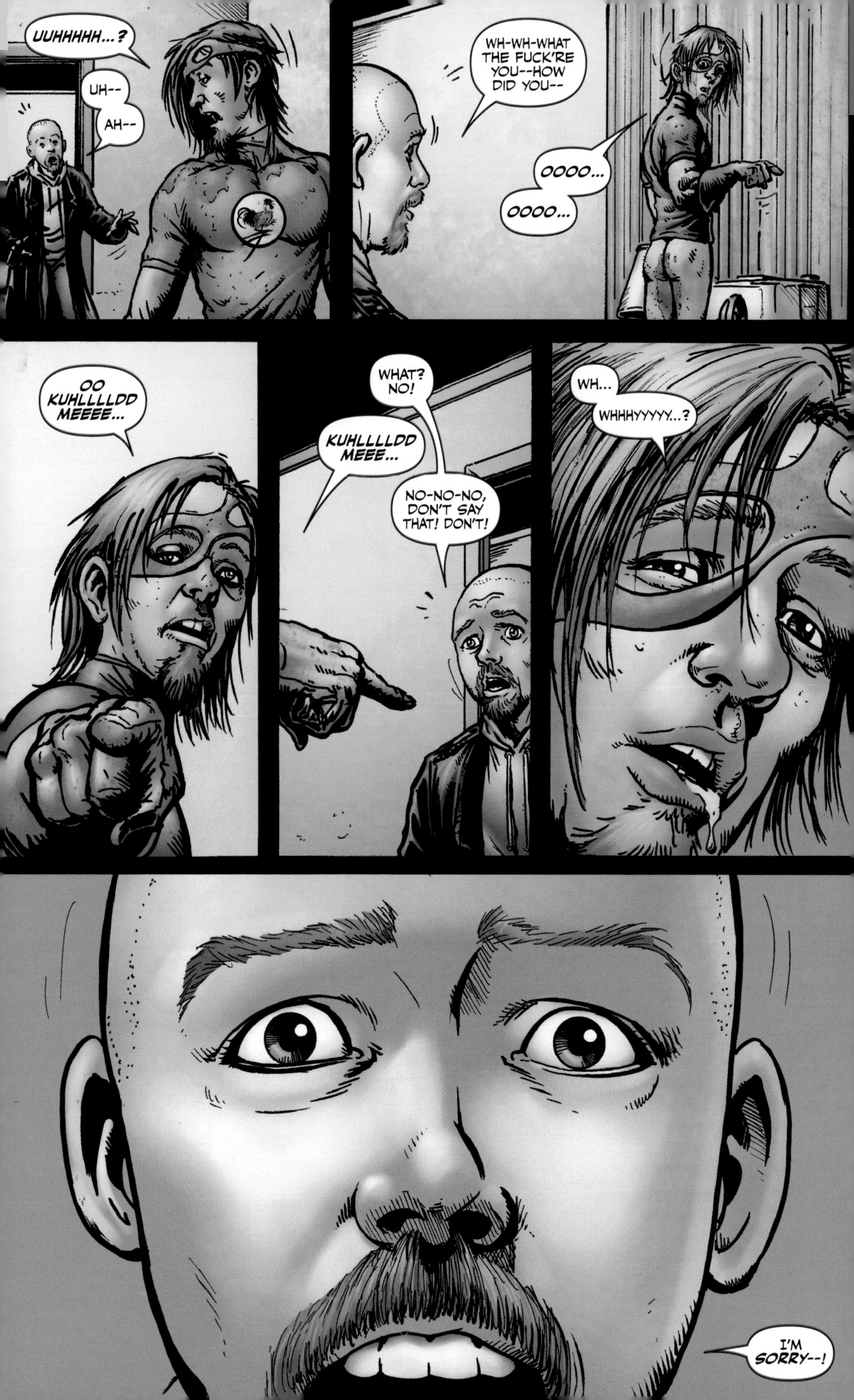
UUHHHHH...?
UH--
AH--
WH-WH-WHAT THE FUCK'RE YOU--HOW DID YOU--
OOOO...
OOOO...
OO KUHLLLLDD MEEEE...
WHAT? NO!
KUHLLLLDD MEEE...
NO-NO-NO, DON'T SAY THAT! DON'T!
WH...
WHHHYYYYY...?
I'M SORRY--!

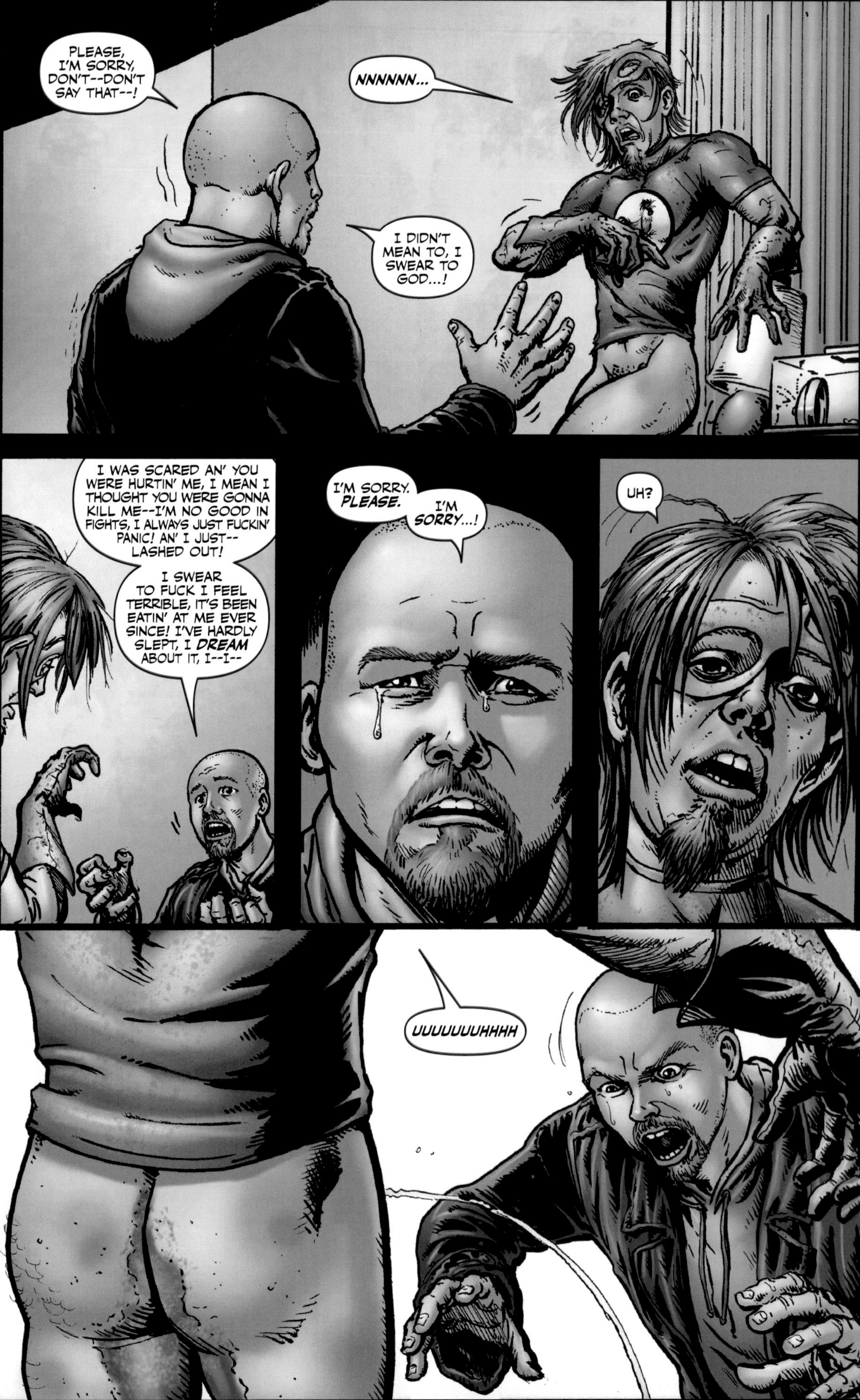
PLEASE, I'M SORRY, DON'T--DON'T SAY THAT--!
NNNNNN...
I DIDN'T MEAN TO, I SWEAR TO GOD...!
I WAS SCARED AN' YOU WERE HURTIN' ME, I MEAN I THOUGHT YOU WERE GONNA KILL ME--I'M NO GOOD IN FIGHTS, I ALWAYS JUST FUCKIN' PANIC! AN' I JUST--LASHED OUT!
I SWEAR TO FUCK I FEEL TERRIBLE, IT'S BEEN EATIN' AT ME EVER SINCE! I'VE HARDLY SLEPT, I DREAM ABOUT IT, I--I--
I'M SORRY. PLEASE.
I'M SORRY...!
UH?
UUUUUUUHHHH

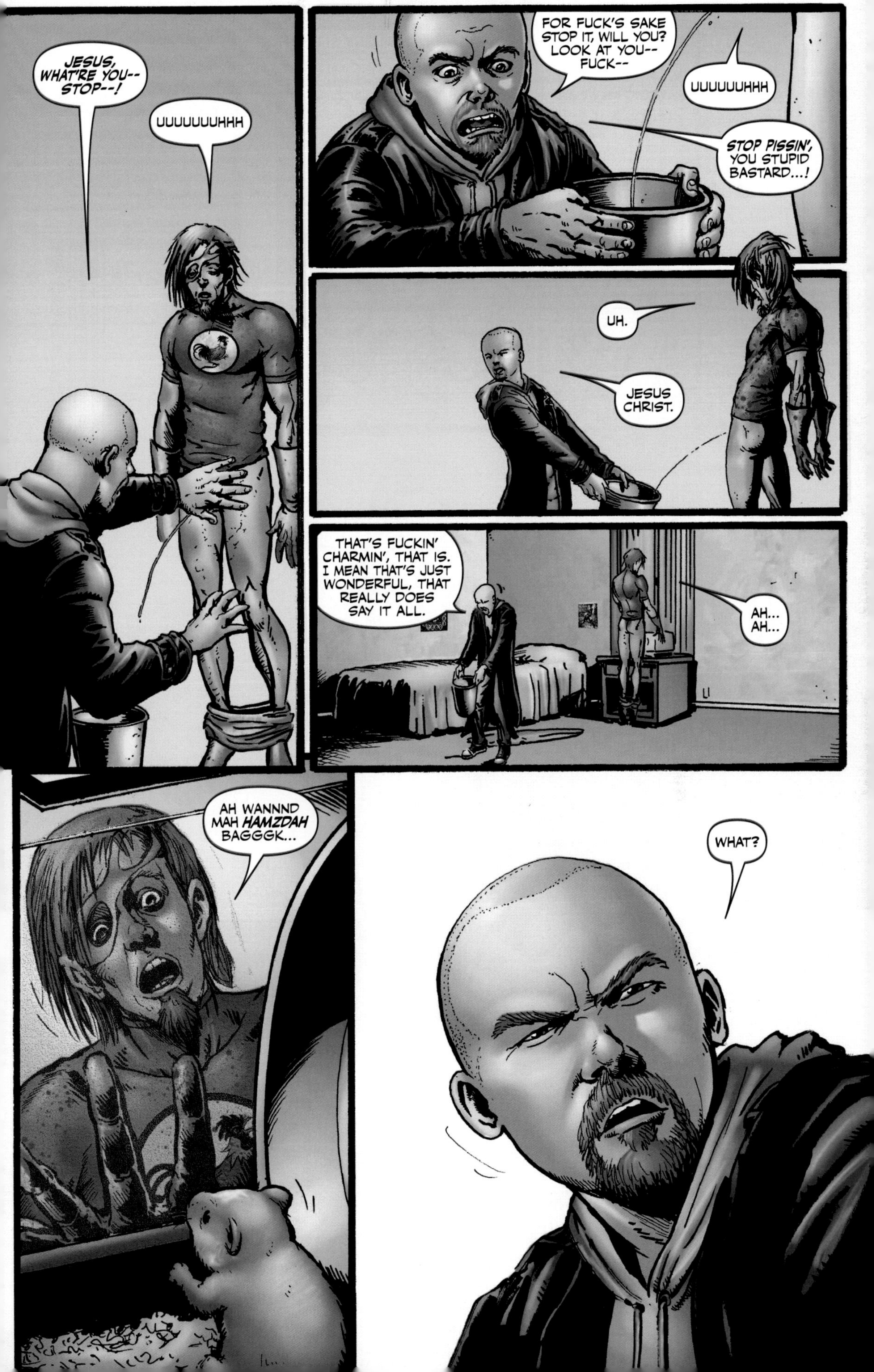
JESUS, WHAT'RE YOU-- STOP--!
UUUUUUUHHH
FOR FUCK'S SAKE STOP IT, WILL YOU? LOOK AT YOU-- FUCK--
UUUUUUHHH
STOP PISSIN', YOU STUPID BASTARD...!
UH.
JESUS CHRIST.
THAT'S FUCKIN' CHARMIN', THAT IS. I MEAN THAT'S JUST WONDERFUL, THAT REALLY DOES SAY IT ALL.
AH... AH...
AH WANNND MAH HAMZDAH BAGGGK...
WHAT?

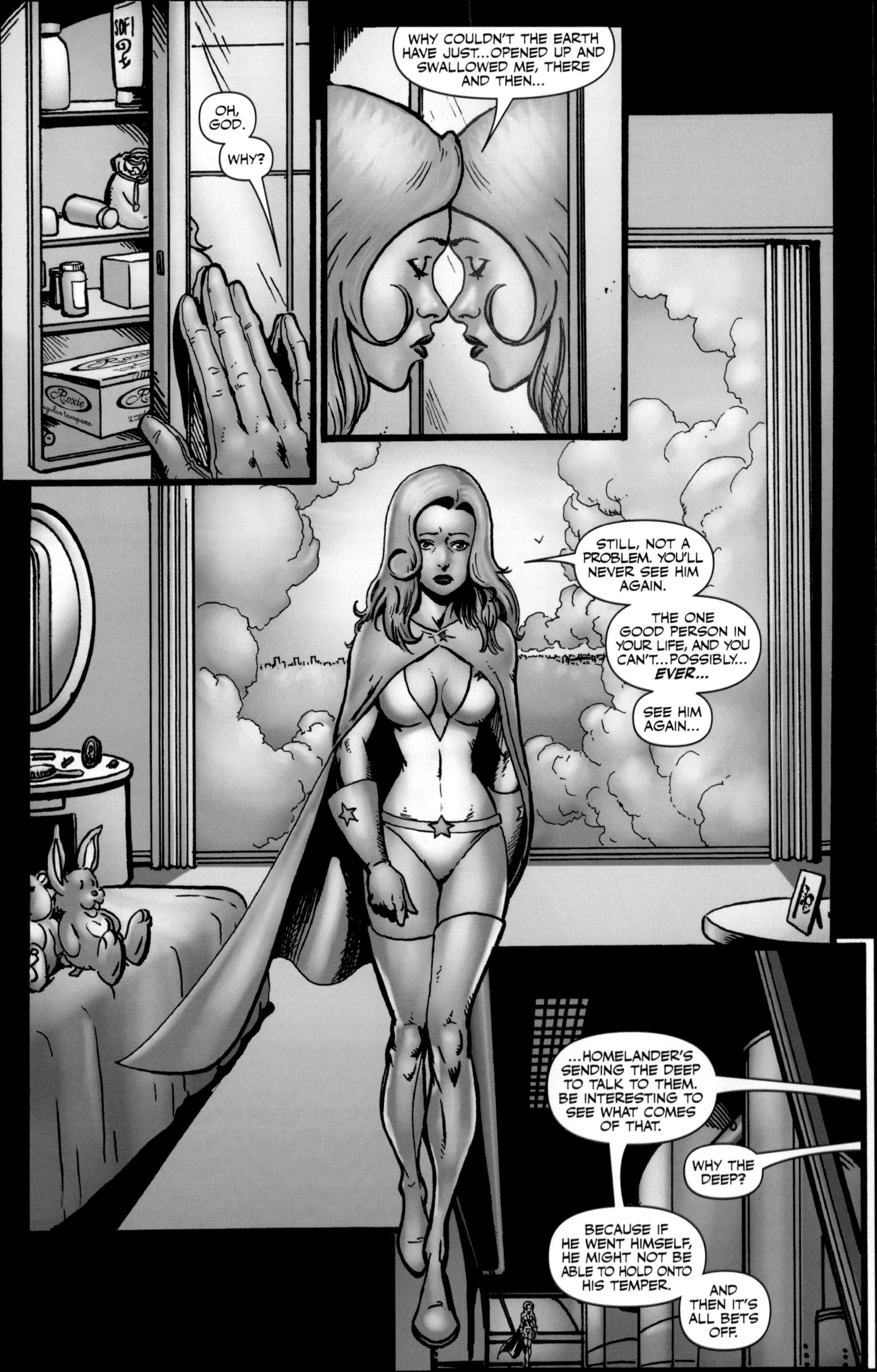
SOFI
Roxie
Roxie
regular tampons
OH, GOD.
WHY?
WHY COULDN'T THE EARTH HAVE JUST...OPENED UP AND SWALLOWED ME, THERE AND THEN...
STILL, NOT A PROBLEM. YOU'LL NEVER SEE HIM AGAIN.
THE ONE GOOD PERSON IN YOUR LIFE, AND YOU CAN'T...POSSIBLY... ***EVER...***
SEE HIM AGAIN...
...HOMELANDER'S SENDING THE DEEP TO TALK TO THEM. BE INTERESTING TO SEE WHAT COMES OF THAT.
WHY THE DEEP?
BECAUSE IF HE WENT HIMSELF, HE MIGHT NOT BE ABLE TO HOLD ONTO HIS TEMPER.
AND THEN IT'S ALL BETS OFF.

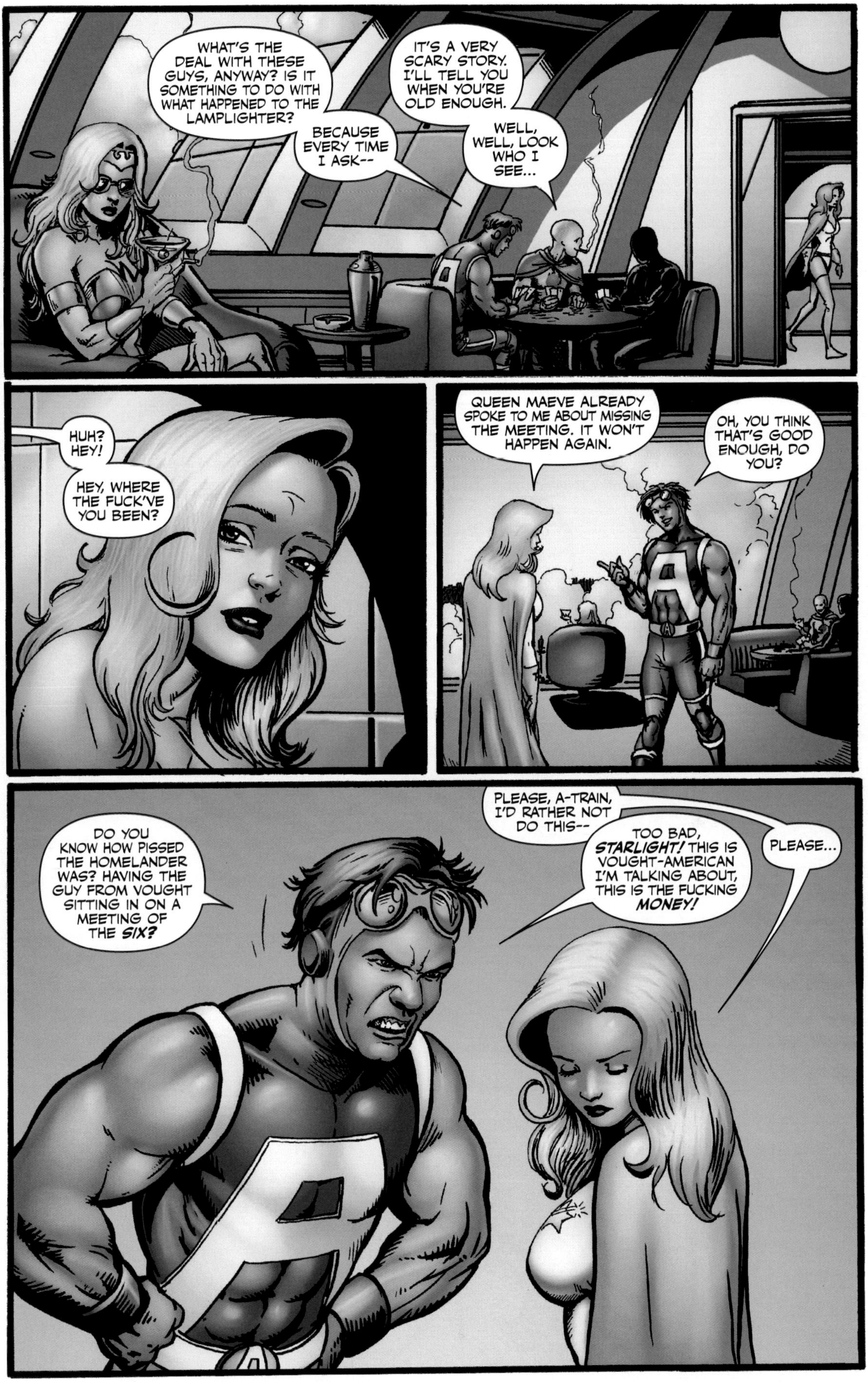
WHAT'S THE DEAL WITH THESE GUYS, ANYWAY? IS IT SOMETHING TO DO WITH WHAT HAPPENED TO THE LAMPLIGHTER?
BECAUSE EVERY TIME I ASK--
IT'S A VERY SCARY STORY. I'LL TELL YOU WHEN YOU'RE OLD ENOUGH.
WELL, WELL, LOOK WHO I SEE...
HUH? HEY!
HEY, WHERE THE FUCK'VE YOU BEEN?
QUEEN MAEVE ALREADY SPOKE TO ME ABOUT MISSING THE MEETING. IT WON'T HAPPEN AGAIN.
OH, YOU THINK THAT'S GOOD ENOUGH, DO YOU?
DO YOU KNOW HOW PISSED THE HOMELANDER WAS? HAVING THE GUY FROM VOUGHT SITTING IN ON A MEETING OF THE SIX?
PLEASE, A-TRAIN, I'D RATHER NOT DO THIS--
TOO BAD, STARLIGHT! THIS IS VOUGHT-AMERICAN I'M TALKING ABOUT, THIS IS THE FUCKING MONEY!
PLEASE...

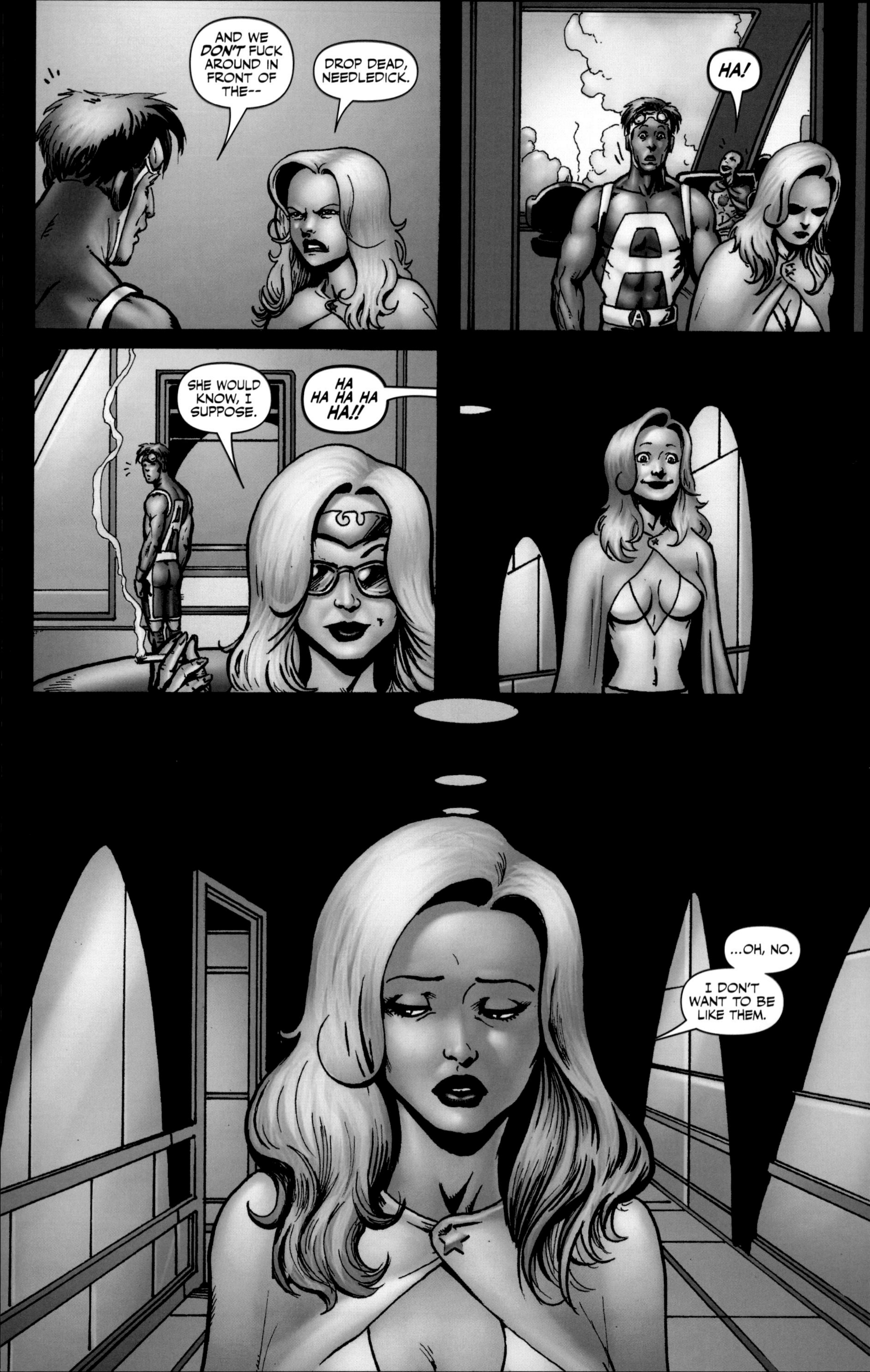
AND WE DON'T FUCK AROUND IN FRONT OF THE--
DROP DEAD, NEEDLEDICK.
HA!
SHE WOULD KNOW, I SUPPOSE.
HA HA HA HA HA!!
...OH, NO.
I DON'T WANT TO BE LIKE THEM.

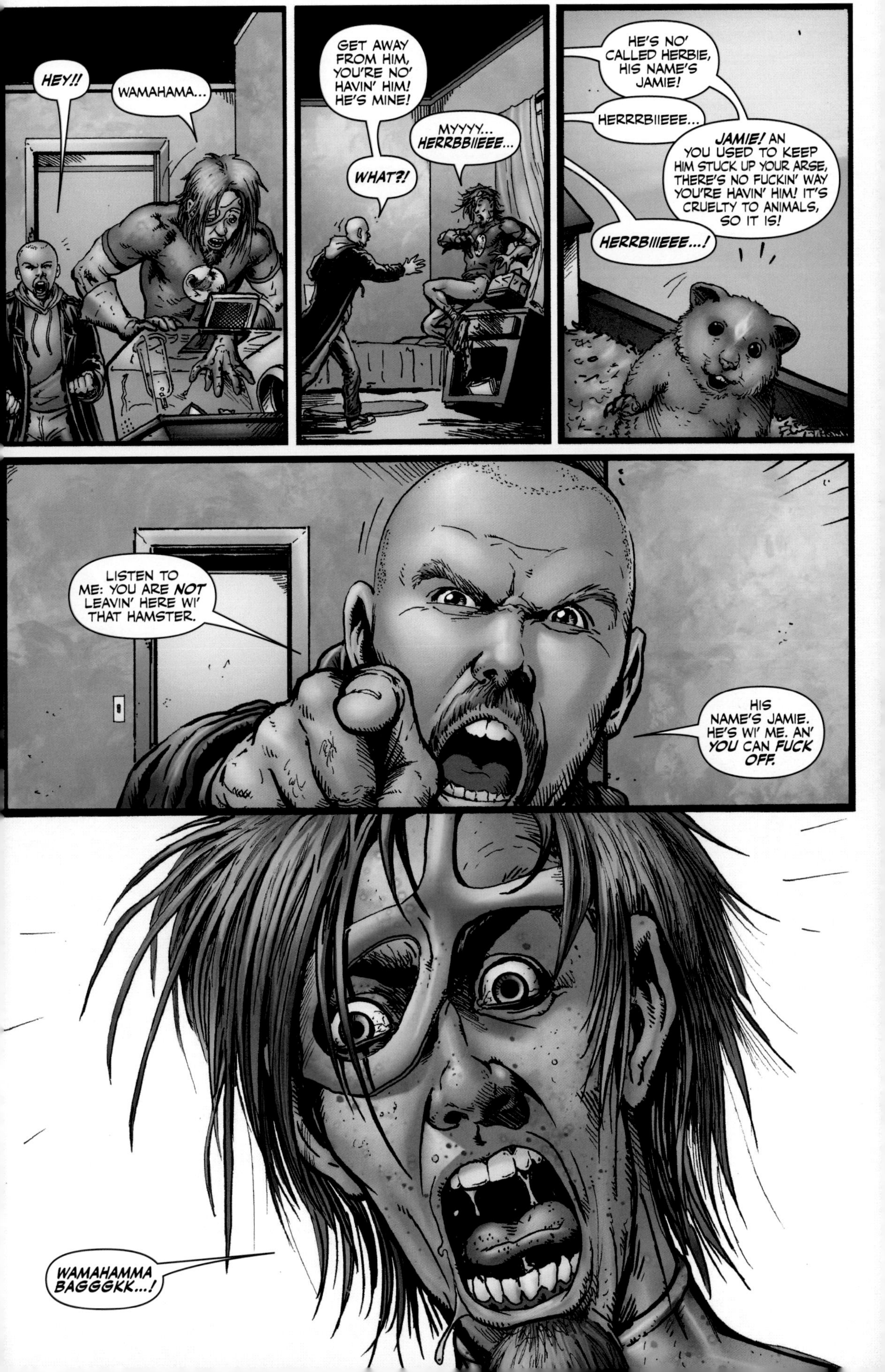
HEY!!
WAMAHAMA...
GET AWAY FROM HIM, YOU'RE NO' HAVIN' HIM! HE'S MINE!
WHAT?!
MYYYY... HERRBBIIEEE...
HE'S NO' CALLED HERBIE, HIS NAME'S JAMIE!
HERRRBIIEEE...
JAMIE! AN YOU USED TO KEEP HIM STUCK UP YOUR ARSE, THERE'S NO FUCKIN' WAY YOU'RE HAVIN' HIM! IT'S CRUELTY TO ANIMALS, SO IT IS!
HERRBIIIEEE...!
LISTEN TO ME: YOU ARE NOT LEAVIN' HERE WI' THAT HAMSTER.
HIS NAME'S JAMIE. HE'S WI' ME. AN' YOU CAN FUCK OFF.
WAMAHAMMA BAGGGKK...!

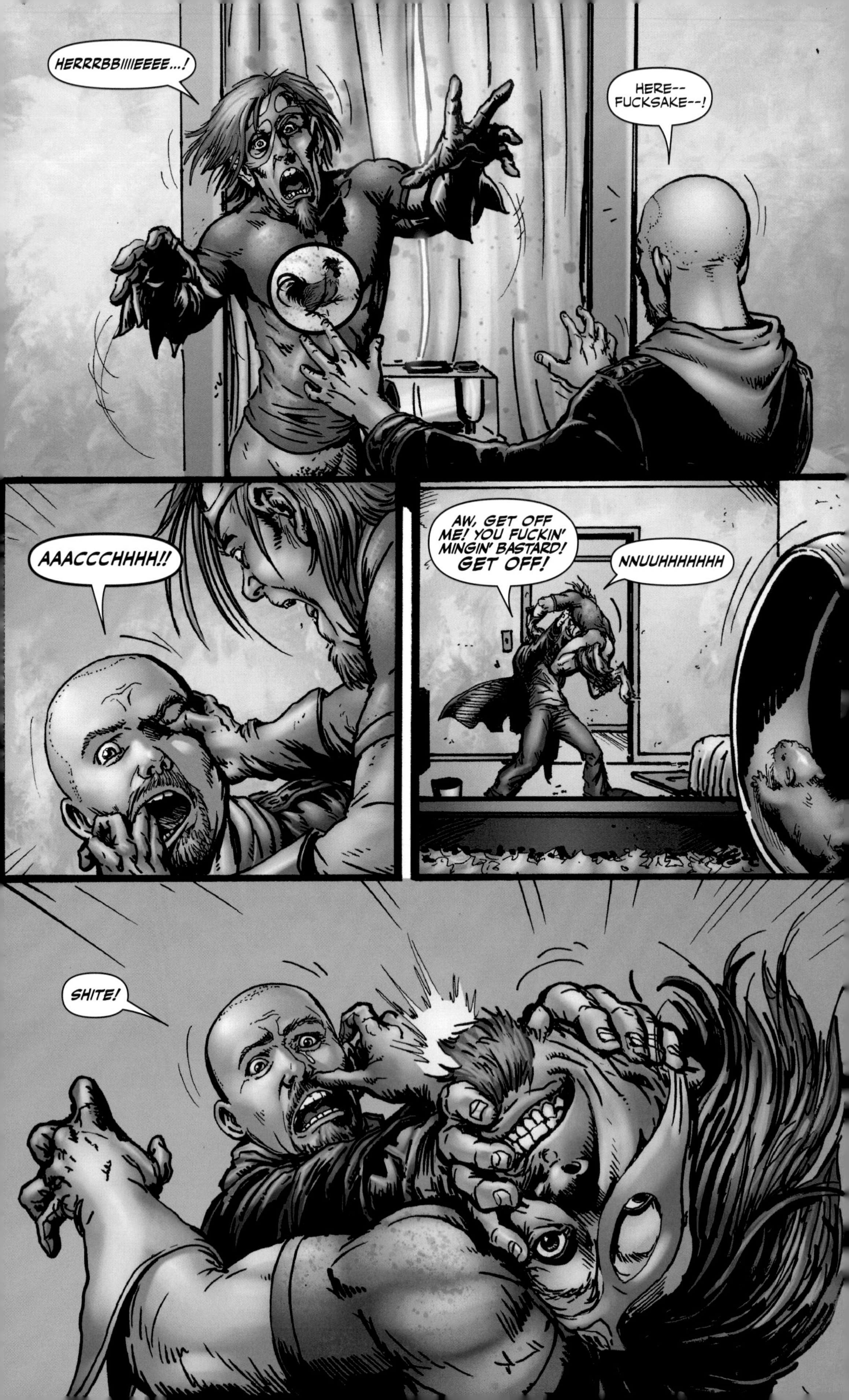
HERRRBBIIIIEEEE...!
HERE--
FUCKSAKE--!
AAACCCHHHH!!
AW, GET OFF
ME! YOU FUCKIN'
MINGIN' BASTARD!
GET OFF!
NNUUHHHHHHHH
SHITE!

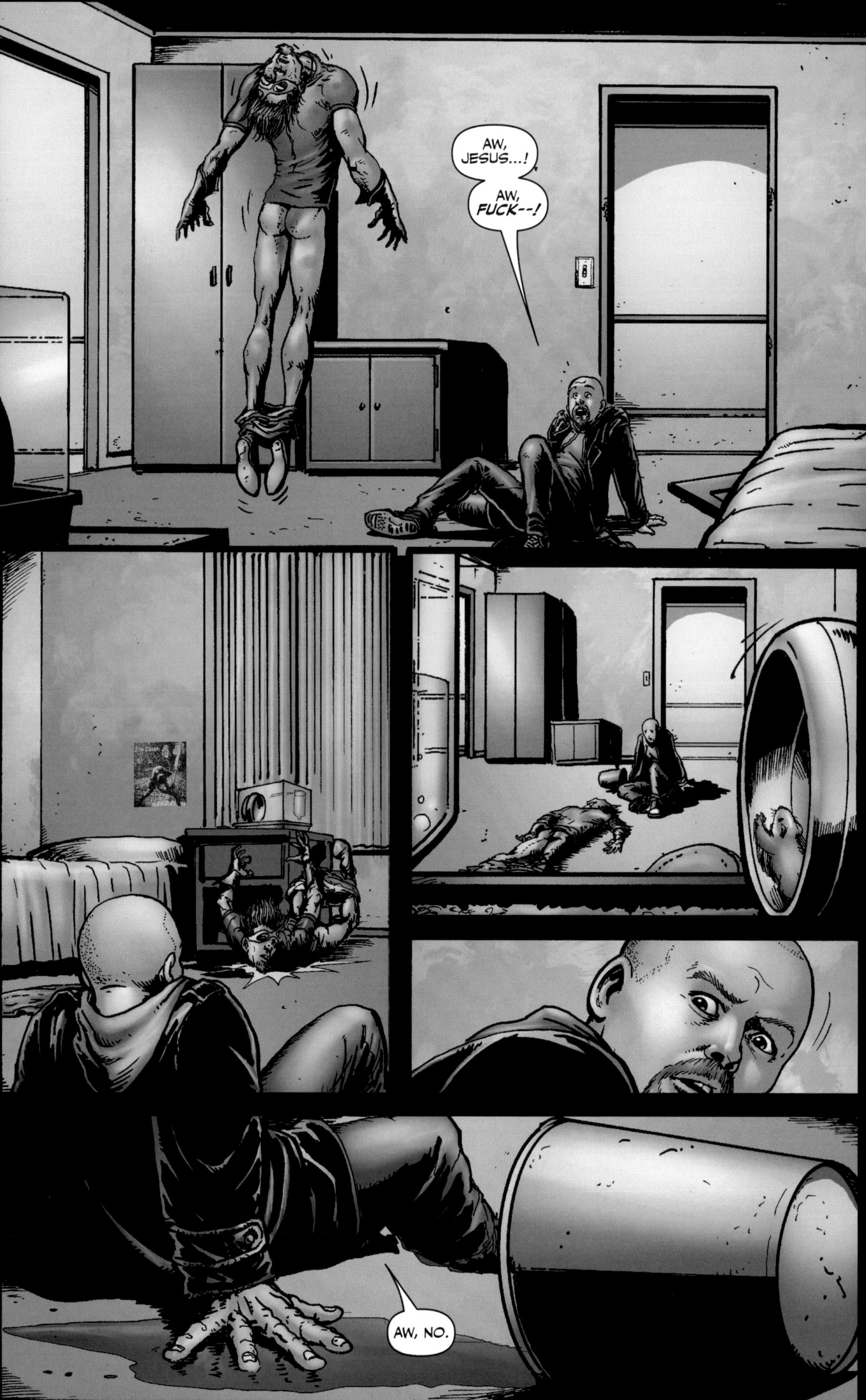
AW, JESUS...!
AW, FUCK--!
AW, NO.

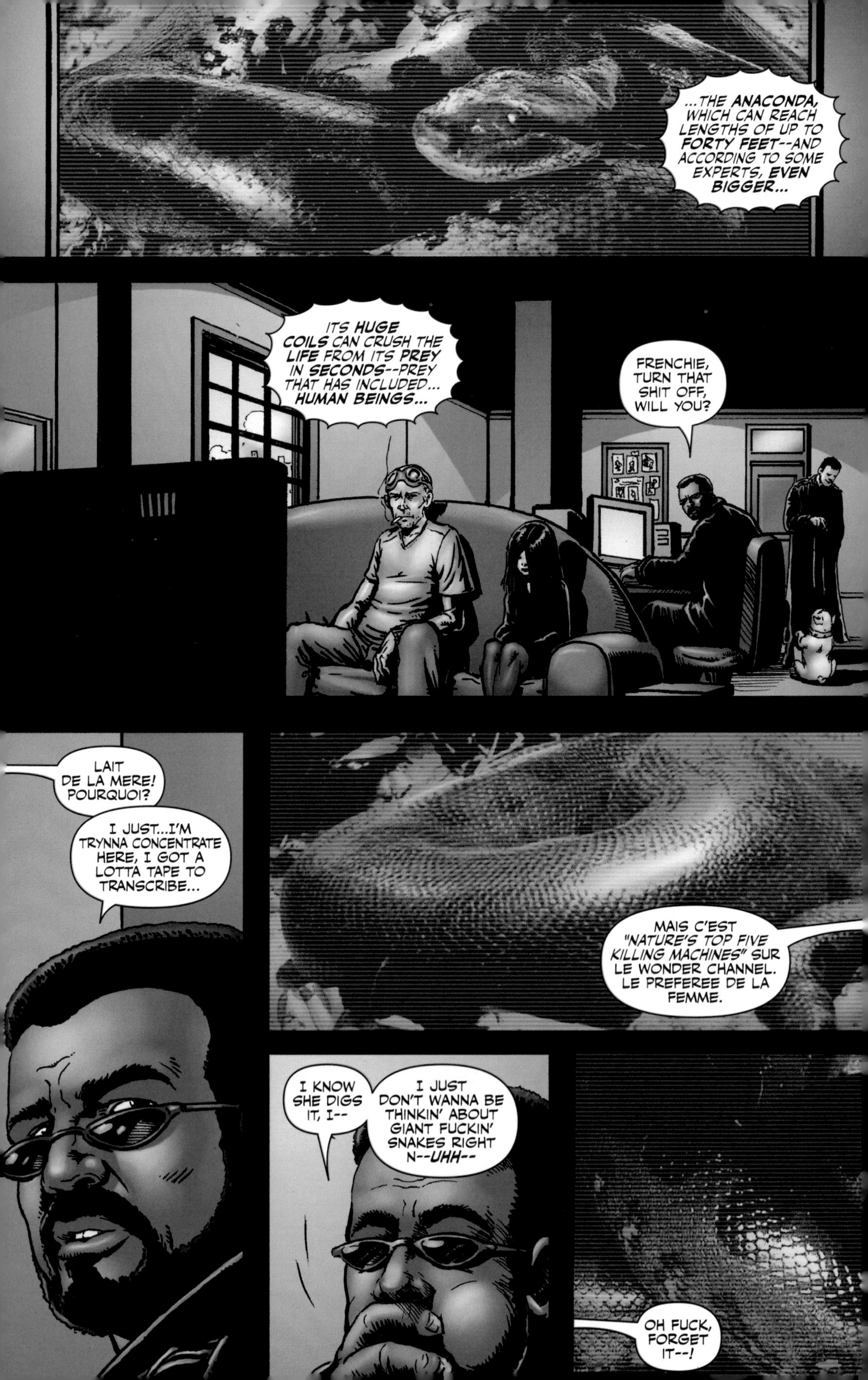
...THE ANACONDA, WHICH CAN REACH LENGTHS OF UP TO FORTY FEET--AND ACCORDING TO SOME EXPERTS, EVEN BIGGER...
ITS HUGE COILS CAN CRUSH THE LIFE FROM ITS PREY IN SECONDS--PREY THAT HAS INCLUDED... HUMAN BEINGS...
FRENCHIE, TURN THAT SHIT OFF, WILL YOU?
LAIT DE LA MERE! POURQUOI?
I JUST...I'M TRYNNA CONCENTRATE HERE, I GOT A LOTTA TAPE TO TRANSCRIBE...
MAIS C'EST "NATURE'S TOP FIVE KILLING MACHINES" SUR LE WONDER CHANNEL. LE PREFEREE DE LA FEMME.
I KNOW SHE DIGS IT, I--
I JUST DON'T WANNA BE THINKIN' ABOUT GIANT FUCKIN' SNAKES RIGHT N--UHH--
OH FUCK, FORGET IT--!

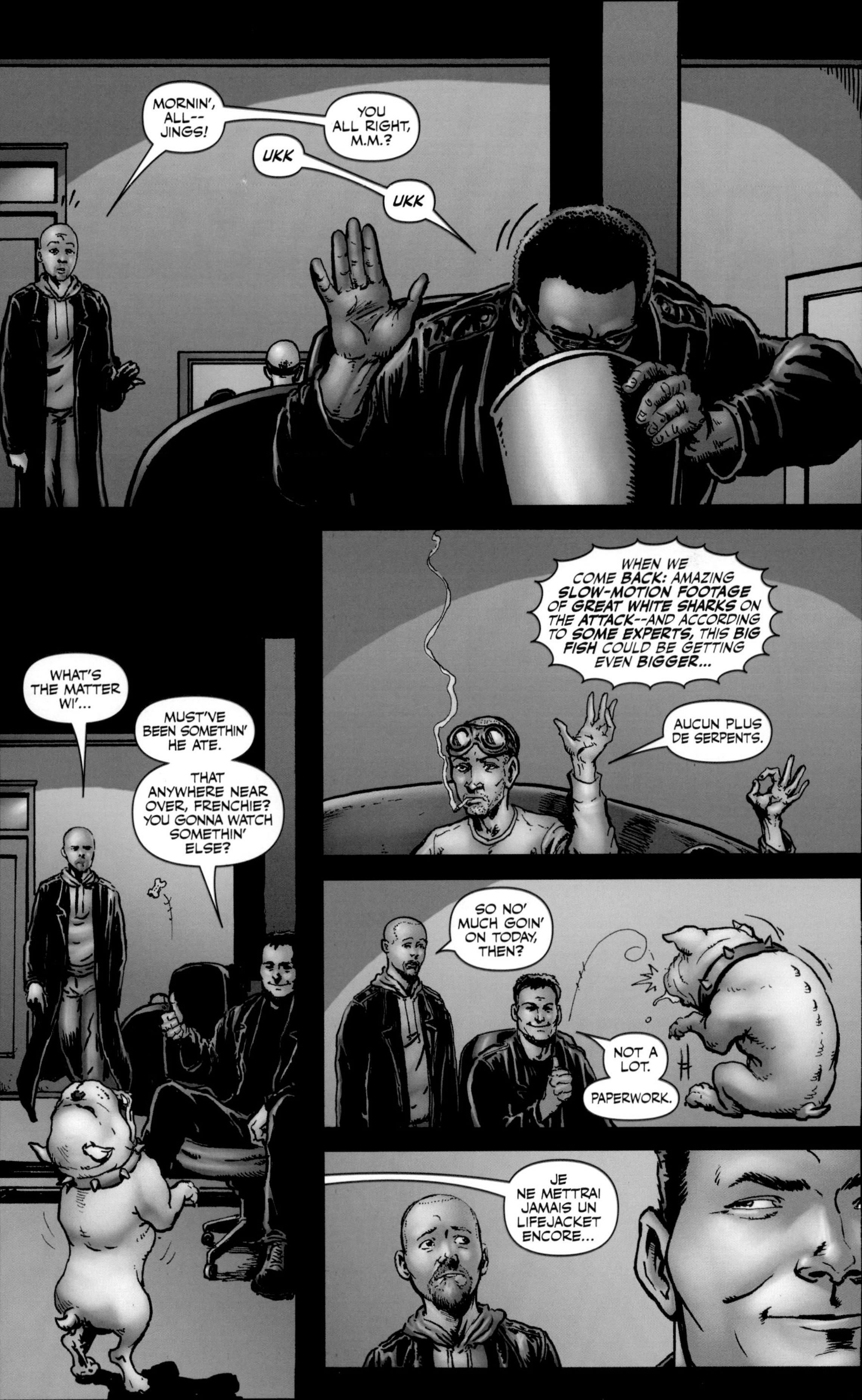

MORNIN', ALL-- JINGS!
YOU ALL RIGHT, M.M.?
UKK
UKK
WHAT'S THE MATTER WI'...
MUST'VE BEEN SOMETHIN' HE ATE.
THAT ANYWHERE NEAR OVER, FRENCHIE? YOU GONNA WATCH SOMETHIN' ELSE?
WHEN WE COME BACK: AMAZING SLOW-MOTION FOOTAGE OF GREAT WHITE SHARKS ON THE ATTACK--AND ACCORDING TO SOME EXPERTS, THIS BIG FISH COULD BE GETTING EVEN BIGGER...
AUCUN PLUS DE SERPENTS.
SO NO' MUCH GOIN' ON TODAY, THEN?
NOT A LOT.
PAPERWORK.
JE NE METTRAI JAMAIS UN LIFEJACKET ENCORE...

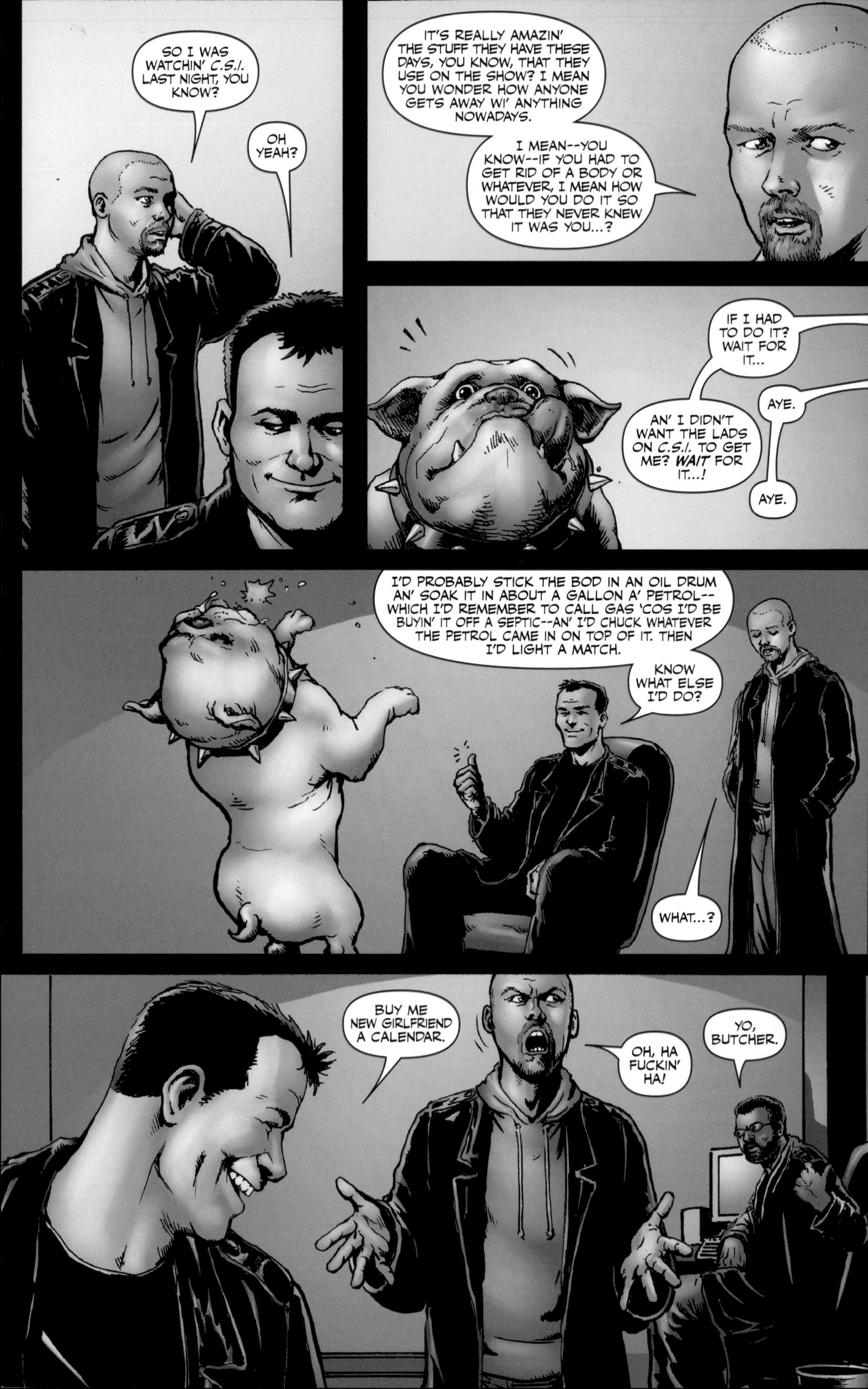
SO I WAS WATCHIN' C.S.I. LAST NIGHT, YOU KNOW?
OH YEAH?
IT'S REALLY AMAZIN' THE STUFF THEY HAVE THESE DAYS, YOU KNOW, THAT THEY USE ON THE SHOW? I MEAN YOU WONDER HOW ANYONE GETS AWAY WI' ANYTHING NOWADAYS.
I MEAN--YOU KNOW--IF YOU HAD TO GET RID OF A BODY OR WHATEVER, I MEAN HOW WOULD YOU DO IT SO THAT THEY NEVER KNEW IT WAS YOU...?
IF I HAD TO DO IT? WAIT FOR IT...
AYE.
AN' I DIDN'T WANT THE LADS ON C.S.I. TO GET ME? WAIT FOR IT...!
AYE.
I'D PROBABLY STICK THE BOD IN AN OIL DRUM AN' SOAK IT IN ABOUT A GALLON A' PETROL--WHICH I'D REMEMBER TO CALL GAS 'COS I'D BE BUYIN' IT OFF A SEPTIC--AN' I'D CHUCK WHATEVER THE PETROL CAME IN ON TOP OF IT. THEN I'D LIGHT A MATCH.
KNOW WHAT ELSE I'D DO?
WHAT...?
BUY ME NEW GIRLFRIEND A CALENDAR.
OH, HA FUCKIN' HA!
YO, BUTCHER.

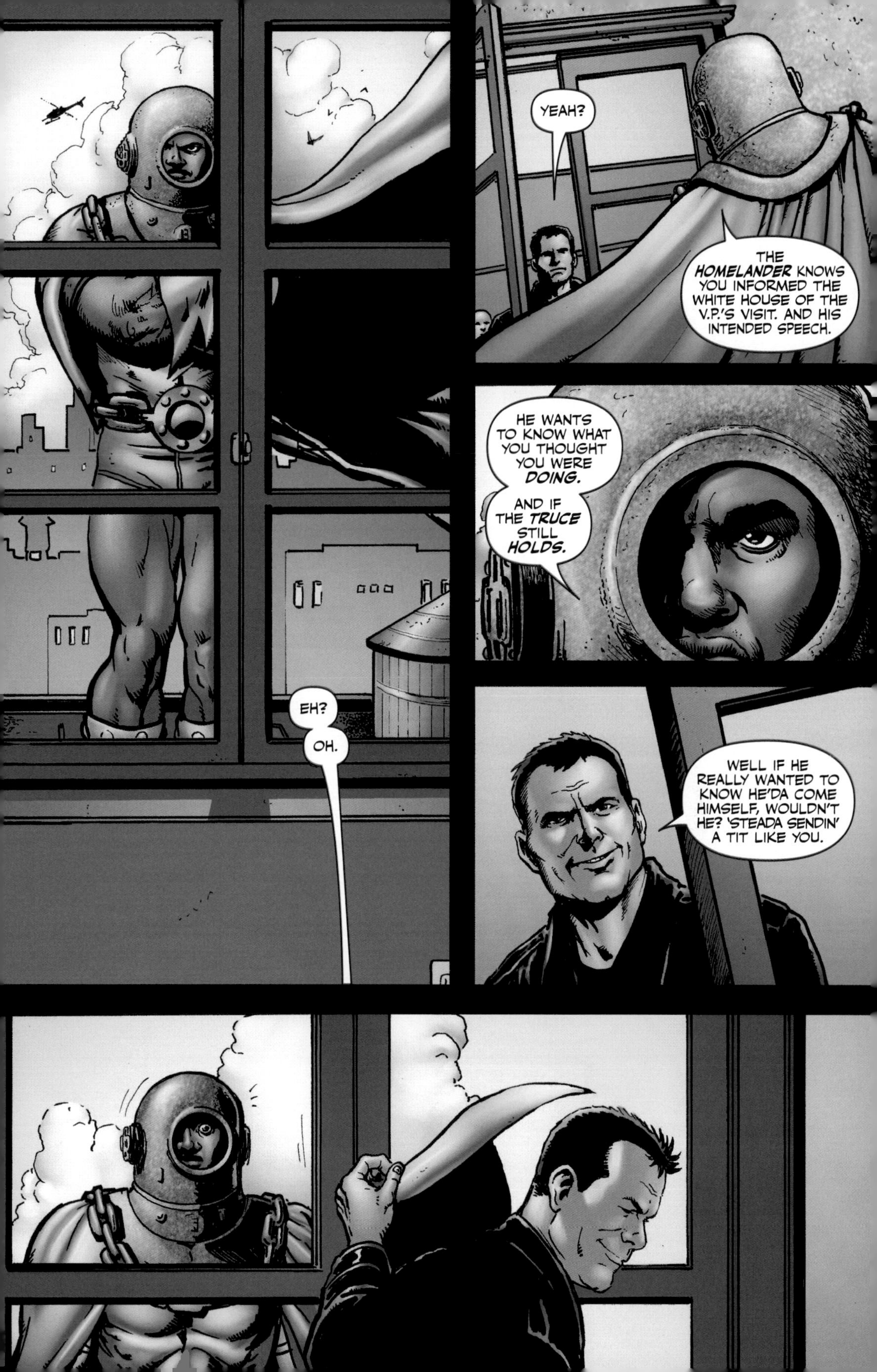
YEAH?
THE *HOMELANDER* KNOWS YOU INFORMED THE WHITE HOUSE OF THE V.P.'S VISIT. AND HIS INTENDED SPEECH.
HE WANTS TO KNOW WHAT YOU THOUGHT YOU WERE *DOING.*
AND IF THE *TRUCE* STILL *HOLDS.*
WELL IF HE REALLY WANTED TO KNOW HE'DA COME HIMSELF, WOULDN'T HE? 'STEADA SENDIN' A TIT LIKE YOU.
EH?
OH.

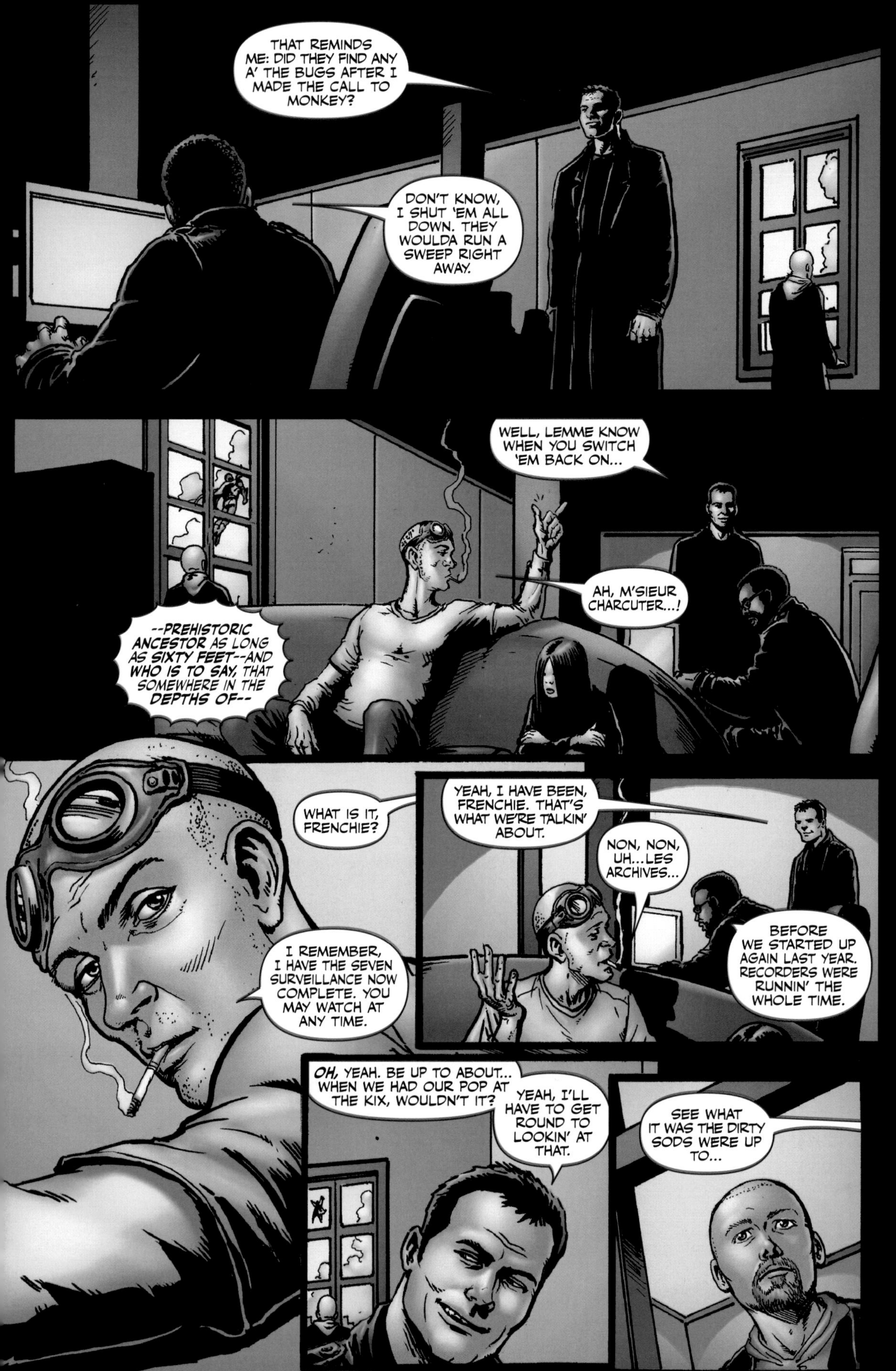
THAT REMINDS ME: DID THEY FIND ANY A' THE BUGS AFTER I MADE THE CALL TO MONKEY?
DON'T KNOW, I SHUT 'EM ALL DOWN. THEY WOULDA RUN A SWEEP RIGHT AWAY.
WELL, LEMME KNOW WHEN YOU SWITCH 'EM BACK ON...
AH, M'SIEUR CHARCUTER...!
--PREHISTORIC ANCESTOR AS LONG AS SIXTY FEET--AND WHO IS TO SAY, THAT SOMEWHERE IN THE DEPTHS OF--
WHAT IS IT, FRENCHIE?
I REMEMBER, I HAVE THE SEVEN SURVEILLANCE NOW COMPLETE. YOU MAY WATCH AT ANY TIME.
YEAH, I HAVE BEEN, FRENCHIE. THAT'S WHAT WE'RE TALKIN' ABOUT.
NON, NON, UH...LES ARCHIVES...
BEFORE WE STARTED UP AGAIN LAST YEAR. RECORDERS WERE RUNNIN' THE WHOLE TIME.
OH, YEAH. BE UP TO ABOUT... WHEN WE HAD OUR POP AT THE KIX, WOULDN'T IT?
YEAH, I'LL HAVE TO GET ROUND TO LOOKIN' AT THAT.
SEE WHAT IT WAS THE DIRTY SODS WERE UP TO...

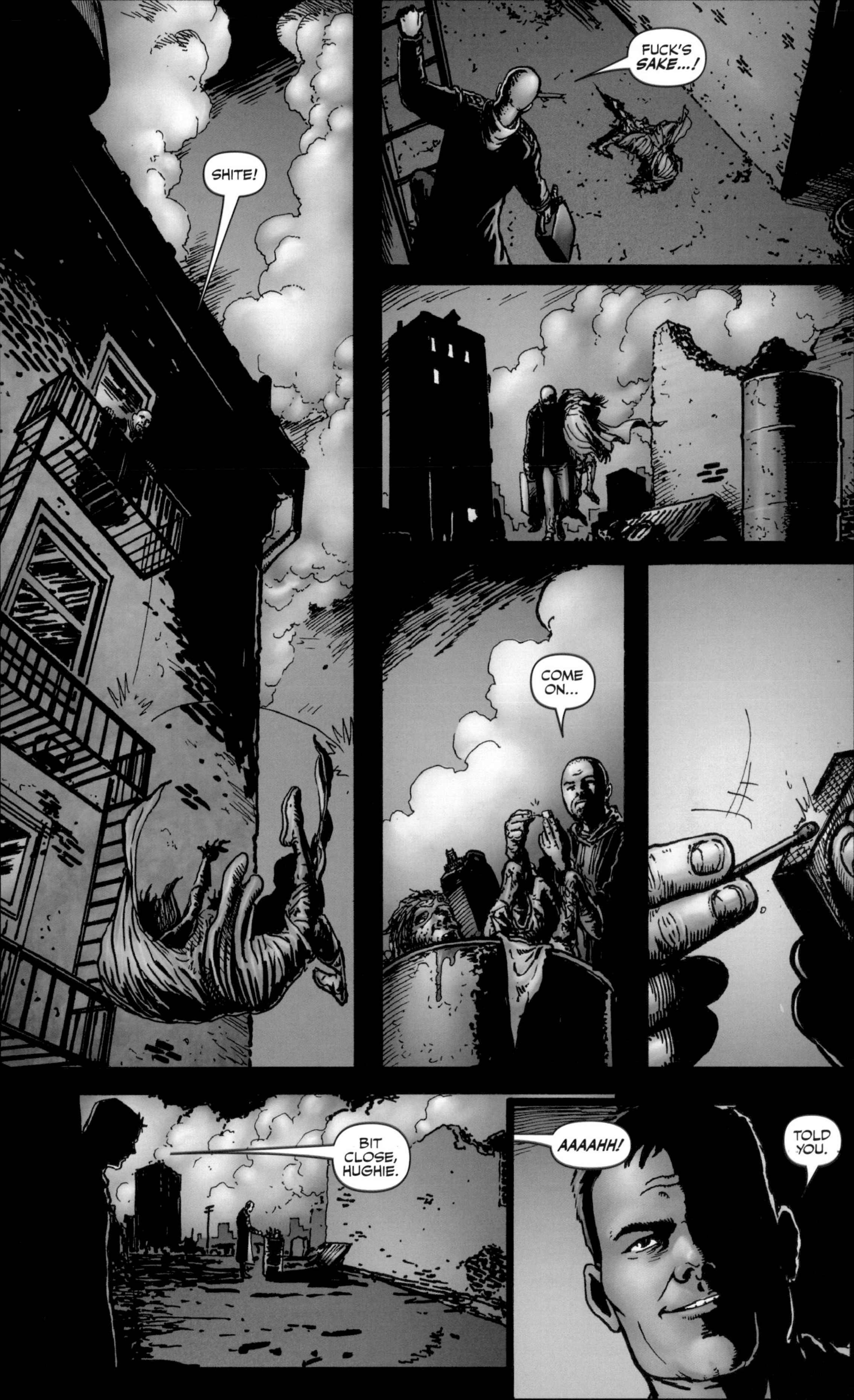
SHITE!
FUCK'S SAKE...!
COME ON...
BIT CLOSE, HUGHIE.
AAAAHH!
TOLD YOU.

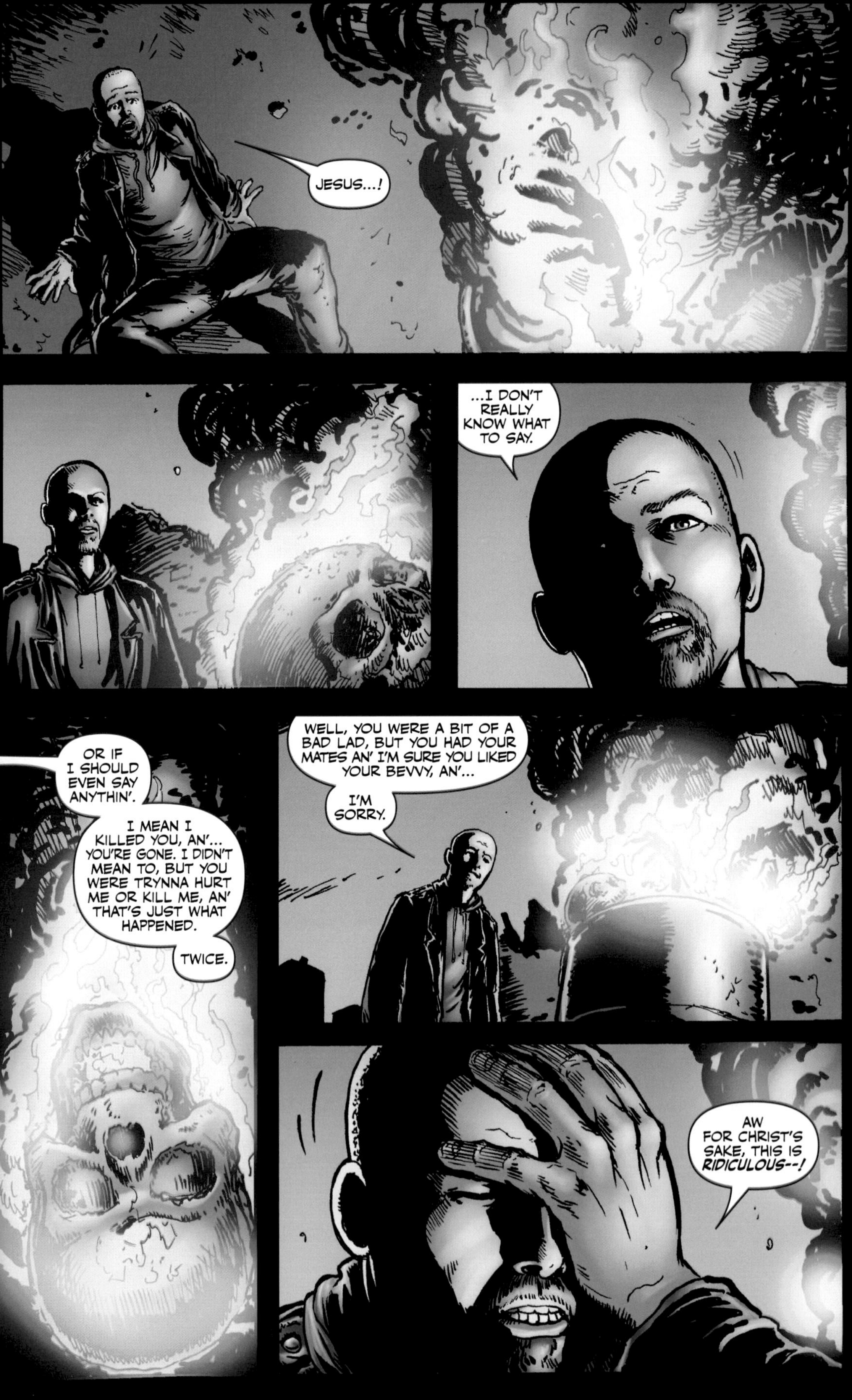
JESUS...!
...I DON'T REALLY KNOW WHAT TO SAY.
OR IF I SHOULD EVEN SAY ANYTHIN'.
I MEAN I KILLED YOU, AN'... YOU'RE GONE. I DIDN'T MEAN TO, BUT YOU WERE TRYNNA HURT ME OR KILL ME, AN' THAT'S JUST WHAT HAPPENED.
TWICE.
WELL, YOU WERE A BIT OF A BAD LAD, BUT YOU HAD YOUR MATES AN' I'M SURE YOU LIKED YOUR BEVVY, AN'...
I'M SORRY.
AW FOR CHRIST'S SAKE, THIS IS *RIDICULOUS--!*

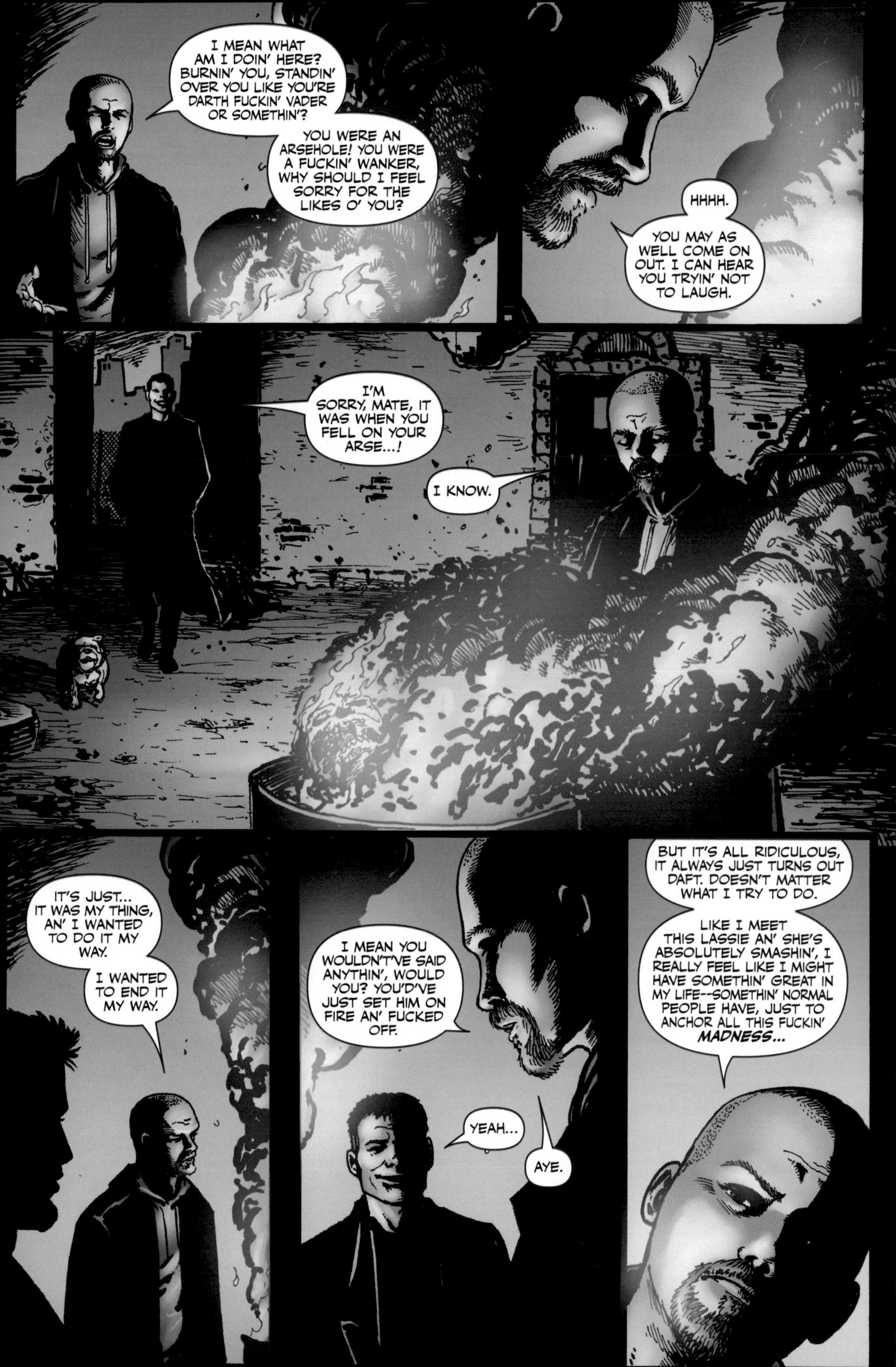
I MEAN WHAT AM I DOIN' HERE? BURNIN' YOU, STANDIN' OVER YOU LIKE YOU'RE DARTH FUCKIN' VADER OR SOMETHIN'?
YOU WERE AN ARSEHOLE! YOU WERE A FUCKIN' WANKER, WHY SHOULD I FEEL SORRY FOR THE LIKES O' YOU?
HHHH.
YOU MAY AS WELL COME ON OUT. I CAN HEAR YOU TRYIN' NOT TO LAUGH.
I'M SORRY, MATE, IT WAS WHEN YOU FELL ON YOUR ARSE...!
I KNOW.
IT'S JUST... IT WAS MY THING, AN' I WANTED TO DO IT MY WAY.
I WANTED TO END IT MY WAY.
I MEAN YOU WOULDN'T'VE SAID ANYTHIN', WOULD YOU? YOU'D'VE JUST SET HIM ON FIRE AN' FUCKED OFF.
YEAH...
AYE.
BUT IT'S ALL RIDICULOUS, IT ALWAYS JUST TURNS OUT DAFT. DOESN'T MATTER WHAT I TRY TO DO.
LIKE I MEET THIS LASSIE AN' SHE'S ABSOLUTELY SMASHIN', I REALLY FEEL LIKE I MIGHT HAVE SOMETHIN' GREAT IN MY LIFE--SOMETHIN' NORMAL PEOPLE HAVE, JUST TO ANCHOR ALL THIS FUCKIN' MADNESS...

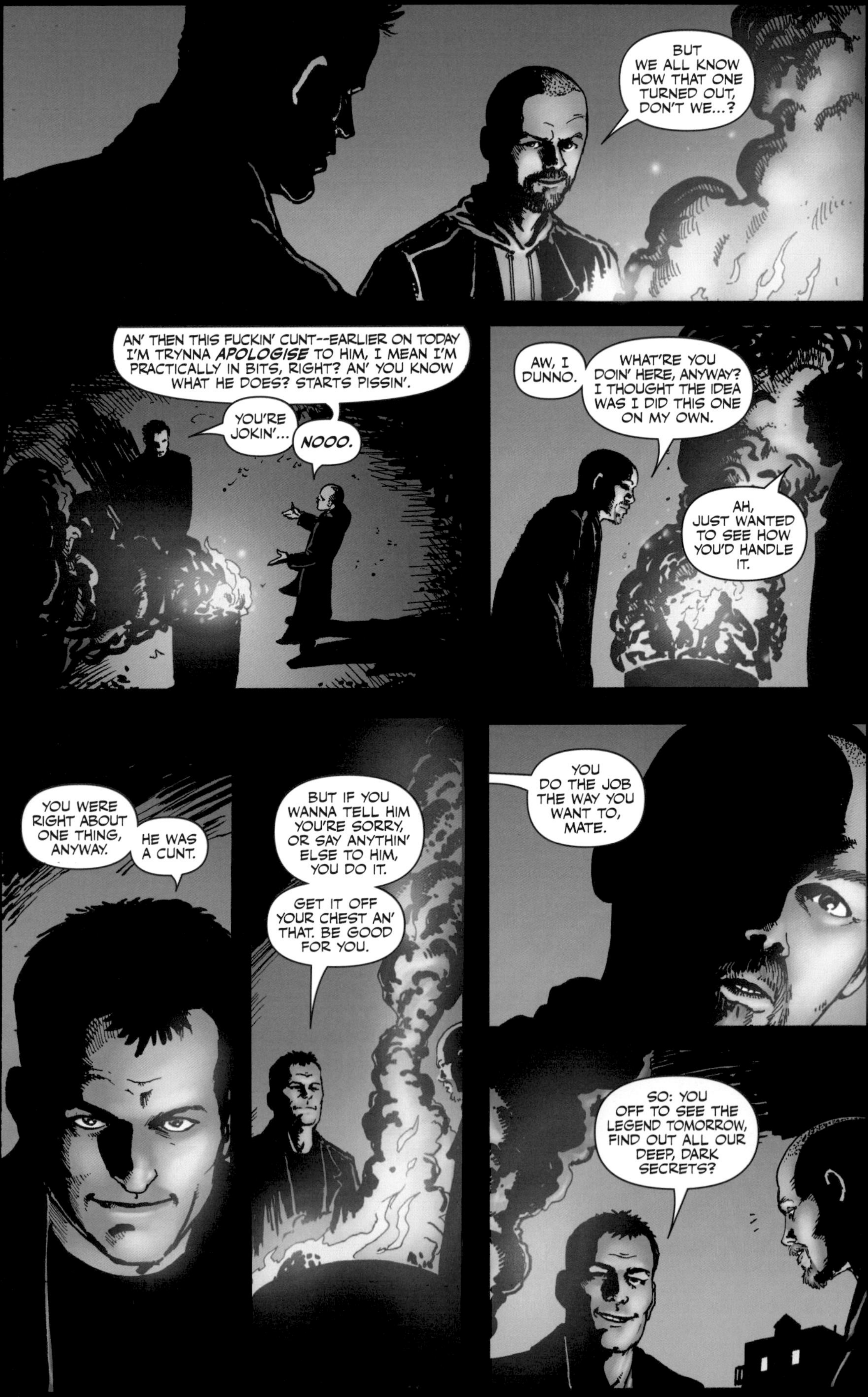
BUT WE ALL KNOW HOW THAT ONE TURNED OUT, DON'T WE...?
AN' THEN THIS FUCKIN' CUNT--EARLIER ON TODAY I'M TRYNNA APOLOGISE TO HIM, I MEAN I'M PRACTICALLY IN BITS, RIGHT? AN' YOU KNOW WHAT HE DOES? STARTS PISSIN'.
YOU'RE JOKIN'...
NOOO.
AW, I DUNNO.
WHAT'RE YOU DOIN' HERE, ANYWAY? I THOUGHT THE IDEA WAS I DID THIS ONE ON MY OWN.
AH, JUST WANTED TO SEE HOW YOU'D HANDLE IT.
YOU WERE RIGHT ABOUT ONE THING, ANYWAY.
HE WAS A CUNT.
BUT IF YOU WANNA TELL HIM YOU'RE SORRY, OR SAY ANYTHIN' ELSE TO HIM, YOU DO IT.
GET IT OFF YOUR CHEST AN' THAT. BE GOOD FOR YOU.
YOU DO THE JOB THE WAY YOU WANT TO, MATE.
SO: YOU OFF TO SEE THE LEGEND TOMORROW, FIND OUT ALL OUR DEEP, DARK SECRETS?

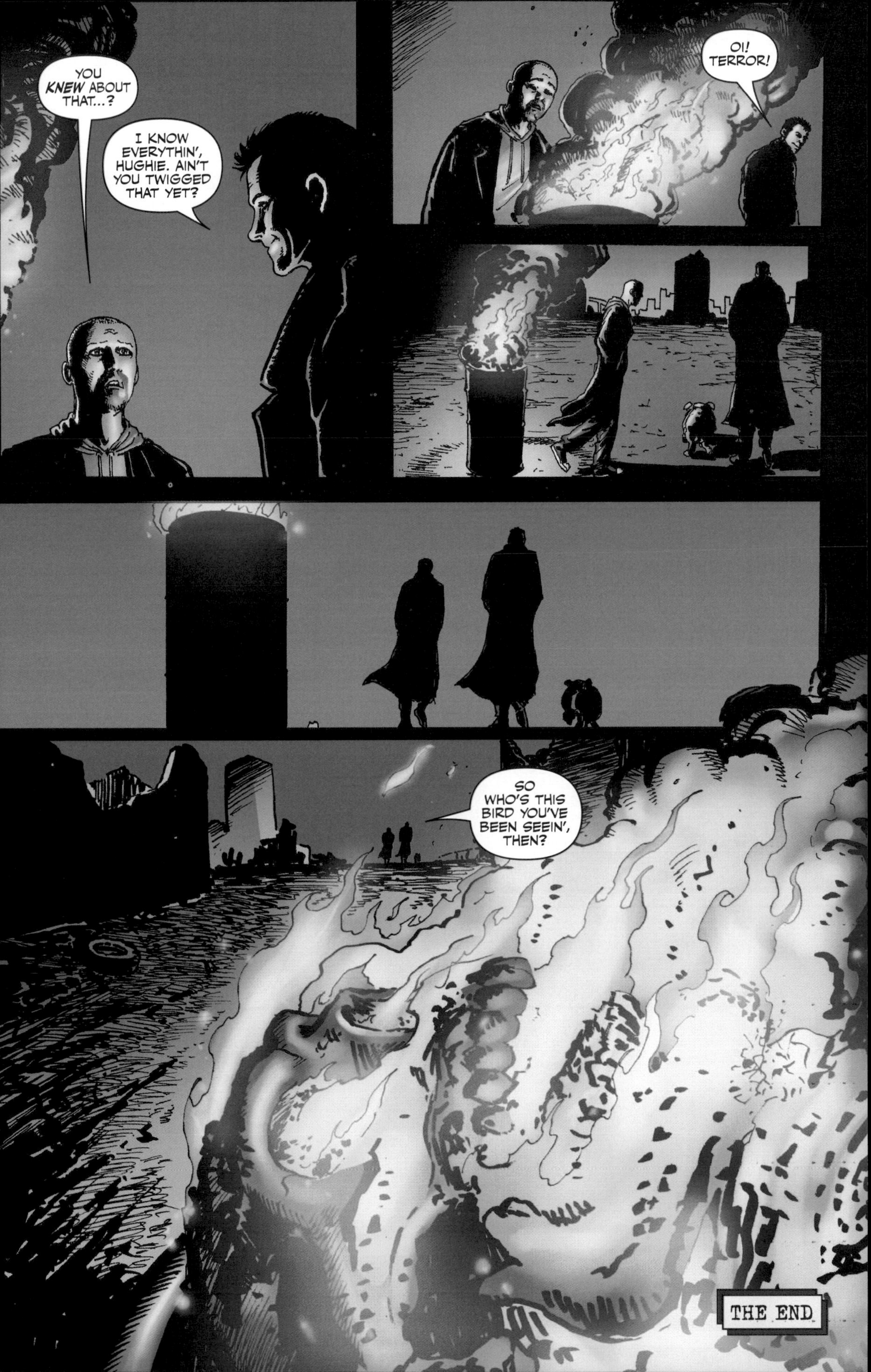

OI! TERROR!
YOU KNEW ABOUT THAT...?
I KNOW EVERYTHIN', HUGHIE. AIN'T YOU TWIGGED THAT YET?
SO WHO'S THIS BIRD YOU'VE BEEN SEEIN', THEN?
THE END

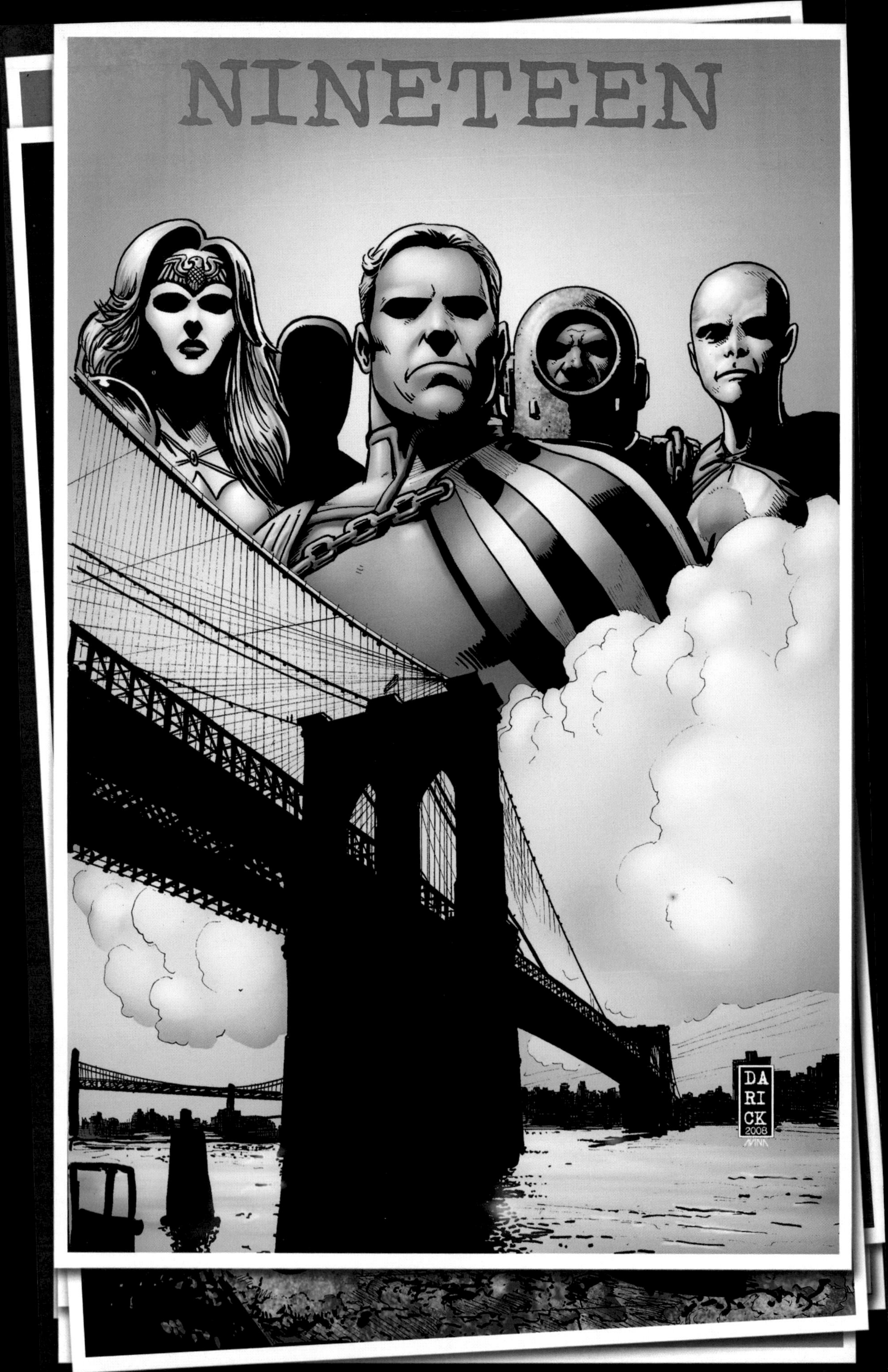
NINETEEN
DA
RI
CK
2008

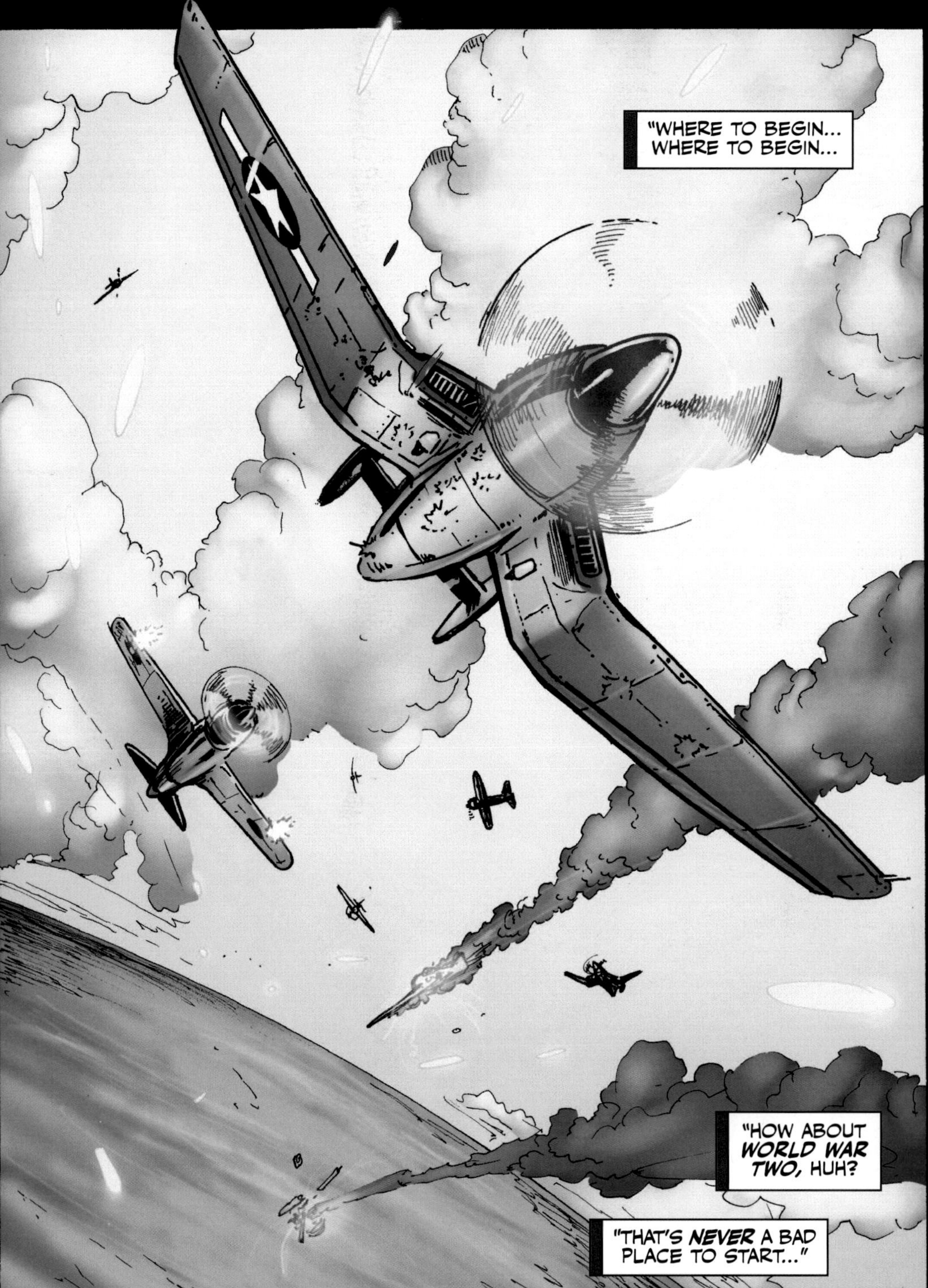
"WHERE TO BEGIN...
WHERE TO BEGIN...
"HOW ABOUT *WORLD WAR TWO,* HUH?
"THAT'S *NEVER* A BAD PLACE TO START..."

I TELL YOU NO LIE, G.I.

part one

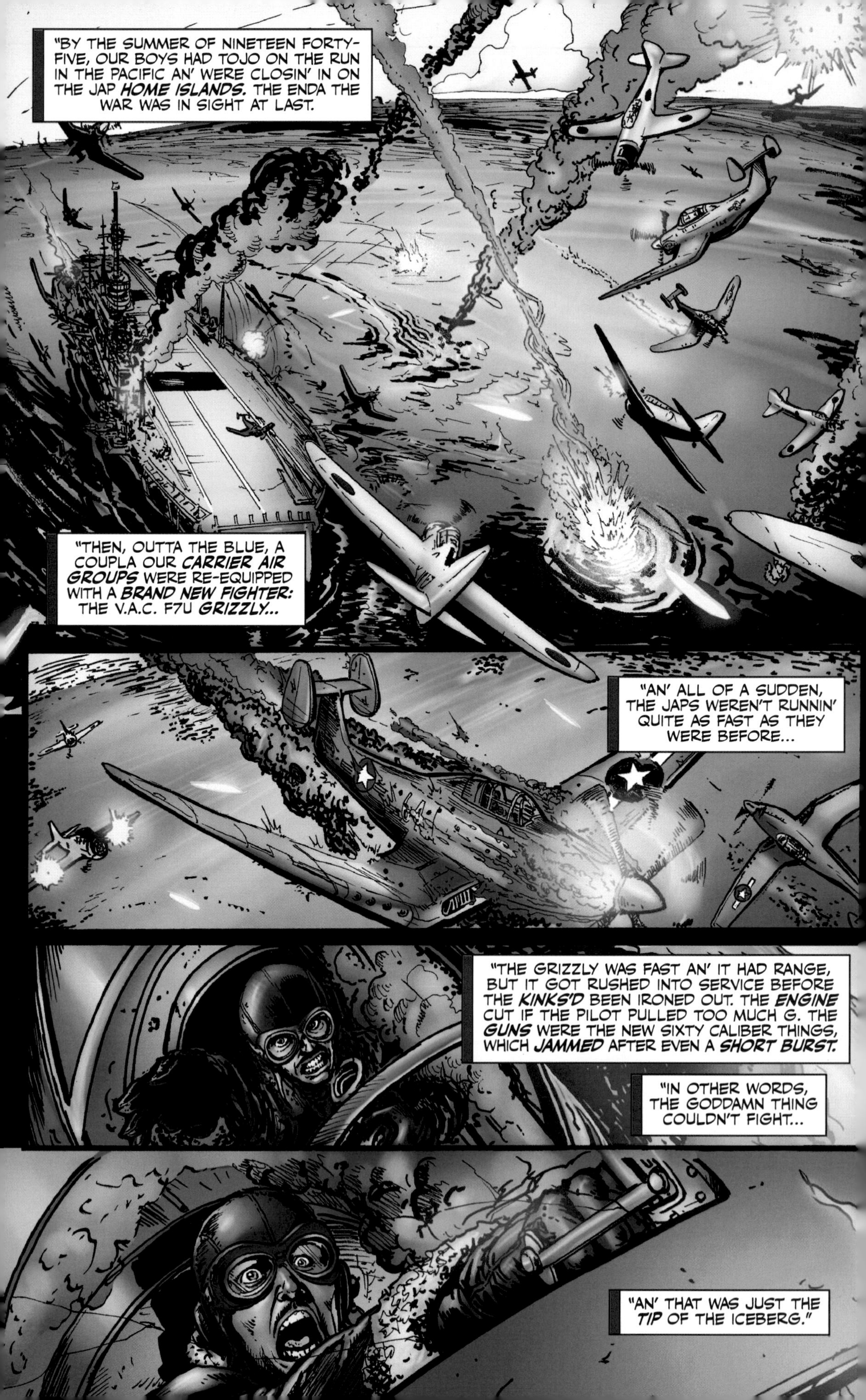
"BY THE SUMMER OF NINETEEN FORTY-FIVE, OUR BOYS HAD TOJO ON THE RUN IN THE PACIFIC AN' WERE CLOSIN' IN ON THE JAP *HOME ISLANDS.* THE ENDA THE WAR WAS IN SIGHT AT LAST.
"THEN, OUTTA THE BLUE, A COUPLA OUR *CARRIER AIR GROUPS* WERE RE-EQUIPPED WITH A *BRAND NEW FIGHTER:* THE V.A.C. F7U *GRIZZLY*...
"AN' ALL OF A SUDDEN, THE JAPS WEREN'T RUNNIN' QUITE AS FAST AS THEY WERE BEFORE...
"THE GRIZZLY WAS FAST AN' IT HAD RANGE, BUT IT GOT RUSHED INTO SERVICE BEFORE THE *KINKS'D* BEEN IRONED OUT. THE *ENGINE* CUT IF THE PILOT PULLED TOO MUCH G. THE *GUNS* WERE THE NEW SIXTY CALIBER THINGS, WHICH *JAMMED* AFTER EVEN A *SHORT BURST.*
"IN OTHER WORDS, THE GODDAMN THING COULDN'T FIGHT...
"AN' THAT WAS JUST THE *TIP* OF THE ICEBERG."

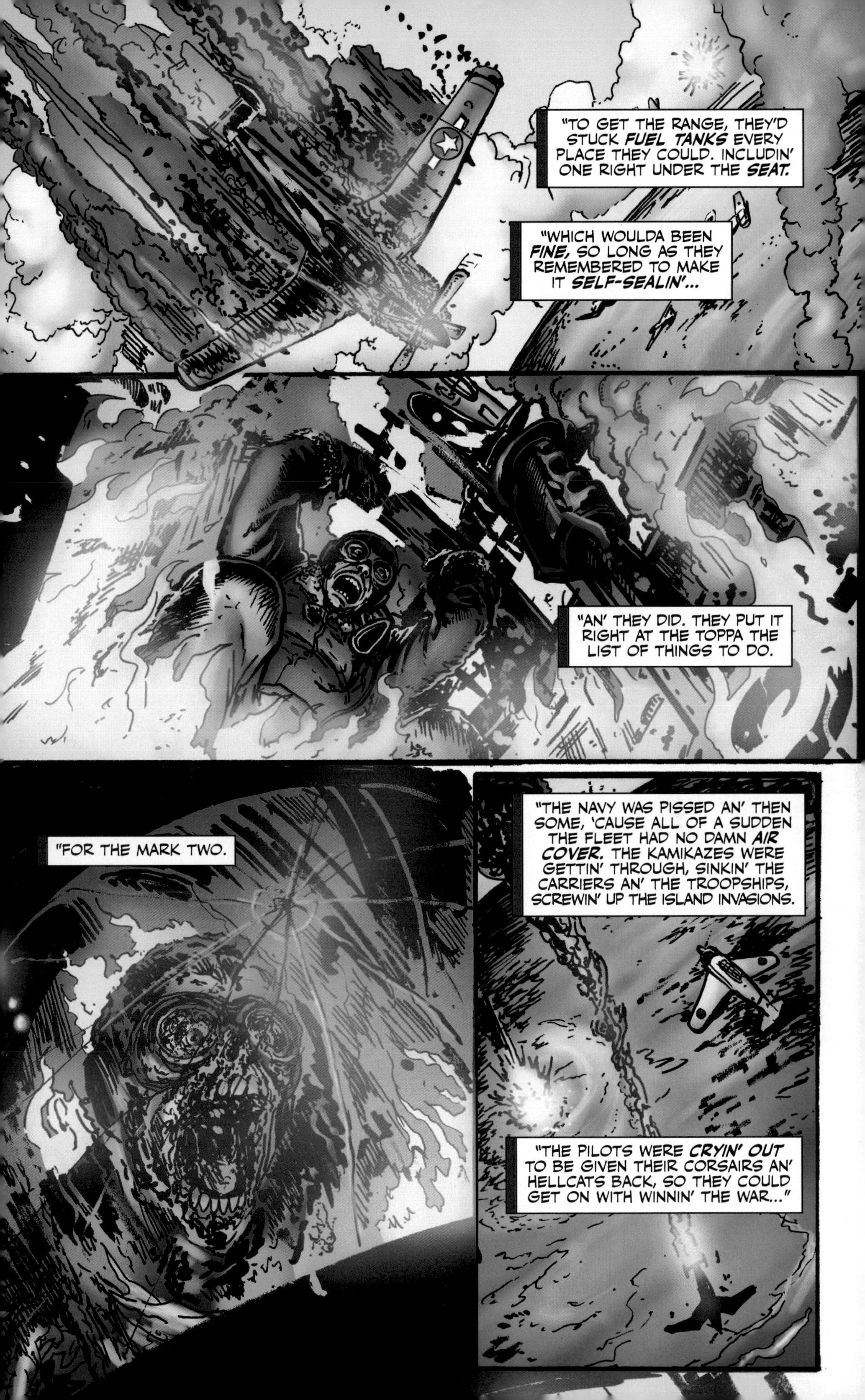
"TO GET THE RANGE, THEY'D STUCK FUEL TANKS EVERY PLACE THEY COULD. INCLUDIN' ONE RIGHT UNDER THE SEAT.
"WHICH WOULDA BEEN FINE, SO LONG AS THEY REMEMBERED TO MAKE IT SELF-SEALIN'...
"AN' THEY DID. THEY PUT IT RIGHT AT THE TOPPA THE LIST OF THINGS TO DO.
"FOR THE MARK TWO.
"THE NAVY WAS PISSED AN' THEN SOME, 'CAUSE ALL OF A SUDDEN THE FLEET HAD NO DAMN AIR COVER. THE KAMIKAZES WERE GETTIN' THROUGH, SINKIN' THE CARRIERS AN' THE TROOPSHIPS, SCREWIN' UP THE ISLAND INVASIONS.
"THE PILOTS WERE CRYIN' OUT TO BE GIVEN THEIR CORSAIRS AN' HELLCATS BACK, SO THEY COULD GET ON WITH WINNIN' THE WAR..."

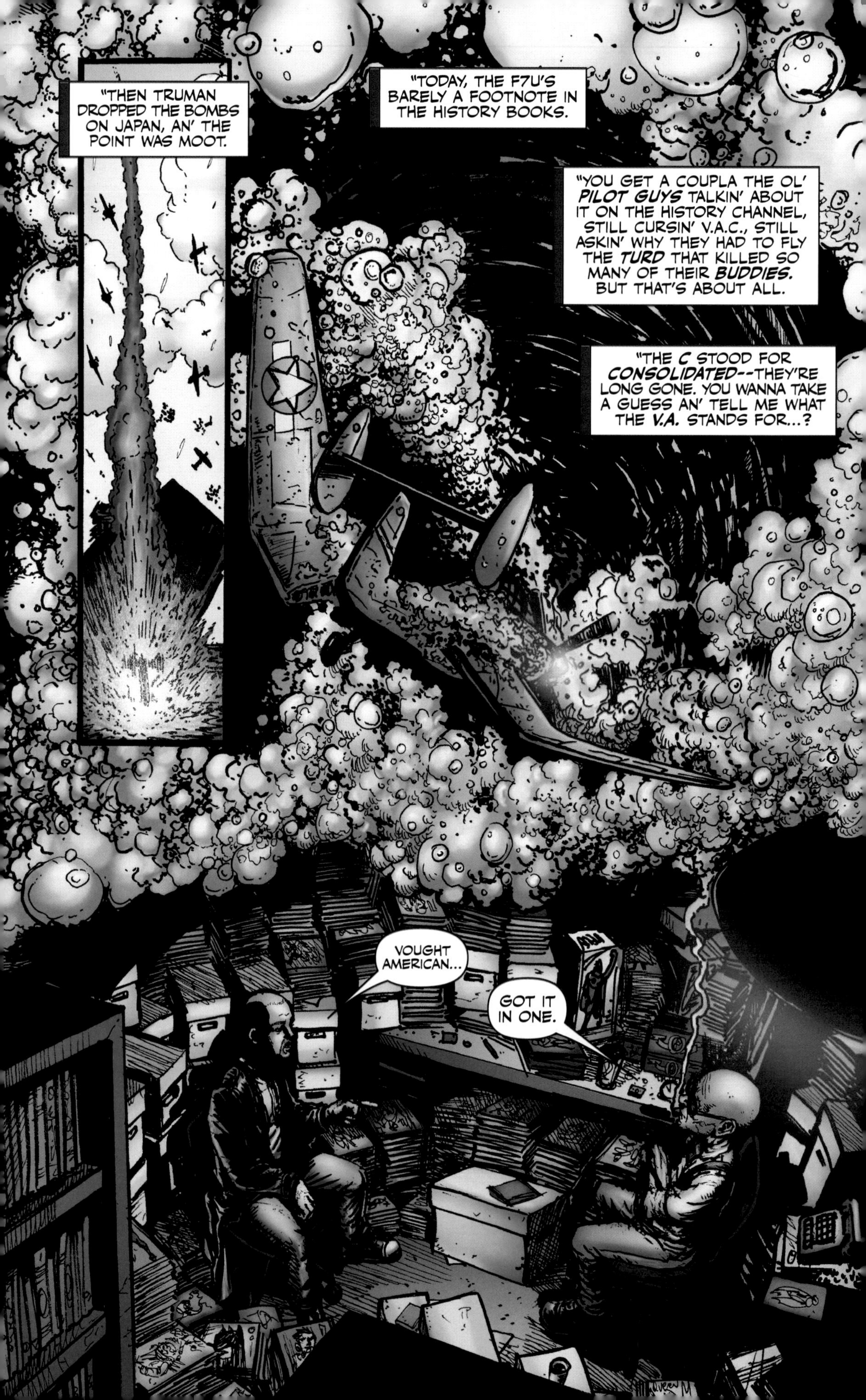
"THEN TRUMAN DROPPED THE BOMBS ON JAPAN, AN' THE POINT WAS MOOT.
"TODAY, THE F7U'S BARELY A FOOTNOTE IN THE HISTORY BOOKS.
"YOU GET A COUPLA THE OL' PILOT GUYS TALKIN' ABOUT IT ON THE HISTORY CHANNEL, STILL CURSIN' V.A.C., STILL ASKIN' WHY THEY HAD TO FLY THE TURD THAT KILLED SO MANY OF THEIR BUDDIES. BUT THAT'S ABOUT ALL.
"THE C STOOD FOR CONSOLIDATED--THEY'RE LONG GONE. YOU WANNA TAKE A GUESS AN' TELL ME WHAT THE V.A. STANDS FOR...?
VOUGHT AMERICAN...
GOT IT IN ONE.

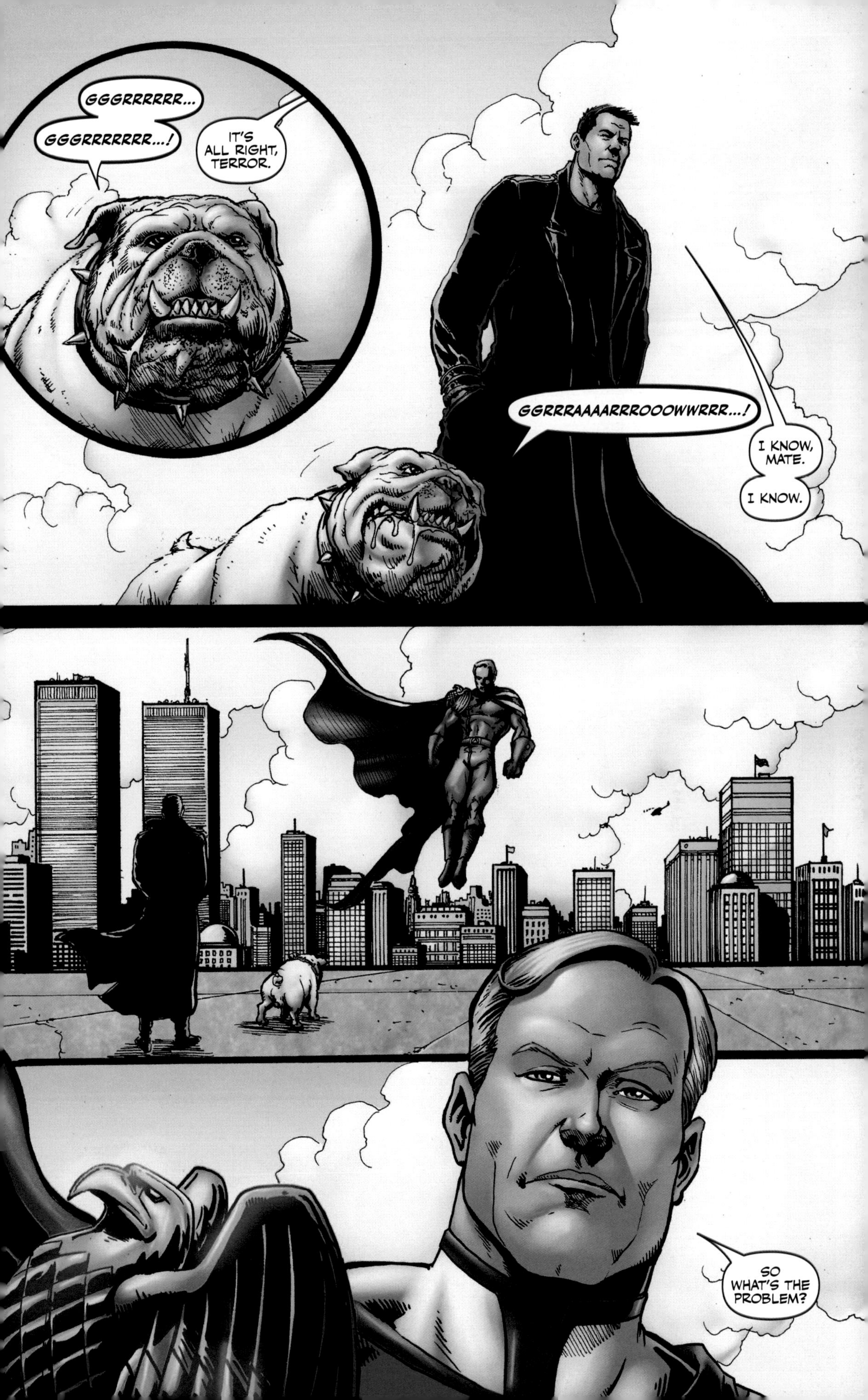
GGGRRRRRR...
GGGRRRRRRR...!
IT'S ALL RIGHT, TERROR.
GGRRRAAAARRROOOWWRRR...!
I KNOW, MATE.
I KNOW.
SO WHAT'S THE PROBLEM?

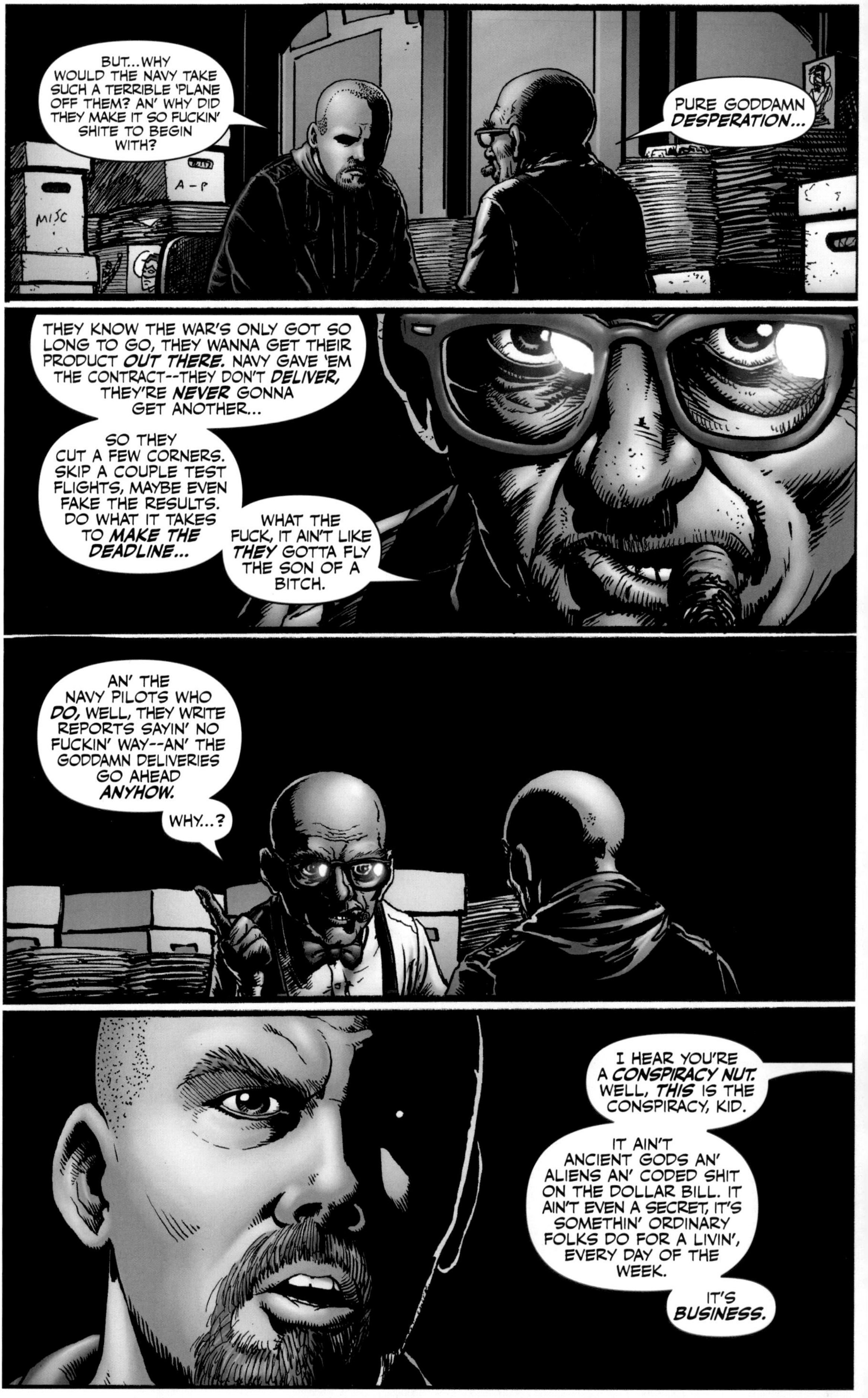
BUT...WHY WOULD THE NAVY TAKE SUCH A TERRIBLE 'PLANE OFF THEM? AN' WHY DID THEY MAKE IT SO FUCKIN' SHITE TO BEGIN WITH?
PURE GODDAMN DESPERATION...
A-P
MISC
THEY KNOW THE WAR'S ONLY GOT SO LONG TO GO, THEY WANNA GET THEIR PRODUCT OUT THERE. NAVY GAVE 'EM THE CONTRACT--THEY DON'T DELIVER, THEY'RE NEVER GONNA GET ANOTHER...
SO THEY CUT A FEW CORNERS. SKIP A COUPLE TEST FLIGHTS, MAYBE EVEN FAKE THE RESULTS. DO WHAT IT TAKES TO MAKE THE DEADLINE...
WHAT THE FUCK, IT AIN'T LIKE THEY GOTTA FLY THE SON OF A BITCH.
AN' THE NAVY PILOTS WHO DO, WELL, THEY WRITE REPORTS SAYIN' NO FUCKIN' WAY--AN' THE GODDAMN DELIVERIES GO AHEAD ANYHOW.
WHY...?
I HEAR YOU'RE A CONSPIRACY NUT. WELL, THIS IS THE CONSPIRACY, KID.
IT AIN'T ANCIENT GODS AN' ALIENS AN' CODED SHIT ON THE DOLLAR BILL. IT AIN'T EVEN A SECRET, IT'S SOMETHIN' ORDINARY FOLKS DO FOR A LIVIN', EVERY DAY OF THE WEEK.
IT'S BUSINESS.

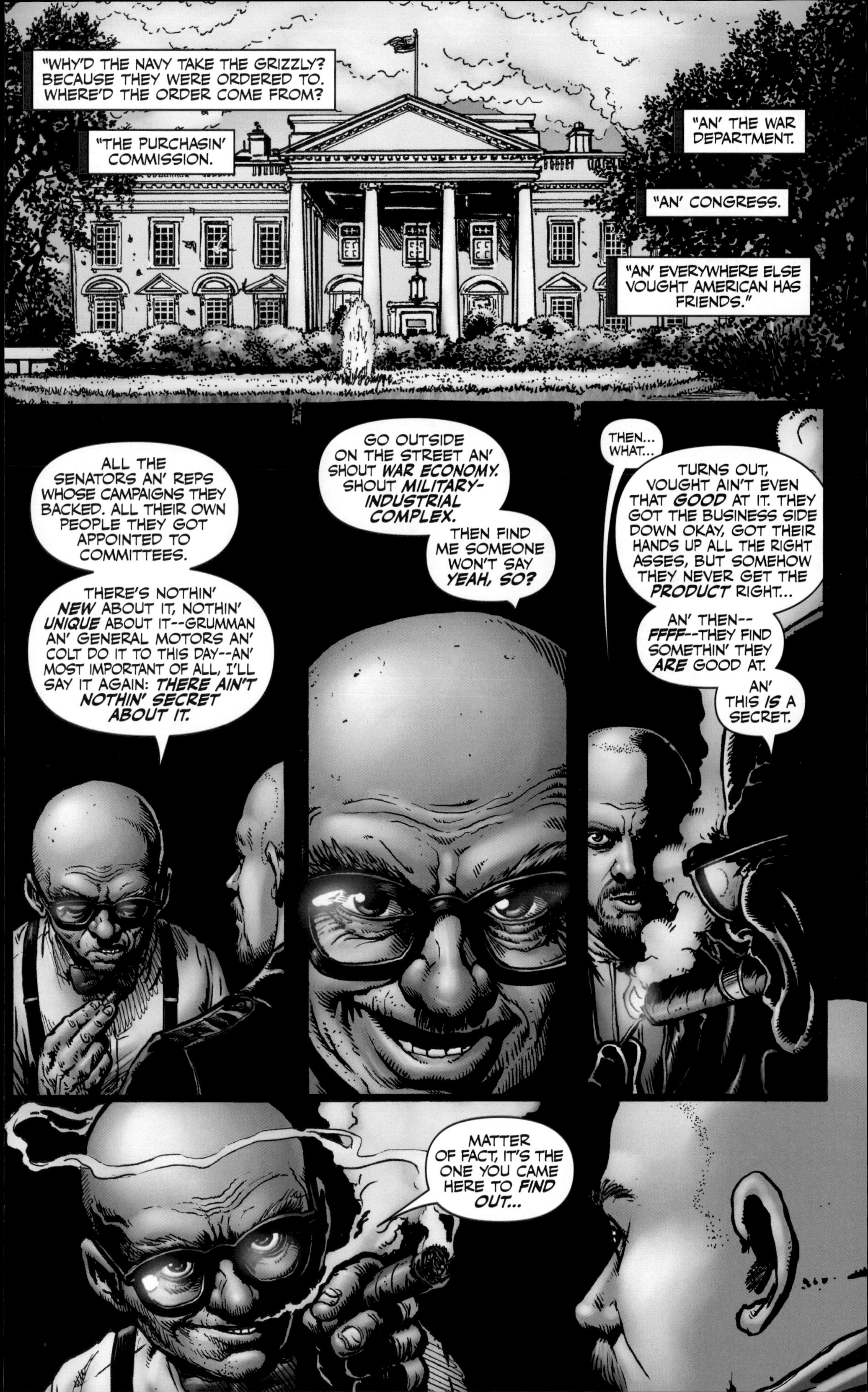

"WHY'D THE NAVY TAKE THE GRIZZLY? BECAUSE THEY WERE ORDERED TO. WHERE'D THE ORDER COME FROM?
"THE PURCHASIN' COMMISSION.
"AN' THE WAR DEPARTMENT.
"AN' CONGRESS.
"AN' EVERYWHERE ELSE VOUGHT AMERICAN HAS FRIENDS."
ALL THE SENATORS AN' REPS WHOSE CAMPAIGNS THEY BACKED. ALL THEIR OWN PEOPLE THEY GOT APPOINTED TO COMMITTEES.
THERE'S NOTHIN' NEW ABOUT IT, NOTHIN' UNIQUE ABOUT IT--GRUMMAN AN' GENERAL MOTORS AN' COLT DO IT TO THIS DAY--AN' MOST IMPORTANT OF ALL, I'LL SAY IT AGAIN: THERE AIN'T NOTHIN' SECRET ABOUT IT.
GO OUTSIDE ON THE STREET AN' SHOUT WAR ECONOMY. SHOUT MILITARY-INDUSTRIAL COMPLEX.
THEN FIND ME SOMEONE WON'T SAY YEAH, SO?
THEN... WHAT...
TURNS OUT, VOUGHT AIN'T EVEN THAT GOOD AT IT. THEY GOT THE BUSINESS SIDE DOWN OKAY, GOT THEIR HANDS UP ALL THE RIGHT ASSES, BUT SOMEHOW THEY NEVER GET THE PRODUCT RIGHT...
AN' THEN--FFFF--THEY FIND SOMETHIN' THEY ARE GOOD AT.
AN' THIS IS A SECRET.
MATTER OF FACT, IT'S THE ONE YOU CAME HERE TO FIND OUT...

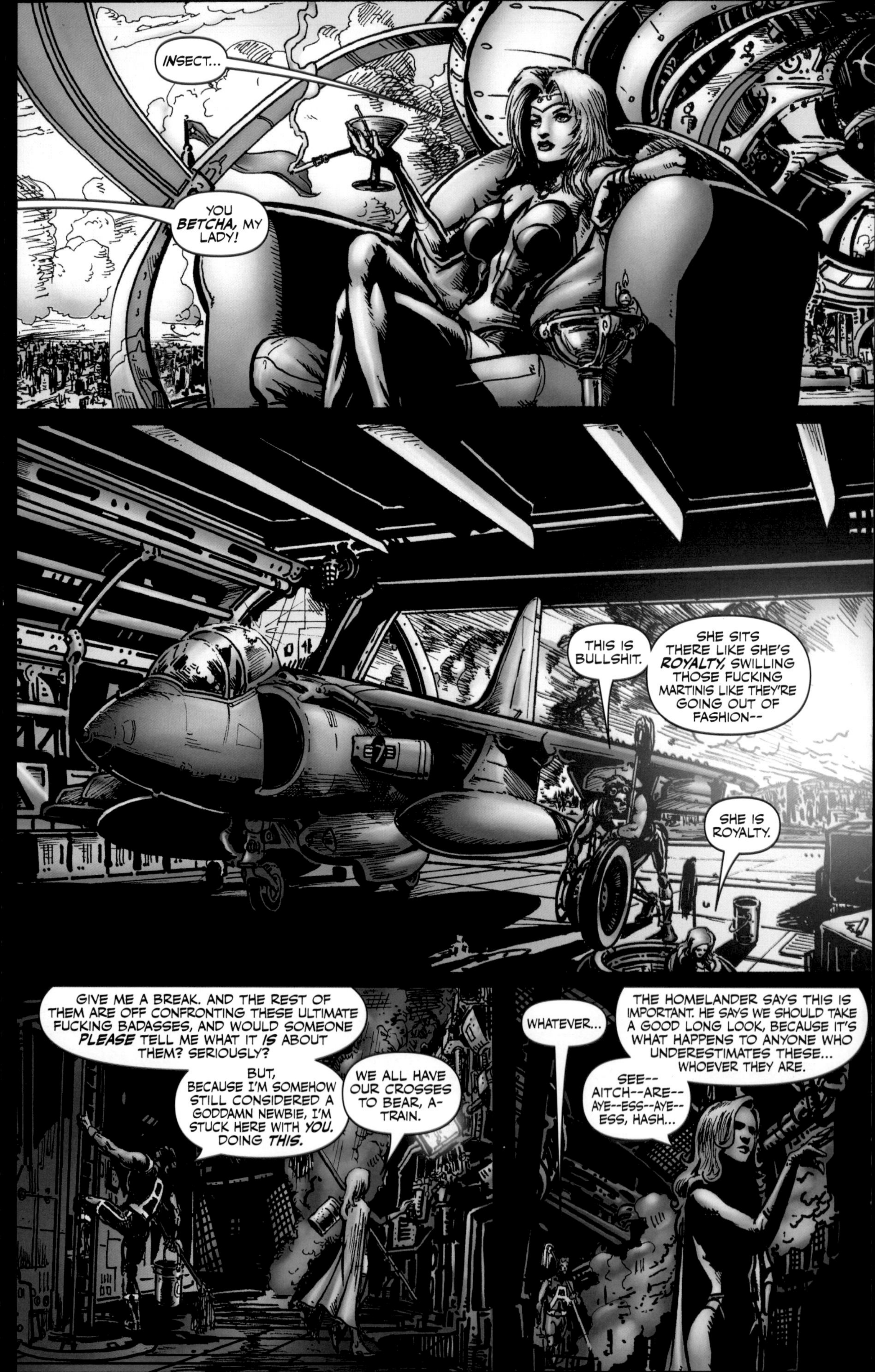
INSECT...
YOU BETCHA, MY LADY!
THIS IS BULLSHIT.
SHE SITS THERE LIKE SHE'S ROYALTY, SWILLING THOSE FUCKING MARTINIS LIKE THEY'RE GOING OUT OF FASHION--
SHE IS ROYALTY.
GIVE ME A BREAK. AND THE REST OF THEM ARE OFF CONFRONTING THESE ULTIMATE FUCKING BADASSES, AND WOULD SOMEONE PLEASE TELL ME WHAT IT IS ABOUT THEM? SERIOUSLY?
BUT, BECAUSE I'M SOMEHOW STILL CONSIDERED A GODDAMN NEWBIE, I'M STUCK HERE WITH YOU. DOING THIS.
WE ALL HAVE OUR CROSSES TO BEAR, A-TRAIN.
WHATEVER...
THE HOMELANDER SAYS THIS IS IMPORTANT. HE SAYS WE SHOULD TAKE A GOOD LONG LOOK, BECAUSE IT'S WHAT HAPPENS TO ANYONE WHO UNDERESTIMATES THESE... WHOEVER THEY ARE.
SEE-- AITCH--ARE-- AYE--ESS--AYE-- ESS, HASH...

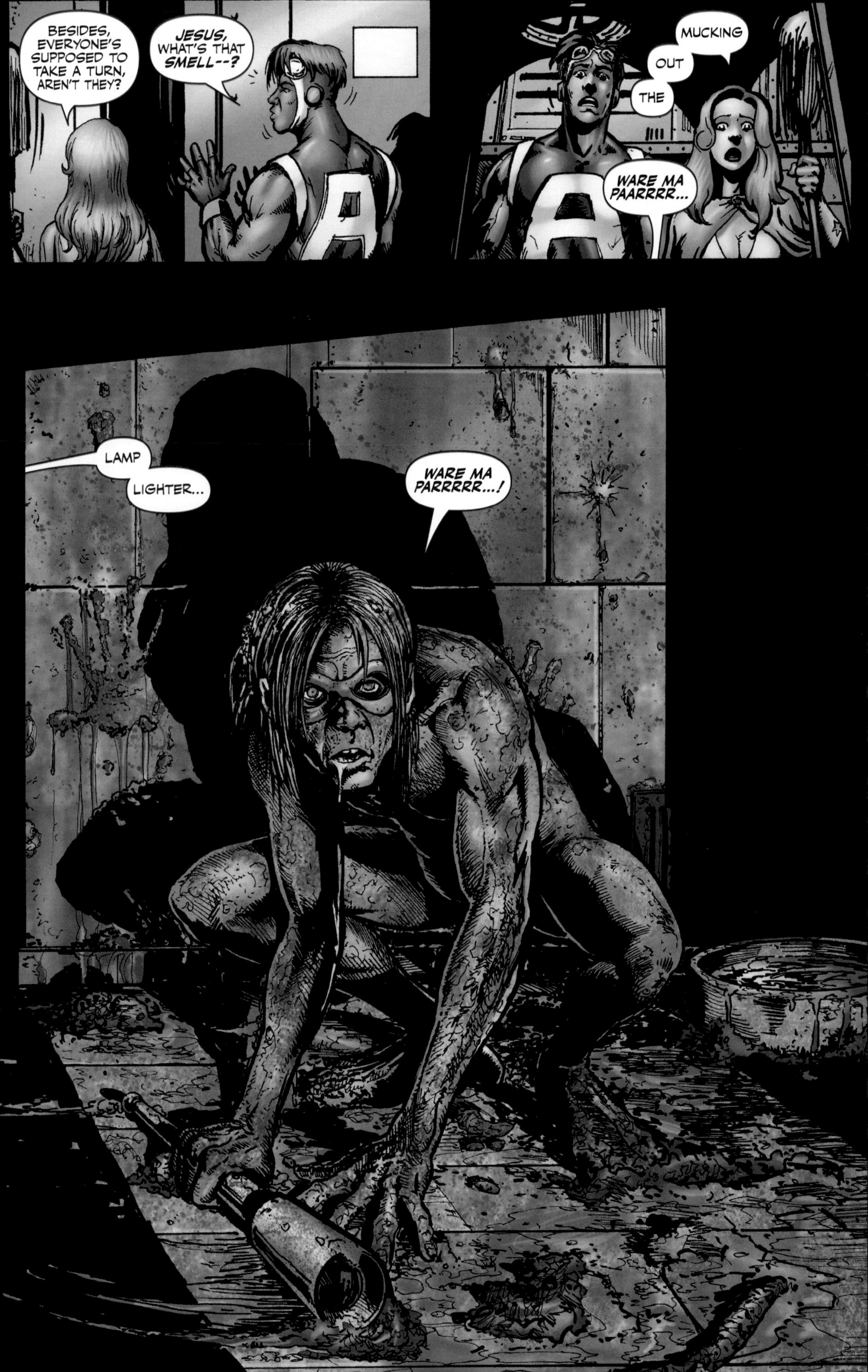

BESIDES, EVERYONE'S SUPPOSED TO TAKE A TURN, AREN'T THEY?
JESUS, WHAT'S THAT SMELL--?
MUCKING
OUT
THE
WARE MA PAARRRR...
LAMP
LIGHTER...
WARE MA PARRRRR...!

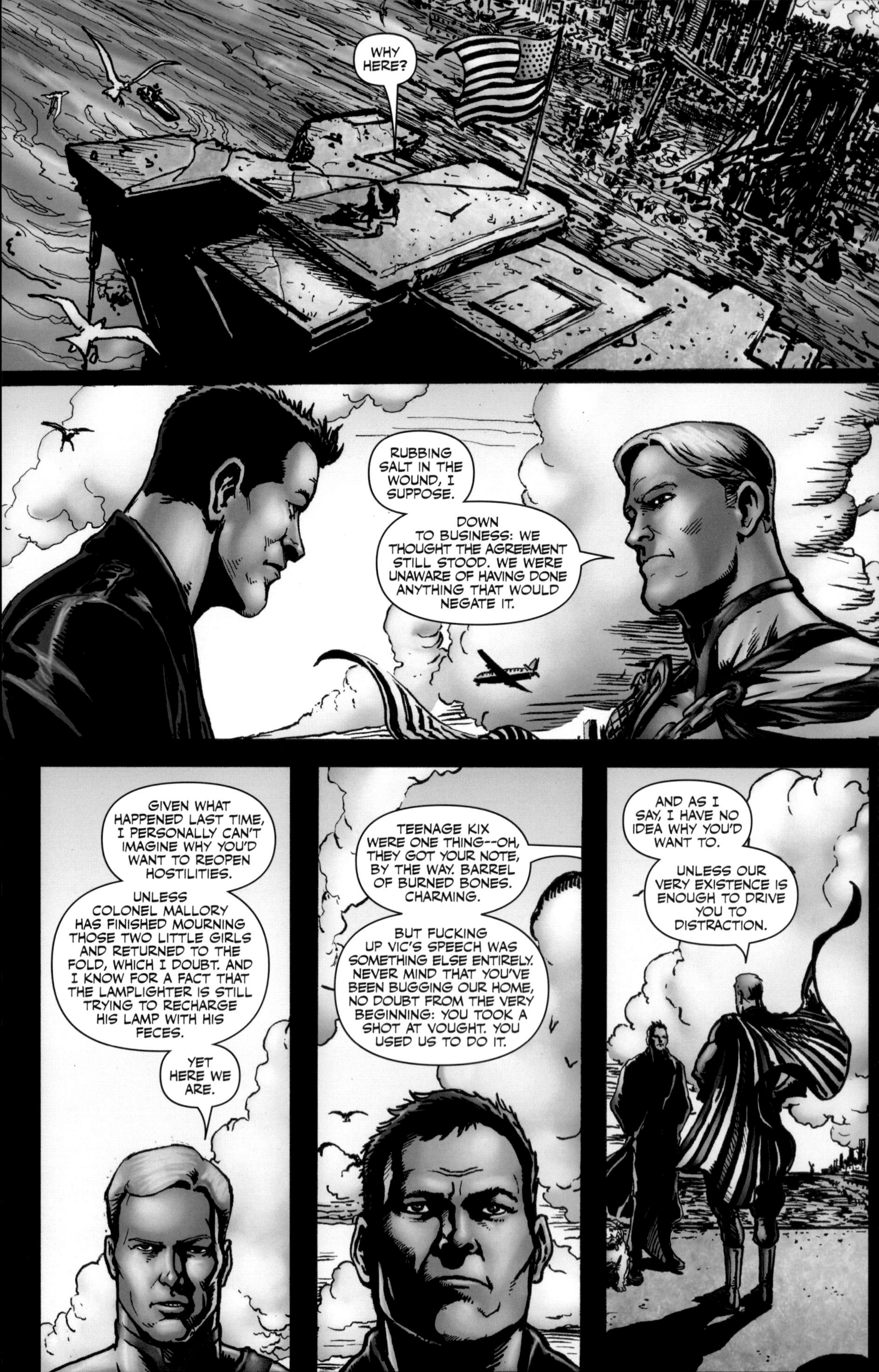
WHY HERE?
RUBBING SALT IN THE WOUND, I SUPPOSE.
DOWN TO BUSINESS: WE THOUGHT THE AGREEMENT STILL STOOD. WE WERE UNAWARE OF HAVING DONE ANYTHING THAT WOULD NEGATE IT.
GIVEN WHAT HAPPENED LAST TIME, I PERSONALLY CAN'T IMAGINE WHY YOU'D WANT TO REOPEN HOSTILITIES.
UNLESS COLONEL MALLORY HAS FINISHED MOURNING THOSE TWO LITTLE GIRLS AND RETURNED TO THE FOLD, WHICH I DOUBT. AND I KNOW FOR A FACT THAT THE LAMPLIGHTER IS STILL TRYING TO RECHARGE HIS LAMP WITH HIS FECES.
YET HERE WE ARE.
TEENAGE KIX WERE ONE THING--OH, THEY GOT YOUR NOTE, BY THE WAY. BARREL OF BURNED BONES. CHARMING.
BUT FUCKING UP VIC'S SPEECH WAS SOMETHING ELSE ENTIRELY. NEVER MIND THAT YOU'VE BEEN BUGGING OUR HOME, NO DOUBT FROM THE VERY BEGINNING: YOU TOOK A SHOT AT VOUGHT. YOU USED US TO DO IT.
AND AS I SAY, I HAVE NO IDEA WHY YOU'D WANT TO.
UNLESS OUR VERY EXISTENCE IS ENOUGH TO DRIVE YOU TO DISTRACTION.

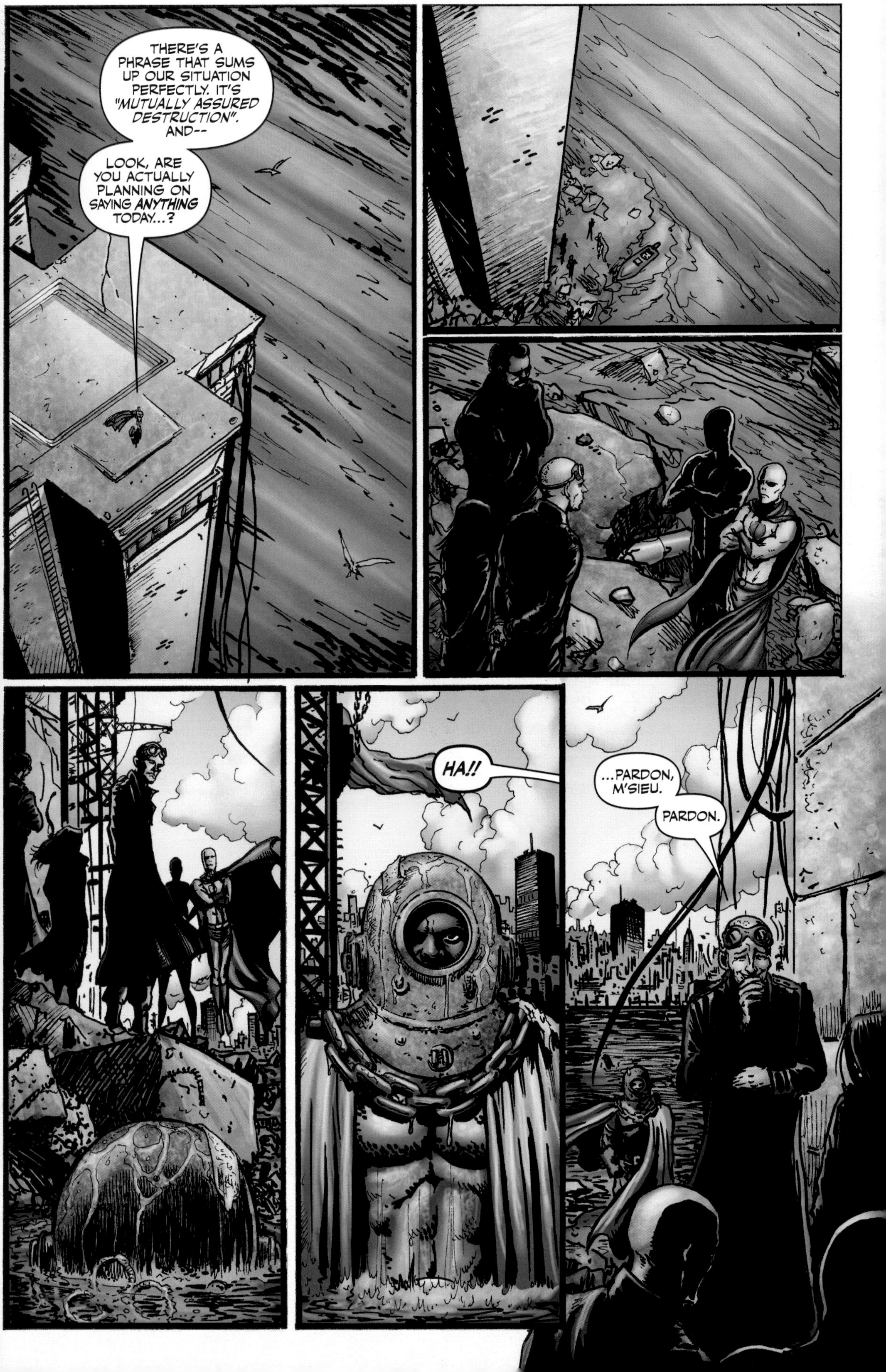

THERE'S A PHRASE THAT SUMS UP OUR SITUATION PERFECTLY. IT'S "*MUTUALLY ASSURED DESTRUCTION*". AND--
LOOK, ARE YOU ACTUALLY PLANNING ON SAYING *ANYTHING* TODAY...?
HA!!
...PARDON, M'SIEU.
PARDON.

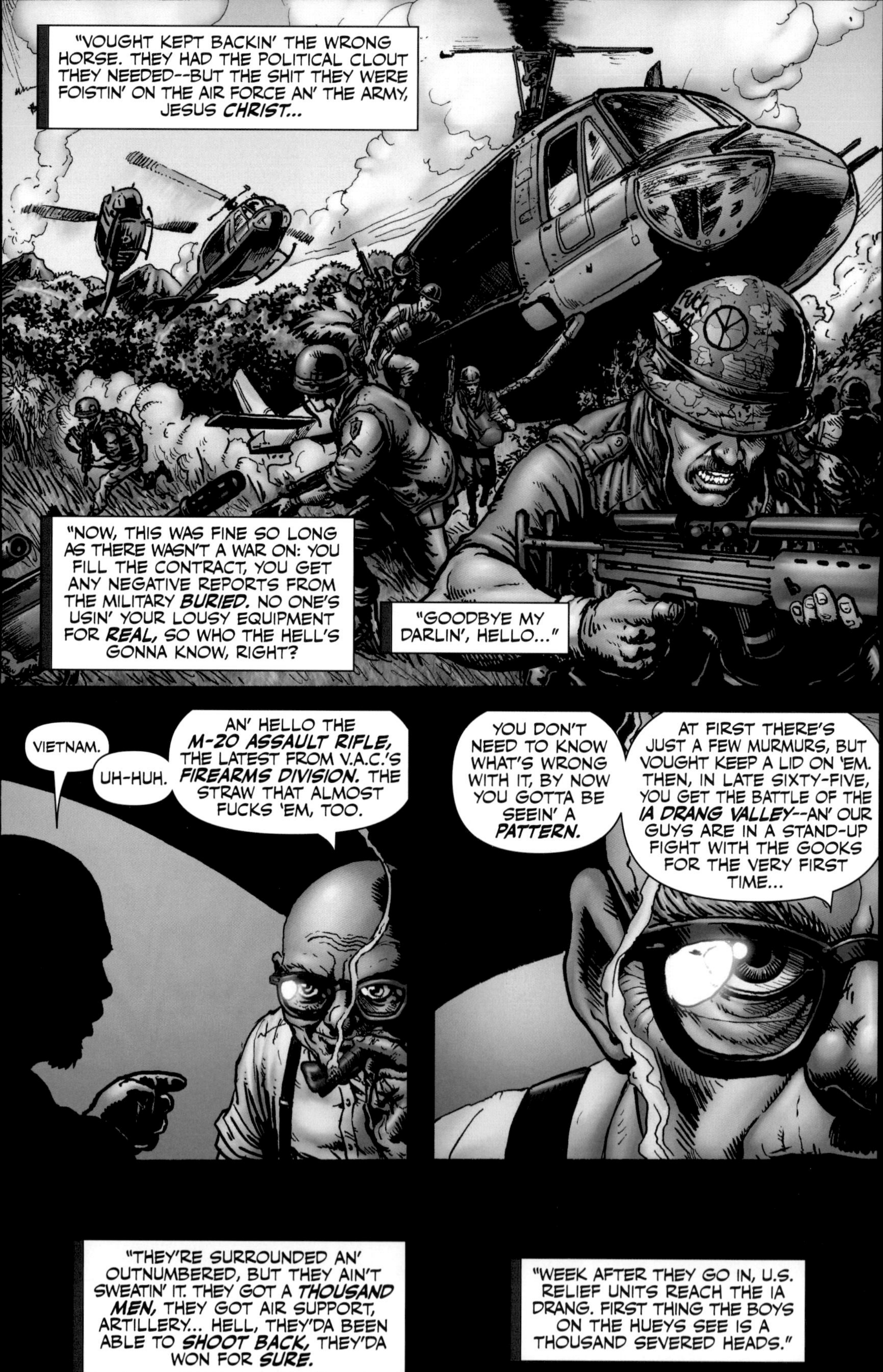
"VOUGHT KEPT BACKIN' THE WRONG HORSE. THEY HAD THE POLITICAL CLOUT THEY NEEDED--BUT THE SHIT THEY WERE FOISTIN' ON THE AIR FORCE AN' THE ARMY, JESUS CHRIST...
"NOW, THIS WAS FINE SO LONG AS THERE WASN'T A WAR ON: YOU FILL THE CONTRACT, YOU GET ANY NEGATIVE REPORTS FROM THE MILITARY BURIED. NO ONE'S USIN' YOUR LOUSY EQUIPMENT FOR REAL, SO WHO THE HELL'S GONNA KNOW, RIGHT?
"GOODBYE MY DARLIN', HELLO..."
VIETNAM.
UH-HUH.
AN' HELLO THE M-20 ASSAULT RIFLE, THE LATEST FROM V.A.C.'S FIREARMS DIVISION. THE STRAW THAT ALMOST FUCKS 'EM, TOO.
YOU DON'T NEED TO KNOW WHAT'S WRONG WITH IT, BY NOW YOU GOTTA BE SEEIN' A PATTERN.
AT FIRST THERE'S JUST A FEW MURMURS, BUT VOUGHT KEEP A LID ON 'EM. THEN, IN LATE SIXTY-FIVE, YOU GET THE BATTLE OF THE IA DRANG VALLEY--AN' OUR GUYS ARE IN A STAND-UP FIGHT WITH THE GOOKS FOR THE VERY FIRST TIME...
"THEY'RE SURROUNDED AN' OUTNUMBERED, BUT THEY AIN'T SWEATIN' IT. THEY GOT A THOUSAND MEN, THEY GOT AIR SUPPORT, ARTILLERY... HELL, THEY'DA BEEN ABLE TO SHOOT BACK, THEY'DA WON FOR SURE.
"WEEK AFTER THEY GO IN, U.S. RELIEF UNITS REACH THE IA DRANG. FIRST THING THE BOYS ON THE HUEYS SEE IS A THOUSAND SEVERED HEADS."

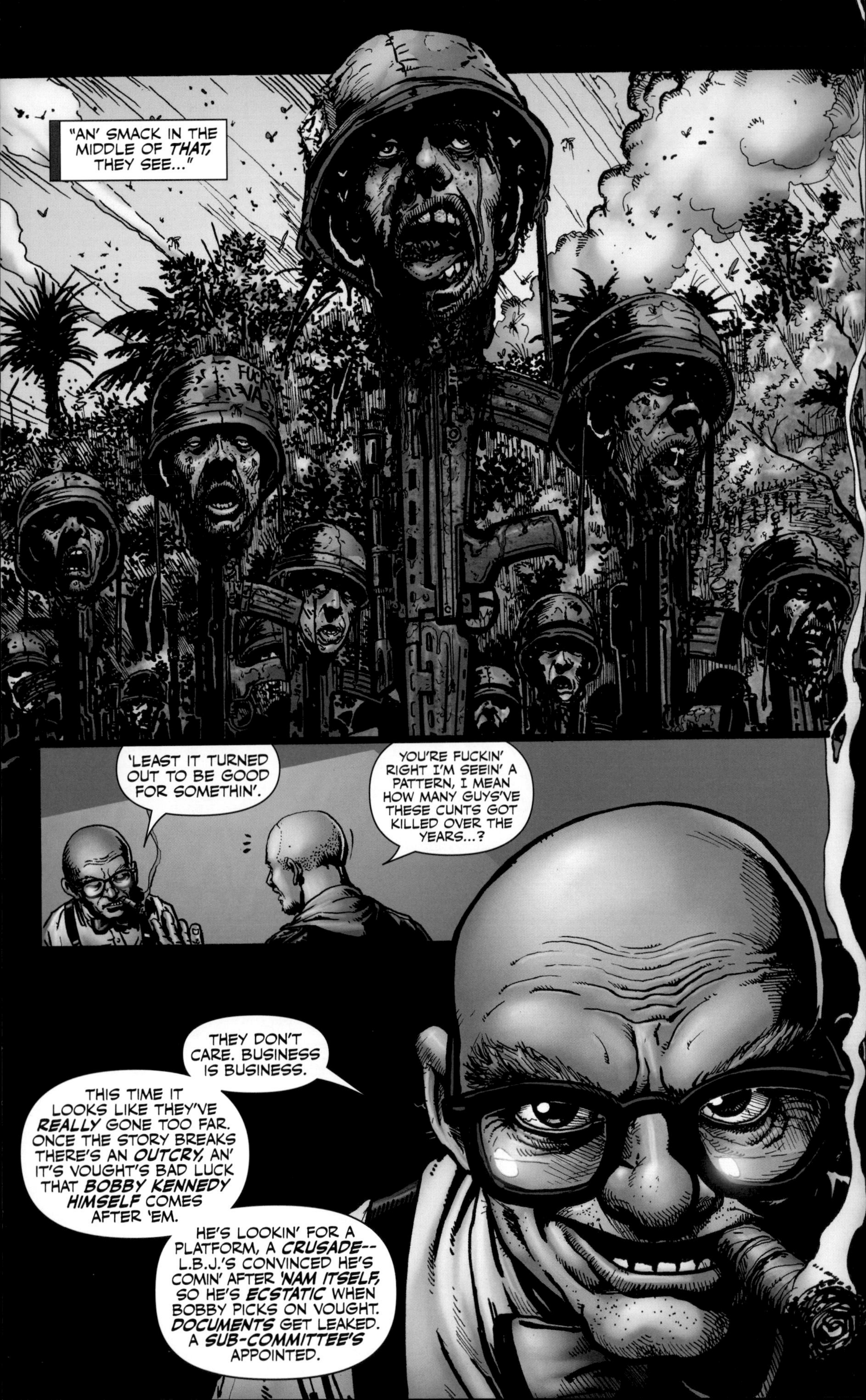
"AN' SMACK IN THE MIDDLE OF THAT, THEY SEE..."
'LEAST IT TURNED OUT TO BE GOOD FOR SOMETHIN'.
YOU'RE FUCKIN' RIGHT I'M SEEIN' A PATTERN, I MEAN HOW MANY GUYS'VE THESE CUNTS GOT KILLED OVER THE YEARS...?
THEY DON'T CARE. BUSINESS IS BUSINESS.
THIS TIME IT LOOKS LIKE THEY'VE REALLY GONE TOO FAR. ONCE THE STORY BREAKS THERE'S AN OUTCRY, AN' IT'S VOUGHT'S BAD LUCK THAT BOBBY KENNEDY HIMSELF COMES AFTER 'EM.
HE'S LOOKIN' FOR A PLATFORM, A CRUSADE-- L.B.J.'S CONVINCED HE'S COMIN' AFTER 'NAM ITSELF, SO HE'S ECSTATIC WHEN BOBBY PICKS ON VOUGHT. DOCUMENTS GET LEAKED. A SUB-COMMITTEE'S APPOINTED.

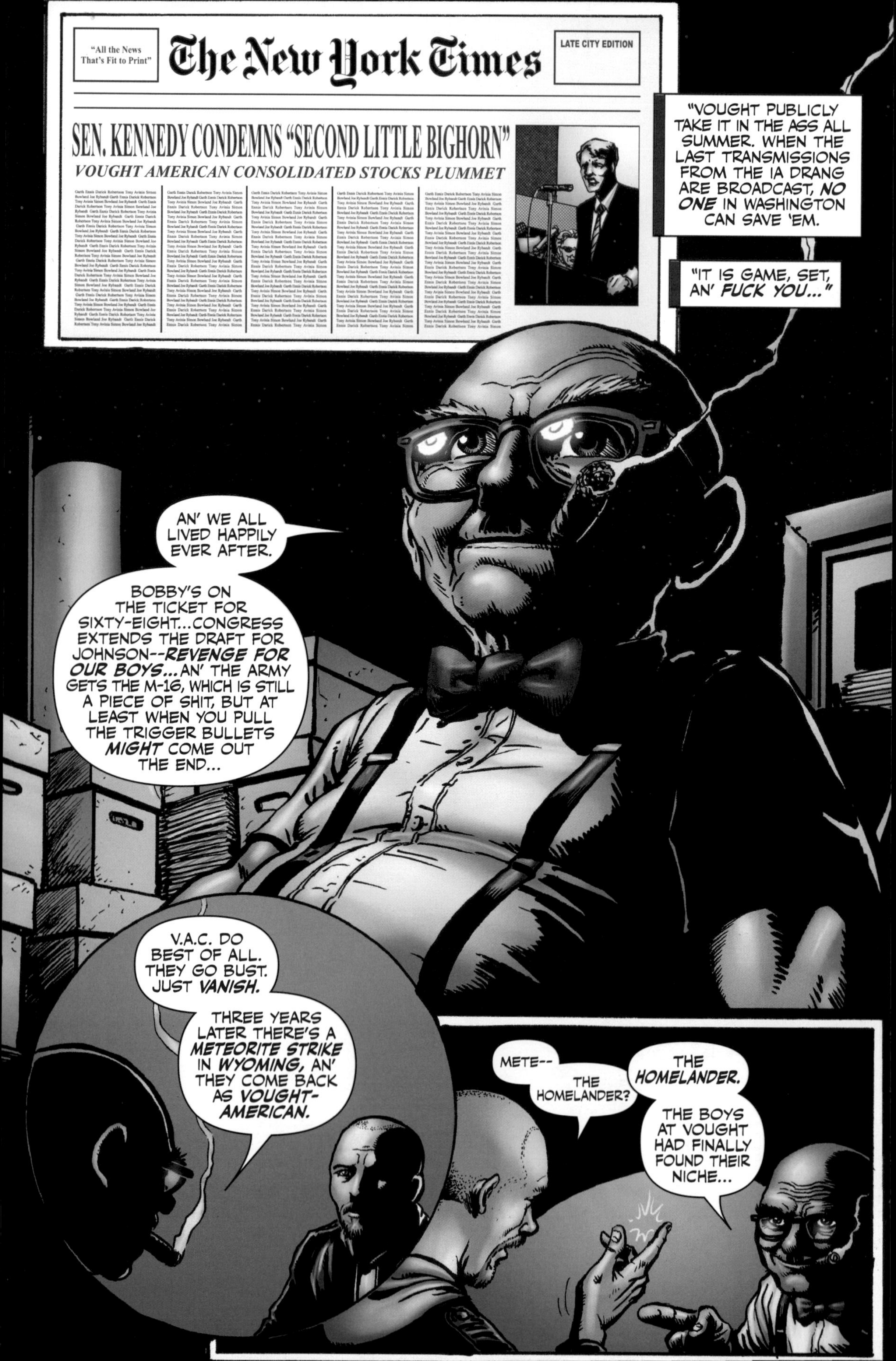
"All the News That's Fit to Print"
The New York Times
LATE CITY EDITION
SEN. KENNEDY CONDEMNS "SECOND LITTLE BIGHORN"
VOUGHT AMERICAN CONSOLIDATED STOCKS PLUMMET
"VOUGHT PUBLICLY TAKE IT IN THE ASS ALL SUMMER. WHEN THE LAST TRANSMISSIONS FROM THE IA DRANG ARE BROADCAST, NO ONE IN WASHINGTON CAN SAVE 'EM.
"IT IS GAME, SET, AN' FUCK YOU..."
AN' WE ALL LIVED HAPPILY EVER AFTER.
BOBBY'S ON THE TICKET FOR SIXTY-EIGHT...CONGRESS EXTENDS THE DRAFT FOR JOHNSON--REVENGE FOR OUR BOYS...AN' THE ARMY GETS THE M-16, WHICH IS STILL A PIECE OF SHIT, BUT AT LEAST WHEN YOU PULL THE TRIGGER BULLETS MIGHT COME OUT THE END...
V.A.C. DO BEST OF ALL. THEY GO BUST. JUST VANISH.
THREE YEARS LATER THERE'S A METEORITE STRIKE IN WYOMING, AN' THEY COME BACK AS VOUGHT-AMERICAN.
METE--
THE HOMELANDER?
THE HOMELANDER.
THE BOYS AT VOUGHT HAD FINALLY FOUND THEIR NICHE...

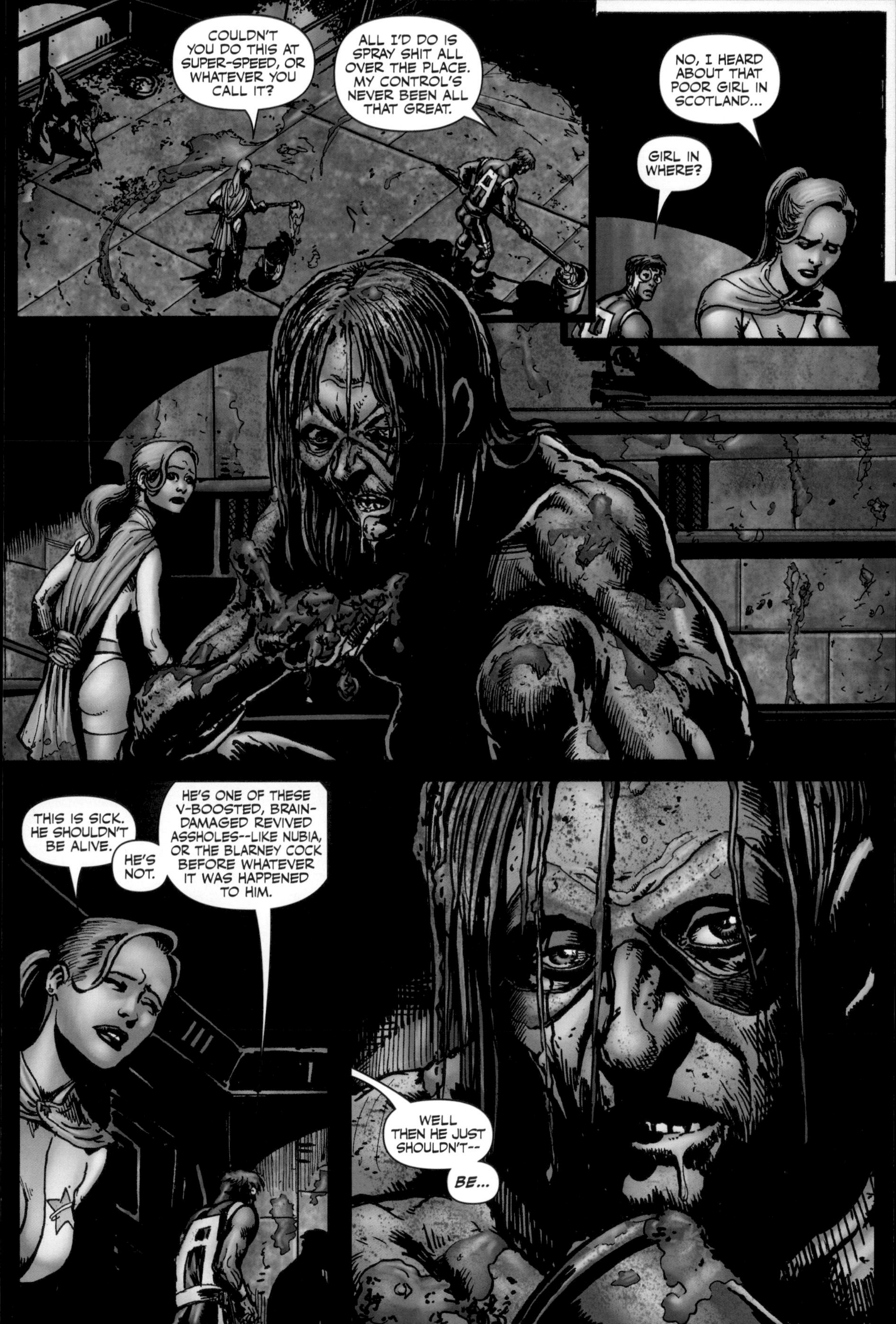
COULDN'T YOU DO THIS AT SUPER-SPEED, OR WHATEVER YOU CALL IT?
ALL I'D DO IS SPRAY SHIT ALL OVER THE PLACE. MY CONTROL'S NEVER BEEN ALL THAT GREAT.
NO, I HEARD ABOUT THAT POOR GIRL IN SCOTLAND...
GIRL IN WHERE?
THIS IS SICK. HE SHOULDN'T BE ALIVE.
HE'S NOT.
HE'S ONE OF THESE V-BOOSTED, BRAIN-DAMAGED REVIVED ASSHOLES--LIKE NUBIA, OR THE BLARNEY COCK BEFORE WHATEVER IT WAS HAPPENED TO HIM.
WELL THEN HE JUST SHOULDN'T--
BE...

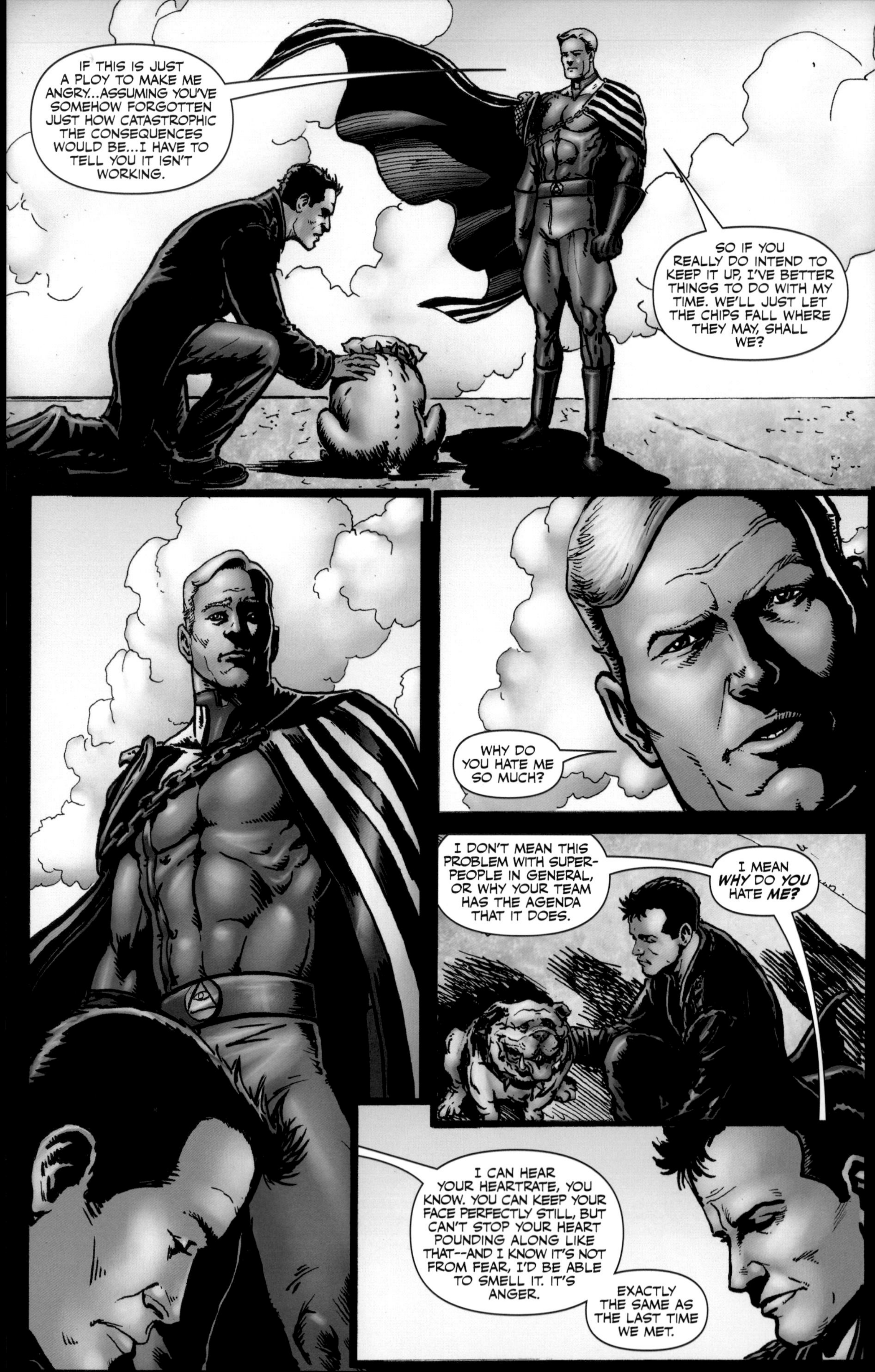
IF THIS IS JUST A PLOY TO MAKE ME ANGRY...ASSUMING YOU'VE SOMEHOW FORGOTTEN JUST HOW CATASTROPHIC THE CONSEQUENCES WOULD BE...I HAVE TO TELL YOU IT ISN'T WORKING.
SO IF YOU REALLY DO INTEND TO KEEP IT UP, I'VE BETTER THINGS TO DO WITH MY TIME. WE'LL JUST LET THE CHIPS FALL WHERE THEY MAY, SHALL WE?
WHY DO YOU HATE ME SO MUCH?
I DON'T MEAN THIS PROBLEM WITH SUPER-PEOPLE IN GENERAL, OR WHY YOUR TEAM HAS THE AGENDA THAT IT DOES.
I MEAN *WHY* DO *YOU* HATE *ME?*
I CAN HEAR YOUR HEARTRATE, YOU KNOW. YOU CAN KEEP YOUR FACE PERFECTLY STILL, BUT CAN'T STOP YOUR HEART POUNDING ALONG LIKE THAT--AND I KNOW IT'S NOT FROM FEAR, I'D BE ABLE TO SMELL IT. IT'S ANGER.
EXACTLY THE SAME AS THE LAST TIME WE MET.

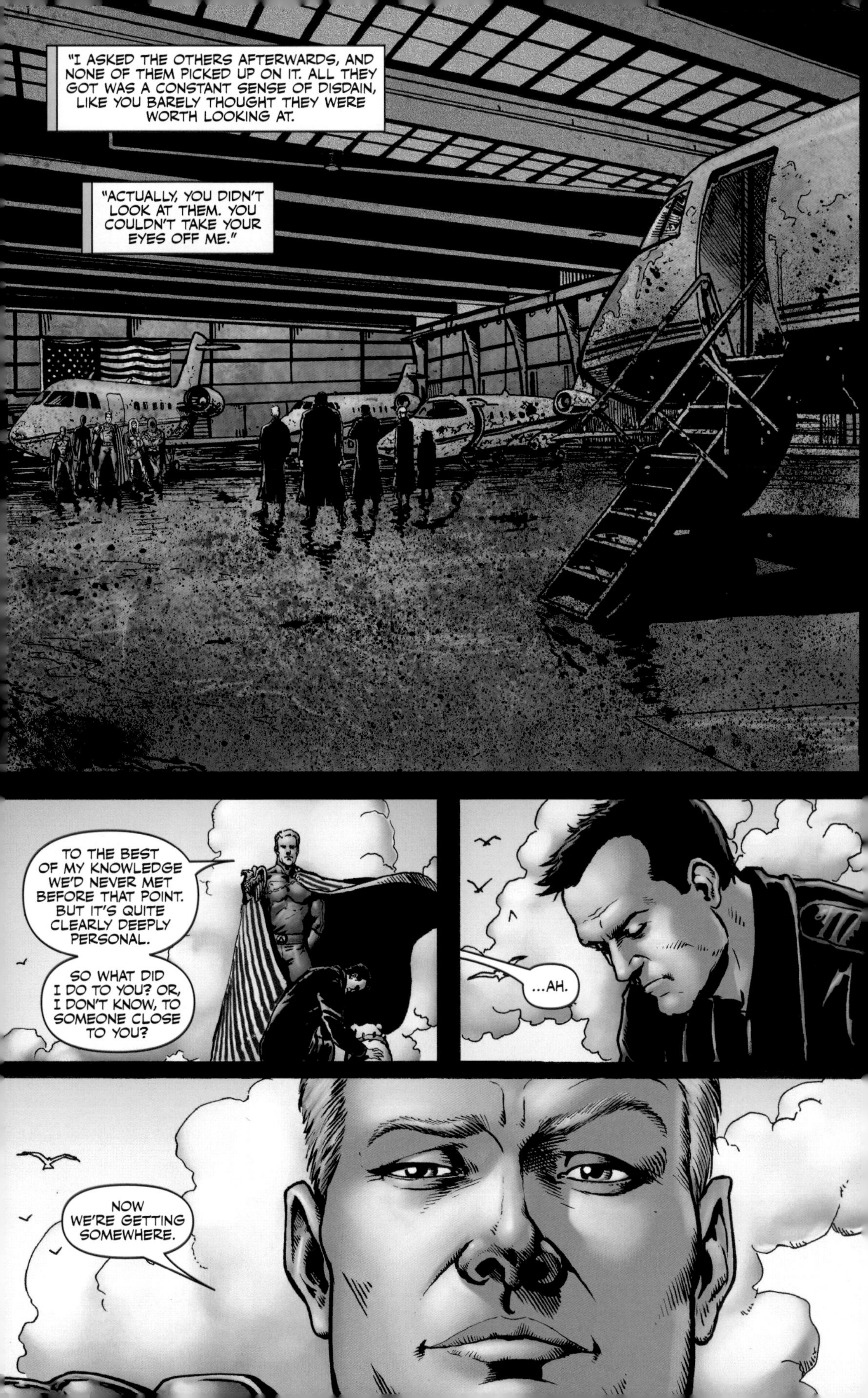
"I ASKED THE OTHERS AFTERWARDS, AND NONE OF THEM PICKED UP ON IT. ALL THEY GOT WAS A CONSTANT SENSE OF DISDAIN, LIKE YOU BARELY THOUGHT THEY WERE WORTH LOOKING AT.
"ACTUALLY, YOU DIDN'T LOOK AT THEM. YOU COULDN'T TAKE YOUR EYES OFF ME."
TO THE BEST OF MY KNOWLEDGE WE'D NEVER MET BEFORE THAT POINT. BUT IT'S QUITE CLEARLY DEEPLY PERSONAL.
SO WHAT DID I DO TO YOU? OR, I DON'T KNOW, TO SOMEONE CLOSE TO YOU?
...AH.
NOW WE'RE GETTING SOMEWHERE.

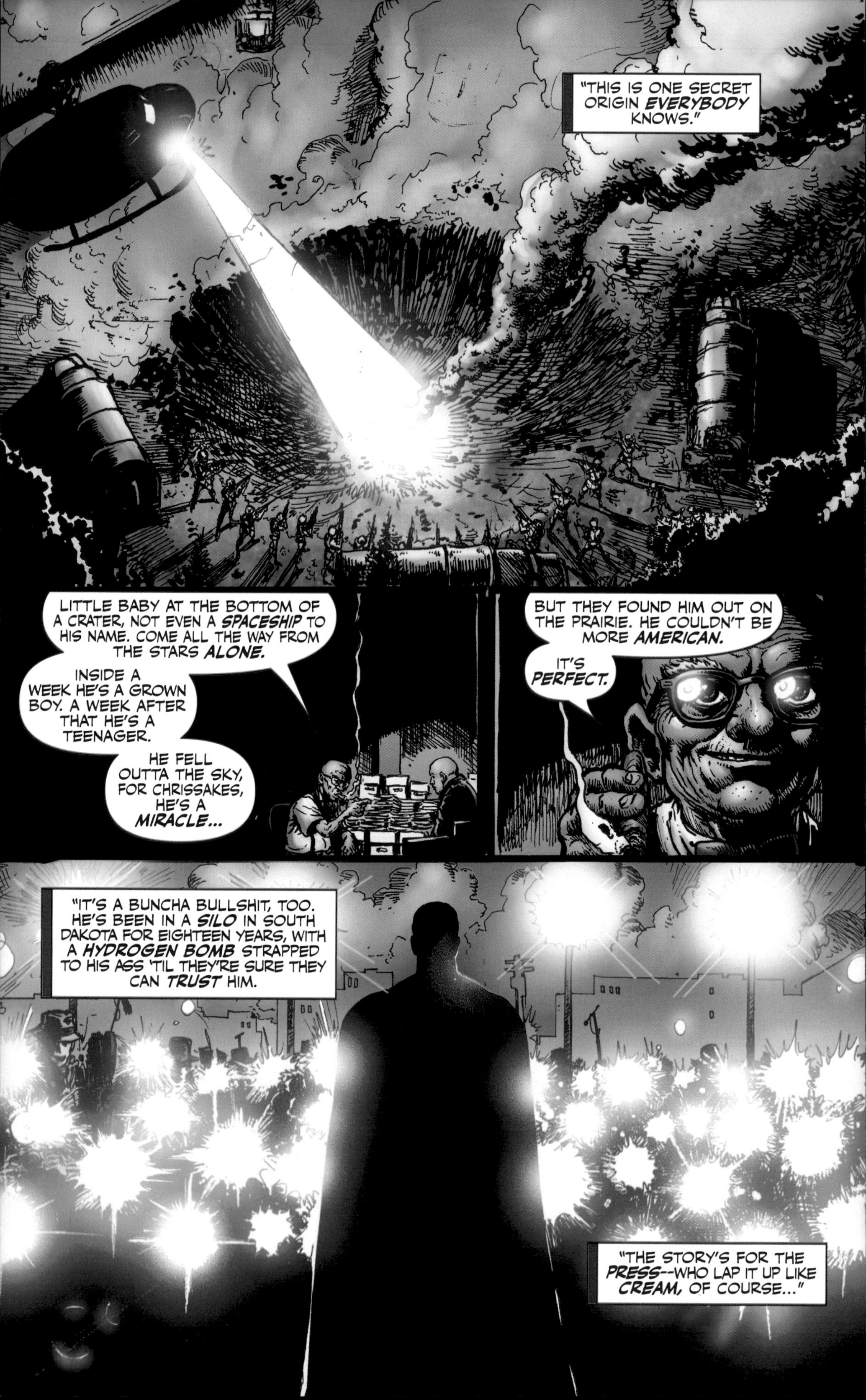
"THIS IS ONE SECRET ORIGIN EVERYBODY KNOWS."
LITTLE BABY AT THE BOTTOM OF A CRATER, NOT EVEN A SPACESHIP TO HIS NAME. COME ALL THE WAY FROM THE STARS ALONE.
INSIDE A WEEK HE'S A GROWN BOY. A WEEK AFTER THAT HE'S A TEENAGER.
HE FELL OUTTA THE SKY, FOR CHRISSAKES, HE'S A MIRACLE...
BUT THEY FOUND HIM OUT ON THE PRAIRIE. HE COULDN'T BE MORE AMERICAN.
IT'S PERFECT.
"IT'S A BUNCHA BULLSHIT, TOO. HE'S BEEN IN A SILO IN SOUTH DAKOTA FOR EIGHTEEN YEARS, WITH A HYDROGEN BOMB STRAPPED TO HIS ASS 'TIL THEY'RE SURE THEY CAN TRUST HIM.
"THE STORY'S FOR THE PRESS--WHO LAP IT UP LIKE CREAM, OF COURSE..."

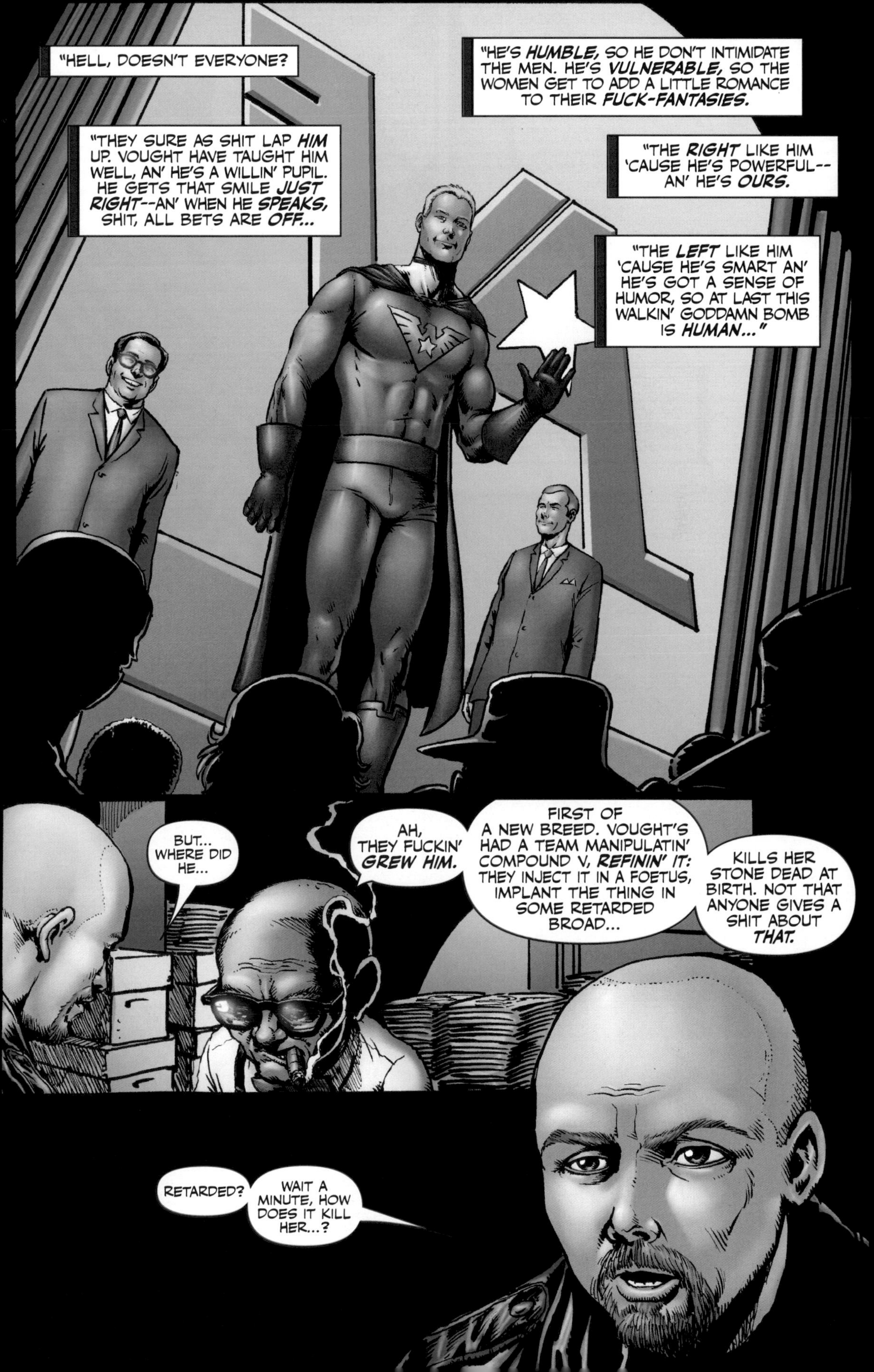
"HELL, DOESN'T EVERYONE?
"THEY SURE AS SHIT LAP HIM UP. VOUGHT HAVE TAUGHT HIM WELL, AN' HE'S A WILLIN' PUPIL. HE GETS THAT SMILE JUST RIGHT--AN' WHEN HE SPEAKS, SHIT, ALL BETS ARE OFF...
"HE'S HUMBLE, SO HE DON'T INTIMIDATE THE MEN. HE'S VULNERABLE, SO THE WOMEN GET TO ADD A LITTLE ROMANCE TO THEIR FUCK-FANTASIES.
"THE RIGHT LIKE HIM 'CAUSE HE'S POWERFUL-- AN' HE'S OURS.
"THE LEFT LIKE HIM 'CAUSE HE'S SMART AN' HE'S GOT A SENSE OF HUMOR, SO AT LAST THIS WALKIN' GODDAMN BOMB IS HUMAN..."
BUT... WHERE DID HE...
AH, THEY FUCKIN' GREW HIM.
FIRST OF A NEW BREED. VOUGHT'S HAD A TEAM MANIPULATIN' COMPOUND V, REFININ' IT: THEY INJECT IT IN A FOETUS, IMPLANT THE THING IN SOME RETARDED BROAD...
KILLS HER STONE DEAD AT BIRTH. NOT THAT ANYONE GIVES A SHIT ABOUT THAT.
RETARDED?
WAIT A MINUTE, HOW DOES IT KILL HER...?

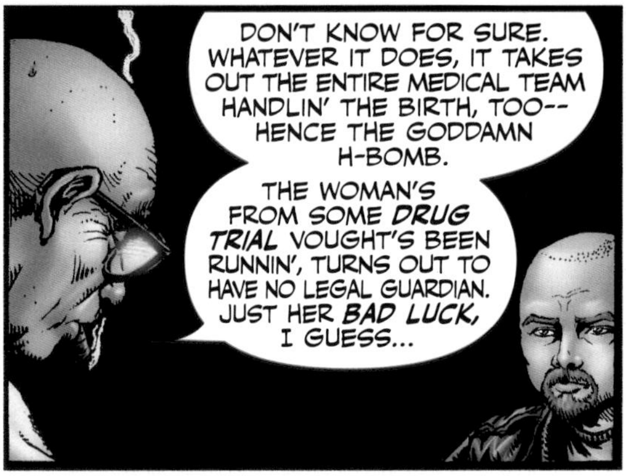
DON'T KNOW FOR SURE. WHATEVER IT DOES, IT TAKES OUT THE ENTIRE MEDICAL TEAM HANDLIN' THE BIRTH, TOO-- HENCE THE GODDAMN H-BOMB.
THE WOMAN'S FROM SOME DRUG TRIAL VOUGHT'S BEEN RUNNIN', TURNS OUT TO HAVE NO LEGAL GUARDIAN. JUST HER BAD LUCK, I GUESS...

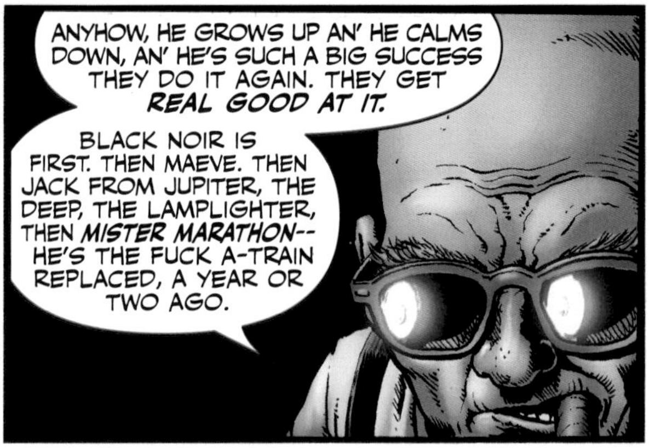
ANYHOW, HE GROWS UP AN' HE CALMS DOWN, AN' HE'S SUCH A BIG SUCCESS THEY DO IT AGAIN. THEY GET REAL GOOD AT IT.
BLACK NOIR IS FIRST. THEN MAEVE. THEN JACK FROM JUPITER, THE DEEP, THE LAMPLIGHTER, THEN MISTER MARATHON-- HE'S THE FUCK A-TRAIN REPLACED, A YEAR OR TWO AGO.

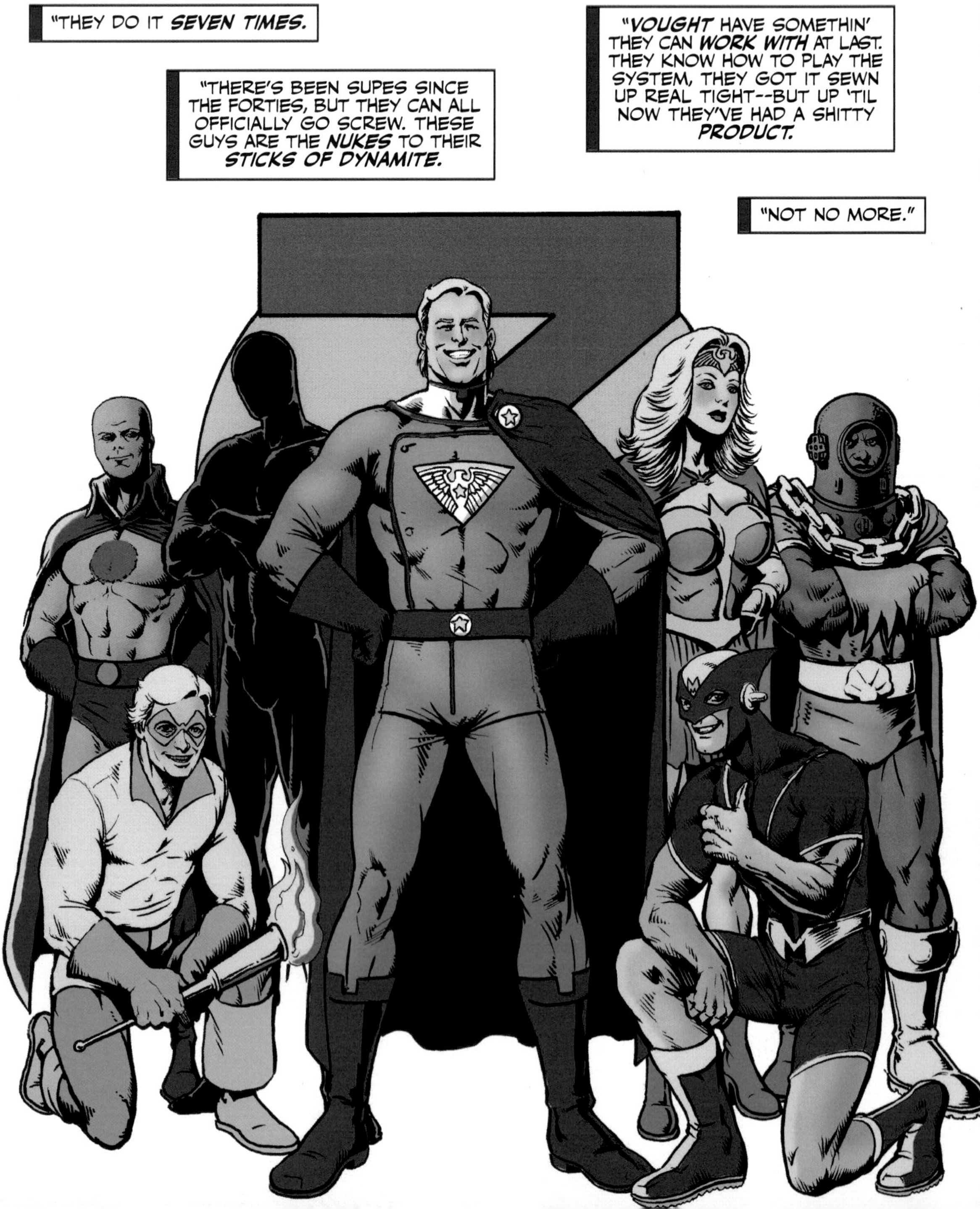
"THEY DO IT SEVEN TIMES.
"THERE'S BEEN SUPES SINCE THE FORTIES, BUT THEY CAN ALL OFFICIALLY GO SCREW. THESE GUYS ARE THE NUKES TO THEIR STICKS OF DYNAMITE.
"VOUGHT HAVE SOMETHIN' THEY CAN WORK WITH AT LAST. THEY KNOW HOW TO PLAY THE SYSTEM, THEY GOT IT SEWN UP REAL TIGHT--BUT UP 'TIL NOW THEY'VE HAD A SHITTY PRODUCT.
"NOT NO MORE."

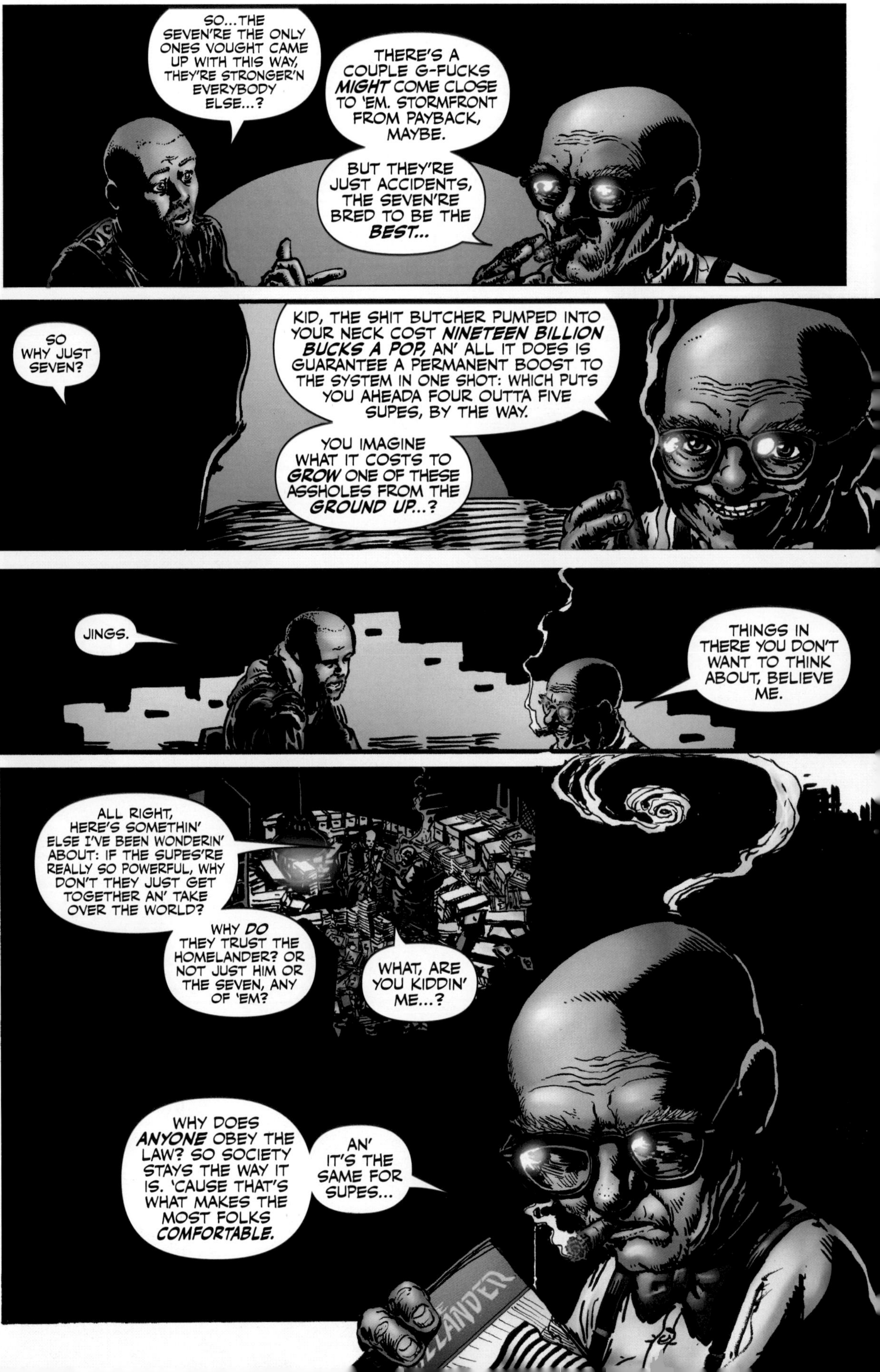
SO... THE SEVEN'RE THE ONLY ONES VOUGHT CAME UP WITH THIS WAY, THEY'RE STRONGER'N EVERYBODY ELSE...?
THERE'S A COUPLE G-FUCKS MIGHT COME CLOSE TO 'EM. STORMFRONT FROM PAYBACK, MAYBE.
BUT THEY'RE JUST ACCIDENTS, THE SEVEN'RE BRED TO BE THE BEST...
SO WHY JUST SEVEN?
KID, THE SHIT BUTCHER PUMPED INTO YOUR NECK COST NINETEEN BILLION BUCKS A POP, AN' ALL IT DOES IS GUARANTEE A PERMANENT BOOST TO THE SYSTEM IN ONE SHOT: WHICH PUTS YOU AHEADA FOUR OUTTA FIVE SUPES, BY THE WAY.
YOU IMAGINE WHAT IT COSTS TO GROW ONE OF THESE ASSHOLES FROM THE GROUND UP...?
JINGS.
THINGS IN THERE YOU DON'T WANT TO THINK ABOUT, BELIEVE ME.
ALL RIGHT, HERE'S SOMETHIN' ELSE I'VE BEEN WONDERIN' ABOUT: IF THE SUPES'RE REALLY SO POWERFUL, WHY DON'T THEY JUST GET TOGETHER AN' TAKE OVER THE WORLD?
WHY DO THEY TRUST THE HOMELANDER? OR NOT JUST HIM OR THE SEVEN, ANY OF 'EM?
WHAT, ARE YOU KIDDIN' ME...?
WHY DOES ANYONE OBEY THE LAW? SO SOCIETY STAYS THE WAY IT IS. 'CAUSE THAT'S WHAT MAKES THE MOST FOLKS COMFORTABLE.
AN' IT'S THE SAME FOR SUPES...

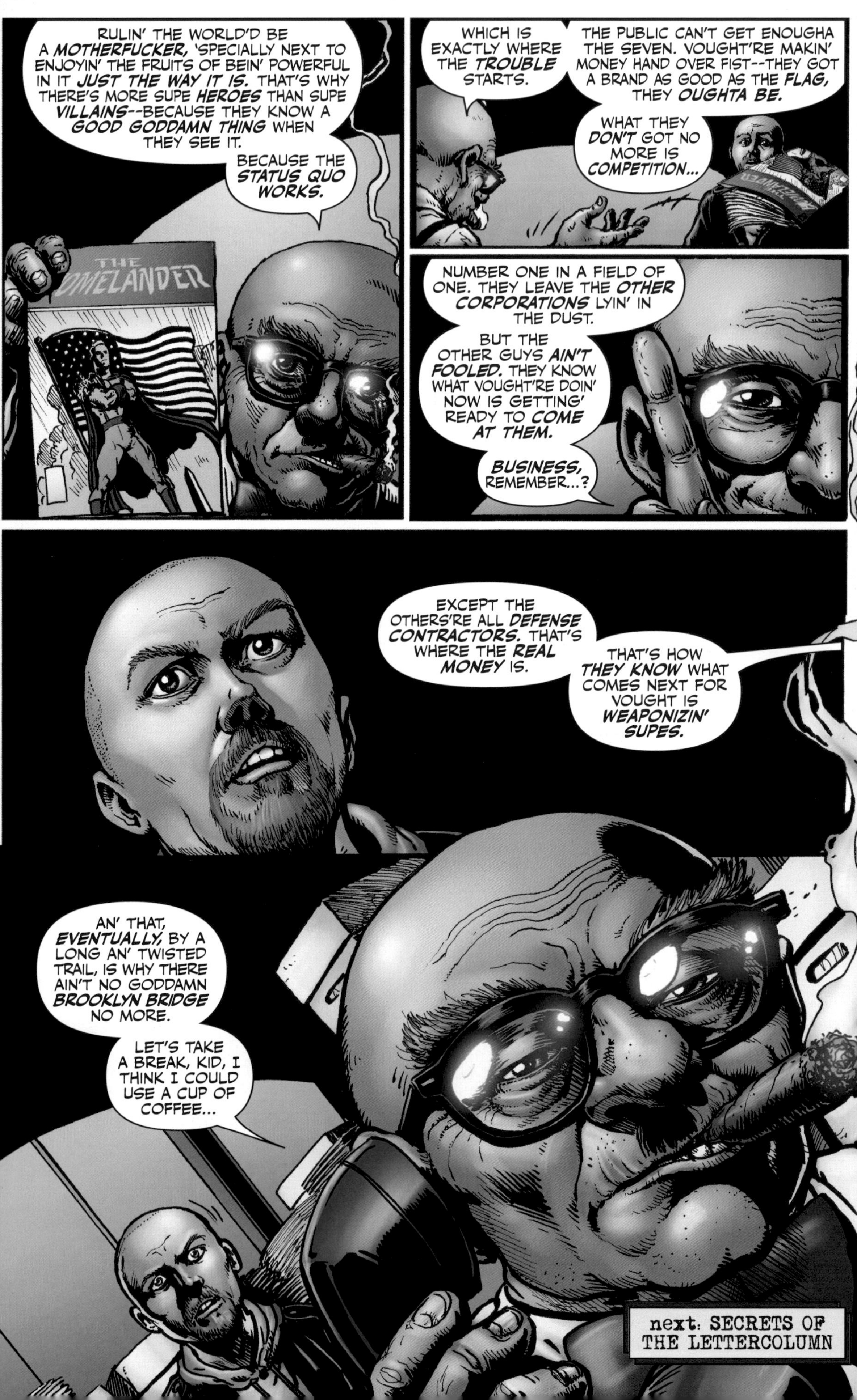
RULIN' THE WORLD'D BE A MOTHERFUCKER, 'SPECIALLY NEXT TO ENJOYIN' THE FRUITS OF BEIN' POWERFUL IN IT JUST THE WAY IT IS. THAT'S WHY THERE'S MORE SUPE HEROES THAN SUPE VILLAINS--BECAUSE THEY KNOW A GOOD GODDAMN THING WHEN THEY SEE IT.
BECAUSE THE STATUS QUO WORKS.
WHICH IS EXACTLY WHERE THE TROUBLE STARTS.
THE PUBLIC CAN'T GET ENOUGHA THE SEVEN. VOUGHT'RE MAKIN' MONEY HAND OVER FIST--THEY GOT A BRAND AS GOOD AS THE FLAG, THEY OUGHTA BE.
WHAT THEY DON'T GOT NO MORE IS COMPETITION...
NUMBER ONE IN A FIELD OF ONE. THEY LEAVE THE OTHER CORPORATIONS LYIN' IN THE DUST.
BUT THE OTHER GUYS AIN'T FOOLED. THEY KNOW WHAT VOUGHT'RE DOIN' NOW IS GETTING' READY TO COME AT THEM.
BUSINESS, REMEMBER...?
EXCEPT THE OTHERS'RE ALL DEFENSE CONTRACTORS. THAT'S WHERE THE REAL MONEY IS.
THAT'S HOW THEY KNOW WHAT COMES NEXT FOR VOUGHT IS WEAPONIZIN' SUPES.
AN' THAT, EVENTUALLY, BY A LONG AN' TWISTED TRAIL, IS WHY THERE AIN'T NO GODDAMN BROOKLYN BRIDGE NO MORE.
LET'S TAKE A BREAK, KID, I THINK I COULD USE A CUP OF COFFEE...
next: SECRETS OF THE LETTERCOLUMN

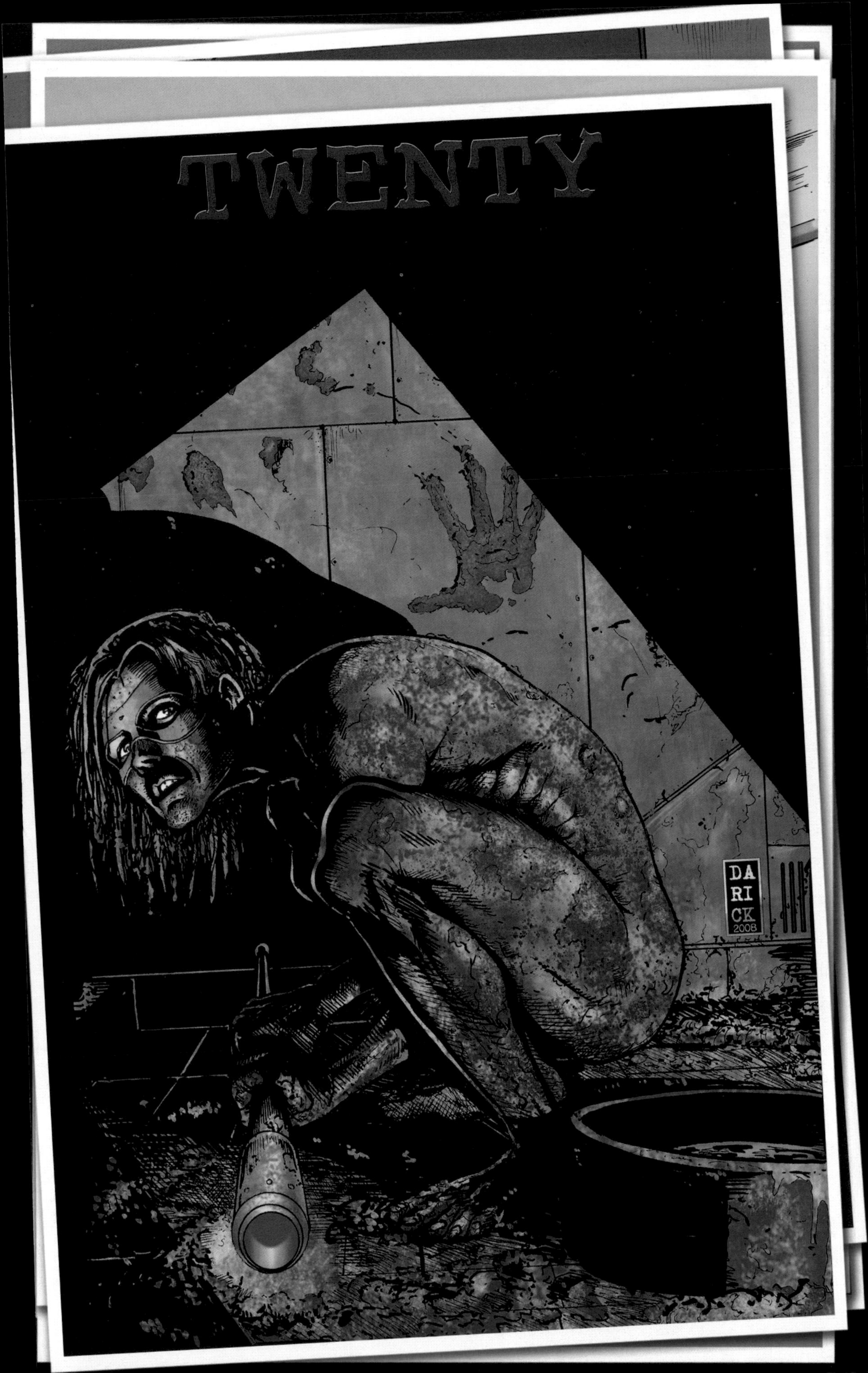
TWENTY
DA
RI
CK
2008

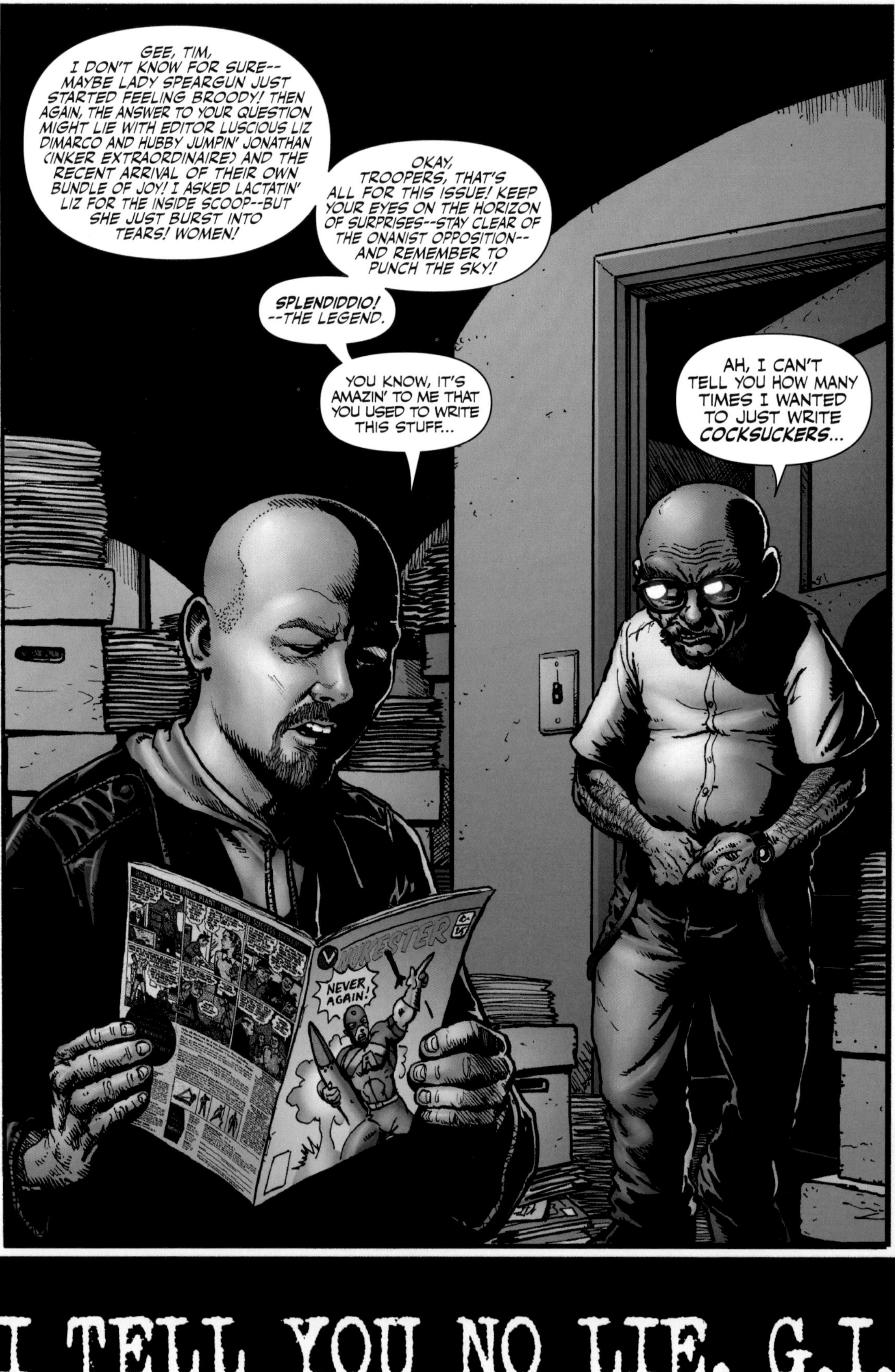
GEE, TIM, I DON'T KNOW FOR SURE-- MAYBE LADY SPEARGUN JUST STARTED FEELING BROODY! THEN AGAIN, THE ANSWER TO YOUR QUESTION MIGHT LIE WITH EDITOR LUSCIOUS LIZ DIMARCO AND HUBBY JUMPIN' JONATHAN (INKER EXTRAORDINAIRE) AND THE RECENT ARRIVAL OF THEIR OWN BUNDLE OF JOY! I ASKED LACTATIN' LIZ FOR THE INSIDE SCOOP--BUT SHE JUST BURST INTO TEARS! WOMEN!
OKAY, TROOPERS, THAT'S ALL FOR THIS ISSUE! KEEP YOUR EYES ON THE HORIZON OF SURPRISES--STAY CLEAR OF THE ONANIST OPPOSITION-- AND REMEMBER TO PUNCH THE SKY!
SPLENDIDDIO! --THE LEGEND.
YOU KNOW, IT'S AMAZIN' TO ME THAT YOU USED TO WRITE THIS STUFF...
AH, I CAN'T TELL YOU HOW MANY TIMES I WANTED TO JUST WRITE COCKSUCKERS...
NEVER AGAIN!

I TELL YOU NO LIE, G.I.

part two

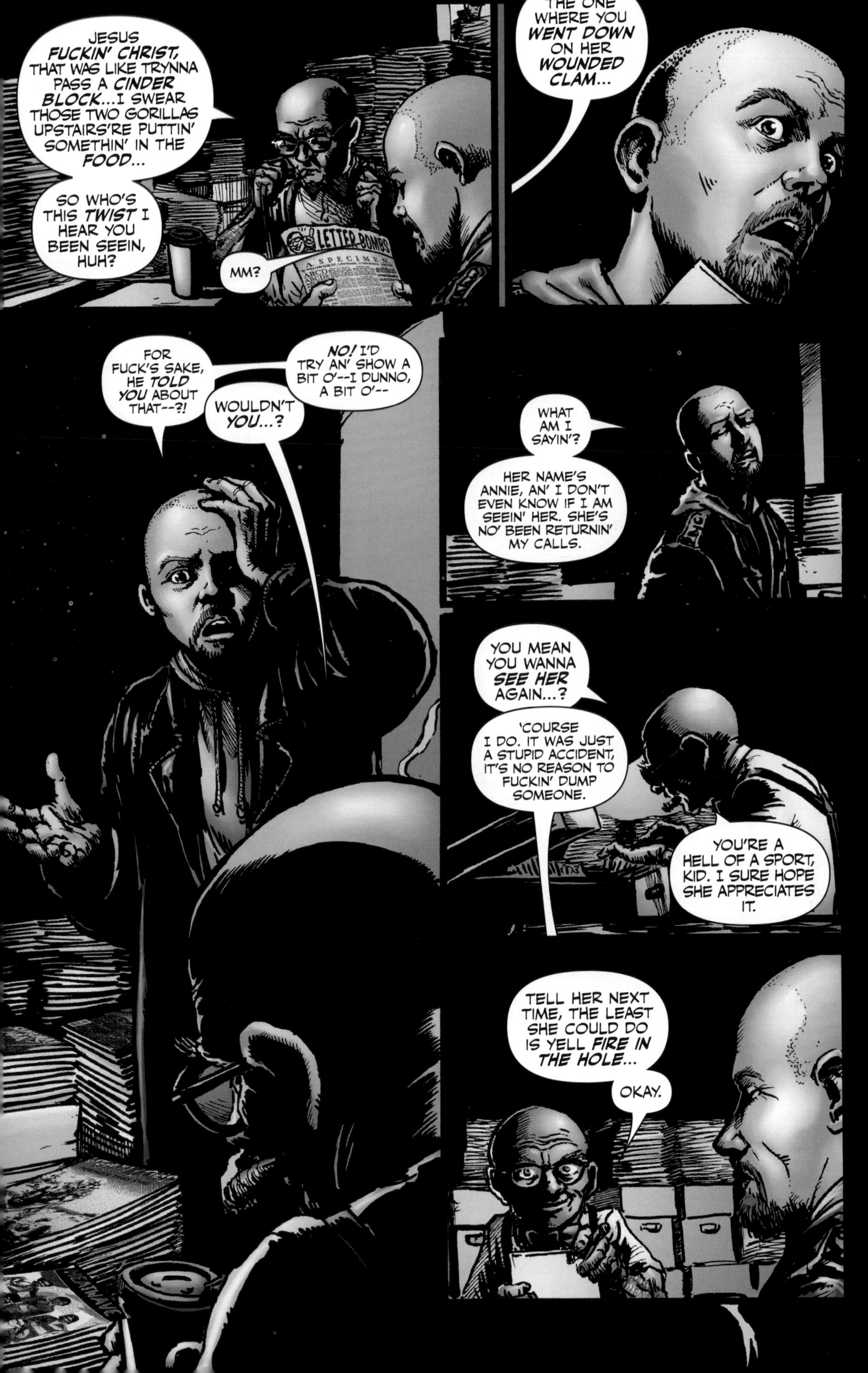
JESUS FUCKIN' CHRIST, THAT WAS LIKE TRYNNA PASS A CINDER BLOCK...I SWEAR THOSE TWO GORILLAS UPSTAIRS'RE PUTTIN' SOMETHIN' IN THE FOOD...
SO WHO'S THIS TWIST I HEAR YOU BEEN SEEIN, HUH?
LETTER BOMBS
A SPECIMEN
MM?
THE ONE WHERE YOU WENT DOWN ON HER WOUNDED CLAM...
FOR FUCK'S SAKE, HE TOLD YOU ABOUT THAT--?!
NO! I'D TRY AN' SHOW A BIT O'--I DUNNO, A BIT O'--
WOULDN'T YOU...?
WHAT AM I SAYIN'?
HER NAME'S ANNIE, AN' I DON'T EVEN KNOW IF I AM SEEIN' HER. SHE'S NO' BEEN RETURNIN' MY CALLS.
YOU MEAN YOU WANNA SEE HER AGAIN...?
'COURSE I DO. IT WAS JUST A STUPID ACCIDENT, IT'S NO REASON TO FUCKIN' DUMP SOMEONE.
YOU'RE A HELL OF A SPORT, KID. I SURE HOPE SHE APPRECIATES IT.
TELL HER NEXT TIME, THE LEAST SHE COULD DO IS YELL FIRE IN THE HOLE...
OKAY.

THE SEVEN TAKE OFF BIG-TIME. HELL, THEY'RE LIKE A *MOVIE* COME TO *LIFE*--THE MERCHANDISIN' *ALONE* DOUBLES VOUGHT-AMERICAN'S PROFITS FOR THE FIRST TWO YEARS...

BELL, DOW, G.E. AN' THE RESTA THEM, THEY'RE WATCHIN' ALLA THIS LIKE *HAWKS.* THEY NEVER UNDERSTOOD BEFORE JUST WHY VOUGHT'S SUNK SO MUCH INTO *SUPES* OVER THE YEARS--THERE WAS A THING IN FORTY-FOUR, WHERE V.A.C. CONVINCED *IKE* TO TRY A TEAM IN THE FRONT LINE, AN' GREG MALLORY CAN TELL YOU HOW *THAT* TURNED OUT--

BUT *CHRIST,* THEY GET IT *NOW*...

THE SEVEN

25¢
FEB

"IT'S THE EARLY SEVENTIES, DON'T FORGET. 'NAM'S WINDIN' DOWN--*BADLY.* AN' THAT'S *THEIR* THING, THAT'S WHAT THE OTHER CORPORATIONS'VE BEEN MAKIN' THEIR MONEY OFF.

HANG ON A MINUTE, WHO'S GREG MALLORY?

ALL IN GOOD TIME, MY FRIEND.

"WELL, IT'S FINISHED NOW, AN' VOUGHT LOOK LIKE THEY'VE GOT THE NEXT TEN YEARS IN THE *BAG.* LET'S FACE IT, WHAT'D *YOU* RATHER WATCH--QUEEN MAEVE'S *TITS,* OR AMERICA *BUGGIN'* OUT...?

"IF EVER ANYONE BACKED THE *WRONG GODDAMNED HORSE...*"

VOUGHT'S COMPETITORS DECIDE TO GO FOR THE JUGULAR. THEY GOT NO CHOICE, IT'S EITHER *STEP UP* OR BE *BOUGHT OUT*...

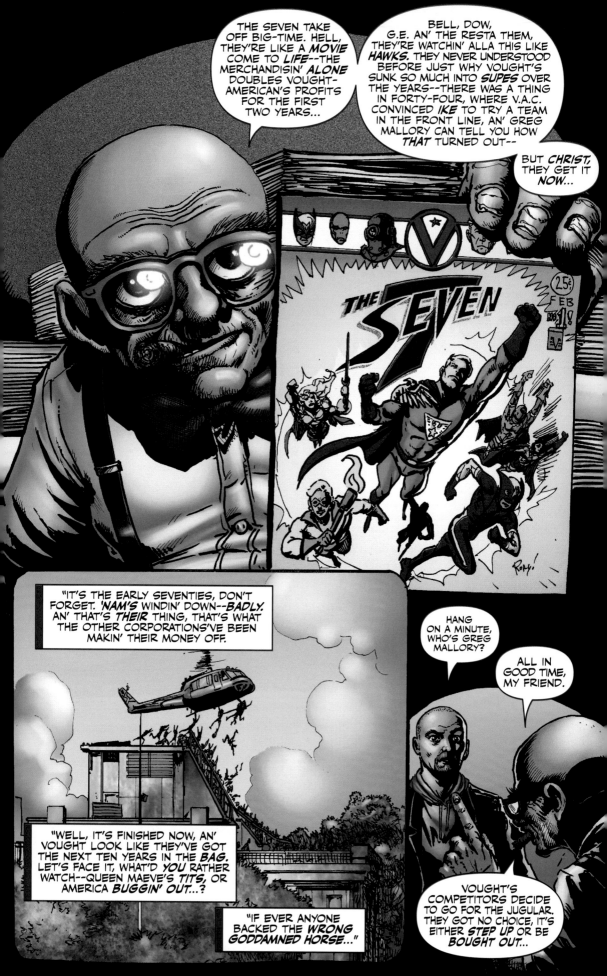

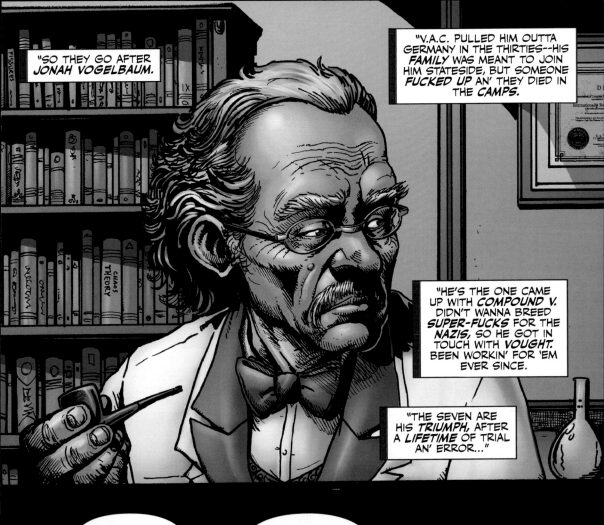

"SO THEY GO AFTER *JONAH VOGELBAUM*.

"V.A.C. PULLED HIM OUTTA GERMANY IN THE THIRTIES--HIS *FAMILY* WAS MEANT TO JOIN HIM STATESIDE, BUT SOMEONE *FUCKED UP* AN' THEY DIED IN THE *CAMPS*.

"HE'S THE ONE CAME UP WITH *COMPOUND V*. DIDN'T WANNA BREED *SUPER-FUCKS* FOR THE *NAZIS*, SO HE GOT IN TOUCH WITH *VOUGHT*. BEEN WORKIN' FOR 'EM EVER SINCE.

"THE SEVEN ARE HIS *TRIUMPH*, AFTER A *LIFETIME* OF TRIAL AN' ERROR..."

BUT HE NEVER SEEMS TO *GIVE A SHIT*. COULD BE THE *WORK* MATTERS MORE THAN THE *RESULT*...

COULD BE HIS *WIFE AN' KIDS* ARE ON HIS MIND, EVERY DAY FOR OVER *FORTY GODDAMN YEARS*.

'CAUSE WHEN THESE ASSHOLES HAVE HIM *KIDNAPPED*...AN' THEY SAY, GUESS WHAT, YOU'RE WORKIN' FOR *US* NOW, YOU'RE GONNA GIVE US SUPES MAKE *VOUGHT'S* TEAM LOOK LIKE *CLOCKWORK TOYS*...

VOGELBAUM'S REACTION IS TO *SLIT HIS FUCKIN' WRISTS*.

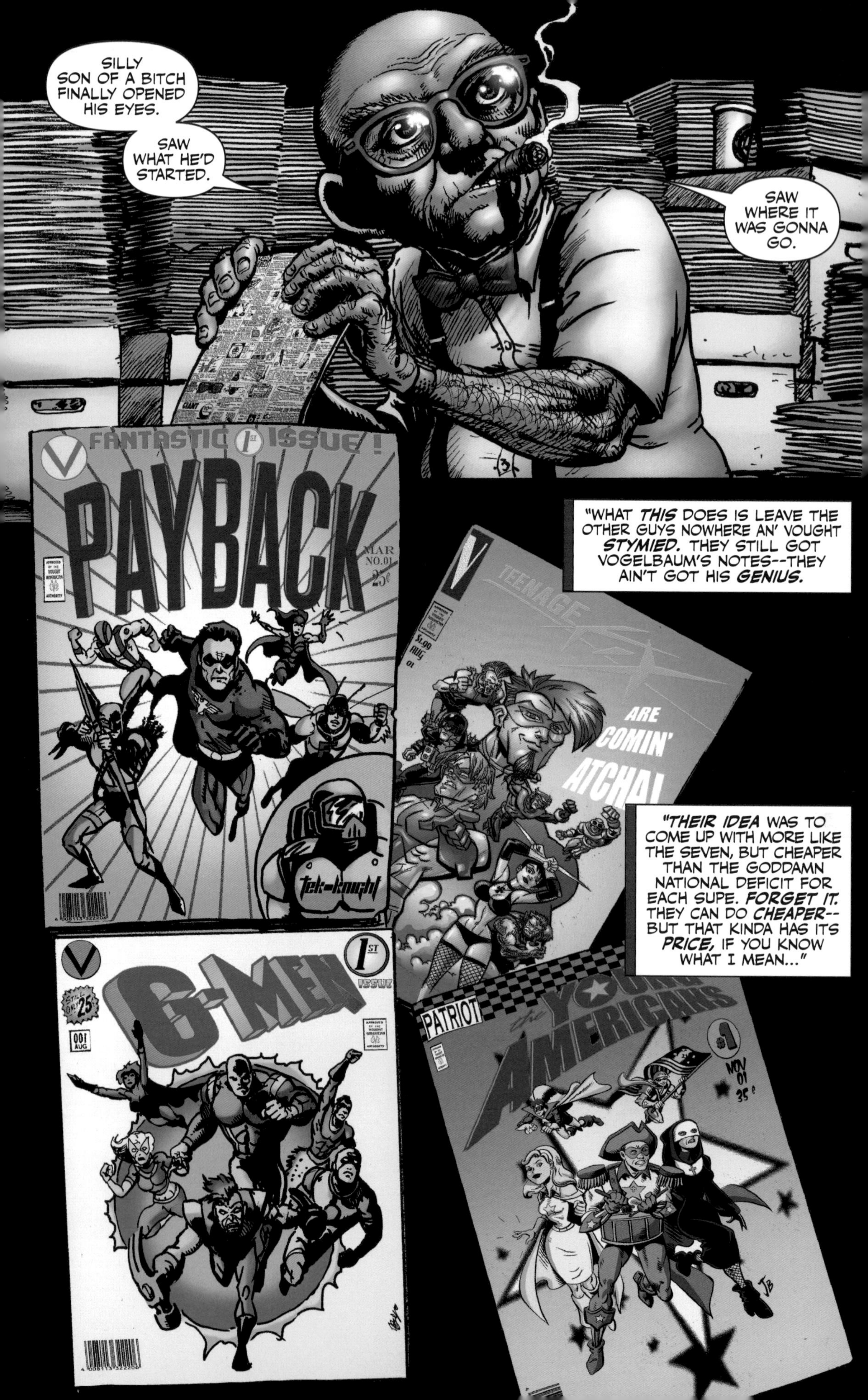

SILLY SON OF A BITCH FINALLY OPENED HIS EYES.
SAW WHAT HE'D STARTED.
SAW WHERE IT WAS GONNA GO.
FANTASTIC 1ST ISSUE!
PAYBACK
MAR NO.01 25¢
tek-knight
"WHAT *THIS* DOES IS LEAVE THE OTHER GUYS NOWHERE AN' VOUGHT *STYMIED.* THEY STILL GOT VOGELBAUM'S NOTES--THEY AIN'T GOT HIS *GENIUS.*
TEENAGE
$1.99 AUG 01
ARE COMIN' ATCHA!
"*THEIR IDEA* WAS TO COME UP WITH MORE LIKE THE SEVEN, BUT CHEAPER THAN THE GODDAMN NATIONAL DEFICIT FOR EACH SUPE. *FORGET IT.* THEY CAN DO *CHEAPER*-- BUT THAT KINDA HAS ITS *PRICE,* IF YOU KNOW WHAT I MEAN..."
1ST ISSUE
G-MEN
STILL ONLY 25¢
001 AUG
PATRIOT
AMERICANS
#1
NOV 01 35¢

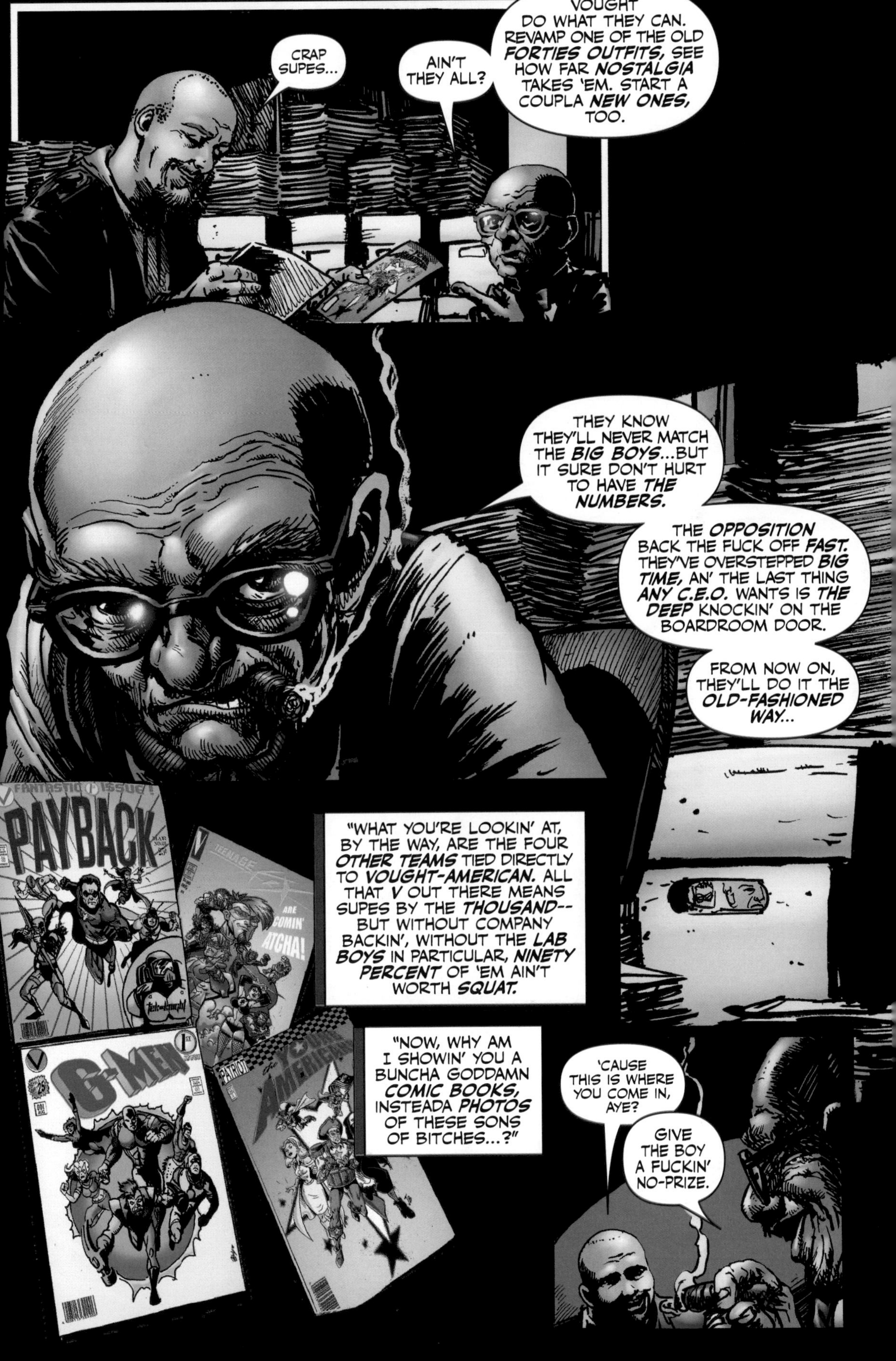

CRAP SUPES...
AIN'T THEY ALL?
VOUGHT DO WHAT THEY CAN. REVAMP ONE OF THE OLD FORTIES OUTFITS, SEE HOW FAR NOSTALGIA TAKES 'EM. START A COUPLA NEW ONES, TOO.
THEY KNOW THEY'LL NEVER MATCH THE BIG BOYS...BUT IT SURE DON'T HURT TO HAVE THE NUMBERS.
THE OPPOSITION BACK THE FUCK OFF FAST. THEY'VE OVERSTEPPED BIG TIME, AN' THE LAST THING ANY C.E.O. WANTS IS THE DEEP KNOCKIN' ON THE BOARDROOM DOOR.
FROM NOW ON, THEY'LL DO IT THE OLD-FASHIONED WAY...
FANTASTIC 1ST ISSUE!
PAYBACK
TEENAGE
ARE COMIN' ATCHA!
"WHAT YOU'RE LOOKIN' AT, BY THE WAY, ARE THE FOUR OTHER TEAMS TIED DIRECTLY TO VOUGHT-AMERICAN. ALL THAT V OUT THERE MEANS SUPES BY THE THOUSAND-- BUT WITHOUT COMPANY BACKIN', WITHOUT THE LAB BOYS IN PARTICULAR, NINETY PERCENT OF 'EM AIN'T WORTH SQUAT.
G-MEN
PATRIOT
"NOW, WHY AM I SHOWIN' YOU A BUNCHA GODDAMN COMIC BOOKS, INSTEADA PHOTOS OF THESE SONS OF BITCHES...?"
'CAUSE THIS IS WHERE YOU COME IN, AYE?
GIVE THE BOY A FUCKIN' NO-PRIZE.

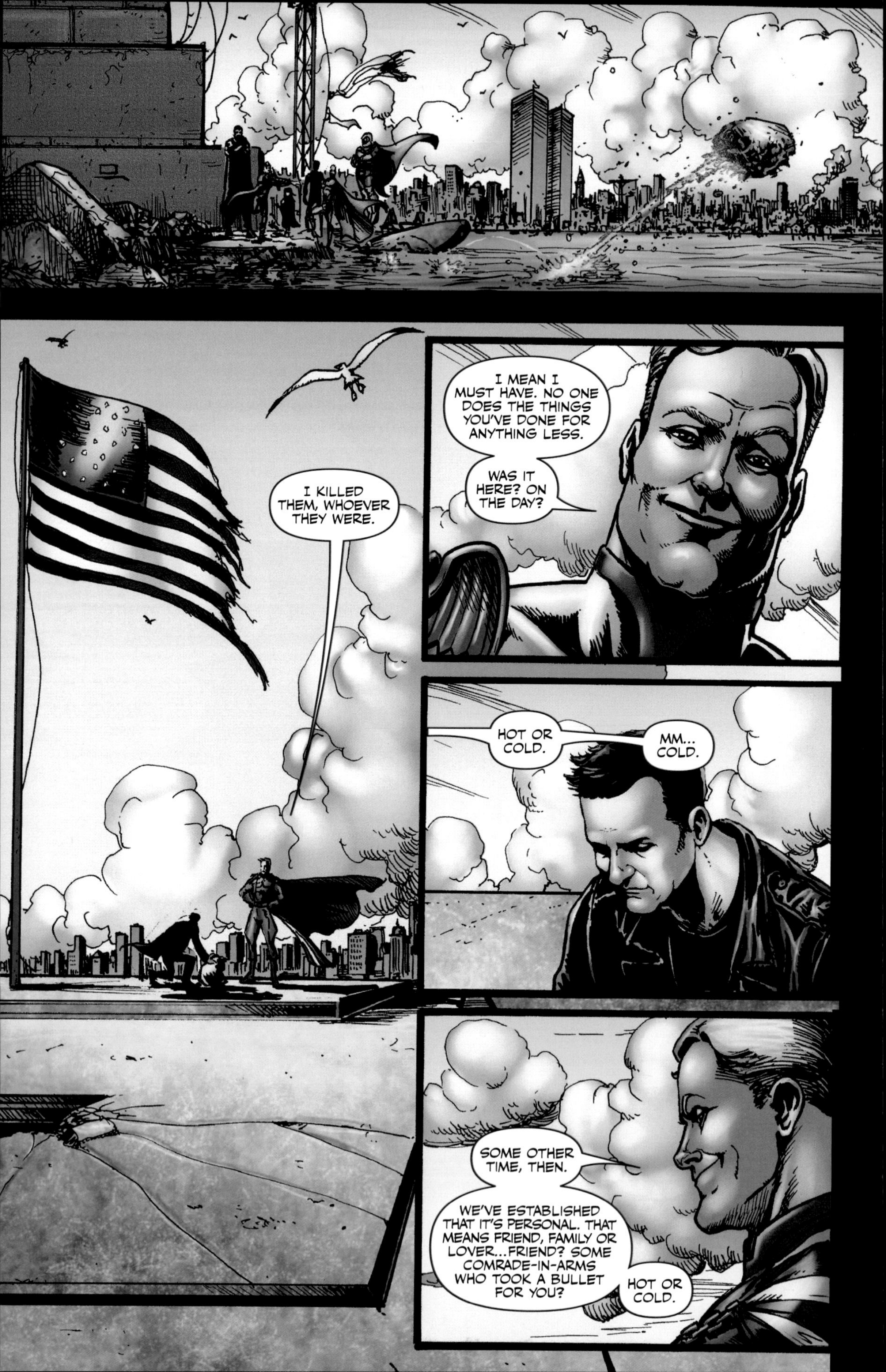
I MEAN I MUST HAVE. NO ONE DOES THE THINGS YOU'VE DONE FOR ANYTHING LESS.
WAS IT HERE? ON THE DAY?
I KILLED THEM, WHOEVER THEY WERE.
HOT OR COLD.
MM... COLD.
SOME OTHER TIME, THEN.
WE'VE ESTABLISHED THAT IT'S PERSONAL. THAT MEANS FRIEND, FAMILY OR LOVER...FRIEND? SOME COMRADE-IN-ARMS WHO TOOK A BULLET FOR YOU?
HOT OR COLD.

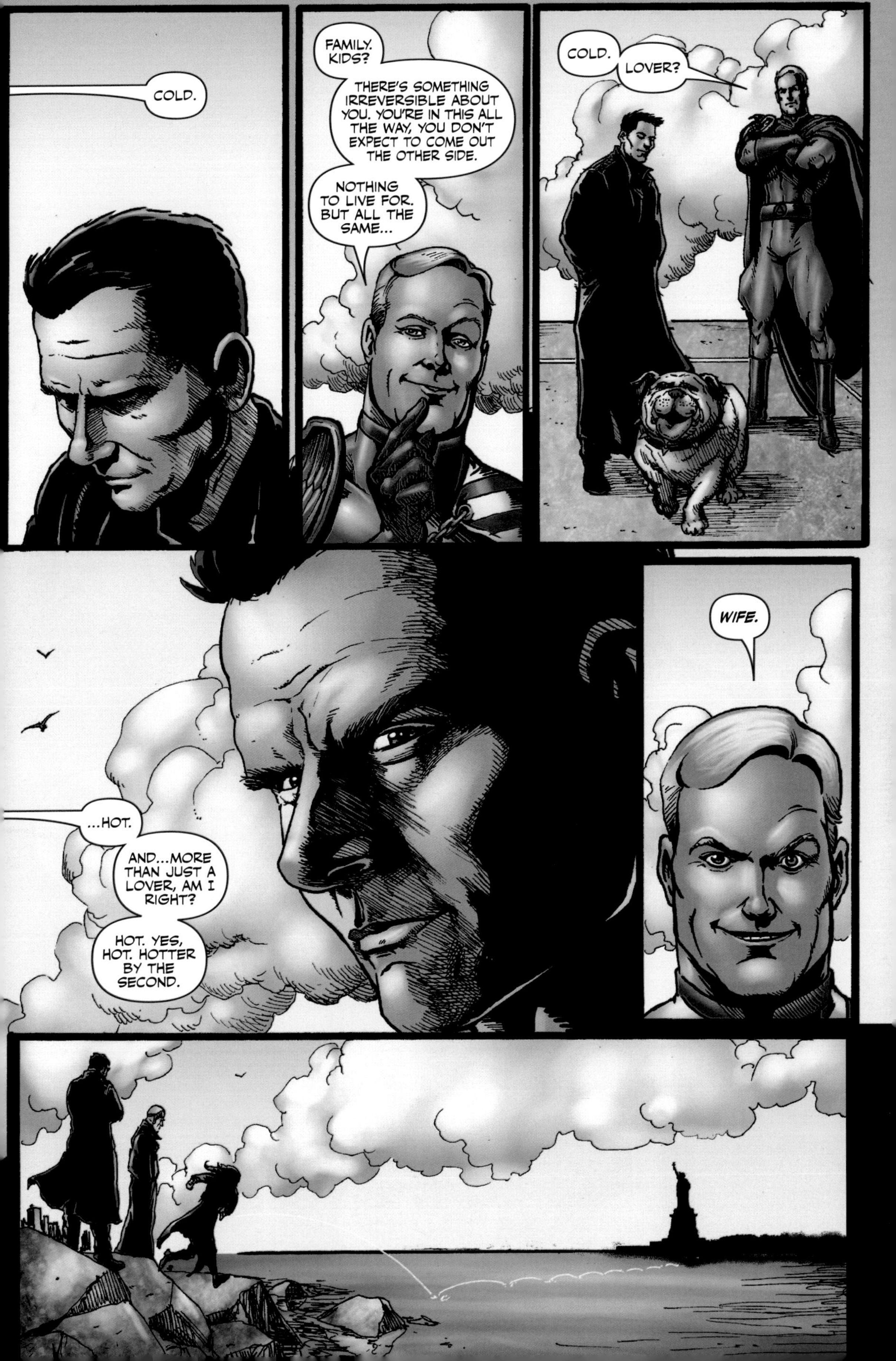
COLD.
FAMILY. KIDS?
THERE'S SOMETHING IRREVERSIBLE ABOUT YOU. YOU'RE IN THIS ALL THE WAY, YOU DON'T EXPECT TO COME OUT THE OTHER SIDE.
NOTHING TO LIVE FOR. BUT ALL THE SAME...
COLD.
LOVER?
...HOT.
AND...MORE THAN JUST A LOVER, AM I RIGHT?
HOT. YES, HOT. HOTTER BY THE SECOND.
WIFE.

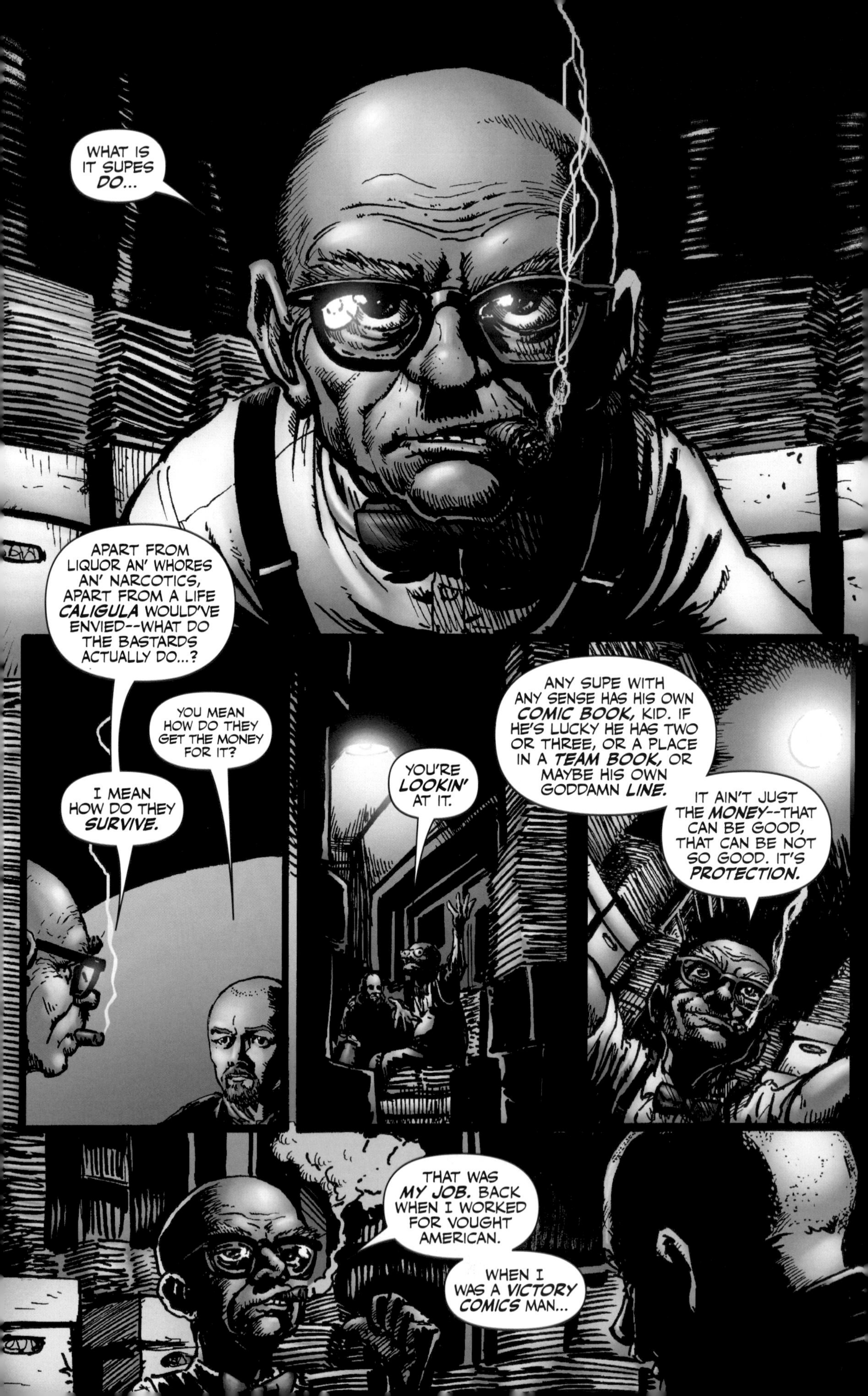
WHAT IS IT SUPES DO...
APART FROM LIQUOR AN' WHORES AN' NARCOTICS, APART FROM A LIFE CALIGULA WOULD'VE ENVIED--WHAT DO THE BASTARDS ACTUALLY DO...?
YOU MEAN HOW DO THEY GET THE MONEY FOR IT?
I MEAN HOW DO THEY SURVIVE.
YOU'RE LOOKIN' AT IT.
ANY SUPE WITH ANY SENSE HAS HIS OWN COMIC BOOK, KID. IF HE'S LUCKY HE HAS TWO OR THREE, OR A PLACE IN A TEAM BOOK, OR MAYBE HIS OWN GODDAMN LINE.
IT AIN'T JUST THE MONEY--THAT CAN BE GOOD, THAT CAN BE NOT SO GOOD. IT'S PROTECTION.
THAT WAS MY JOB. BACK WHEN I WORKED FOR VOUGHT AMERICAN.
WHEN I WAS A VICTORY COMICS MAN...

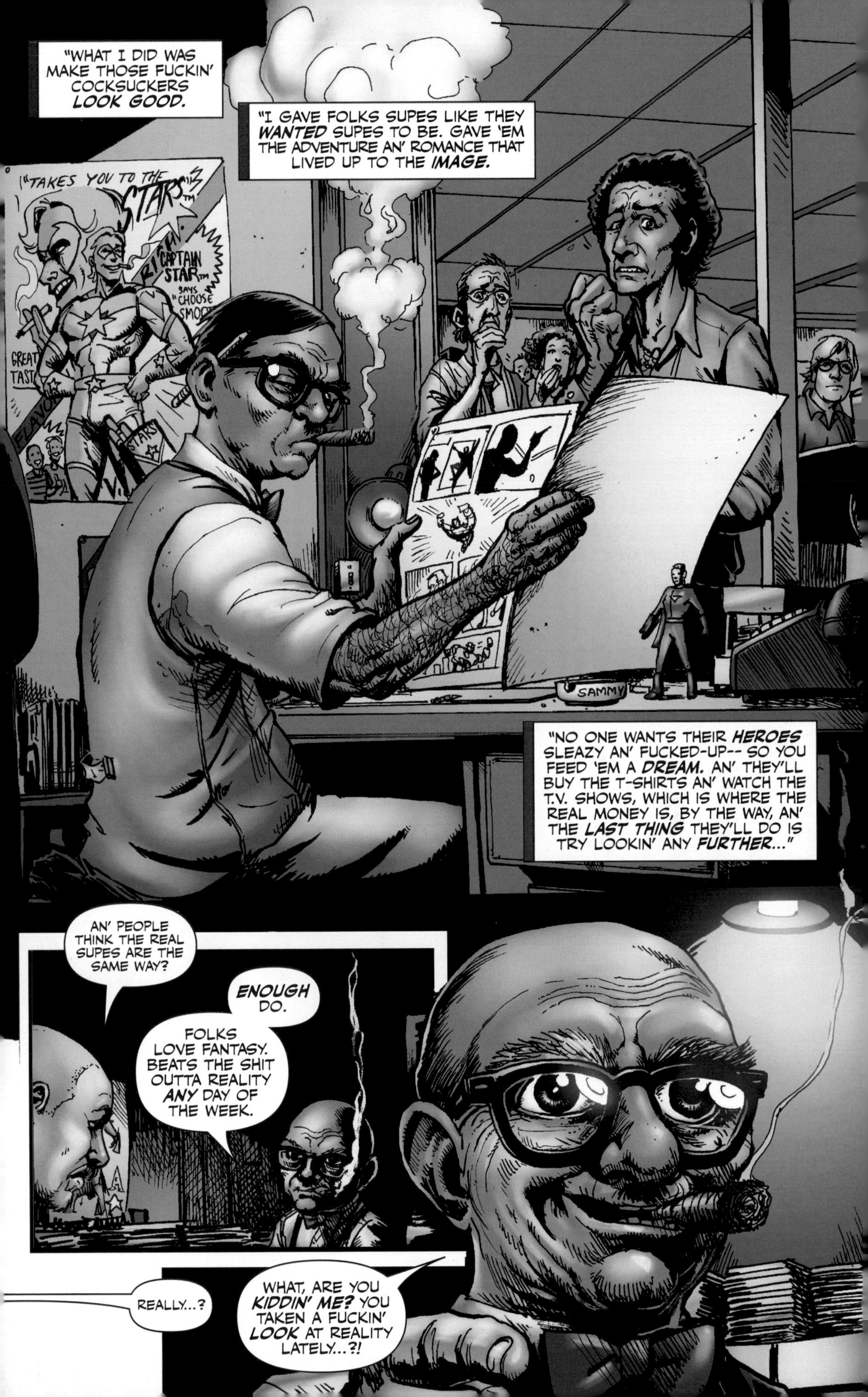
"WHAT I DID WAS MAKE THOSE FUCKIN' COCKSUCKERS LOOK GOOD.
"I GAVE FOLKS SUPES LIKE THEY WANTED SUPES TO BE. GAVE 'EM THE ADVENTURE AN' ROMANCE THAT LIVED UP TO THE IMAGE.
"TAKES YOU TO THE STARS"
CAPTAIN STAR SAYS "CHOOSE SMOO
GREAT TAST
SAMMY
"NO ONE WANTS THEIR HEROES SLEAZY AN' FUCKED-UP-- SO YOU FEED 'EM A DREAM. AN' THEY'LL BUY THE T-SHIRTS AN' WATCH THE T.V. SHOWS, WHICH IS WHERE THE REAL MONEY IS, BY THE WAY, AN' THE LAST THING THEY'LL DO IS TRY LOOKIN' ANY FURTHER..."
AN' PEOPLE THINK THE REAL SUPES ARE THE SAME WAY?
ENOUGH DO.
FOLKS LOVE FANTASY. BEATS THE SHIT OUTTA REALITY ANY DAY OF THE WEEK.
REALLY...?
WHAT, ARE YOU KIDDIN' ME? YOU TAKEN A FUCKIN' LOOK AT REALITY LATELY...?!

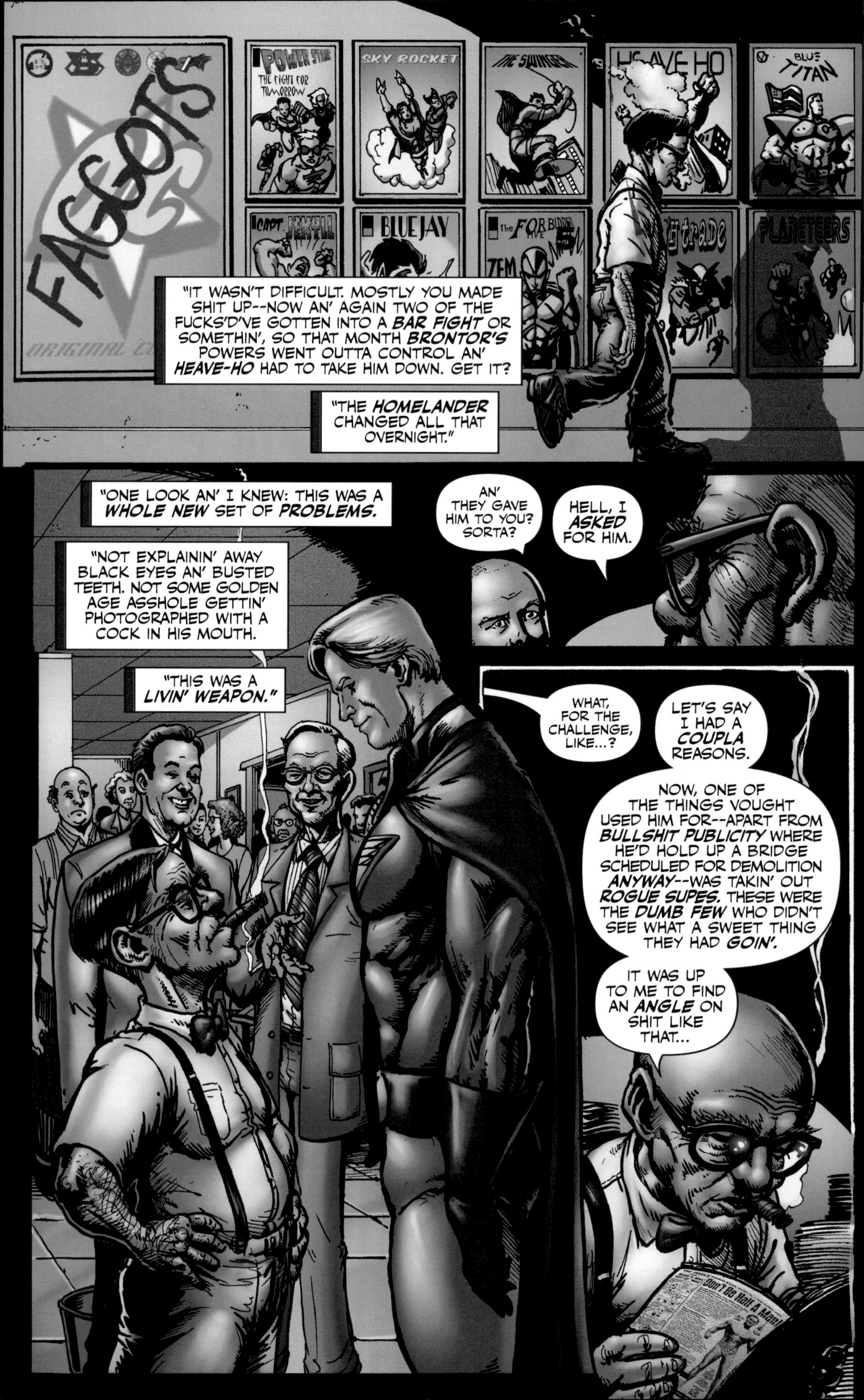
FAGGOTS
THE FIGHT FOR TOMORROW
SKY ROCKET
THE SWINGER
HEAVE HO
BLUE TITAN
BLUEJAY
PLANETEERS
"IT WASN'T DIFFICULT. MOSTLY YOU MADE SHIT UP--NOW AN' AGAIN TWO OF THE FUCKS'D'VE GOTTEN INTO A BAR FIGHT OR SOMETHIN', SO THAT MONTH BRONTOR'S POWERS WENT OUTTA CONTROL AN' HEAVE-HO HAD TO TAKE HIM DOWN. GET IT?
"THE HOMELANDER CHANGED ALL THAT OVERNIGHT."
"ONE LOOK AN' I KNEW: THIS WAS A WHOLE NEW SET OF PROBLEMS.
"NOT EXPLAININ' AWAY BLACK EYES AN' BUSTED TEETH. NOT SOME GOLDEN AGE ASSHOLE GETTIN' PHOTOGRAPHED WITH A COCK IN HIS MOUTH.
"THIS WAS A LIVIN' WEAPON."
AN' THEY GAVE HIM TO YOU? SORTA?
HELL, I ASKED FOR HIM.
WHAT, FOR THE CHALLENGE, LIKE...?
LET'S SAY I HAD A COUPLA REASONS.
NOW, ONE OF THE THINGS VOUGHT USED HIM FOR--APART FROM BULLSHIT PUBLICITY WHERE HE'D HOLD UP A BRIDGE SCHEDULED FOR DEMOLITION ANYWAY--WAS TAKIN' OUT ROGUE SUPES. THESE WERE THE DUMB FEW WHO DIDN'T SEE WHAT A SWEET THING THEY HAD GOIN'.
IT WAS UP TO ME TO FIND AN ANGLE ON SHIT LIKE THAT...
Don't Be Half A Man!

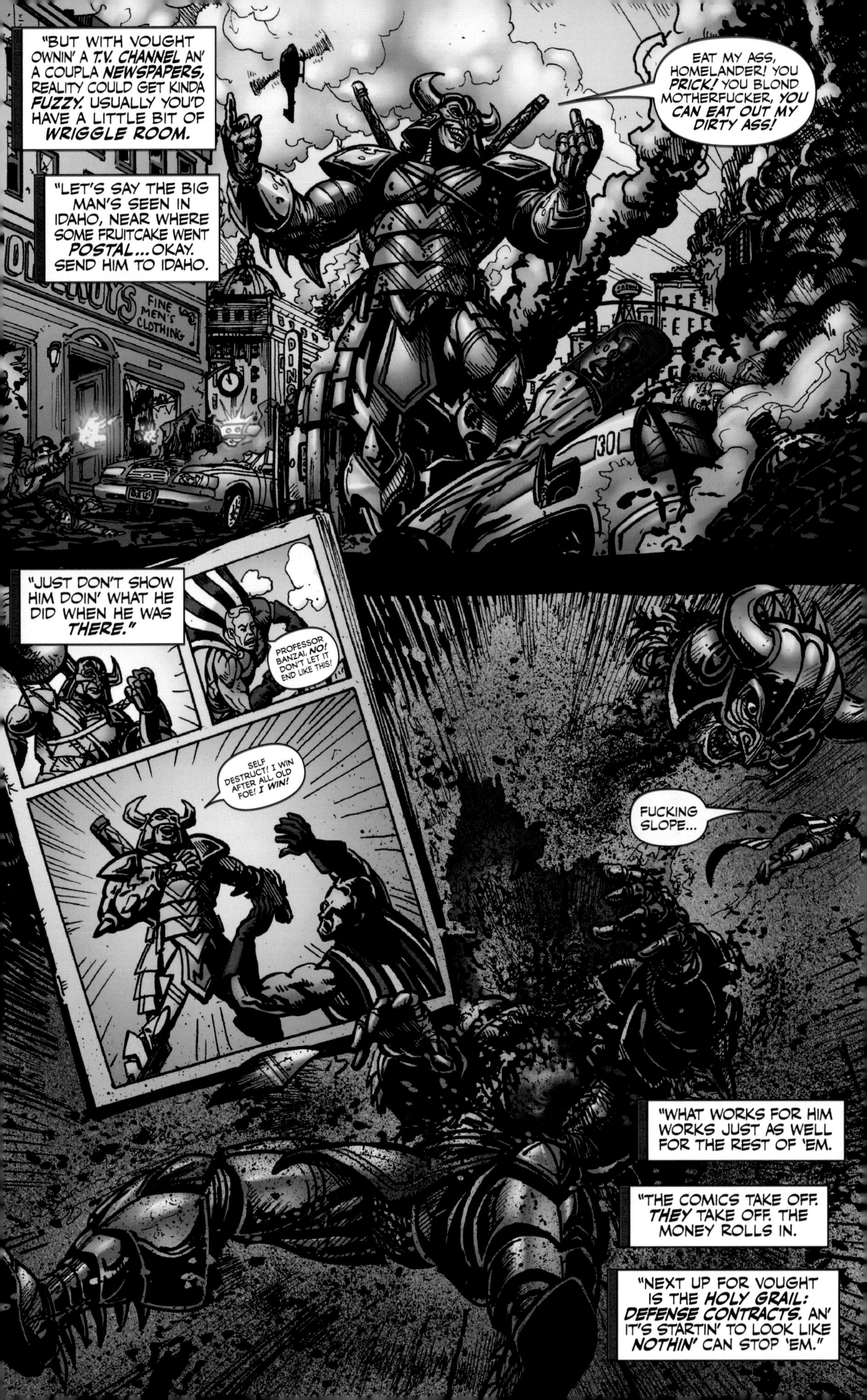
"BUT WITH VOUGHT OWNIN' A T.V. CHANNEL AN' A COUPLA NEWSPAPERS, REALITY COULD GET KINDA FUZZY. USUALLY YOU'D HAVE A LITTLE BIT OF WRIGGLE ROOM.
EAT MY ASS, HOMELANDER! YOU PRICK! YOU BLOND MOTHERFUCKER, YOU CAN EAT OUT MY DIRTY ASS!
"LET'S SAY THE BIG MAN'S SEEN IN IDAHO, NEAR WHERE SOME FRUITCAKE WENT POSTAL...OKAY. SEND HIM TO IDAHO.
FINE MEN'S CLOTHING
"JUST DON'T SHOW HIM DOIN' WHAT HE DID WHEN HE WAS THERE."
PROFESSOR BANZAI, NO! DON'T LET IT END LIKE THIS!
SELF DESTRUCT! I WIN AFTER ALL, OLD FOE! I WIN!
FUCKING SLOPE...
"WHAT WORKS FOR HIM WORKS JUST AS WELL FOR THE REST OF 'EM.
"THE COMICS TAKE OFF. THEY TAKE OFF. THE MONEY ROLLS IN.
"NEXT UP FOR VOUGHT IS THE HOLY GRAIL: DEFENSE CONTRACTS. AN' IT'S STARTIN' TO LOOK LIKE NOTHIN' CAN STOP 'EM."

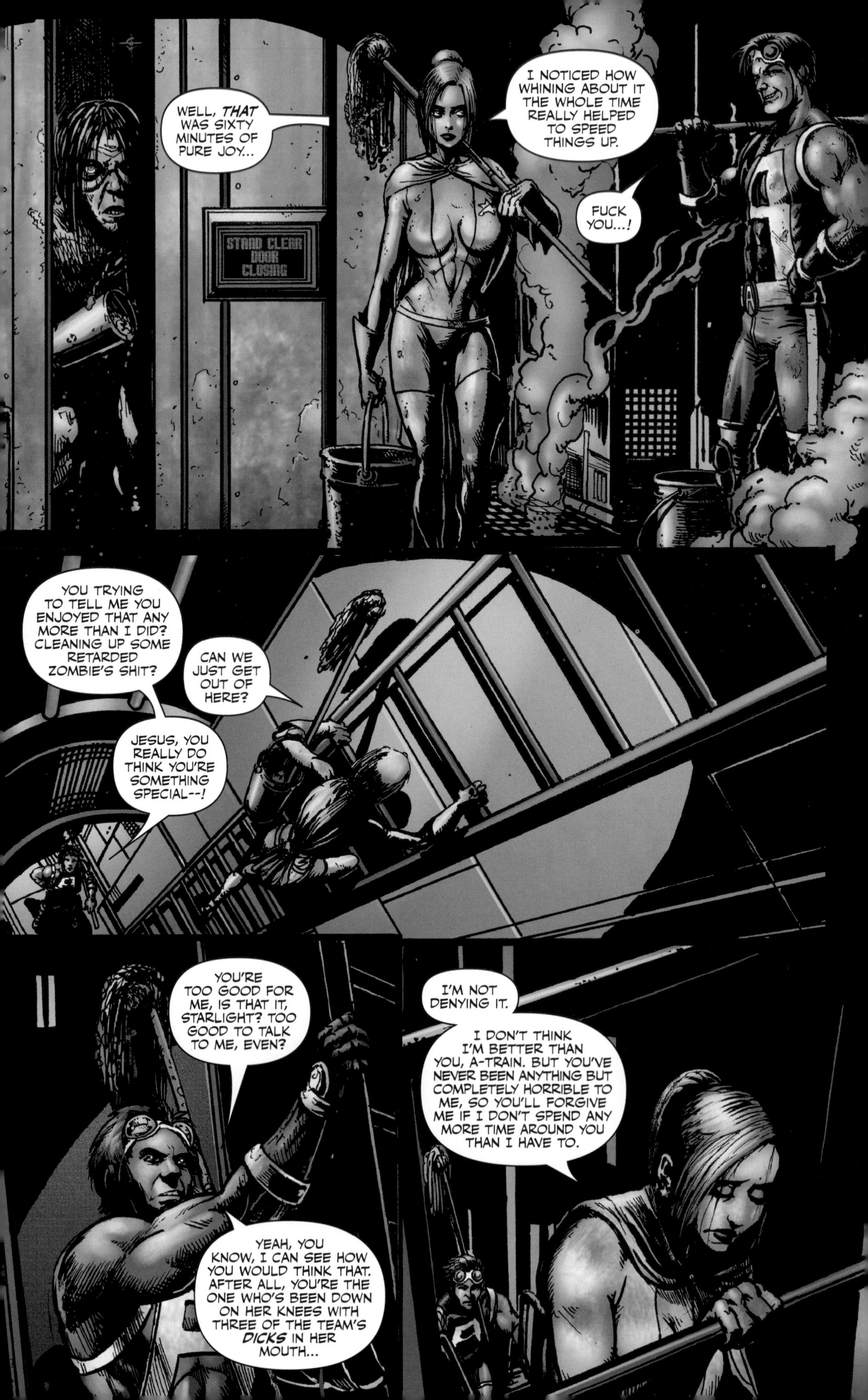
WELL, *THAT* WAS SIXTY MINUTES OF PURE JOY...
I NOTICED HOW WHINING ABOUT IT THE WHOLE TIME REALLY HELPED TO SPEED THINGS UP.
FUCK YOU...!
STAND CLEAR DOOR CLOSING
YOU TRYING TO TELL ME YOU ENJOYED THAT ANY MORE THAN I DID? CLEANING UP SOME RETARDED ZOMBIE'S SHIT?
CAN WE JUST GET OUT OF HERE?
JESUS, YOU REALLY DO THINK YOU'RE SOMETHING SPECIAL--!
YOU'RE TOO GOOD FOR ME, IS THAT IT, STARLIGHT? TOO GOOD TO TALK TO ME, EVEN?
YEAH, YOU KNOW, I CAN SEE HOW YOU WOULD THINK THAT. AFTER ALL, YOU'RE THE ONE WHO'S BEEN DOWN ON HER KNEES WITH THREE OF THE TEAM'S *DICKS* IN HER MOUTH...
I'M NOT DENYING IT.
I DON'T THINK I'M BETTER THAN YOU, A-TRAIN. BUT YOU'VE NEVER BEEN ANYTHING BUT COMPLETELY HORRIBLE TO ME, SO YOU'LL FORGIVE ME IF I DON'T SPEND ANY MORE TIME AROUND YOU THAN I HAVE TO.

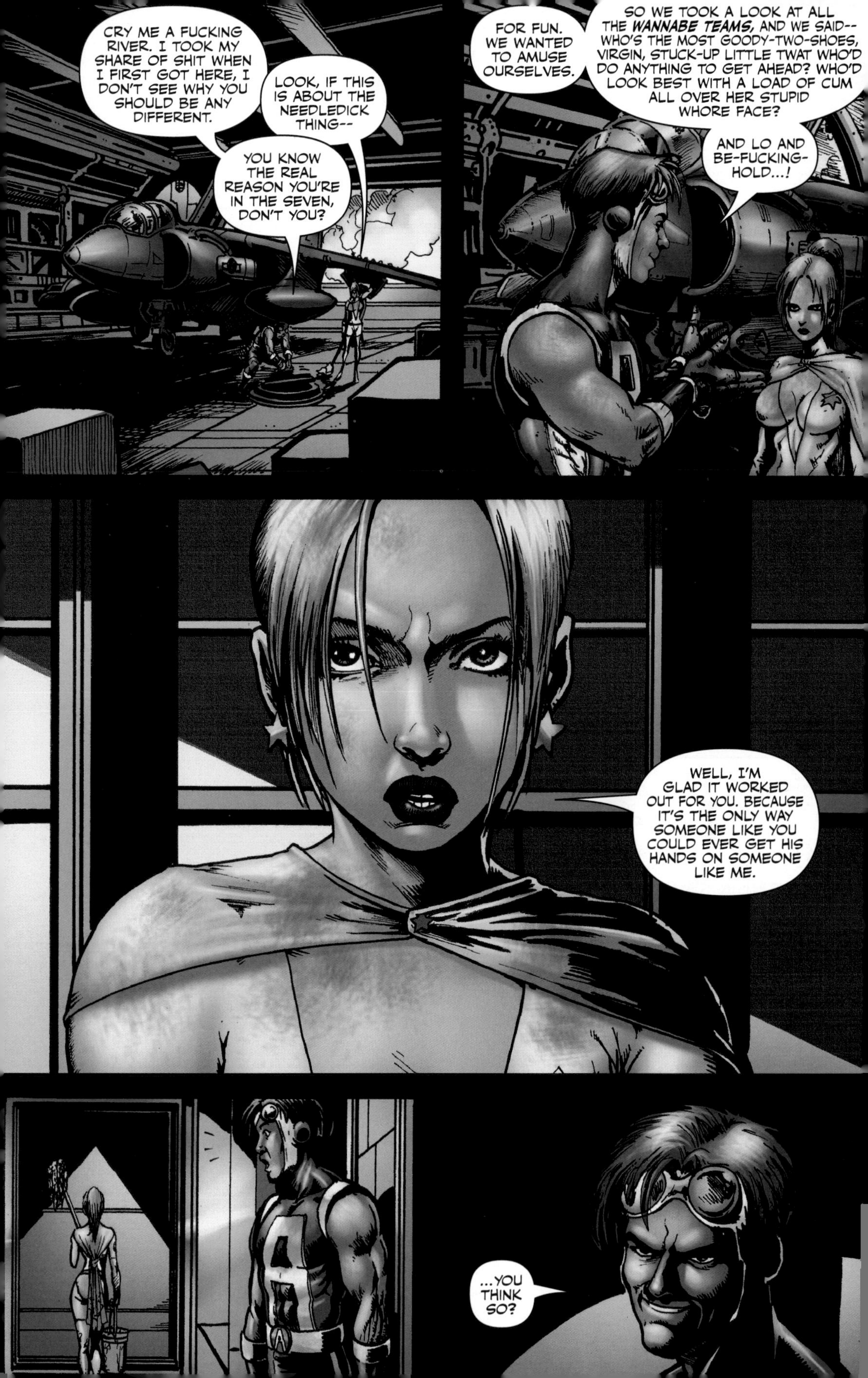
CRY ME A FUCKING RIVER. I TOOK MY SHARE OF SHIT WHEN I FIRST GOT HERE, I DON'T SEE WHY YOU SHOULD BE ANY DIFFERENT.
LOOK, IF THIS IS ABOUT THE NEEDLEDICK THING--
YOU KNOW THE REAL REASON YOU'RE IN THE SEVEN, DON'T YOU?
FOR FUN. WE WANTED TO AMUSE OURSELVES.
SO WE TOOK A LOOK AT ALL THE WANNABE TEAMS, AND WE SAID-- WHO'S THE MOST GOODY-TWO-SHOES, VIRGIN, STUCK-UP LITTLE TWAT WHO'D DO ANYTHING TO GET AHEAD? WHO'D LOOK BEST WITH A LOAD OF CUM ALL OVER HER STUPID WHORE FACE?
AND LO AND BE-FUCKING-HOLD...!
WELL, I'M GLAD IT WORKED OUT FOR YOU. BECAUSE IT'S THE ONLY WAY SOMEONE LIKE YOU COULD EVER GET HIS HANDS ON SOMEONE LIKE ME.
...YOU THINK SO?

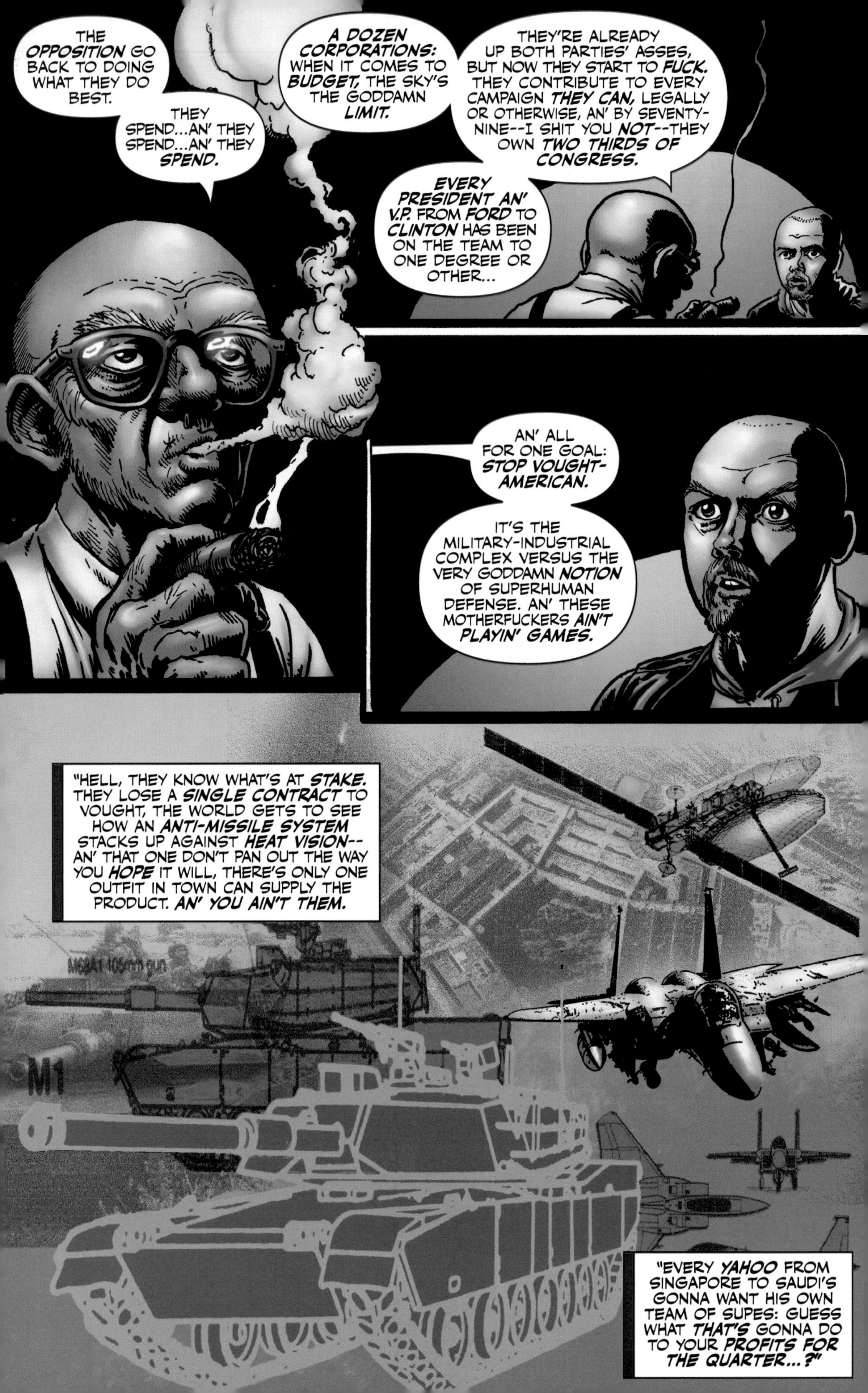
THE OPPOSITION GO BACK TO DOING WHAT THEY DO BEST.
THEY SPEND...AN' THEY SPEND...AN' THEY SPEND.
A DOZEN CORPORATIONS: WHEN IT COMES TO BUDGET, THE SKY'S THE GODDAMN LIMIT.
THEY'RE ALREADY UP BOTH PARTIES' ASSES, BUT NOW THEY START TO FUCK. THEY CONTRIBUTE TO EVERY CAMPAIGN THEY CAN, LEGALLY OR OTHERWISE, AN' BY SEVENTY-NINE--I SHIT YOU NOT--THEY OWN TWO THIRDS OF CONGRESS.
EVERY PRESIDENT AN' V.P. FROM FORD TO CLINTON HAS BEEN ON THE TEAM TO ONE DEGREE OR OTHER...
AN' ALL FOR ONE GOAL: STOP VOUGHT-AMERICAN.
IT'S THE MILITARY-INDUSTRIAL COMPLEX VERSUS THE VERY GODDAMN NOTION OF SUPERHUMAN DEFENSE. AN' THESE MOTHERFUCKERS AIN'T PLAYIN' GAMES.
"HELL, THEY KNOW WHAT'S AT STAKE. THEY LOSE A SINGLE CONTRACT TO VOUGHT, THE WORLD GETS TO SEE HOW AN ANTI-MISSILE SYSTEM STACKS UP AGAINST HEAT VISION--AN' THAT ONE DON'T PAN OUT THE WAY YOU HOPE IT WILL, THERE'S ONLY ONE OUTFIT IN TOWN CAN SUPPLY THE PRODUCT. AN' YOU AIN'T THEM.
M68A1 105mm gun
M1
"EVERY YAHOO FROM SINGAPORE TO SAUDI'S GONNA WANT HIS OWN TEAM OF SUPES: GUESS WHAT THAT'S GONNA DO TO YOUR PROFITS FOR THE QUARTER...?"

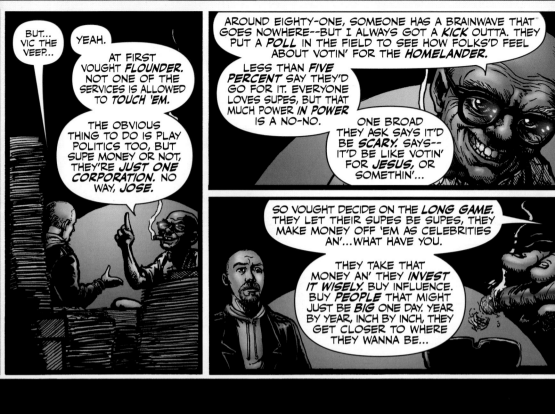

BUT... VIC THE VEEP...

YEAH. AT FIRST VOUGHT *FLOUNDER*. NOT ONE OF THE SERVICES IS ALLOWED TO *TOUCH 'EM*.

THE OBVIOUS THING TO DO IS PLAY POLITICS TOO, BUT SUPE MONEY OR NOT, THEY'RE *JUST ONE CORPORATION*. NO WAY, *JOSE*.

AROUND EIGHTY-ONE, SOMEONE HAS A BRAINWAVE THAT GOES NOWHERE--BUT I ALWAYS GOT A *KICK* OUTTA. THEY PUT A *POLL* IN THE FIELD TO SEE HOW FOLKS'D FEEL ABOUT VOTIN' FOR THE *HOMELANDER*.

LESS THAN *FIVE PERCENT* SAY THEY'D GO FOR IT. EVERYONE LOVES SUPES, BUT THAT MUCH POWER *IN POWER* IS A NO-NO.

ONE BROAD THEY ASK SAYS IT'D BE *SCARY*. SAYS-- IT'D BE LIKE VOTIN' FOR *JESUS*, OR SOMETHIN'...

SO VOUGHT DECIDE ON THE *LONG GAME*. THEY LET THEIR SUPES BE SUPES, THEY MAKE MONEY OFF 'EM AS CELEBRITIES AN'...WHAT HAVE YOU.

THEY TAKE THAT MONEY AN' THEY *INVEST IT WISELY*. BUY INFLUENCE. BUY *PEOPLE* THAT MIGHT JUST BE *BIG* ONE DAY. YEAR BY YEAR, INCH BY INCH, THEY GET CLOSER TO WHERE THEY WANNA BE...

"AN' ALL OF A SUDDEN IT'S THE YEAR TWO THOUSAND, AN' THE OPPOSITION HAVE FOUND THE *PERFECT CANDIDATE* FOR *NOVEMBER*...

"*DAKOTA BOB SHAEFER:* OLD SCHOOL REPUBLICAN, HALIBURTON MAN, AN' HARD AN' COLD AS THE *BADLANDS THEMSELVES*."

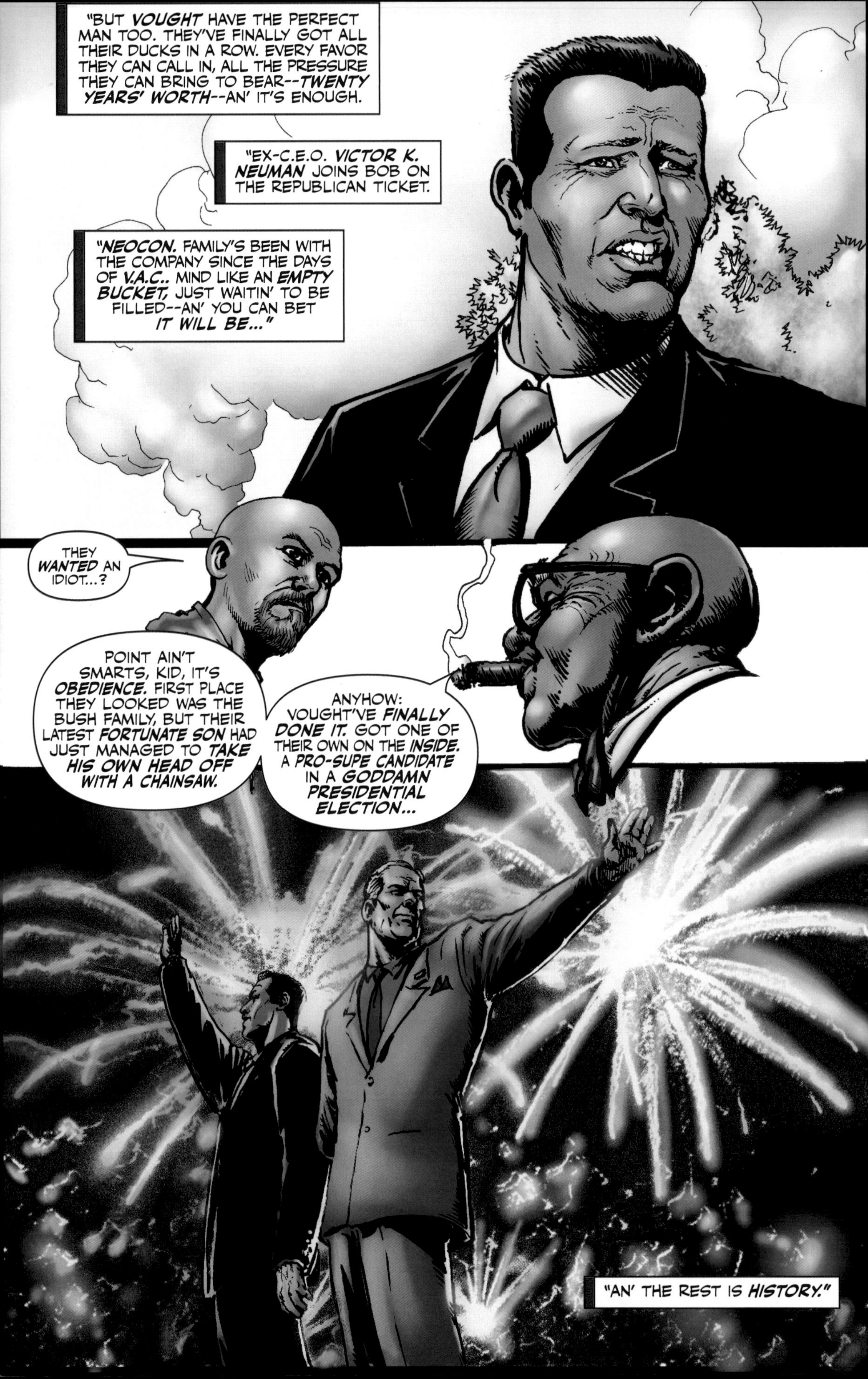
"BUT VOUGHT HAVE THE PERFECT MAN TOO. THEY'VE FINALLY GOT ALL THEIR DUCKS IN A ROW. EVERY FAVOR THEY CAN CALL IN, ALL THE PRESSURE THEY CAN BRING TO BEAR--TWENTY YEARS' WORTH--AN' IT'S ENOUGH.
"EX-C.E.O. VICTOR K. NEUMAN JOINS BOB ON THE REPUBLICAN TICKET.
"NEOCON. FAMILY'S BEEN WITH THE COMPANY SINCE THE DAYS OF V.A.C.. MIND LIKE AN EMPTY BUCKET, JUST WAITIN' TO BE FILLED--AN' YOU CAN BET IT WILL BE..."
THEY WANTED AN IDIOT...?
POINT AIN'T SMARTS, KID, IT'S OBEDIENCE. FIRST PLACE THEY LOOKED WAS THE BUSH FAMILY, BUT THEIR LATEST FORTUNATE SON HAD JUST MANAGED TO TAKE HIS OWN HEAD OFF WITH A CHAINSAW.
ANYHOW: VOUGHT'VE FINALLY DONE IT. GOT ONE OF THEIR OWN ON THE INSIDE. A PRO-SUPE CANDIDATE IN A GODDAMN PRESIDENTIAL ELECTION...
"AN' THE REST IS HISTORY."

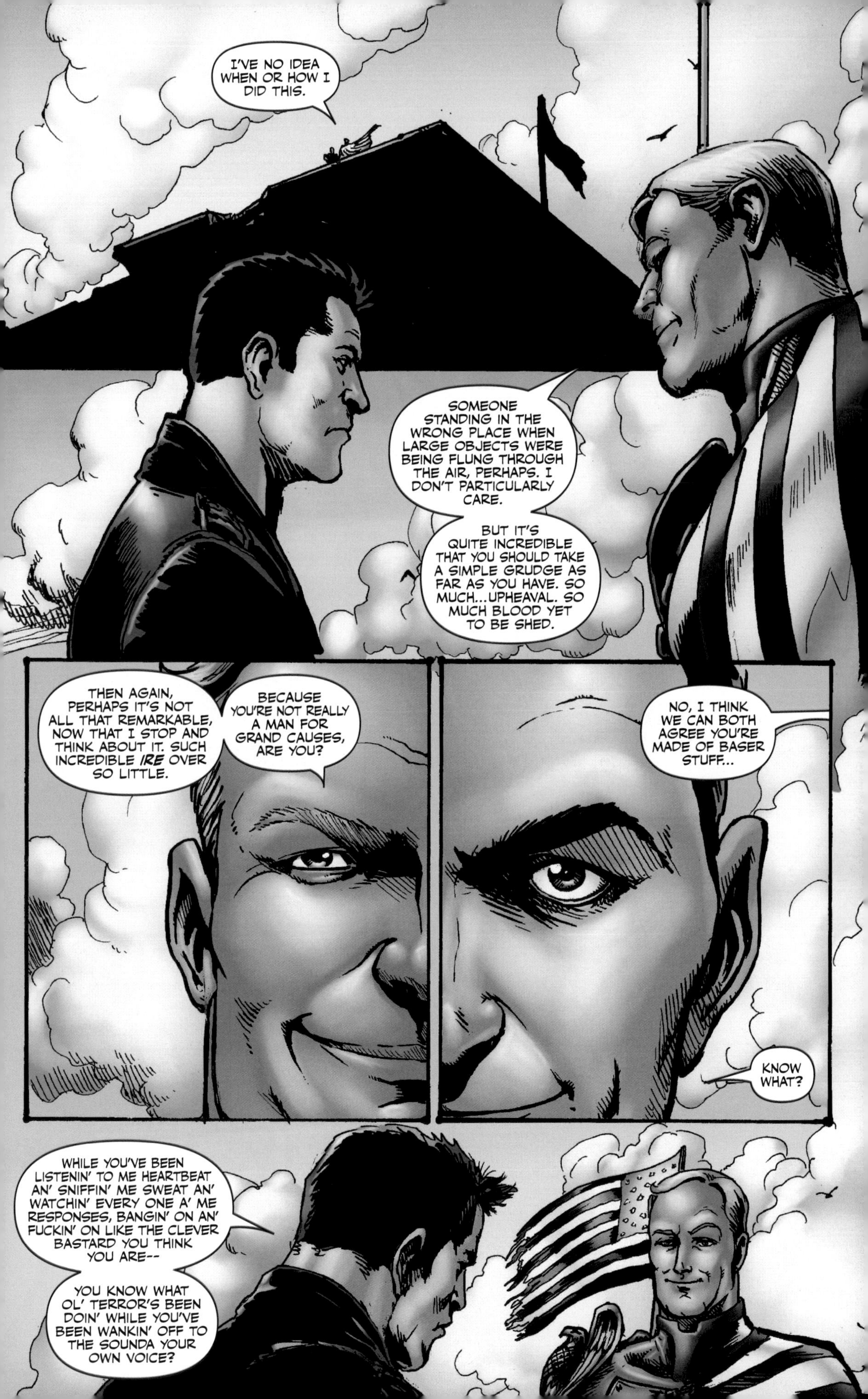
I'VE NO IDEA WHEN OR HOW I DID THIS.
SOMEONE STANDING IN THE WRONG PLACE WHEN LARGE OBJECTS WERE BEING FLUNG THROUGH THE AIR, PERHAPS. I DON'T PARTICULARLY CARE.
BUT IT'S QUITE INCREDIBLE THAT YOU SHOULD TAKE A SIMPLE GRUDGE AS FAR AS YOU HAVE. SO MUCH...UPHEAVAL. SO MUCH BLOOD YET TO BE SHED.
THEN AGAIN, PERHAPS IT'S NOT ALL THAT REMARKABLE, NOW THAT I STOP AND THINK ABOUT IT. SUCH INCREDIBLE *IRE* OVER SO LITTLE.
BECAUSE YOU'RE NOT REALLY A MAN FOR GRAND CAUSES, ARE YOU?
NO, I THINK WE CAN BOTH AGREE YOU'RE MADE OF BASER STUFF...
KNOW WHAT?
WHILE YOU'VE BEEN LISTENIN' TO ME HEARTBEAT AN' SNIFFIN' ME SWEAT AN' WATCHIN' EVERY ONE A' ME RESPONSES, BANGIN' ON AN' FUCKIN' ON LIKE THE CLEVER BASTARD YOU THINK YOU ARE--
YOU KNOW WHAT OL' TERROR'S BEEN DOIN' WHILE YOU'VE BEEN WANKIN' OFF TO THE SOUNDA YOUR OWN VOICE?

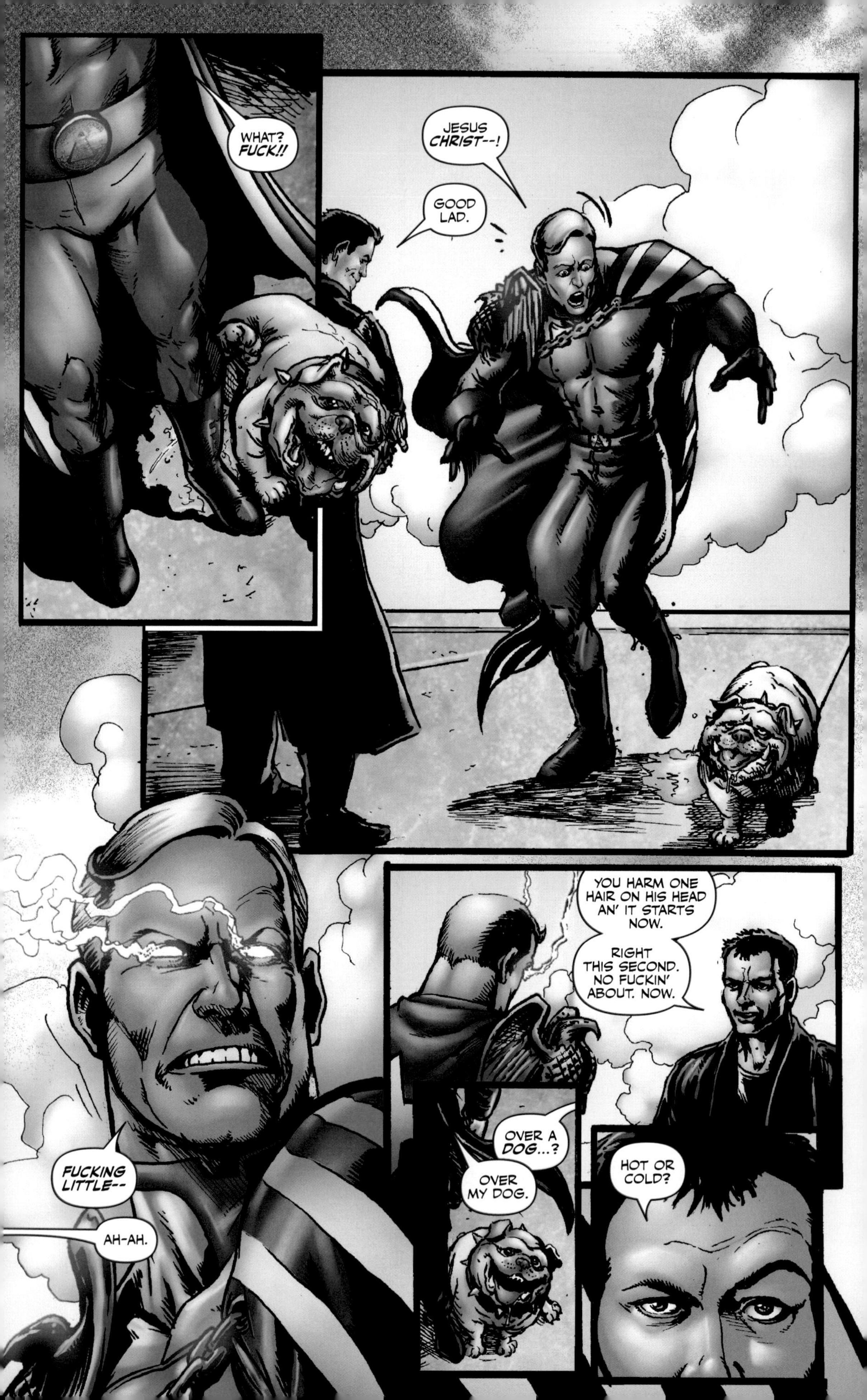
WHAT? FUCK!!
JESUS CHRIST--!
GOOD LAD.
FUCKING LITTLE--
AH-AH.
YOU HARM ONE HAIR ON HIS HEAD AN' IT STARTS NOW.
RIGHT THIS SECOND. NO FUCKIN' ABOUT. NOW.
OVER A DOG...?
OVER MY DOG.
HOT OR COLD?

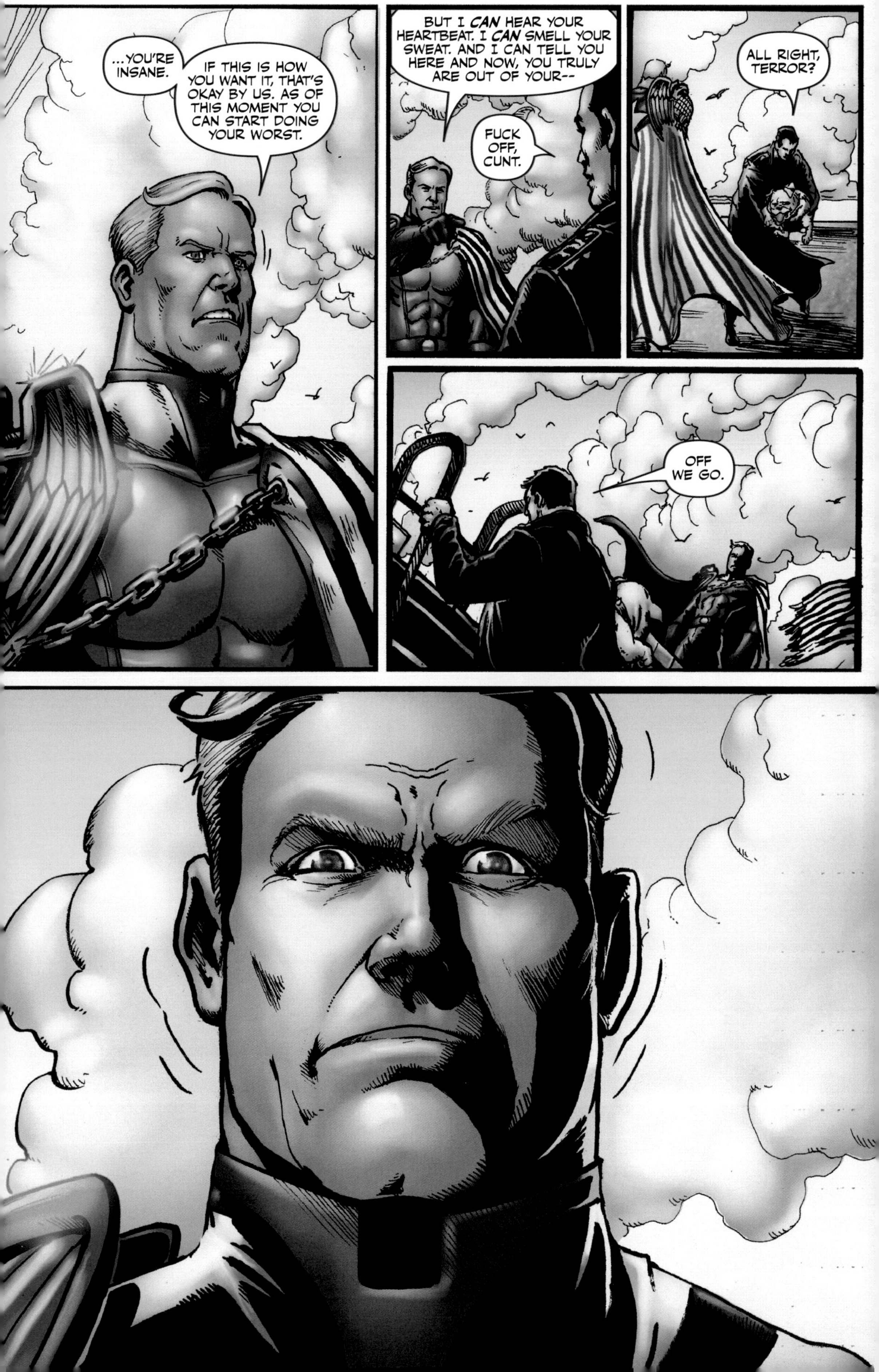
...YOU'RE INSANE.
IF THIS IS HOW YOU WANT IT, THAT'S OKAY BY US. AS OF THIS MOMENT YOU CAN START DOING YOUR WORST.
BUT I CAN HEAR YOUR HEARTBEAT. I CAN SMELL YOUR SWEAT. AND I CAN TELL YOU HERE AND NOW, YOU TRULY ARE OUT OF YOUR--
FUCK OFF, CUNT.
ALL RIGHT, TERROR?
OFF WE GO.

NOTHIN' MUCH *HAPPENS* FOR THE FIRST EIGHT MONTHS OF THE SHAEFER-NEUMAN ADMINISTRATION.

THEN COMES SEPTEMBER.

CAN YOU TELL ME WHAT HAPPENS IN *SEPTEMBER,* KID...?

WHO CAN'T?

GO AHEAD.

THEY CRASH A 'PLANE INTO THE BROOKLYN BRIDGE. KILL ABOUT A THOUSAND PEOPLE.

NEXT THING YOU KNOW WE'VE INVADED PAKISTAN.

WHO CRASHES IT...?

TERRORISTS, FOR FUCK'S SAKE.

THE *TERRORISTS* DON'T CRASH SHIT INTO SHIT.

THEY BOARD THE FLIGHT AT BOSTON LOGAN. SEIZE CONTROL RIGHT AFTER *TAKE-OFF.*

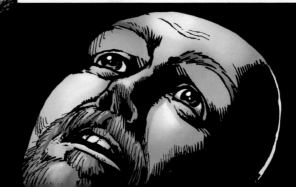

PLAN IS TO FLY THE THING INTO THE SOUTH TOWER OF THE *WORLD TRADE CENTER;* THEY DON'T GIVE A *FUCK* ABOUT THE *BROOKLYN BRIDGE...*

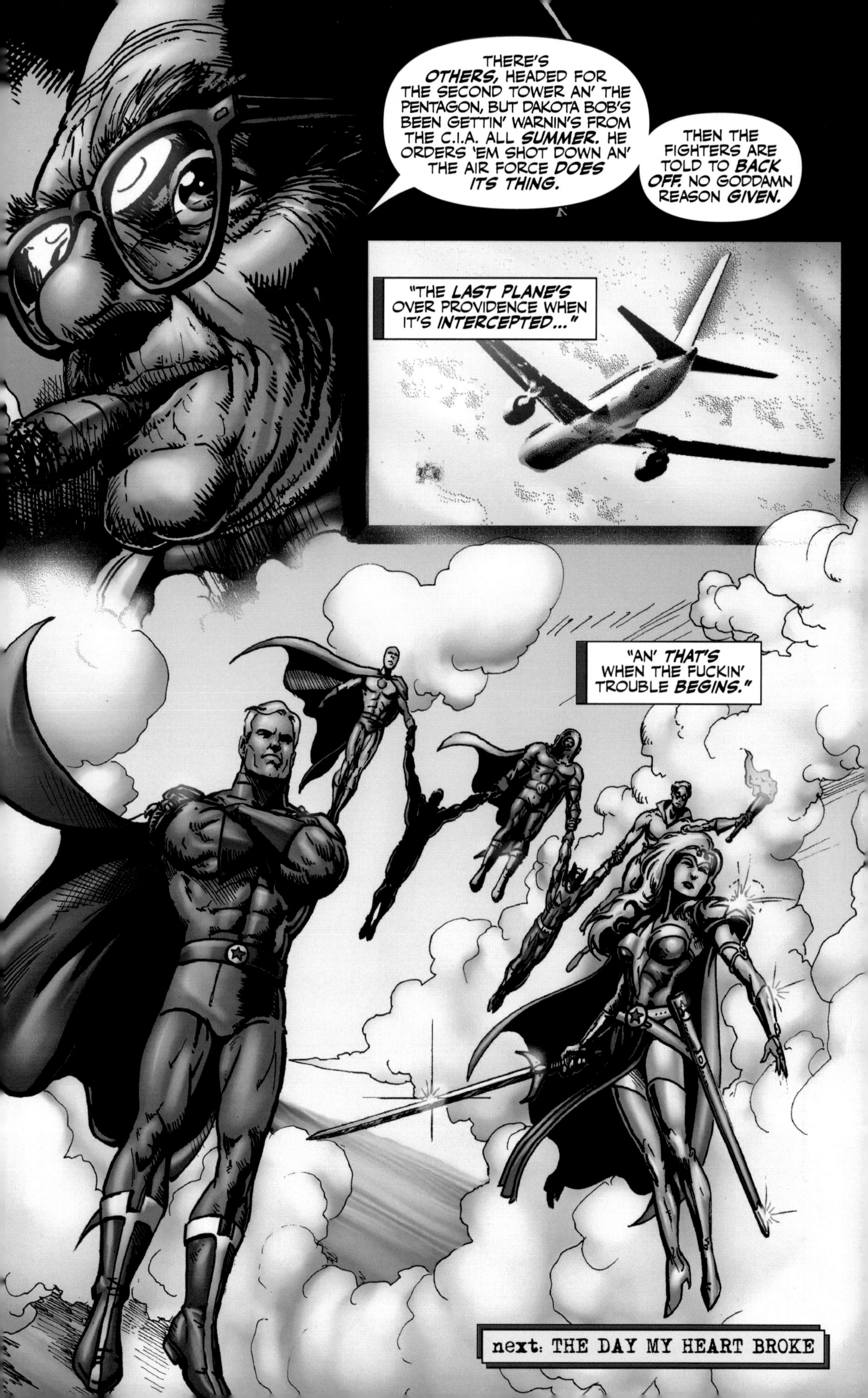
THERE'S OTHERS, HEADED FOR THE SECOND TOWER AN' THE PENTAGON, BUT DAKOTA BOB'S BEEN GETTIN' WARNIN'S FROM THE C.I.A. ALL SUMMER. HE ORDERS 'EM SHOT DOWN AN' THE AIR FORCE DOES ITS THING.
THEN THE FIGHTERS ARE TOLD TO BACK OFF. NO GODDAMN REASON GIVEN.
"THE LAST PLANE'S OVER PROVIDENCE WHEN IT'S INTERCEPTED..."
"AN' THAT'S WHEN THE FUCKIN' TROUBLE BEGINS."
next: THE DAY MY HEART BROKE

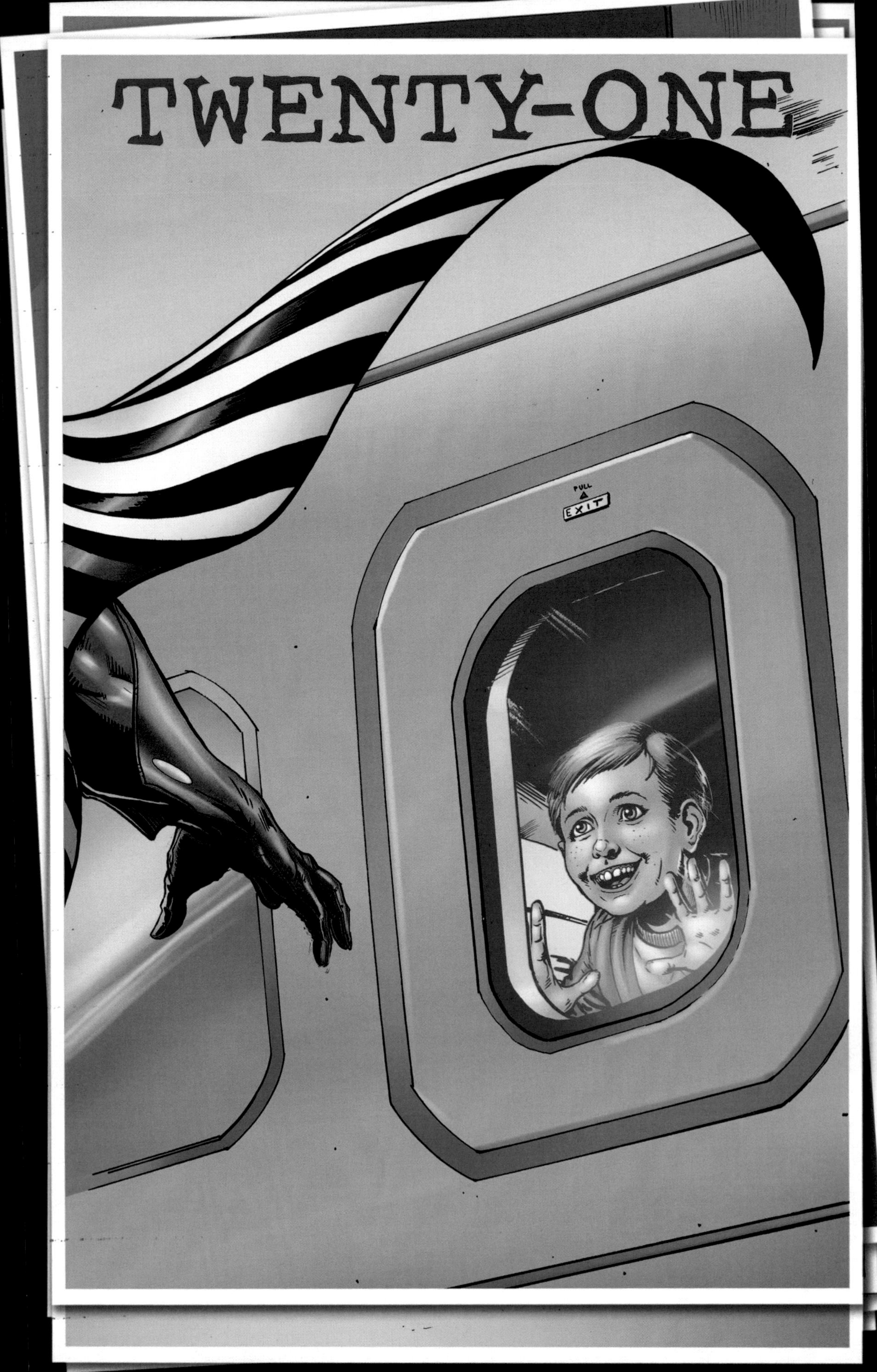
TWENTY-ONE
PULL
EXIT

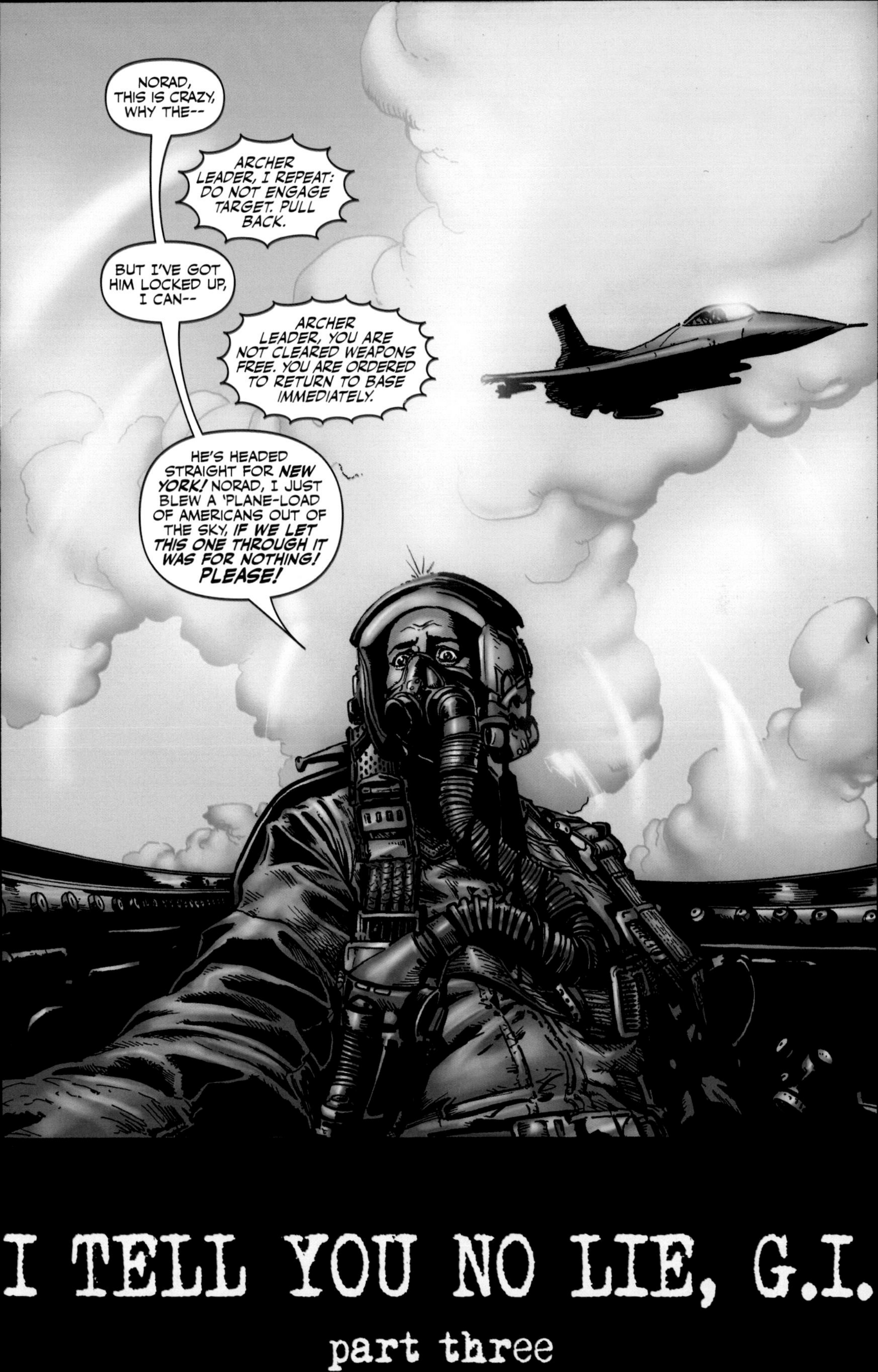
NORAD, THIS IS CRAZY, WHY THE--
ARCHER LEADER, I REPEAT: DO NOT ENGAGE TARGET. PULL BACK.
BUT I'VE GOT HIM LOCKED UP, I CAN--
ARCHER LEADER, YOU ARE NOT CLEARED WEAPONS FREE. YOU ARE ORDERED TO RETURN TO BASE IMMEDIATELY.
HE'S HEADED STRAIGHT FOR NEW YORK! NORAD, I JUST BLEW A 'PLANE-LOAD OF AMERICANS OUT OF THE SKY, IF WE LET THIS ONE THROUGH IT WAS FOR NOTHING! PLEASE!

I TELL YOU NO LIE, G.I.

part three

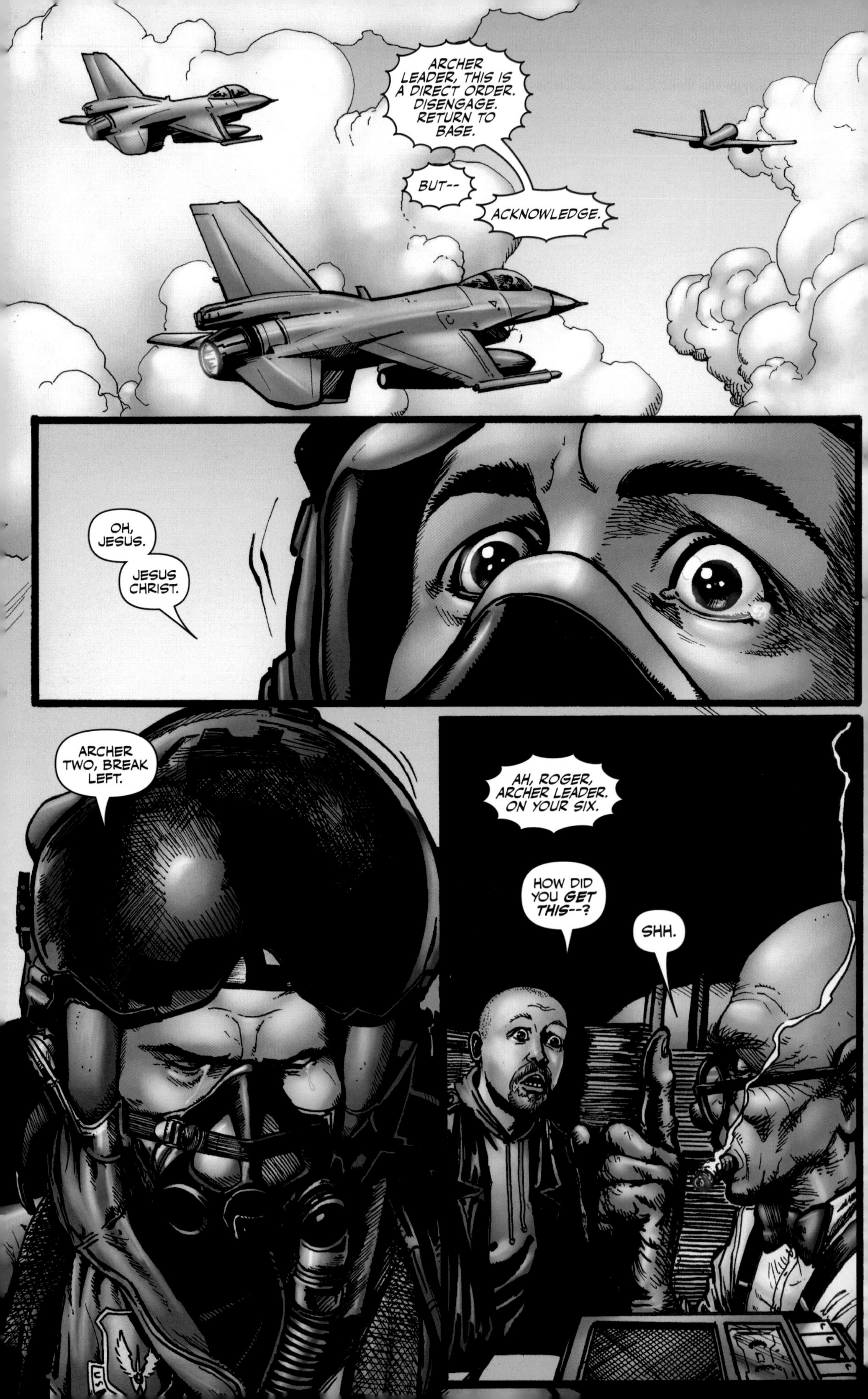
ARCHER LEADER, THIS IS A DIRECT ORDER. DISENGAGE. RETURN TO BASE.
BUT--
ACKNOWLEDGE.
OH, JESUS.
JESUS CHRIST.
ARCHER TWO, BREAK LEFT.
AH, ROGER, ARCHER LEADER. ON YOUR SIX.
HOW DID YOU **GET THIS**--?
SHH.

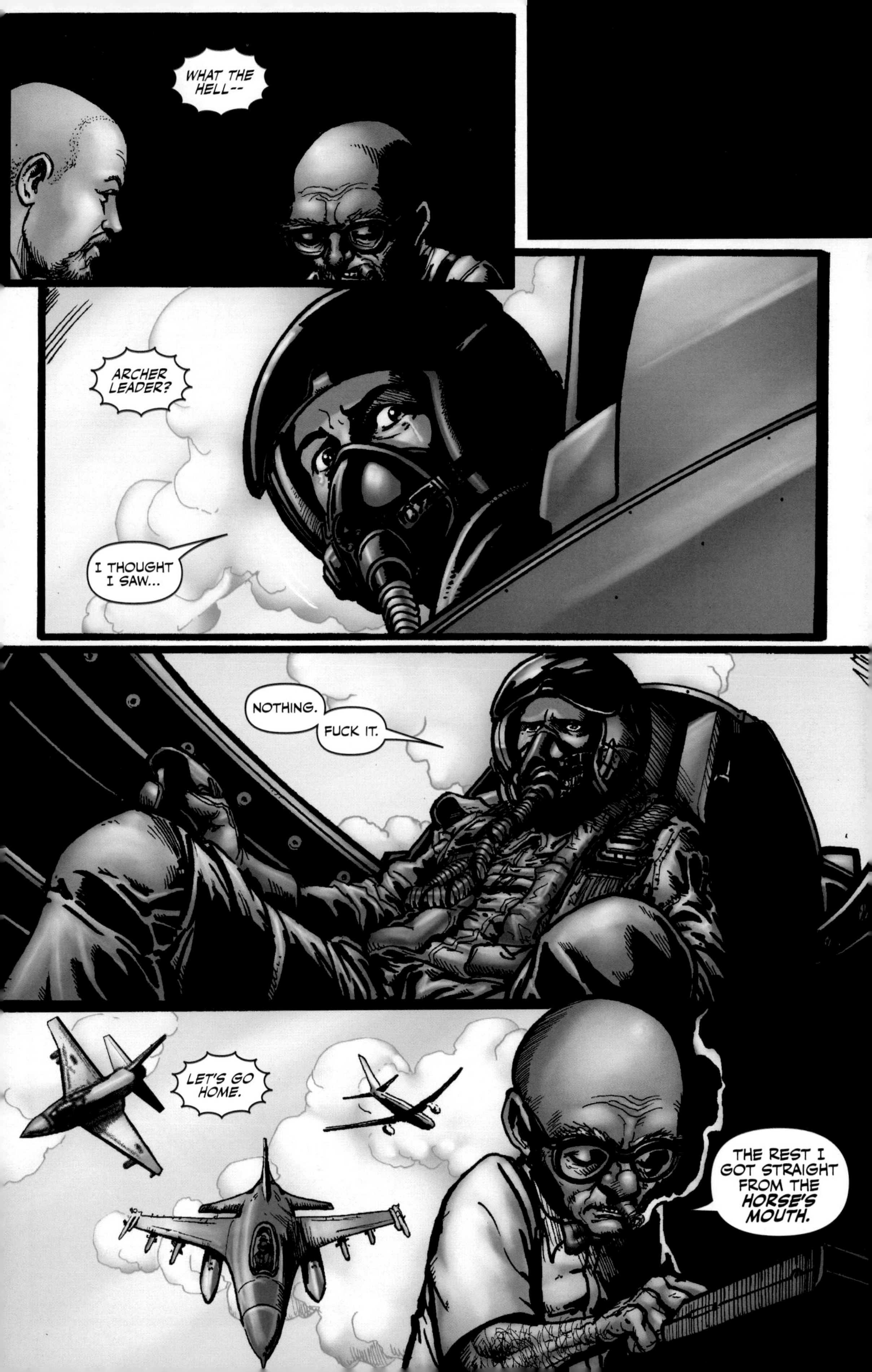
WHAT THE HELL--
ARCHER LEADER?
I THOUGHT I SAW...
NOTHING.
FUCK IT.
LET'S GO HOME.
THE REST I GOT STRAIGHT FROM THE *HORSE'S MOUTH.*

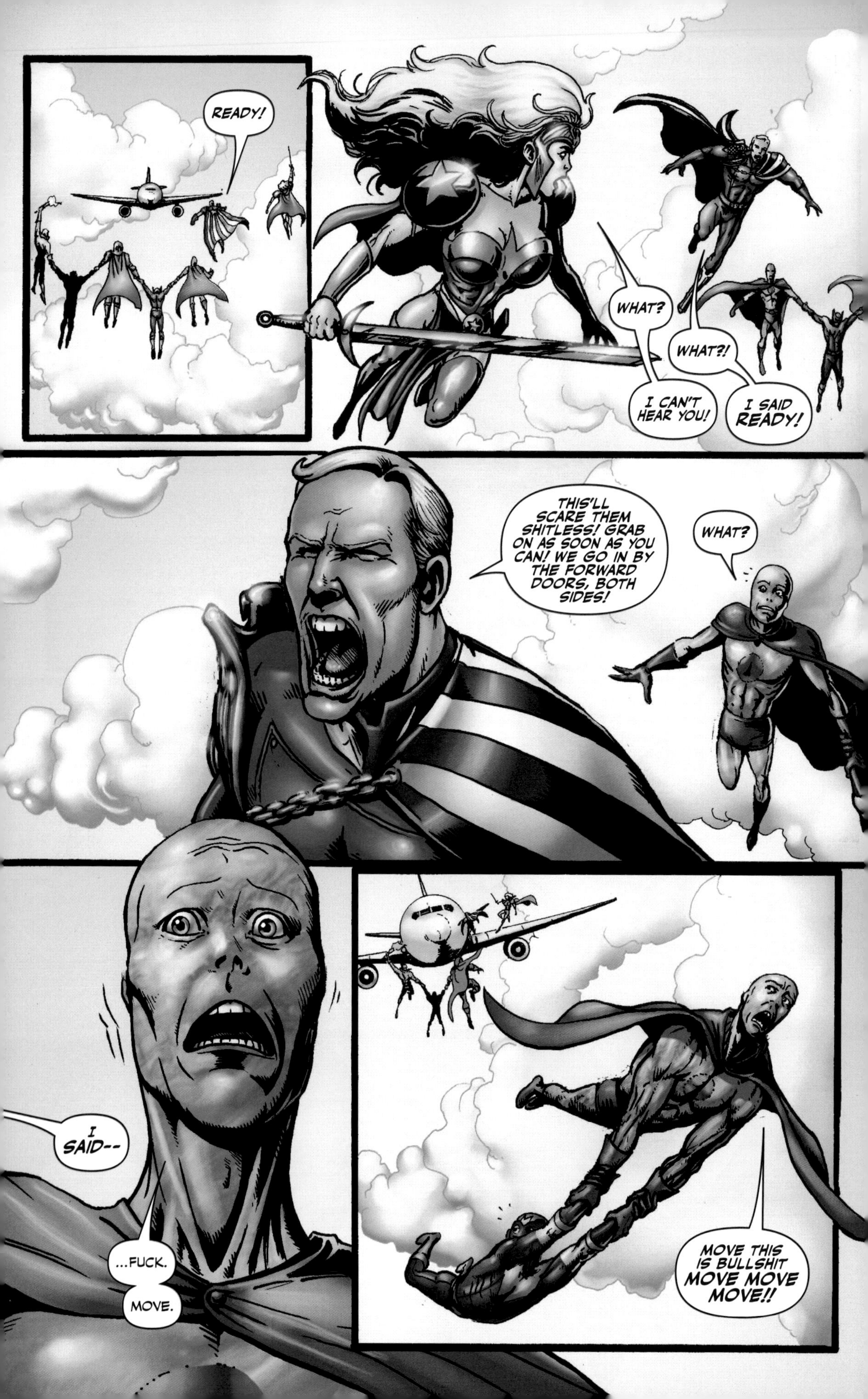
READY!
WHAT?
WHAT?!
I CAN'T HEAR YOU!
I SAID READY!
THIS'LL SCARE THEM SHITLESS! GRAB ON AS SOON AS YOU CAN! WE GO IN BY THE FORWARD DOORS, BOTH SIDES!
WHAT?
I SAID--
...FUCK.
MOVE.
MOVE THIS IS BULLSHIT MOVE MOVE MOVE!!

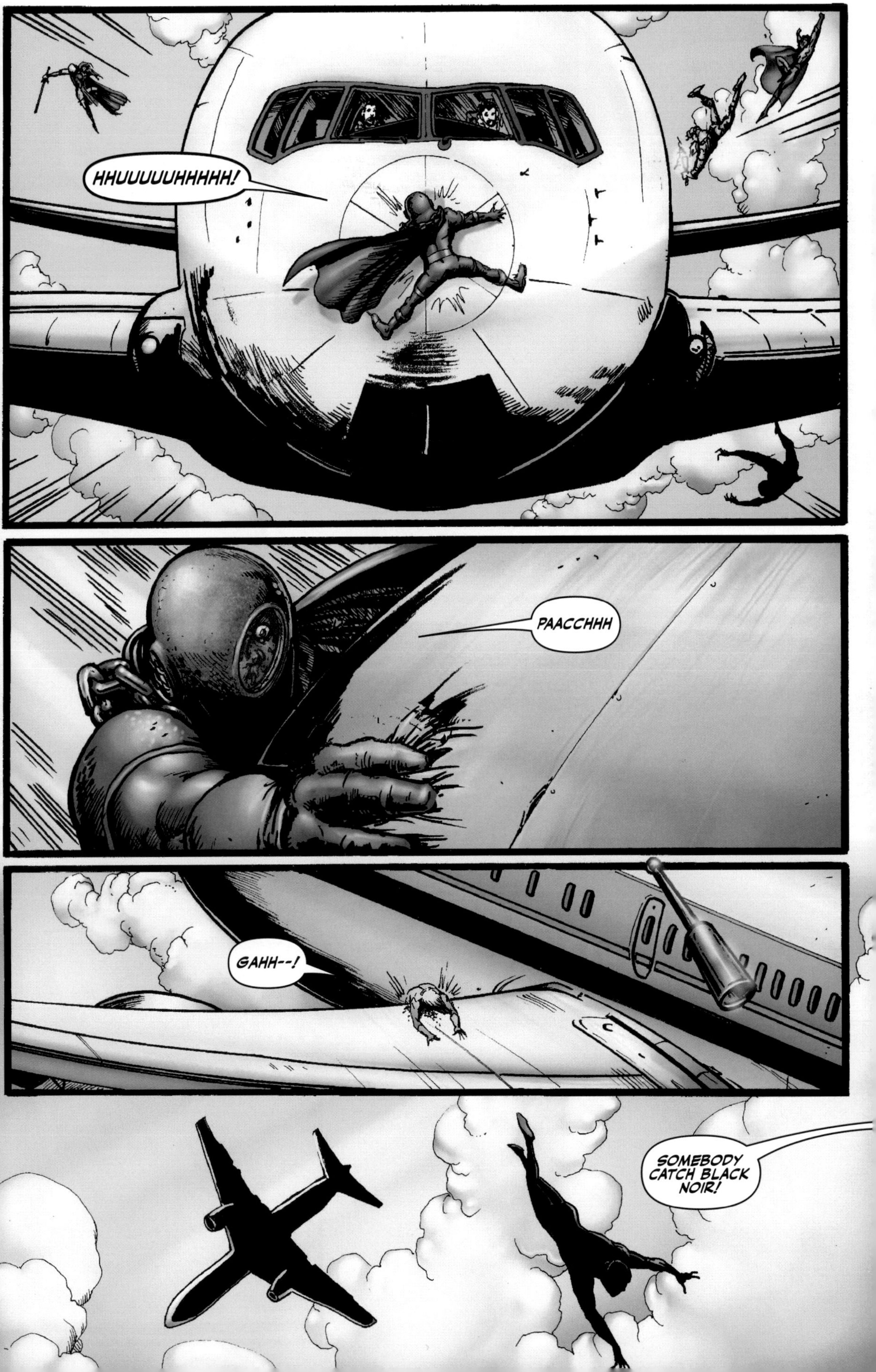
HHUUUUUHHHHH!
PAACCHHH
GAHH--!
SOMEBODY CATCH BLACK NOIR!

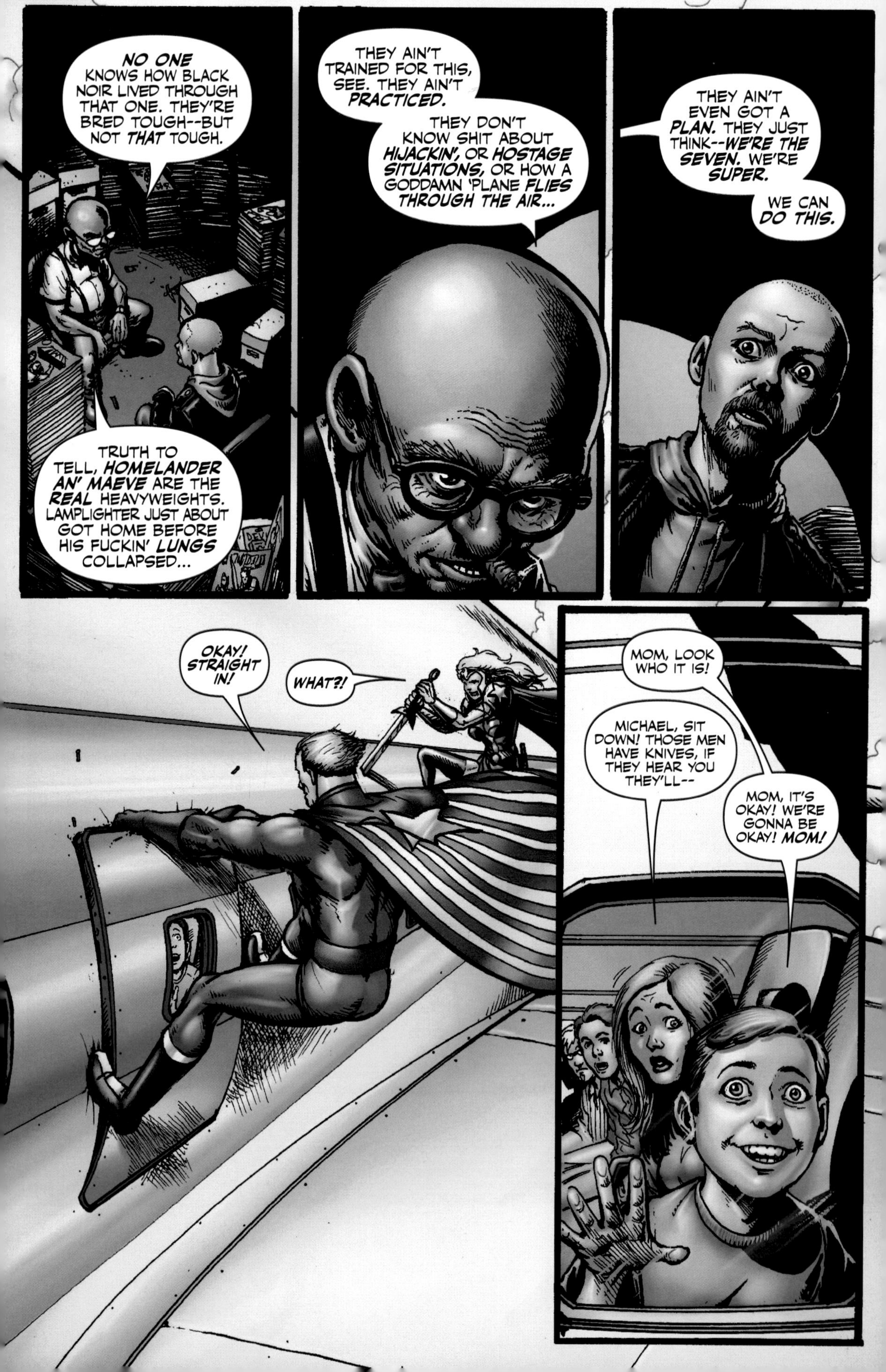
NO ONE KNOWS HOW BLACK NOIR LIVED THROUGH THAT ONE. THEY'RE BRED TOUGH--BUT NOT THAT TOUGH.
TRUTH TO TELL, HOMELANDER AN' MAEVE ARE THE REAL HEAVYWEIGHTS. LAMPLIGHTER JUST ABOUT GOT HOME BEFORE HIS FUCKIN' LUNGS COLLAPSED...
THEY AIN'T TRAINED FOR THIS, SEE. THEY AIN'T PRACTICED.
THEY DON'T KNOW SHIT ABOUT HIJACKIN', OR HOSTAGE SITUATIONS, OR HOW A GODDAMN 'PLANE FLIES THROUGH THE AIR...
THEY AIN'T EVEN GOT A PLAN. THEY JUST THINK--WE'RE THE SEVEN. WE'RE SUPER.
WE CAN DO THIS.
OKAY! STRAIGHT IN!
WHAT?!
MOM, LOOK WHO IT IS!
MICHAEL, SIT DOWN! THOSE MEN HAVE KNIVES, IF THEY HEAR YOU THEY'LL--
MOM, IT'S OKAY! WE'RE GONNA BE OKAY! MOM!

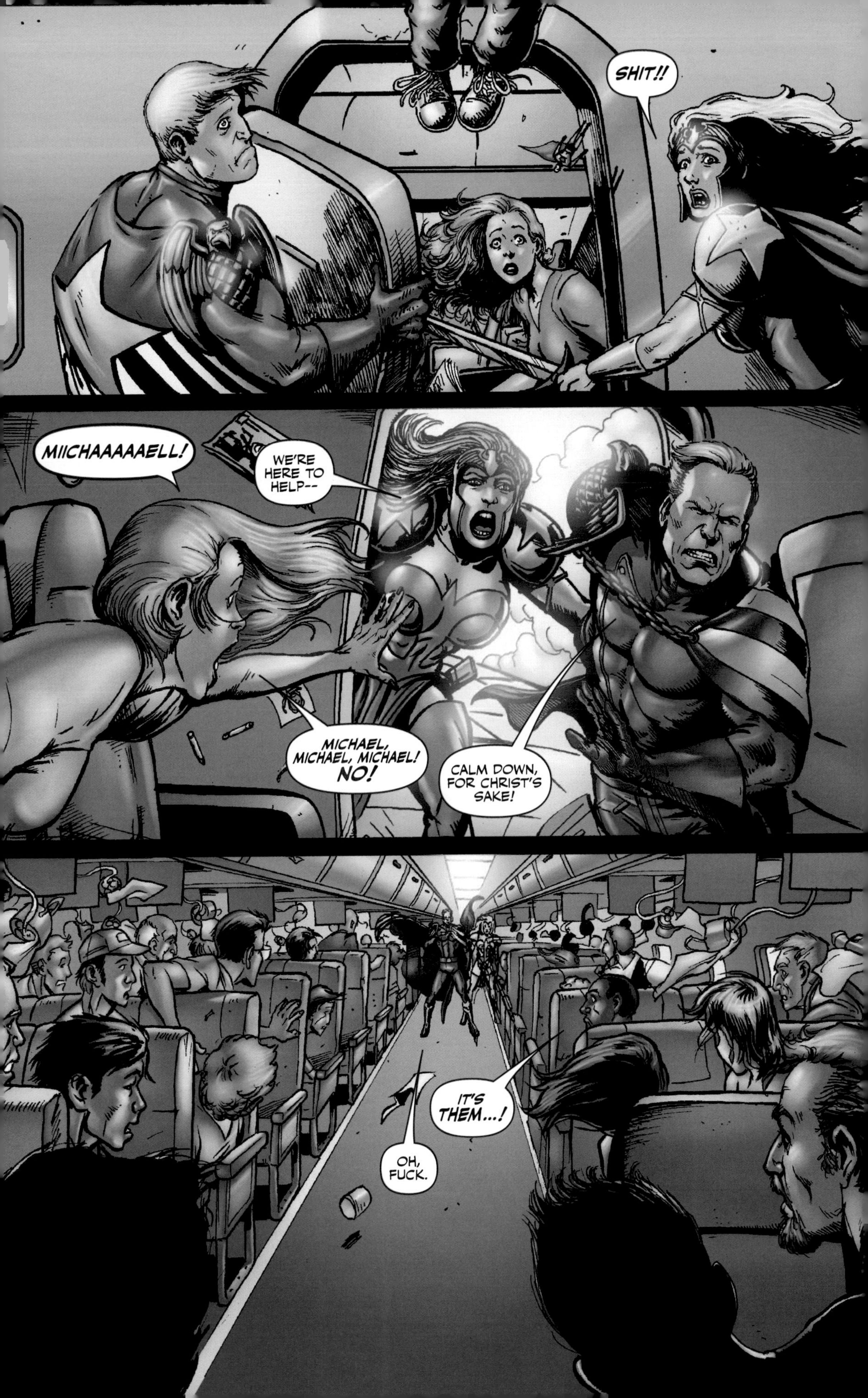
SHIT!!
MIICHAAAAAELL!
WE'RE HERE TO HELP--
MICHAEL, MICHAEL, MICHAEL! NO!
CALM DOWN, FOR CHRIST'S SAKE!
IT'S THEM...!
OH, FUCK.

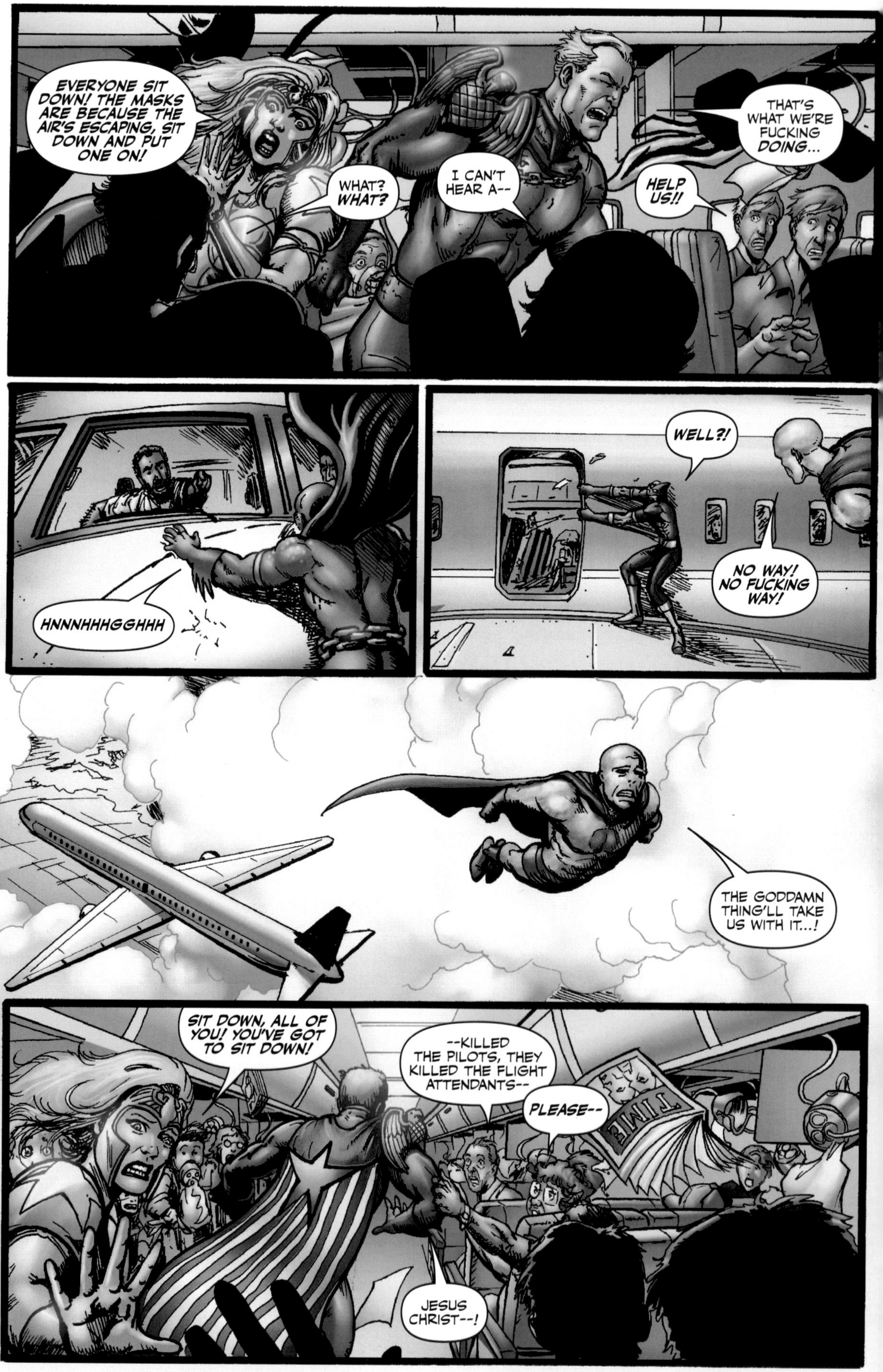
EVERYONE SIT DOWN! THE MASKS ARE BECAUSE THE AIR'S ESCAPING, SIT DOWN AND PUT ONE ON!
WHAT? WHAT?
I CAN'T HEAR A--
HELP US!!
THAT'S WHAT WE'RE FUCKING DOING...
HNNNHHHGGHHH
WELL?!
NO WAY! NO FUCKING WAY!
THE GODDAMN THING'LL TAKE US WITH IT...!
SIT DOWN, ALL OF YOU! YOU'VE GOT TO SIT DOWN!
--KILLED THE PILOTS, THEY KILLED THE FLIGHT ATTENDANTS--
PLEASE--
JESUS CHRIST--!

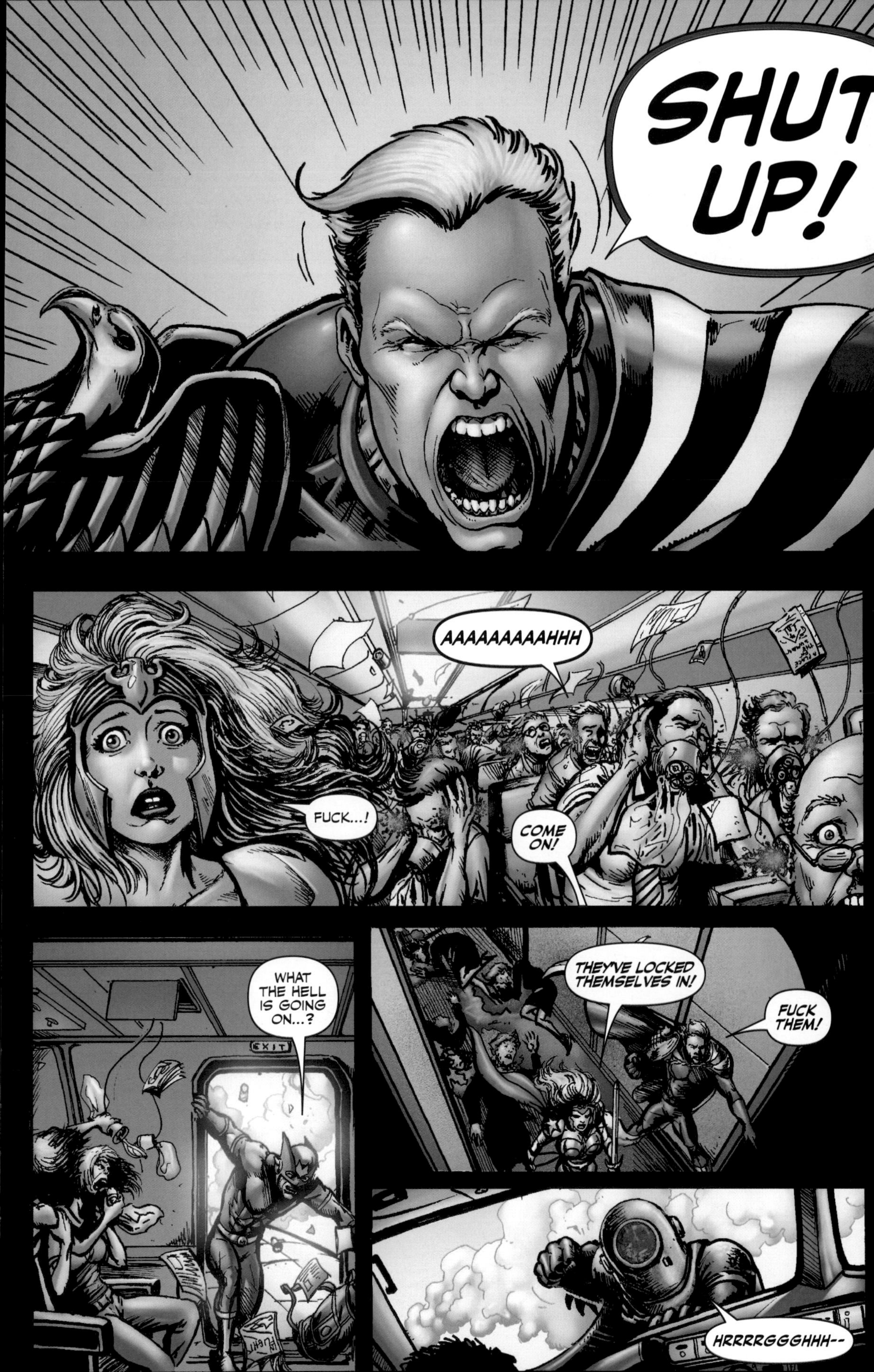
SHUT UP!
AAAAAAAAAHHH
FUCK...!
COME ON!
WHAT THE HELL IS GOING ON...?
THEY'VE LOCKED THEMSELVES IN!
FUCK THEM!
HRRRRGGGHHH--

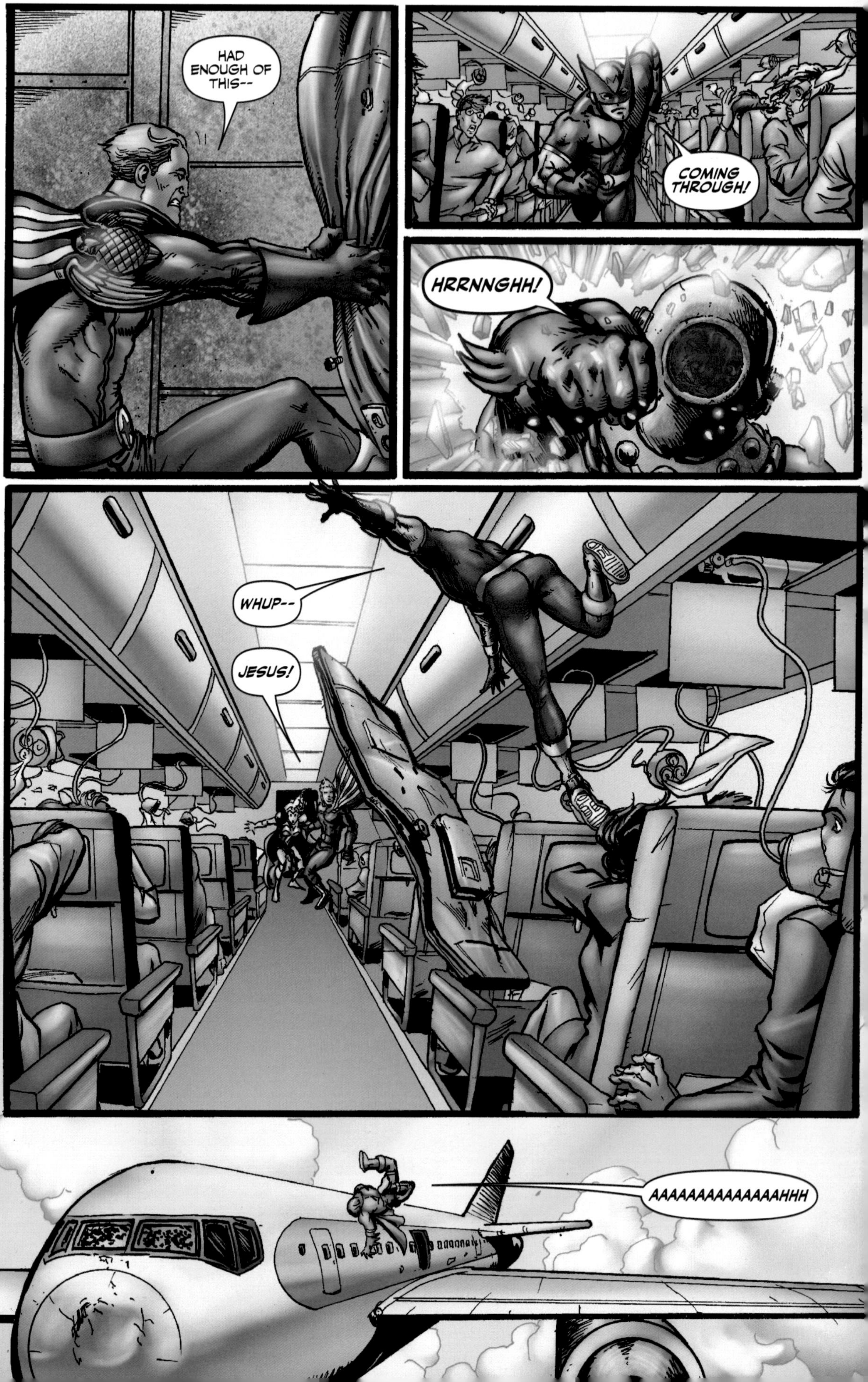
HAD ENOUGH OF THIS--
COMING THROUGH!
HRRNNGHH!
WHUP--
JESUS!
AAAAAAAAAAAAAAHHH

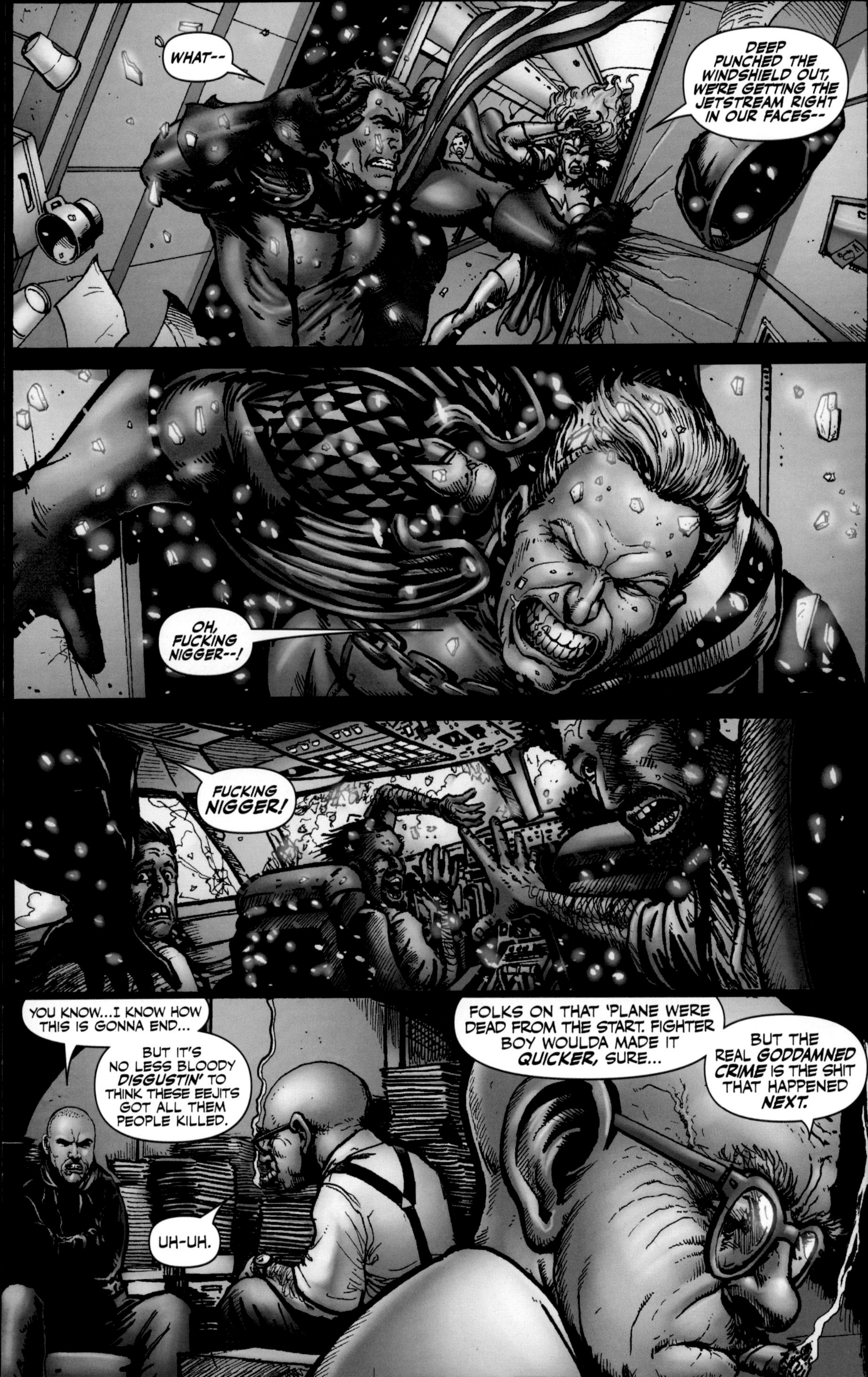
WHAT--
DEEP PUNCHED THE WINDSHIELD OUT, WE'RE GETTING THE JETSTREAM RIGHT IN OUR FACES--
OH, FUCKING NIGGER--!
FUCKING NIGGER!
YOU KNOW...I KNOW HOW THIS IS GONNA END...
BUT IT'S NO LESS BLOODY DISGUSTIN' TO THINK THESE EEJITS GOT ALL THEM PEOPLE KILLED.
UH-UH.
FOLKS ON THAT 'PLANE WERE DEAD FROM THE START. FIGHTER BOY WOULDA MADE IT QUICKER, SURE...
BUT THE REAL GODDAMNED CRIME IS THE SHIT THAT HAPPENED NEXT.

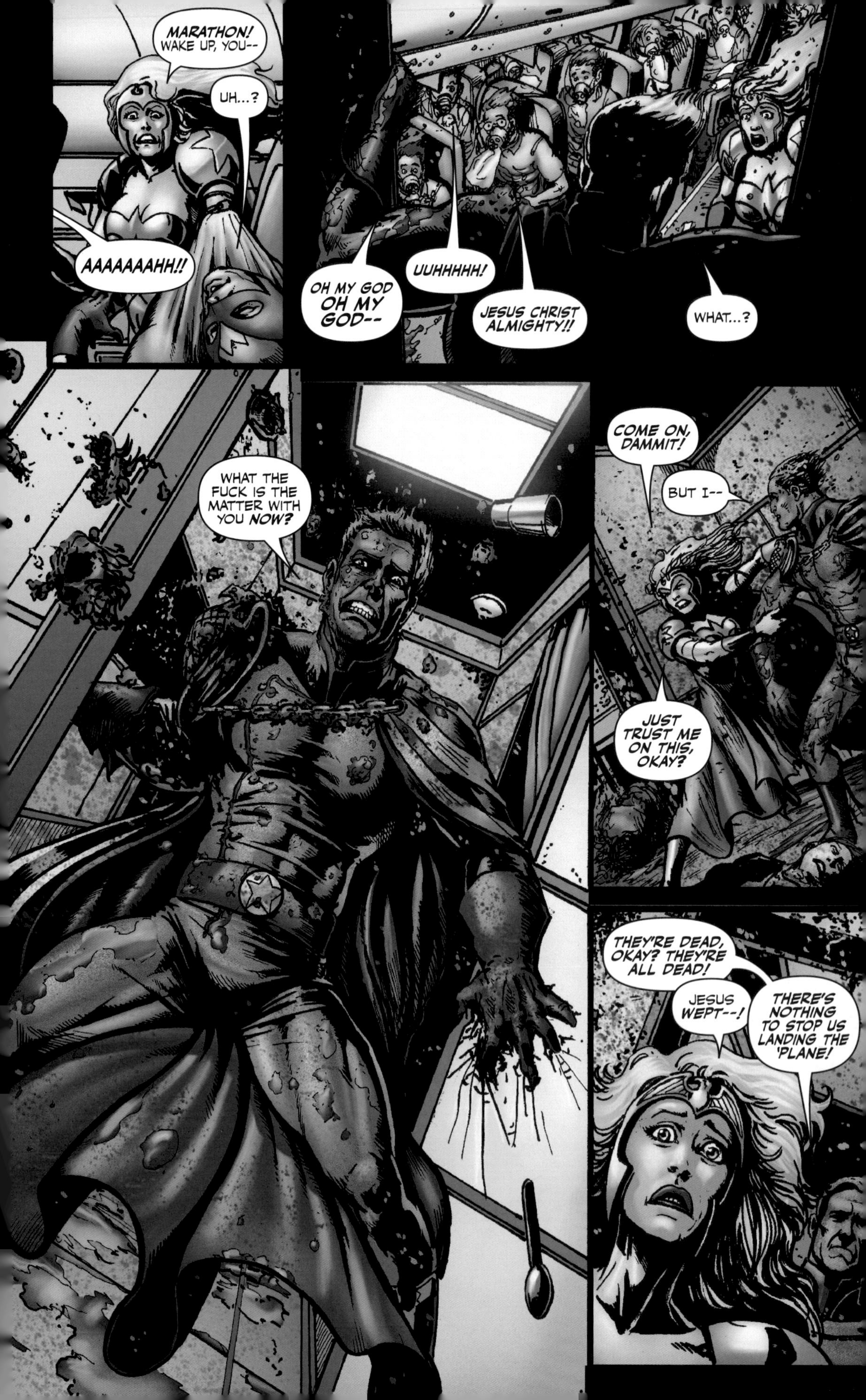
MARATHON! WAKE UP, YOU--
UH...?
AAAAAAAHH!!
OH MY GOD OH MY GOD--
UUHHHHH!
JESUS CHRIST ALMIGHTY!!
WHAT...?
WHAT THE FUCK IS THE MATTER WITH YOU NOW?
COME ON, DAMMIT!
BUT I--
JUST TRUST ME ON THIS, OKAY?
THEY'RE DEAD, OKAY? THEY'RE ALL DEAD!
JESUS WEPT--!
THERE'S NOTHING TO STOP US LANDING THE 'PLANE!

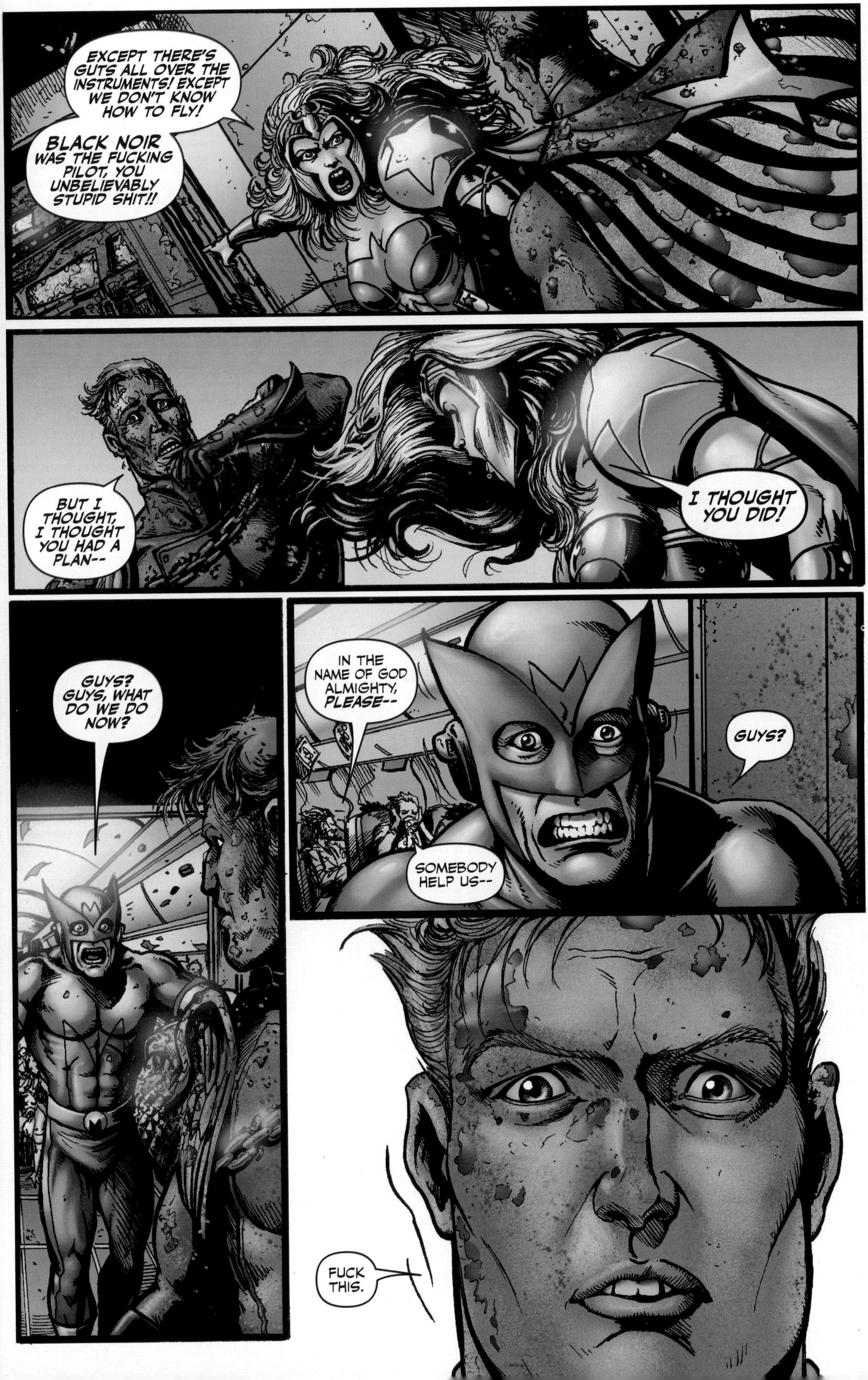
EXCEPT THERE'S GUTS ALL OVER THE INSTRUMENTS! EXCEPT WE DON'T KNOW HOW TO FLY!
BLACK NOIR WAS THE FUCKING PILOT, YOU UNBELIEVABLY STUPID SHIT!!
BUT I THOUGHT, I THOUGHT YOU HAD A PLAN--
I THOUGHT YOU DID!
GUYS? GUYS, WHAT DO WE DO NOW?
IN THE NAME OF GOD ALMIGHTY, PLEASE--
GUYS?
SOMEBODY HELP US--
FUCK THIS.

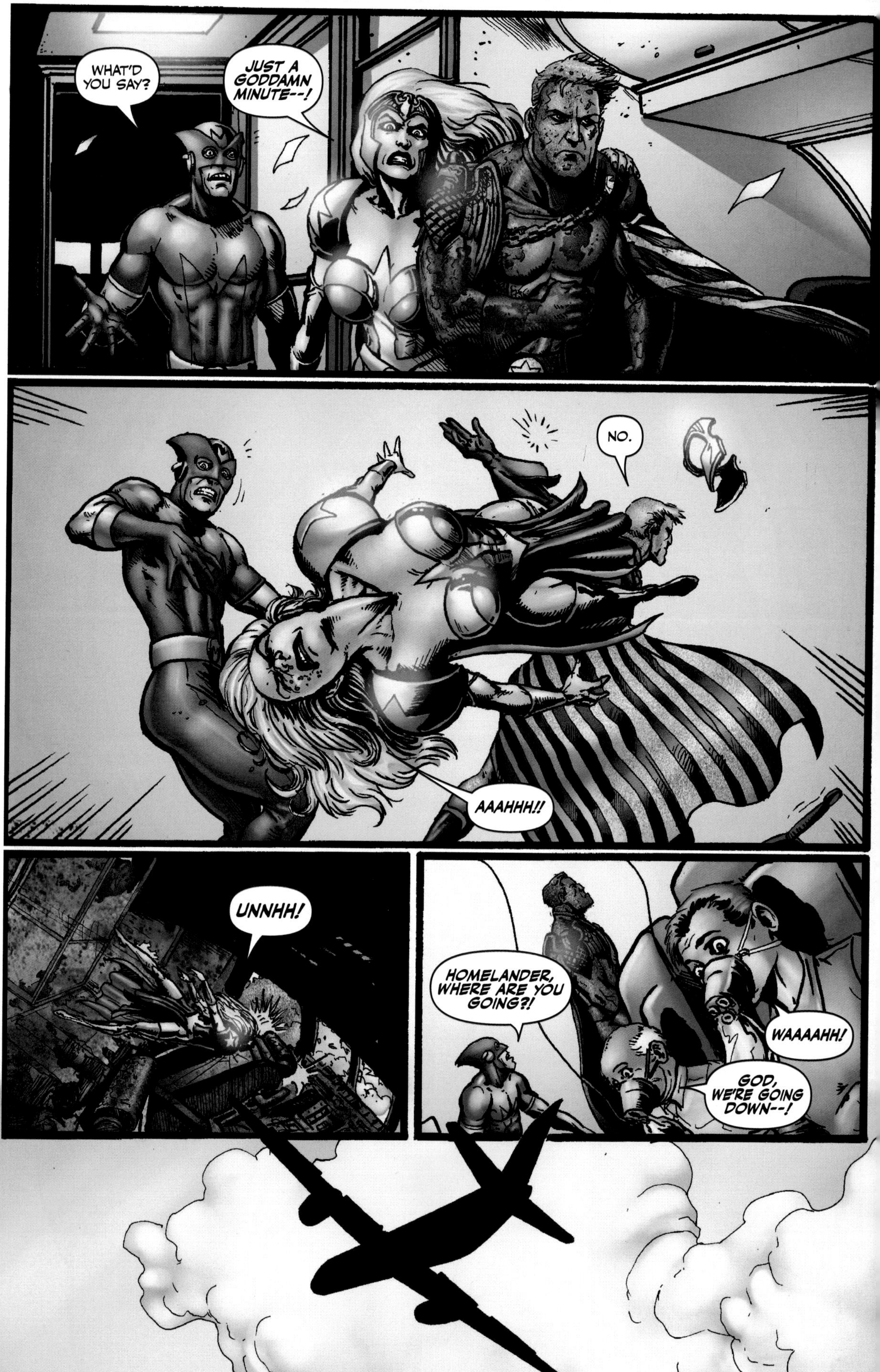
WHAT'D YOU SAY?
JUST A GODDAMN MINUTE--!
NO.
AAAHHH!!
UNNHH!
HOMELANDER, WHERE ARE YOU GOING?!
WAAAAHH!
GOD, WE'RE GOING DOWN--!

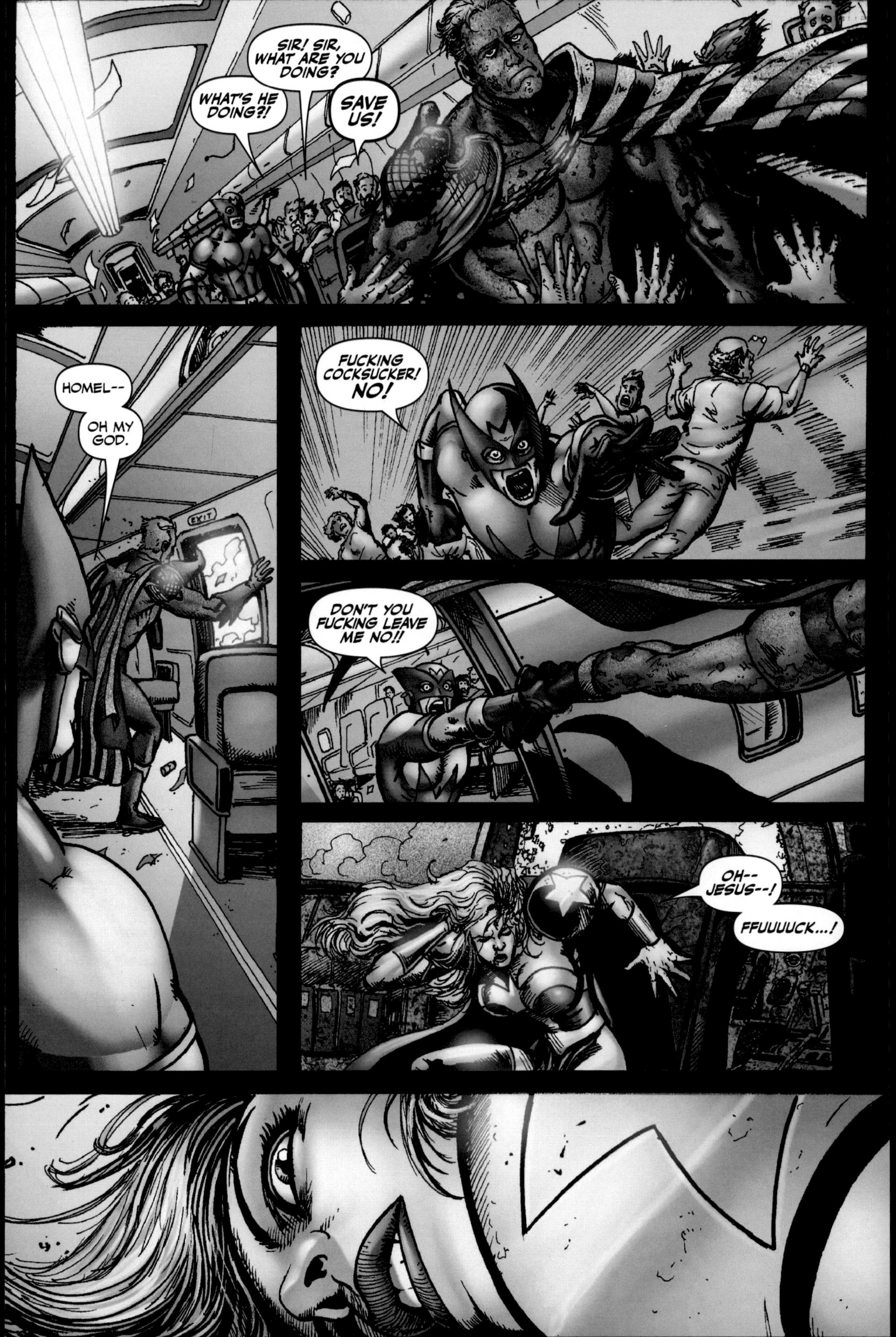

SIR! SIR, WHAT ARE YOU DOING?
WHAT'S HE DOING?!
SAVE US!
HOMEL--
OH MY GOD.
EXIT
FUCKING COCKSUCKER! NO!
DON'T YOU FUCKING LEAVE ME NO!!
OH-- JESUS--!
FFUUUUCK...!

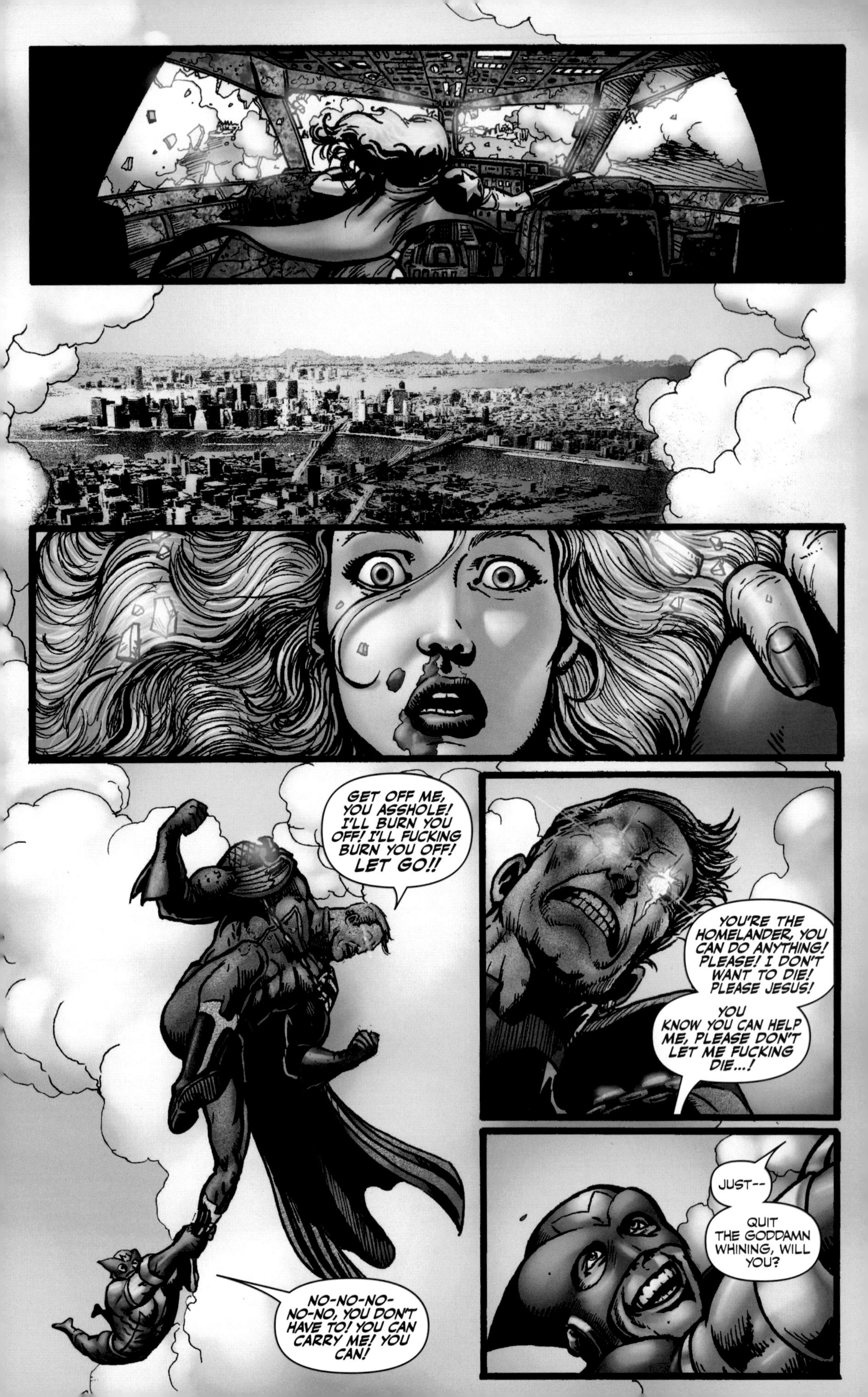
GET OFF ME, YOU ASSHOLE! I'LL BURN YOU OFF! I'LL FUCKING BURN YOU OFF! LET GO!!
NO-NO-NO-NO-NO, YOU DON'T HAVE TO! YOU CAN CARRY ME! YOU CAN!
YOU'RE THE HOMELANDER, YOU CAN DO ANYTHING! PLEASE! I DON'T WANT TO DIE! PLEASE JESUS!
YOU KNOW YOU CAN HELP ME, PLEASE DON'T LET ME FUCKING DIE...!
JUST--
QUIT THE GODDAMN WHINING, WILL YOU?

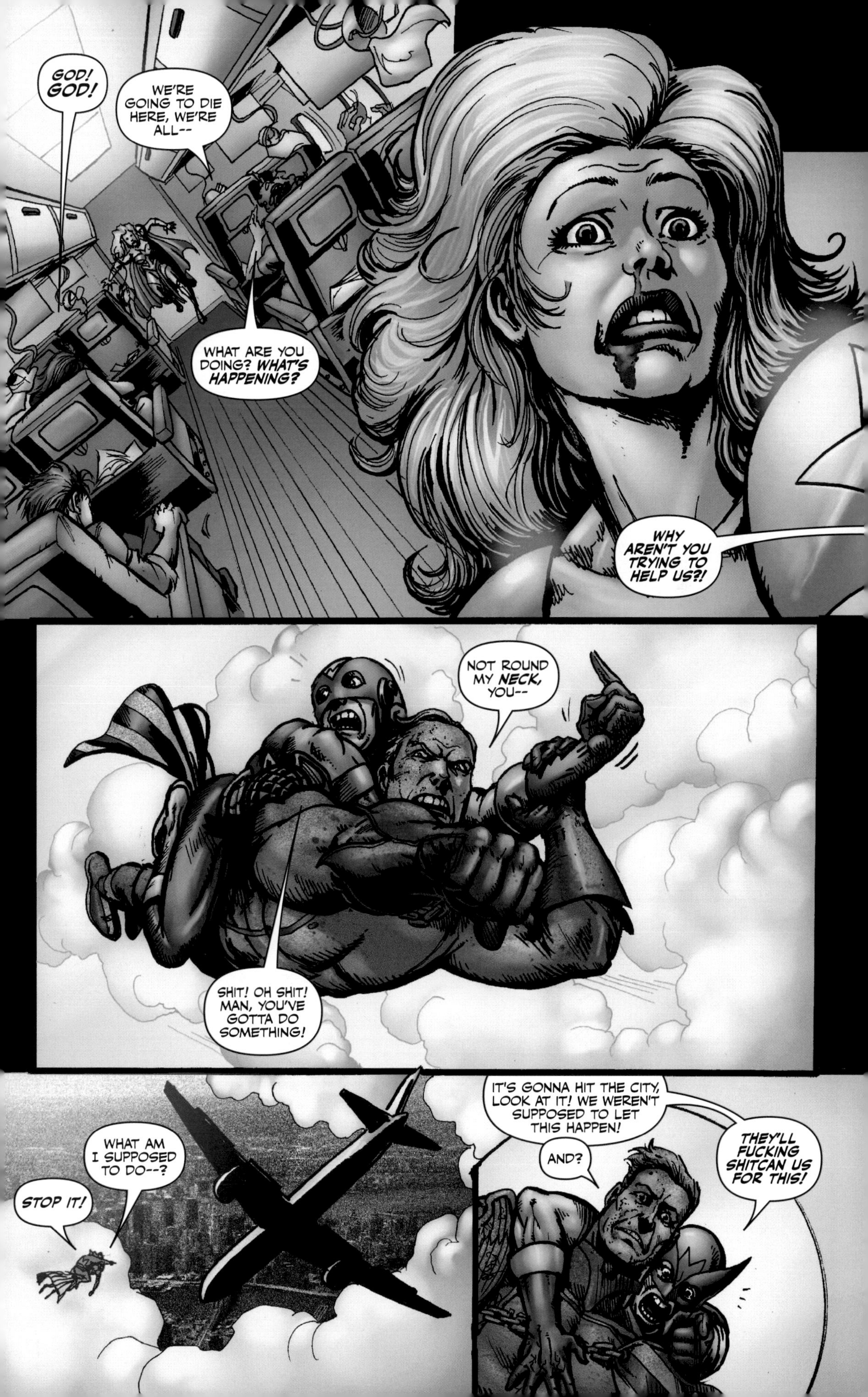
GOD! GOD!
WE'RE GOING TO DIE HERE, WE'RE ALL--
WHAT ARE YOU DOING? WHAT'S HAPPENING?
WHY AREN'T YOU TRYING TO HELP US?!
NOT ROUND MY NECK, YOU--
SHIT! OH SHIT! MAN, YOU'VE GOTTA DO SOMETHING!
WHAT AM I SUPPOSED TO DO--?
STOP IT!
IT'S GONNA HIT THE CITY, LOOK AT IT! WE WEREN'T SUPPOSED TO LET THIS HAPPEN!
AND?
THEY'LL FUCKING SHITCAN US FOR THIS!

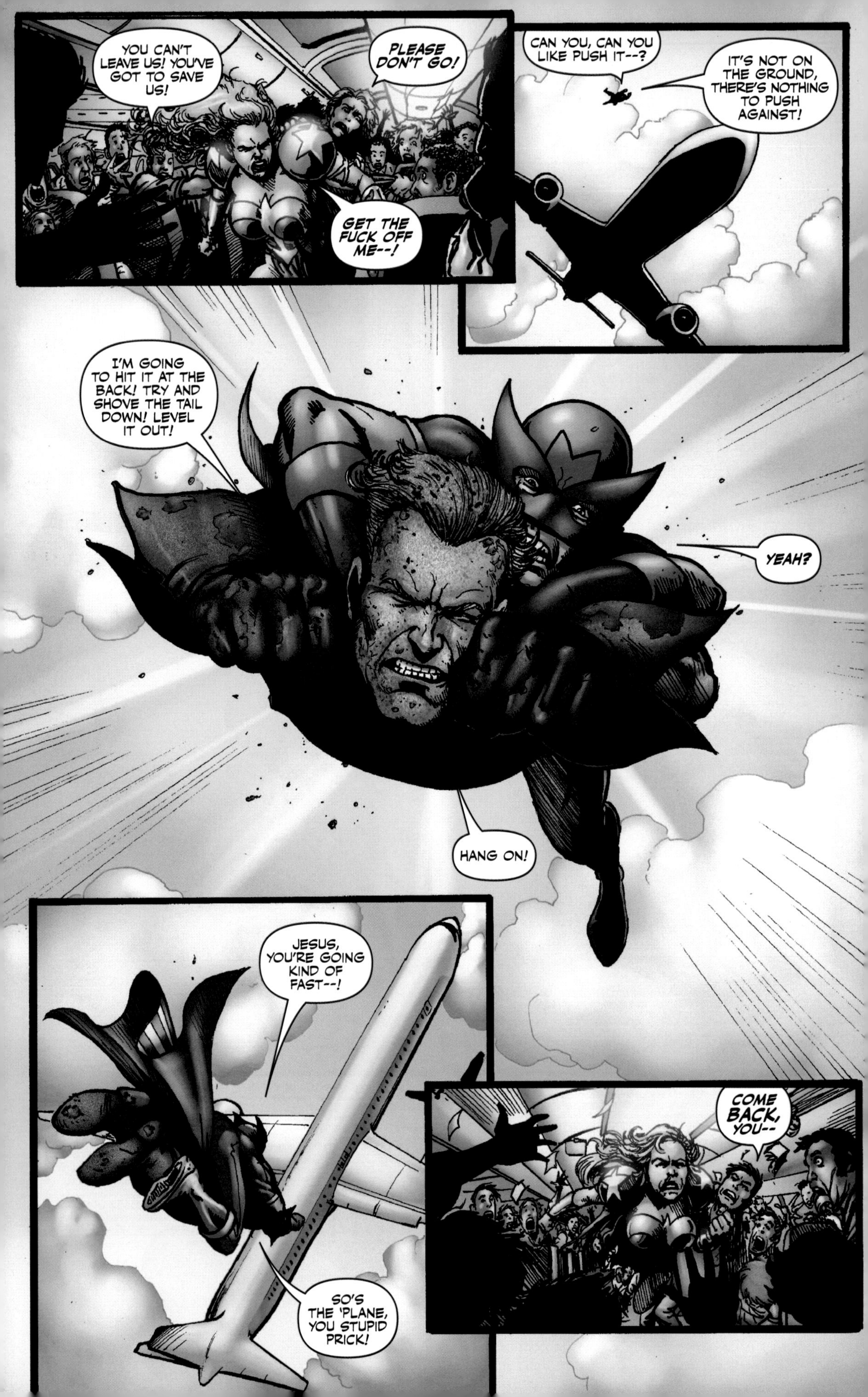
YOU CAN'T LEAVE US! YOU'VE GOT TO SAVE US!
PLEASE DON'T GO!
GET THE FUCK OFF ME--!
CAN YOU, CAN YOU LIKE PUSH IT--?
IT'S NOT ON THE GROUND, THERE'S NOTHING TO PUSH AGAINST!
I'M GOING TO HIT IT AT THE BACK! TRY AND SHOVE THE TAIL DOWN! LEVEL IT OUT!
YEAH?
HANG ON!
JESUS, YOU'RE GOING KIND OF FAST--!
SO'S THE 'PLANE, YOU STUPID PRICK!
COME BACK, YOU--

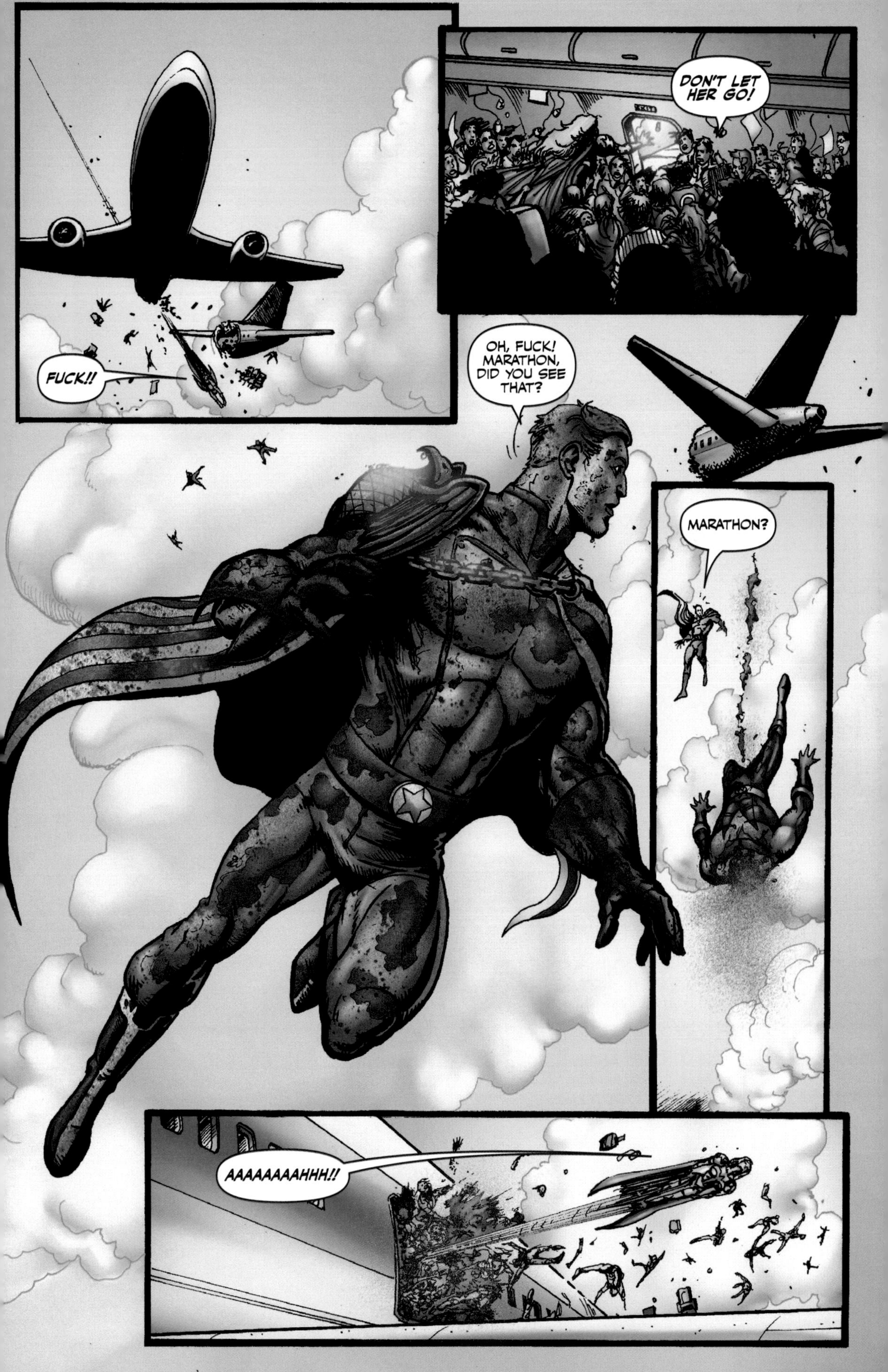
FUCK!!
DON'T LET HER GO!
OH, FUCK! MARATHON, DID YOU SEE THAT?
MARATHON?
AAAAAAAAHHH!!

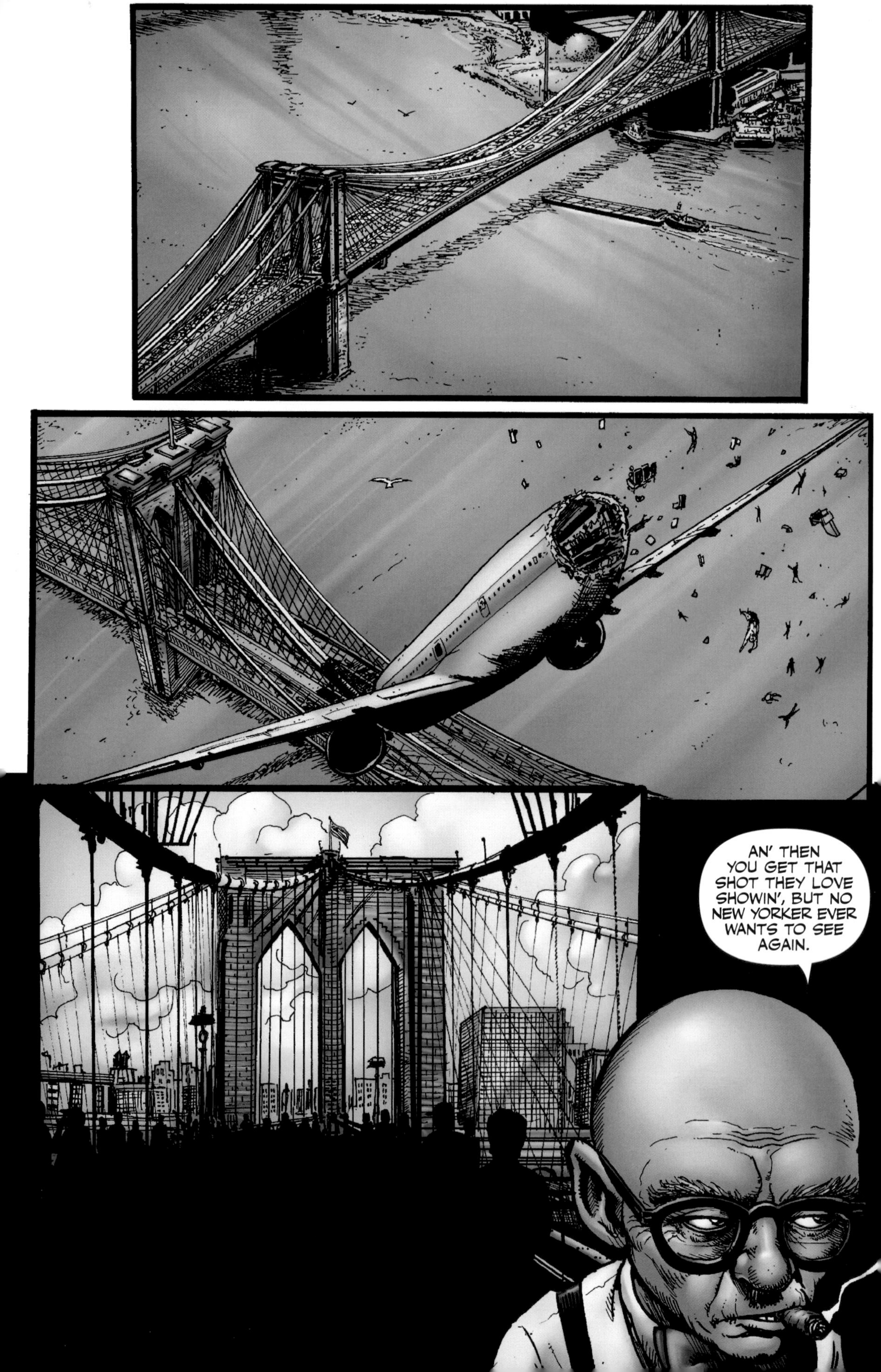
AN' THEN YOU GET THAT SHOT THEY LOVE SHOWIN', BUT NO NEW YORKER EVER WANTS TO SEE AGAIN.

I REMEMBER SEEIN' IT.

I WAS THOUSANDS O' MILES AWAY. I'D NO' EVEN BEEN TO NEW YORK AT THAT STAGE.

BUT I REMEMBER THINKIN'--NOTHIN'S GONNA BE ANY *GOOD* ANYMORE.

IT WASN'T JUST ALL THE PEOPLE GETTIN' KILLED, THOUGH THAT WAS AWFUL. IT WASN'T EVEN WHAT WAS COMIN' NEXT--I MEAN YOU KNEW THEY WERE GONNA USE IT AS AN EXCUSE FOR THE SHITE THEY'D BEEN WANTIN' TO DO FOR AGES, THE FUCKIN' PATRIOT ACT AN' PAKISTAN AN' ALL.

IT WAS JUST THE THOUGHT...THAT THERE WAS STUFF LIKE THIS LOOSE IN THE WORLD.

THEY SURE DIDN'T WASTE ANY TIME.

DAKOTA BOB WENT ON T.V. RIGHT AWAY, ADMITTED ORDERIN' THE 'PLANES SHOT DOWN. HE PLAYED IT JUST RIGHT, IT FIT WELL WITH HIS IMAGE. NO ONE WAS ABOUT TO BLAME HIM.

HELL, HE DID *GREAT.* HE'D LISTENED TO THE SPOOKS WHEN THEY TOLD HIM IT WAS COMIN', HAD FIGHTERS PATROLLIN' COMMERCIAL AIRSPACE ALL SUMMER LONG.

PEOPLE LOVE HIM. HIS *BACKERS* LOVE HIM. HE TAKES US STRAIGHT INTO PAKISTAN, SO *DEFENSE* GETS THE BIG BUCKS AN' *FUCK* SOCIAL SPENDING...

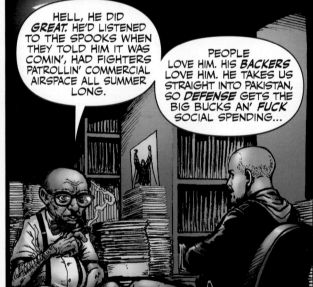

BUT HE SAID THE AIR FORCE SHOT 'EM *ALL* DOWN, NOT JUST THE FIRST ONE AN' THE ONE THEY THINK WAS GOIN' FOR *D.C.*. HE'S COVERIN' UP--AN' NOT JUST THE GODDAMN *SEVEN*...

NO WAY IN *SHIT* DOES *BOB* CALL OFF THE FIGHTERS FOR *VOUGHT-AMERICAN'S SUPES.* THE MAN WHO WOULD IS *VIC THE VEEP*-- BUT *HE* AIN'T SUPPOSED TO BE IN CHARGE...!

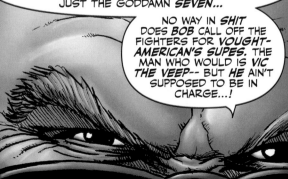

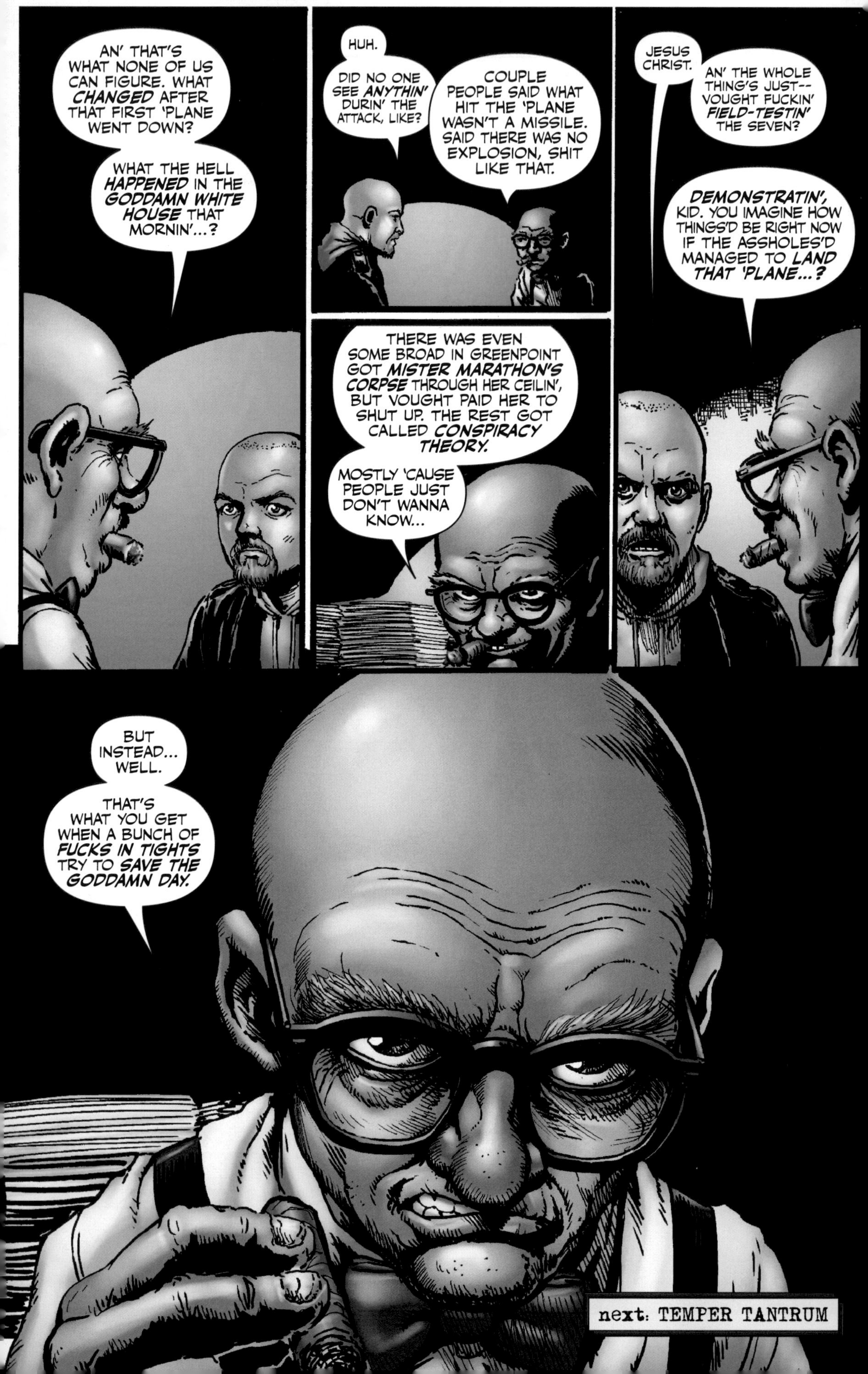
AN' THAT'S WHAT NONE OF US CAN FIGURE. WHAT *CHANGED* AFTER THAT FIRST 'PLANE WENT DOWN?
WHAT THE HELL *HAPPENED* IN THE *GODDAMN WHITE HOUSE* THAT MORNIN'...?
HUH.
DID NO ONE SEE *ANYTHIN'* DURIN' THE ATTACK, LIKE?
COUPLE PEOPLE SAID WHAT HIT THE 'PLANE WASN'T A MISSILE. SAID THERE WAS NO EXPLOSION, SHIT LIKE THAT.
THERE WAS EVEN SOME BROAD IN GREENPOINT GOT *MISTER MARATHON'S CORPSE* THROUGH HER CEILIN', BUT VOUGHT PAID HER TO SHUT UP. THE REST GOT CALLED *CONSPIRACY THEORY.*
MOSTLY 'CAUSE PEOPLE JUST DON'T WANNA KNOW...
JESUS CHRIST.
AN' THE WHOLE THING'S JUST-- VOUGHT FUCKIN' *FIELD-TESTIN'* THE SEVEN?
DEMONSTRATIN', KID. YOU IMAGINE HOW THINGS'D BE RIGHT NOW IF THE ASSHOLES'D MANAGED TO *LAND THAT 'PLANE...?*
BUT INSTEAD... WELL.
THAT'S WHAT YOU GET WHEN A BUNCH OF *FUCKS IN TIGHTS* TRY TO *SAVE THE GODDAMN DAY.*
next: TEMPER TANTRUM

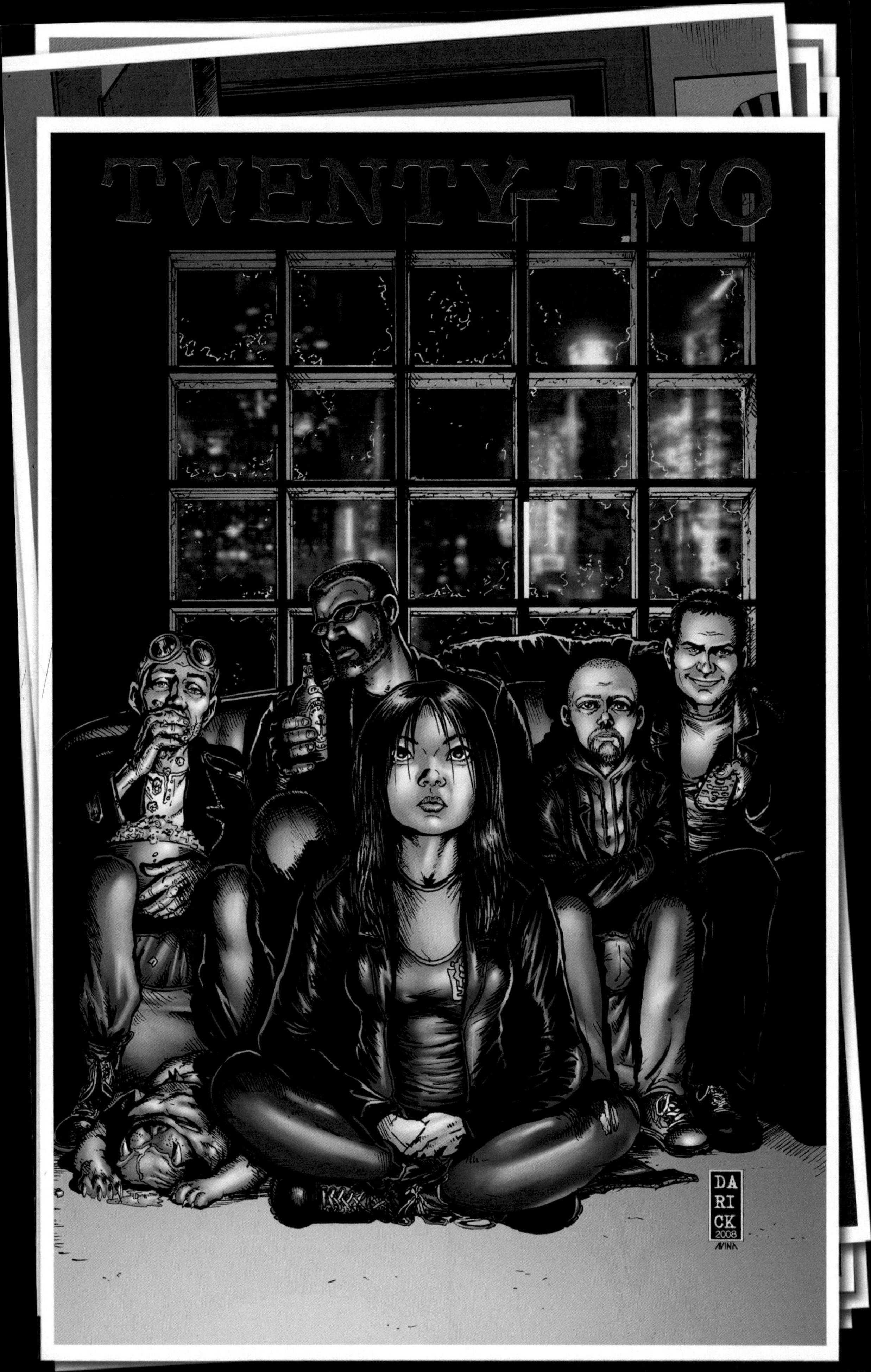
TWENTY-TWO
DA
RI
CK
2008
AVINA

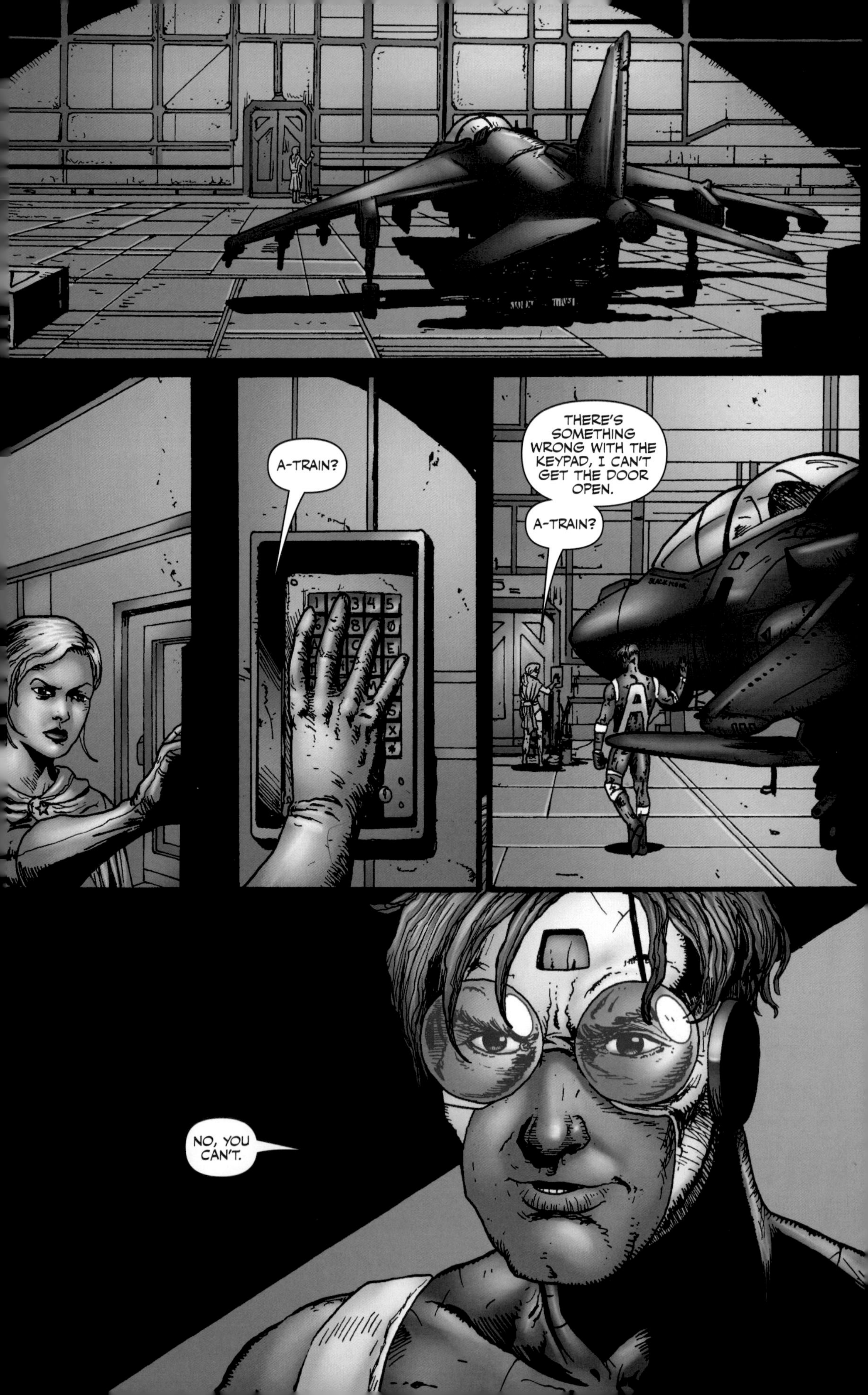
A-TRAIN?
THERE'S SOMETHING WRONG WITH THE KEYPAD, I CAN'T GET THE DOOR OPEN.
A-TRAIN?
NO, YOU CAN'T.

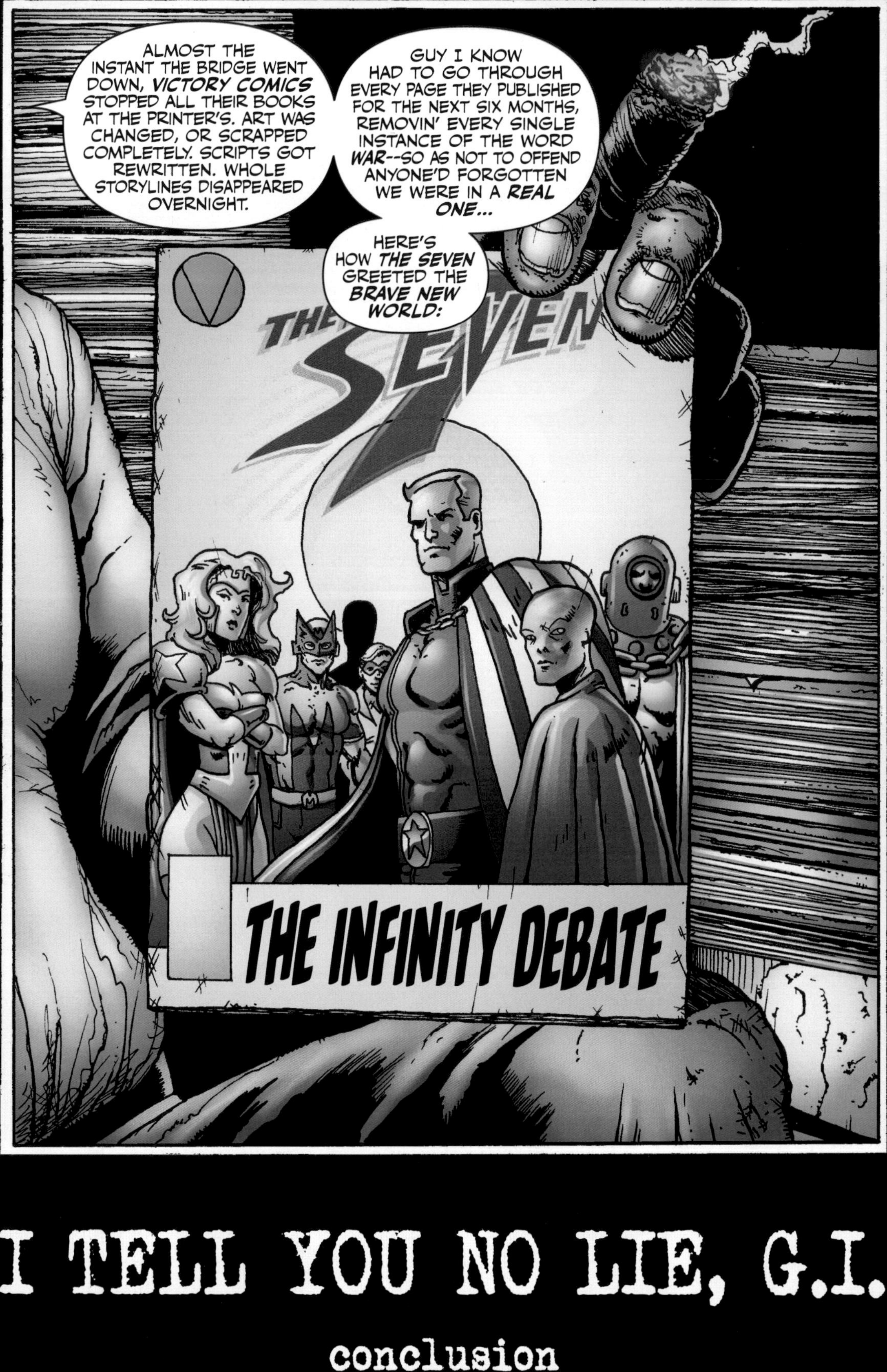
ALMOST THE INSTANT THE BRIDGE WENT DOWN, VICTORY COMICS STOPPED ALL THEIR BOOKS AT THE PRINTER'S. ART WAS CHANGED, OR SCRAPPED COMPLETELY. SCRIPTS GOT REWRITTEN. WHOLE STORYLINES DISAPPEARED OVERNIGHT.
GUY I KNOW HAD TO GO THROUGH EVERY PAGE THEY PUBLISHED FOR THE NEXT SIX MONTHS, REMOVIN' EVERY SINGLE INSTANCE OF THE WORD WAR--SO AS NOT TO OFFEND ANYONE'D FORGOTTEN WE WERE IN A REAL ONE...
HERE'S HOW THE SEVEN GREETED THE BRAVE NEW WORLD:
SEVEN
THE INFINITY DEBATE

I TELL YOU NO LIE, G.I.

conclusion

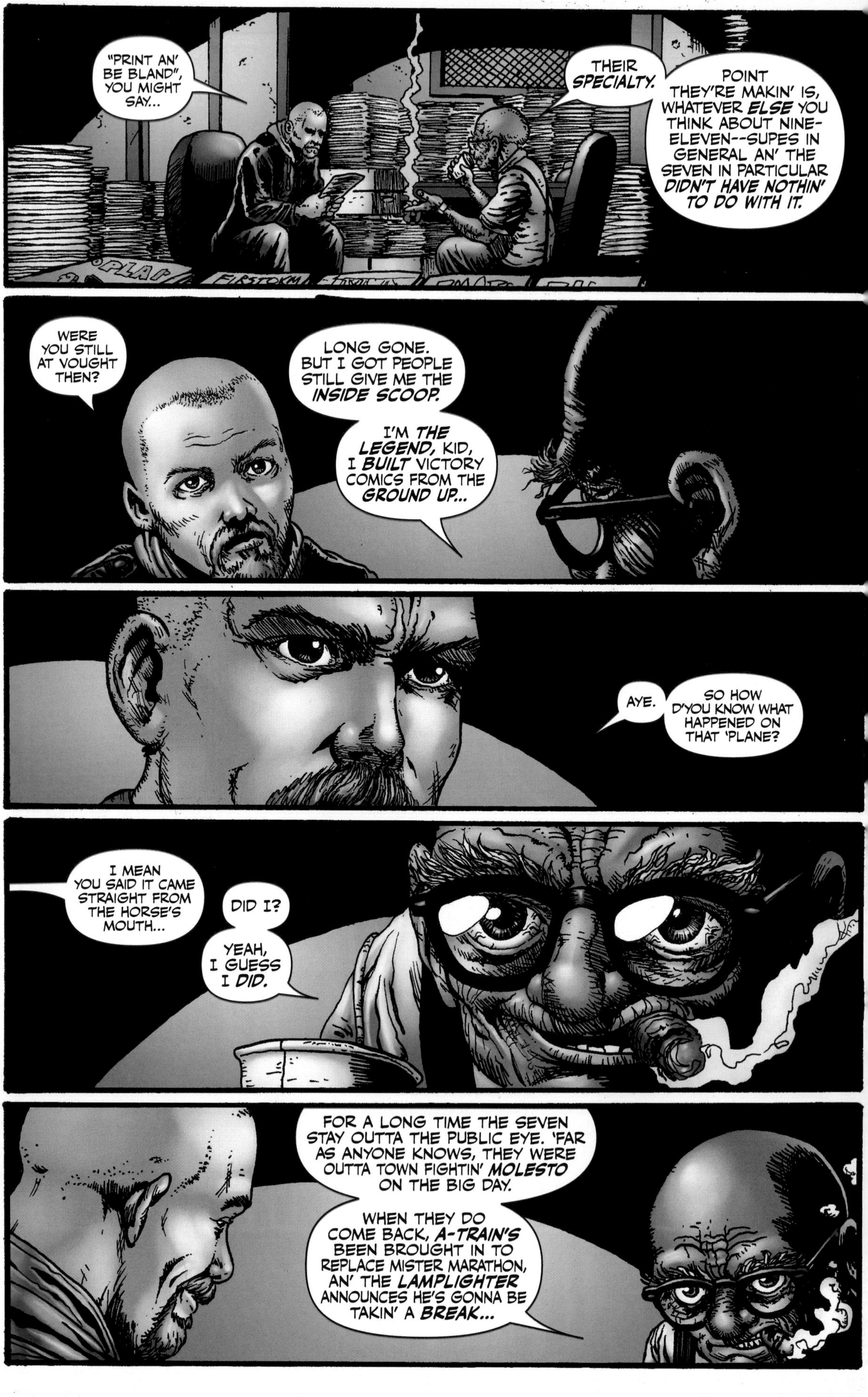
"PRINT AN' BE BLAND", YOU MIGHT SAY...
THEIR SPECIALTY.
POINT THEY'RE MAKIN' IS, WHATEVER ELSE YOU THINK ABOUT NINE-ELEVEN--SUPES IN GENERAL AN' THE SEVEN IN PARTICULAR DIDN'T HAVE NOTHIN' TO DO WITH IT.
WERE YOU STILL AT VOUGHT THEN?
LONG GONE. BUT I GOT PEOPLE STILL GIVE ME THE INSIDE SCOOP.
I'M THE LEGEND, KID, I BUILT VICTORY COMICS FROM THE GROUND UP...
AYE.
SO HOW D'YOU KNOW WHAT HAPPENED ON THAT 'PLANE?
I MEAN YOU SAID IT CAME STRAIGHT FROM THE HORSE'S MOUTH...
DID I?
YEAH, I GUESS I DID.
FOR A LONG TIME THE SEVEN STAY OUTTA THE PUBLIC EYE. 'FAR AS ANYONE KNOWS, THEY WERE OUTTA TOWN FIGHTIN' MOLESTO ON THE BIG DAY.
WHEN THEY DO COME BACK, A-TRAIN'S BEEN BROUGHT IN TO REPLACE MISTER MARATHON, AN' THE LAMPLIGHTER ANNOUNCES HE'S GONNA BE TAKIN' A BREAK...

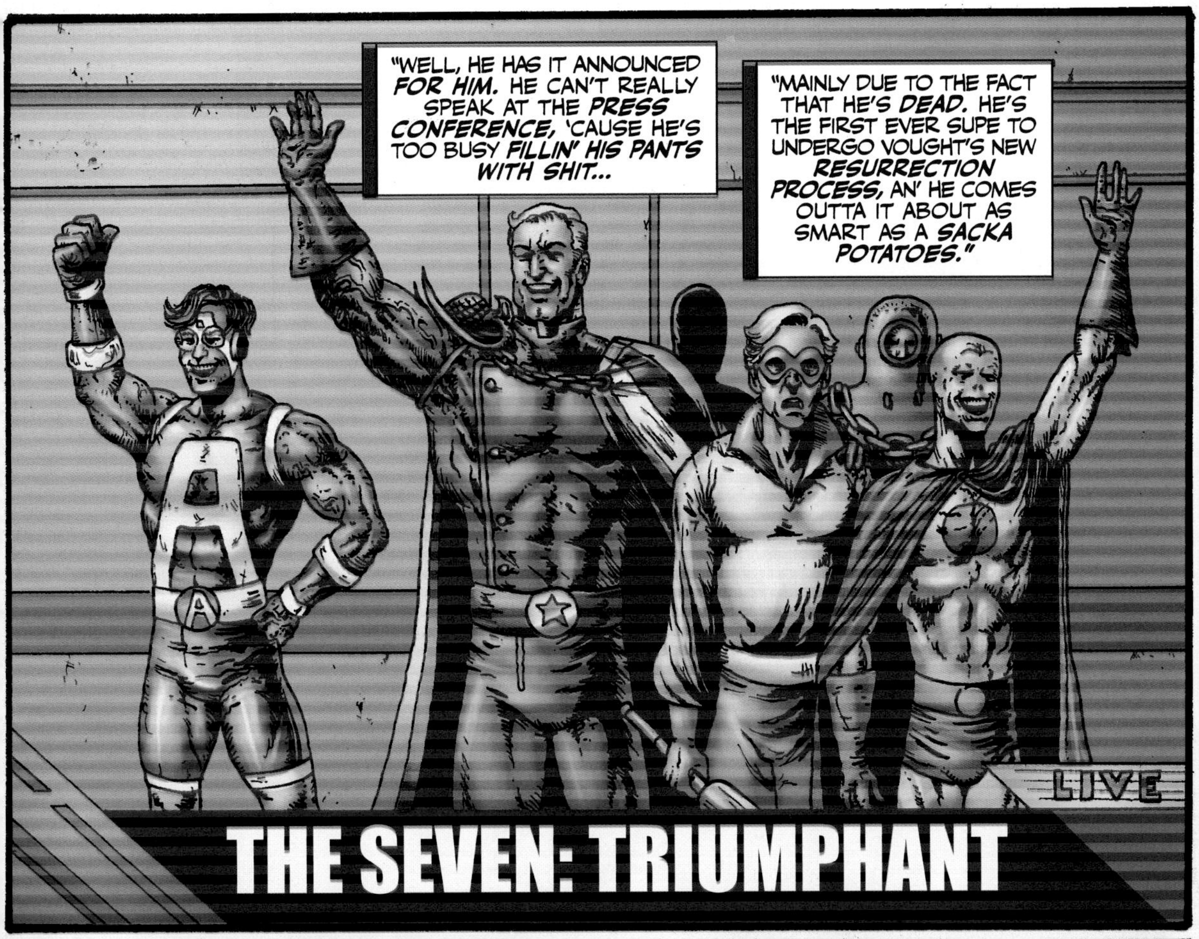
"WELL, HE HAS IT ANNOUNCED FOR HIM. HE CAN'T REALLY SPEAK AT THE PRESS CONFERENCE, 'CAUSE HE'S TOO BUSY FILLIN' HIS PANTS WITH SHIT...
"MAINLY DUE TO THE FACT THAT HE'S DEAD. HE'S THE FIRST EVER SUPE TO UNDERGO VOUGHT'S NEW RESURRECTION PROCESS, AN' HE COMES OUTTA IT ABOUT AS SMART AS A SACKA POTATOES."
LIVE
THE SEVEN: TRIUMPHANT

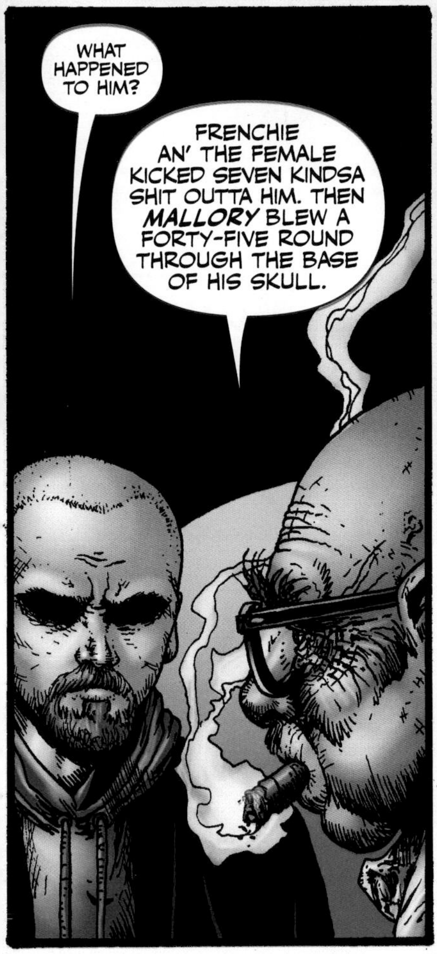
WHAT HAPPENED TO HIM?
FRENCHIE AN' THE FEMALE KICKED SEVEN KINDSA SHIT OUTTA HIM. THEN MALLORY BLEW A FORTY-FIVE ROUND THROUGH THE BASE OF HIS SKULL.

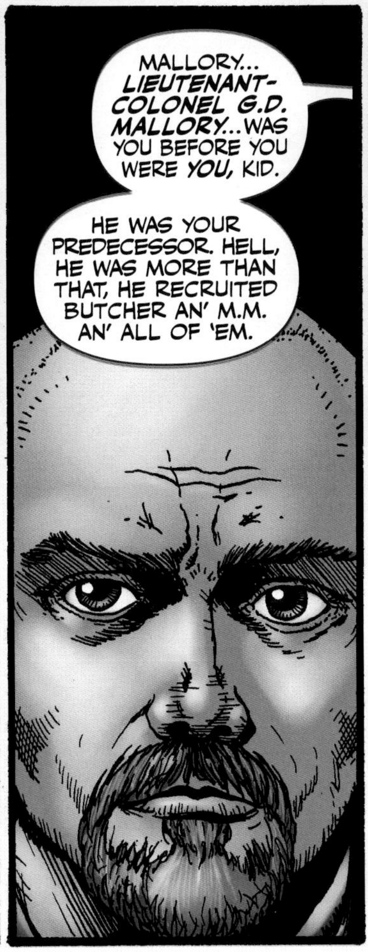
MALLORY... LIEUTENANT-COLONEL G.D. MALLORY...WAS YOU BEFORE YOU WERE YOU, KID.
HE WAS YOUR PREDECESSOR. HELL, HE WAS MORE THAN THAT, HE RECRUITED BUTCHER AN' M.M. AN' ALL OF 'EM.

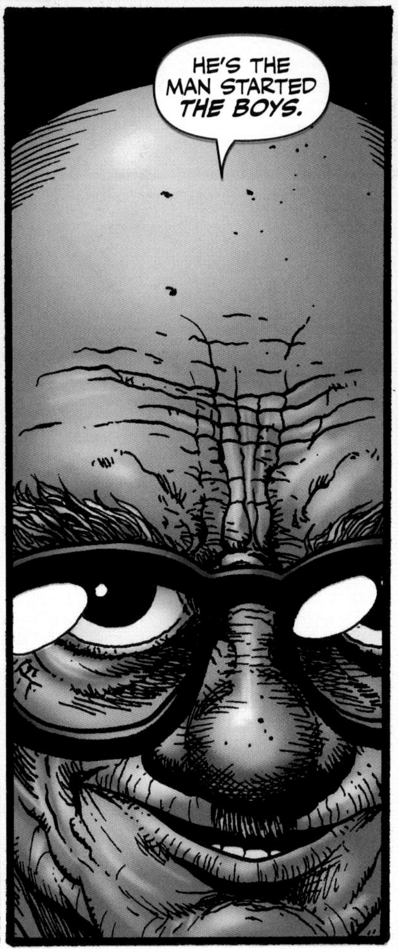
HE'S THE MAN STARTED THE BOYS.

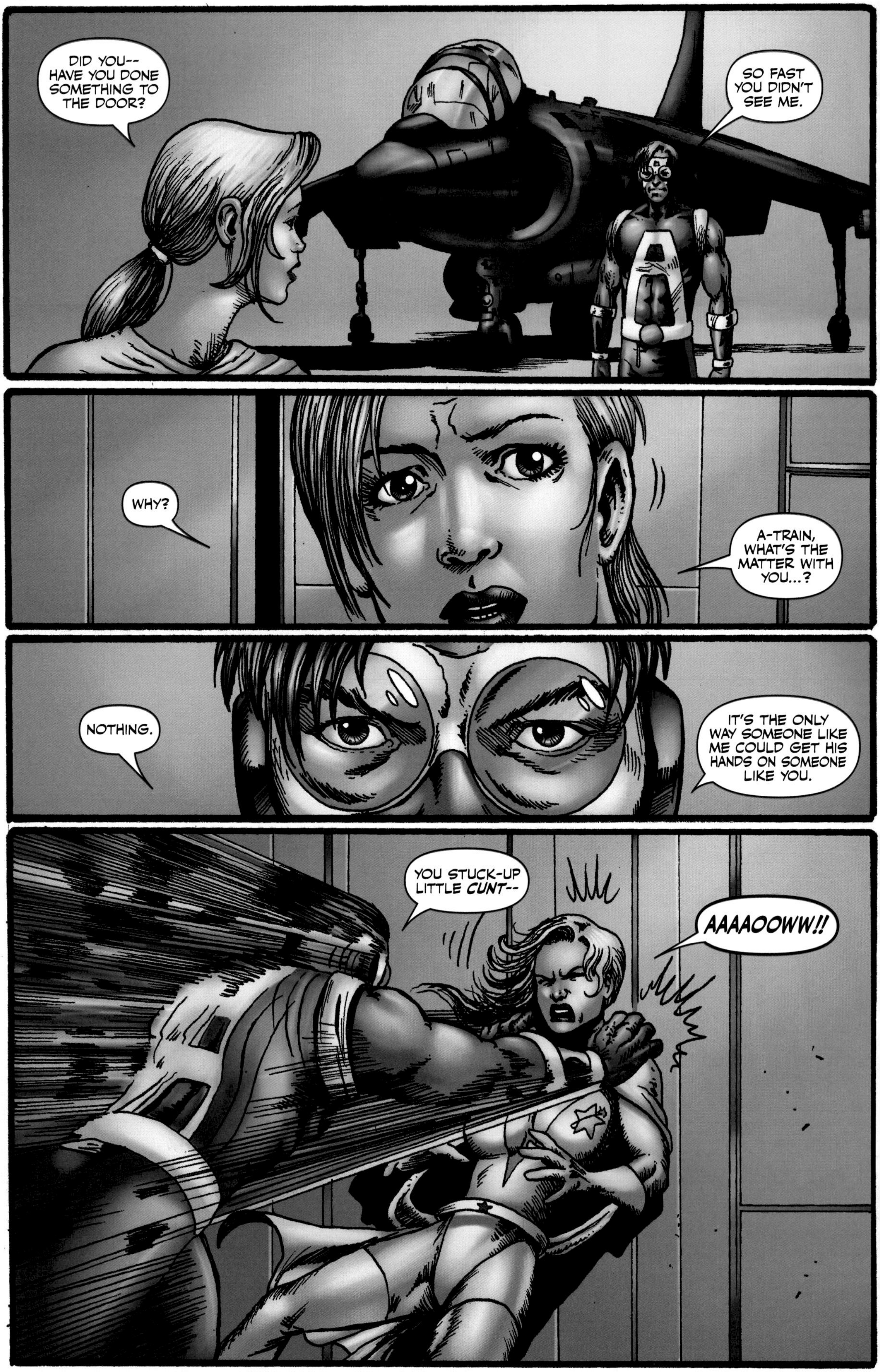
DID YOU-- HAVE YOU DONE SOMETHING TO THE DOOR?
SO FAST YOU DIDN'T SEE ME.
WHY?
A-TRAIN, WHAT'S THE MATTER WITH YOU...?
NOTHING.
IT'S THE ONLY WAY SOMEONE LIKE ME COULD GET HIS HANDS ON SOMEONE LIKE YOU.
YOU STUCK-UP LITTLE *CUNT*--
AAAAOOWW!!

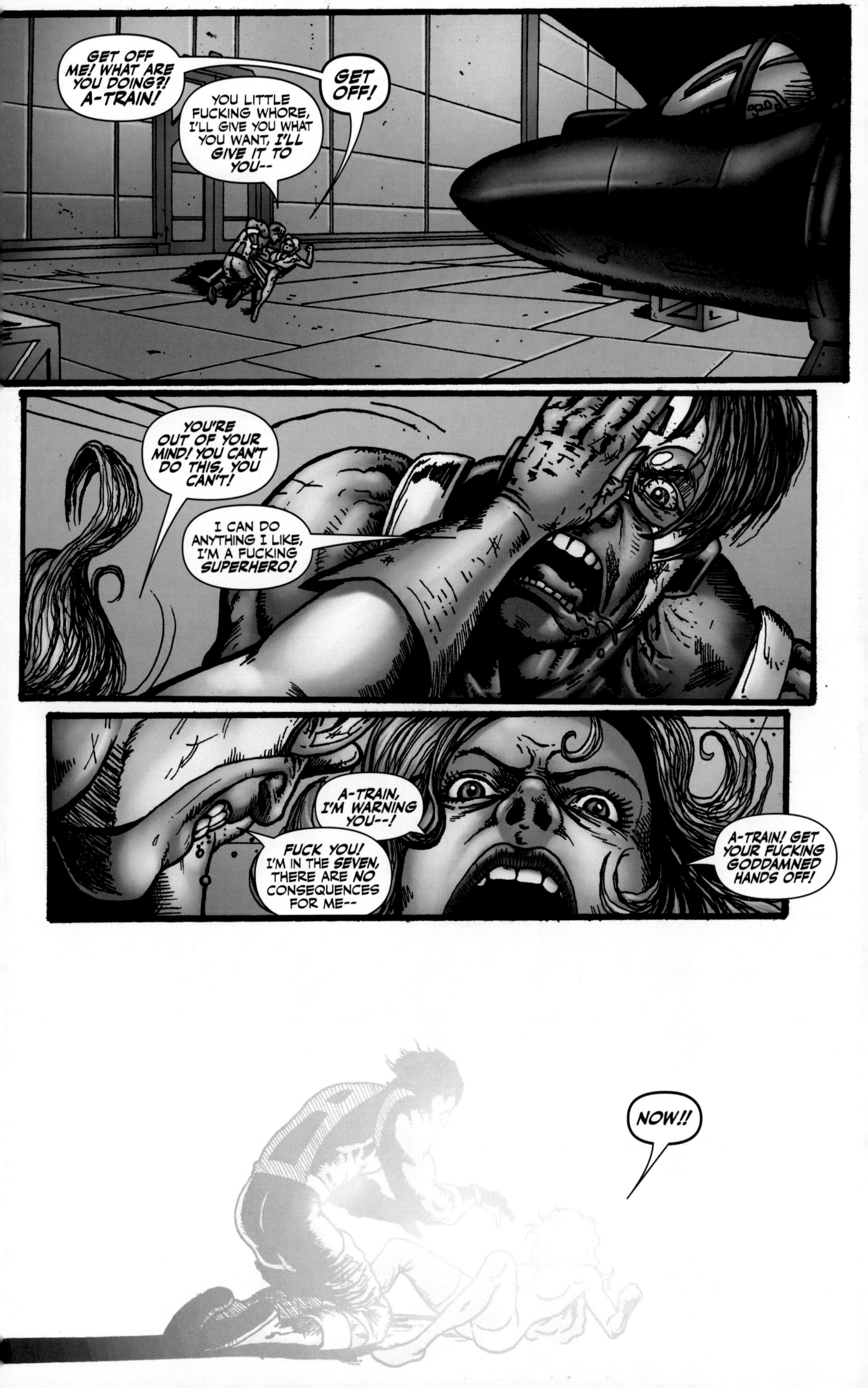
GET OFF ME! WHAT ARE YOU DOING?! A-TRAIN!
GET OFF!
YOU LITTLE FUCKING WHORE, I'LL GIVE YOU WHAT YOU WANT, I'LL GIVE IT TO YOU--
YOU'RE OUT OF YOUR MIND! YOU CAN'T DO THIS, YOU CAN'T!
I CAN DO ANYTHING I LIKE, I'M A FUCKING SUPERHERO!
A-TRAIN, I'M WARNING YOU--!
FUCK YOU! I'M IN THE SEVEN, THERE ARE NO CONSEQUENCES FOR ME--
A-TRAIN! GET YOUR FUCKING GODDAMNED HANDS OFF!
NOW!!

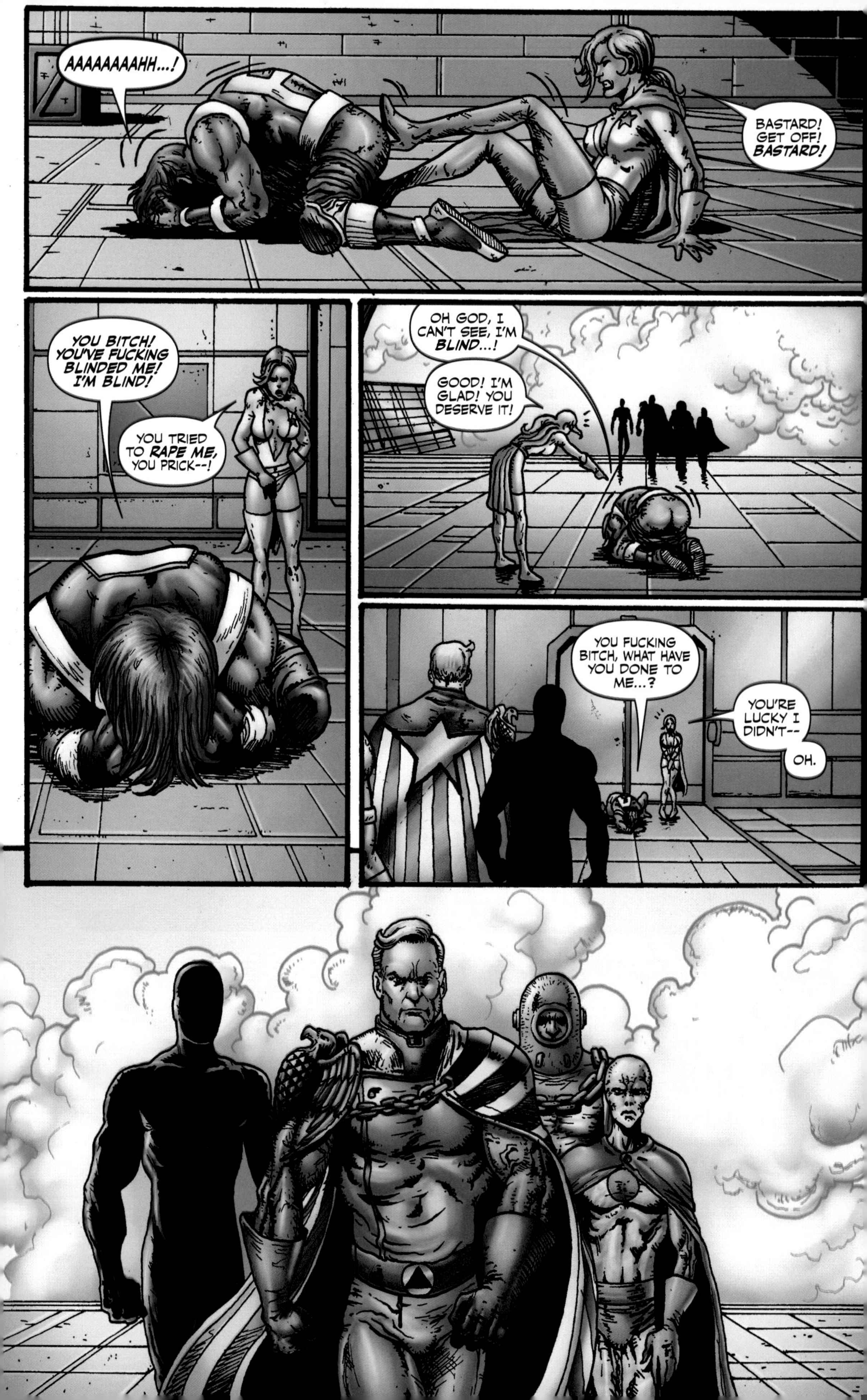
AAAAAAAAHH...!
BASTARD! GET OFF! BASTARD!
YOU BITCH! YOU'VE FUCKING BLINDED ME! I'M BLIND!
YOU TRIED TO RAPE ME, YOU PRICK--!
OH GOD, I CAN'T SEE, I'M BLIND...!
GOOD! I'M GLAD! YOU DESERVE IT!
YOU FUCKING BITCH, WHAT HAVE YOU DONE TO ME...?
YOU'RE LUCKY I DIDN'T--
OH.

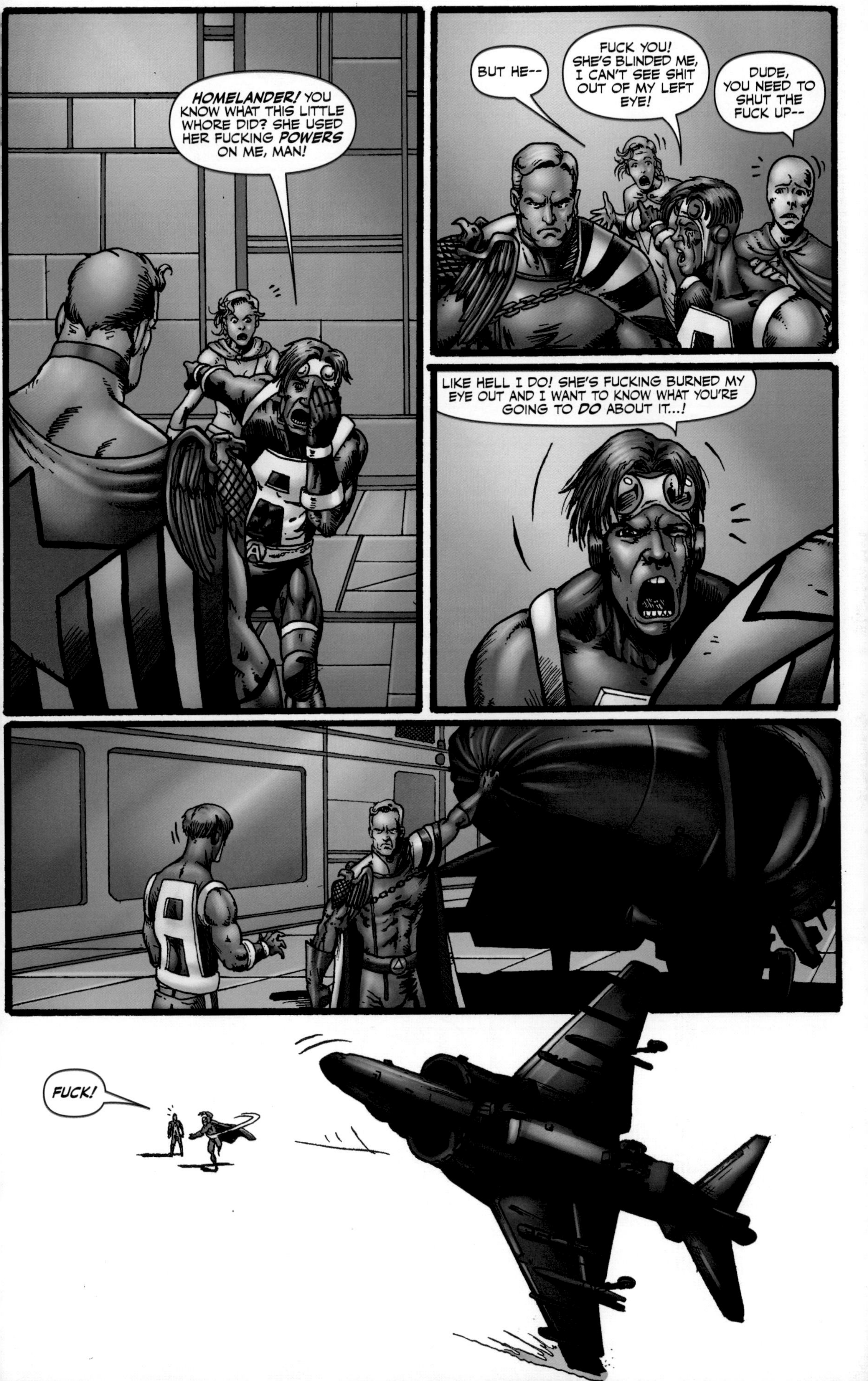
HOMELANDER! YOU KNOW WHAT THIS LITTLE WHORE DID? SHE USED HER FUCKING POWERS ON ME, MAN!
BUT HE--
FUCK YOU! SHE'S BLINDED ME, I CAN'T SEE SHIT OUT OF MY LEFT EYE!
DUDE, YOU NEED TO SHUT THE FUCK UP--
LIKE HELL I DO! SHE'S FUCKING BURNED MY EYE OUT AND I WANT TO KNOW WHAT YOU'RE GOING TO DO ABOUT IT...!
FUCK!

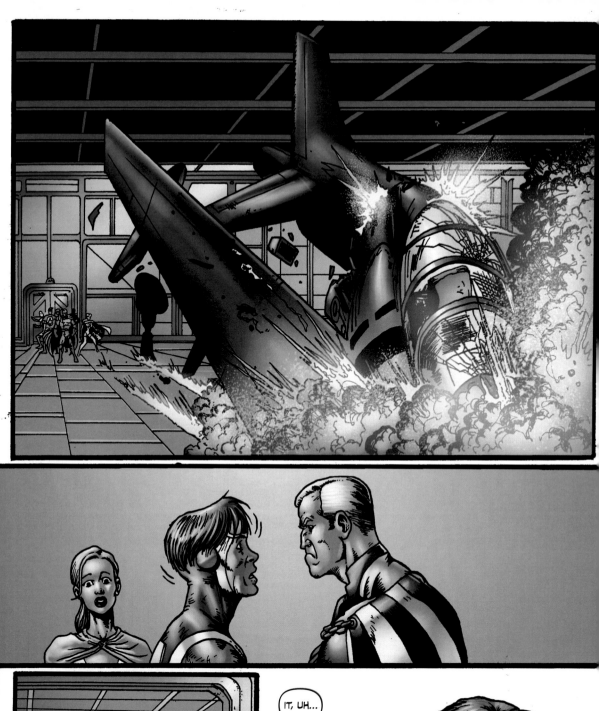

IT, UH...

IT HASN'T BEEN A VERY GOOD DAY.

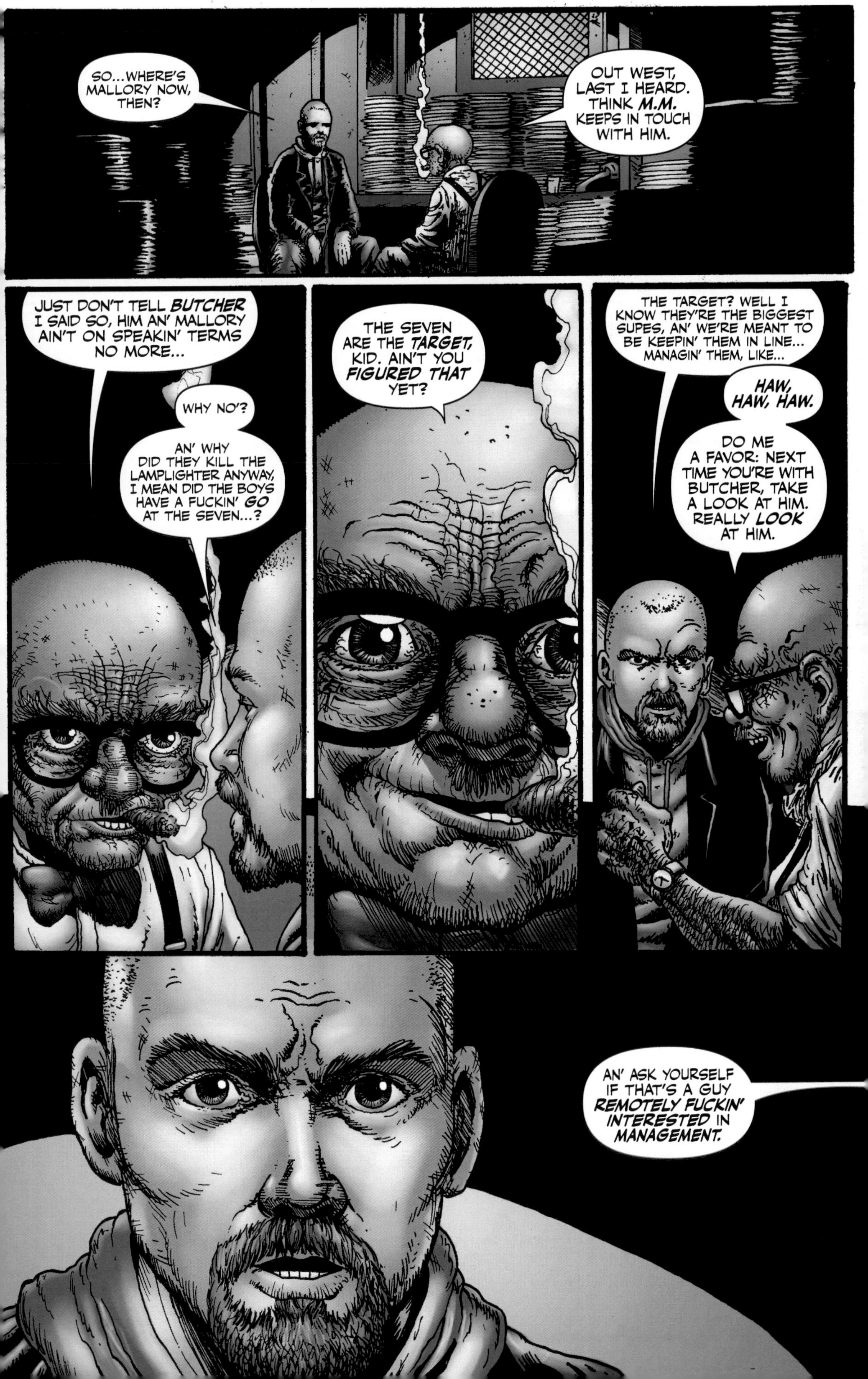
SO...WHERE'S MALLORY NOW, THEN?
OUT WEST, LAST I HEARD. THINK M.M. KEEPS IN TOUCH WITH HIM.
JUST DON'T TELL BUTCHER I SAID SO, HIM AN' MALLORY AIN'T ON SPEAKIN' TERMS NO MORE...
WHY NO'?
AN' WHY DID THEY KILL THE LAMPLIGHTER ANYWAY, I MEAN DID THE BOYS HAVE A FUCKIN' GO AT THE SEVEN...?
THE SEVEN ARE THE TARGET, KID. AIN'T YOU FIGURED THAT YET?
THE TARGET? WELL I KNOW THEY'RE THE BIGGEST SUPES, AN' WE'RE MEANT TO BE KEEPIN' THEM IN LINE... MANAGIN' THEM, LIKE...
HAW, HAW, HAW.
DO ME A FAVOR: NEXT TIME YOU'RE WITH BUTCHER, TAKE A LOOK AT HIM. REALLY LOOK AT HIM.
AN' ASK YOURSELF IF THAT'S A GUY REMOTELY FUCKIN' INTERESTED IN MANAGEMENT.

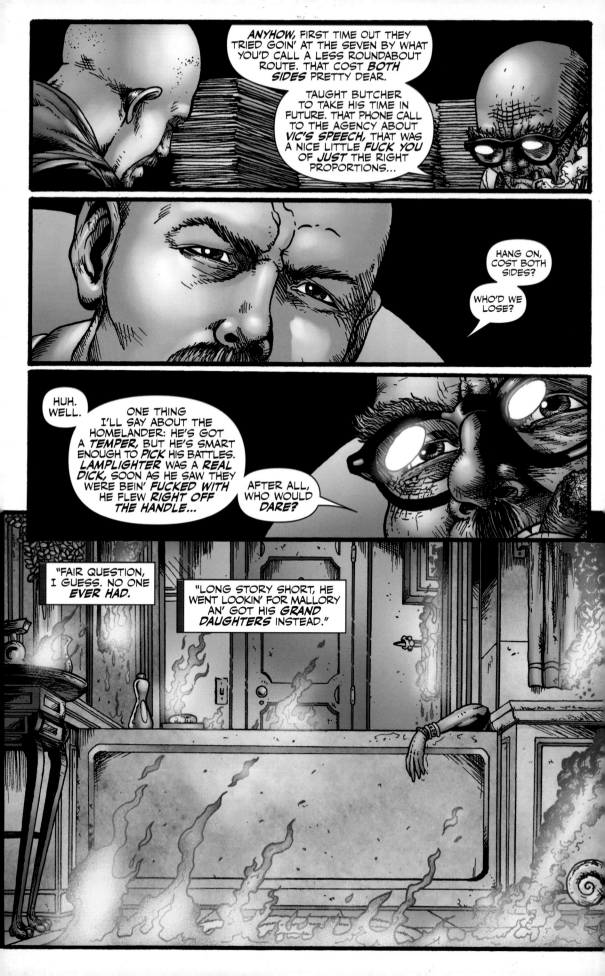

ANYHOW, FIRST TIME OUT THEY TRIED GOIN' AT THE SEVEN BY WHAT YOU'D CALL A LESS ROUNDABOUT ROUTE. THAT COST *BOTH SIDES* PRETTY DEAR.

TAUGHT BUTCHER TO TAKE HIS TIME IN FUTURE. THAT PHONE CALL TO THE AGENCY ABOUT *VIC'S SPEECH,* THAT WAS A NICE LITTLE *FUCK YOU* OF *JUST* THE RIGHT PROPORTIONS...

HANG ON, COST BOTH SIDES?

WHO'D WE LOSE?

HUH. WELL.

ONE THING I'LL SAY ABOUT THE HOMELANDER: HE'S GOT A *TEMPER,* BUT HE'S SMART ENOUGH TO *PICK* HIS BATTLES. *LAMPLIGHTER* WAS A *REAL DICK,* SOON AS HE SAW THEY WERE BEIN' *FUCKED WITH* HE FLEW *RIGHT OFF THE HANDLE...*

AFTER ALL, WHO WOULD *DARE?*

"FAIR QUESTION, I GUESS. NO ONE *EVER HAD.*

"LONG STORY SHORT, HE WENT LOOKIN' FOR MALLORY AN' GOT HIS *GRAND DAUGHTERS* INSTEAD."

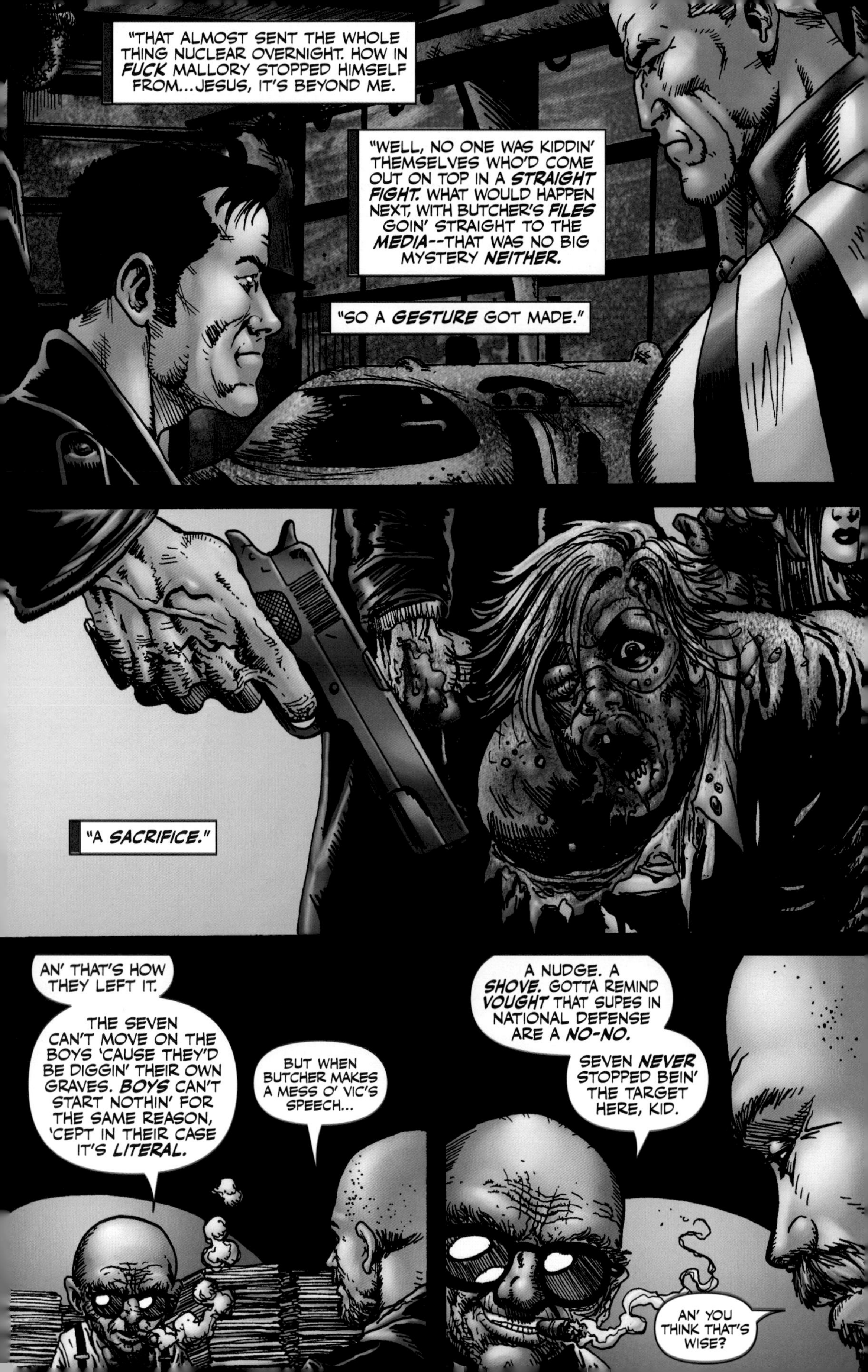
"THAT ALMOST SENT THE WHOLE THING NUCLEAR OVERNIGHT. HOW IN *FUCK* MALLORY STOPPED HIMSELF FROM...JESUS, IT'S BEYOND ME.
"WELL, NO ONE WAS KIDDIN' THEMSELVES WHO'D COME OUT ON TOP IN A *STRAIGHT FIGHT.* WHAT WOULD HAPPEN NEXT, WITH BUTCHER'S *FILES* GOIN' STRAIGHT TO THE *MEDIA*--THAT WAS NO BIG MYSTERY *NEITHER.*
"SO A *GESTURE* GOT MADE."
"A *SACRIFICE.*"
AN' THAT'S HOW THEY LEFT IT.
THE SEVEN CAN'T MOVE ON THE BOYS 'CAUSE THEY'D BE DIGGIN' THEIR OWN GRAVES. *BOYS* CAN'T START NOTHIN' FOR THE SAME REASON, 'CEPT IN THEIR CASE IT'S *LITERAL.*
BUT WHEN BUTCHER MAKES A MESS O' VIC'S SPEECH...
A NUDGE. A *SHOVE.* GOTTA REMIND *VOUGHT* THAT SUPES IN NATIONAL DEFENSE ARE A *NO-NO.*
SEVEN *NEVER* STOPPED BEIN' THE TARGET HERE, KID.
AN' YOU THINK THAT'S WISE?

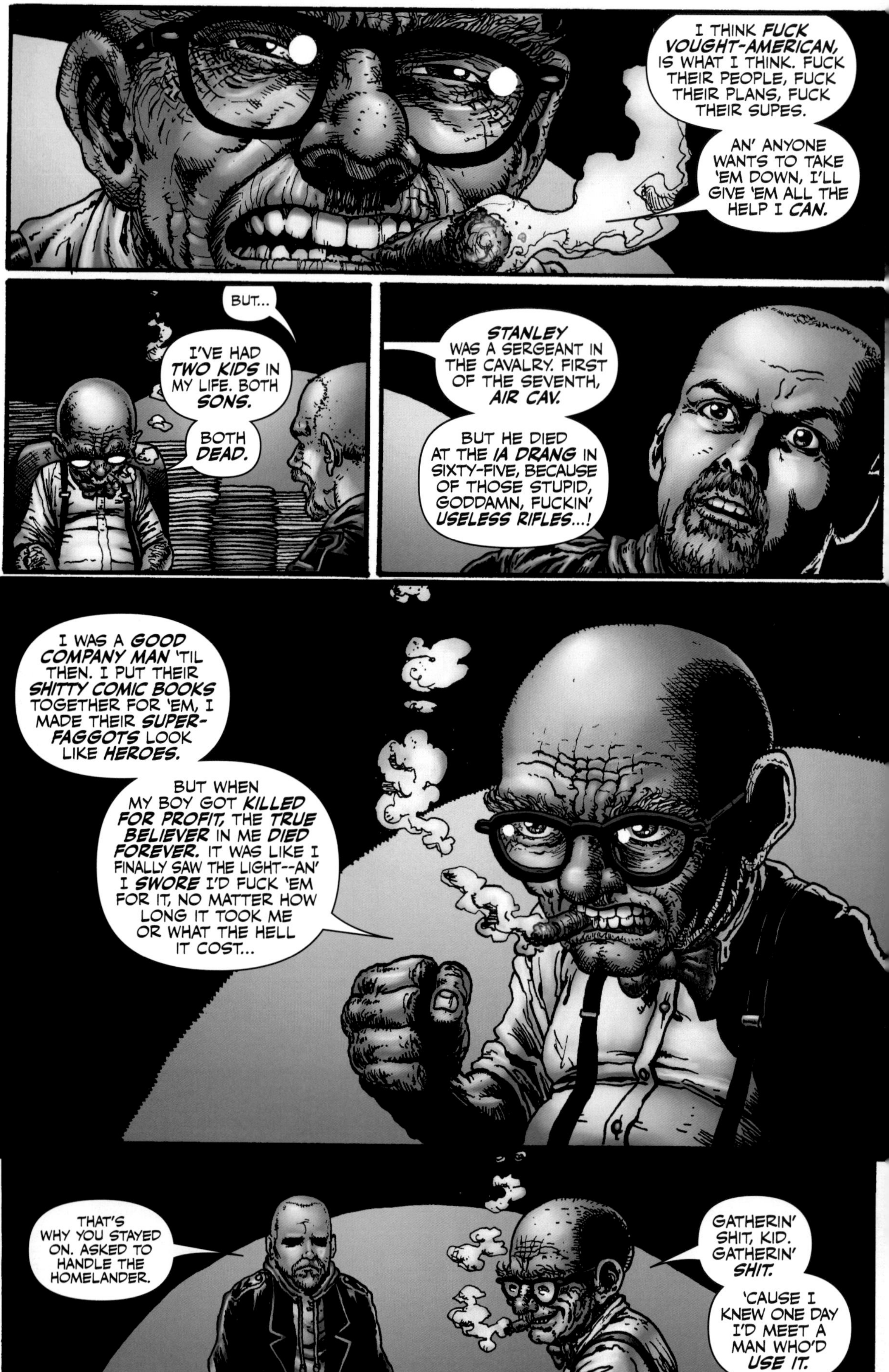

I THINK FUCK VOUGHT-AMERICAN, IS WHAT I THINK. FUCK THEIR PEOPLE, FUCK THEIR PLANS, FUCK THEIR SUPES.
AN' ANYONE WANTS TO TAKE 'EM DOWN, I'LL GIVE 'EM ALL THE HELP I CAN.
BUT...
I'VE HAD TWO KIDS IN MY LIFE. BOTH SONS.
BOTH DEAD.
STANLEY WAS A SERGEANT IN THE CAVALRY. FIRST OF THE SEVENTH, AIR CAV.
BUT HE DIED AT THE IA DRANG IN SIXTY-FIVE, BECAUSE OF THOSE STUPID, GODDAMN, FUCKIN' USELESS RIFLES...!
I WAS A GOOD COMPANY MAN 'TIL THEN. I PUT THEIR SHITTY COMIC BOOKS TOGETHER FOR 'EM, I MADE THEIR SUPER-FAGGOTS LOOK LIKE HEROES.
BUT WHEN MY BOY GOT KILLED FOR PROFIT, THE TRUE BELIEVER IN ME DIED FOREVER. IT WAS LIKE I FINALLY SAW THE LIGHT--AN' I SWORE I'D FUCK 'EM FOR IT, NO MATTER HOW LONG IT TOOK ME OR WHAT THE HELL IT COST...
THAT'S WHY YOU STAYED ON. ASKED TO HANDLE THE HOMELANDER.
GATHERIN' SHIT, KID. GATHERIN' SHIT.
'CAUSE I KNEW ONE DAY I'D MEET A MAN WHO'D USE IT.

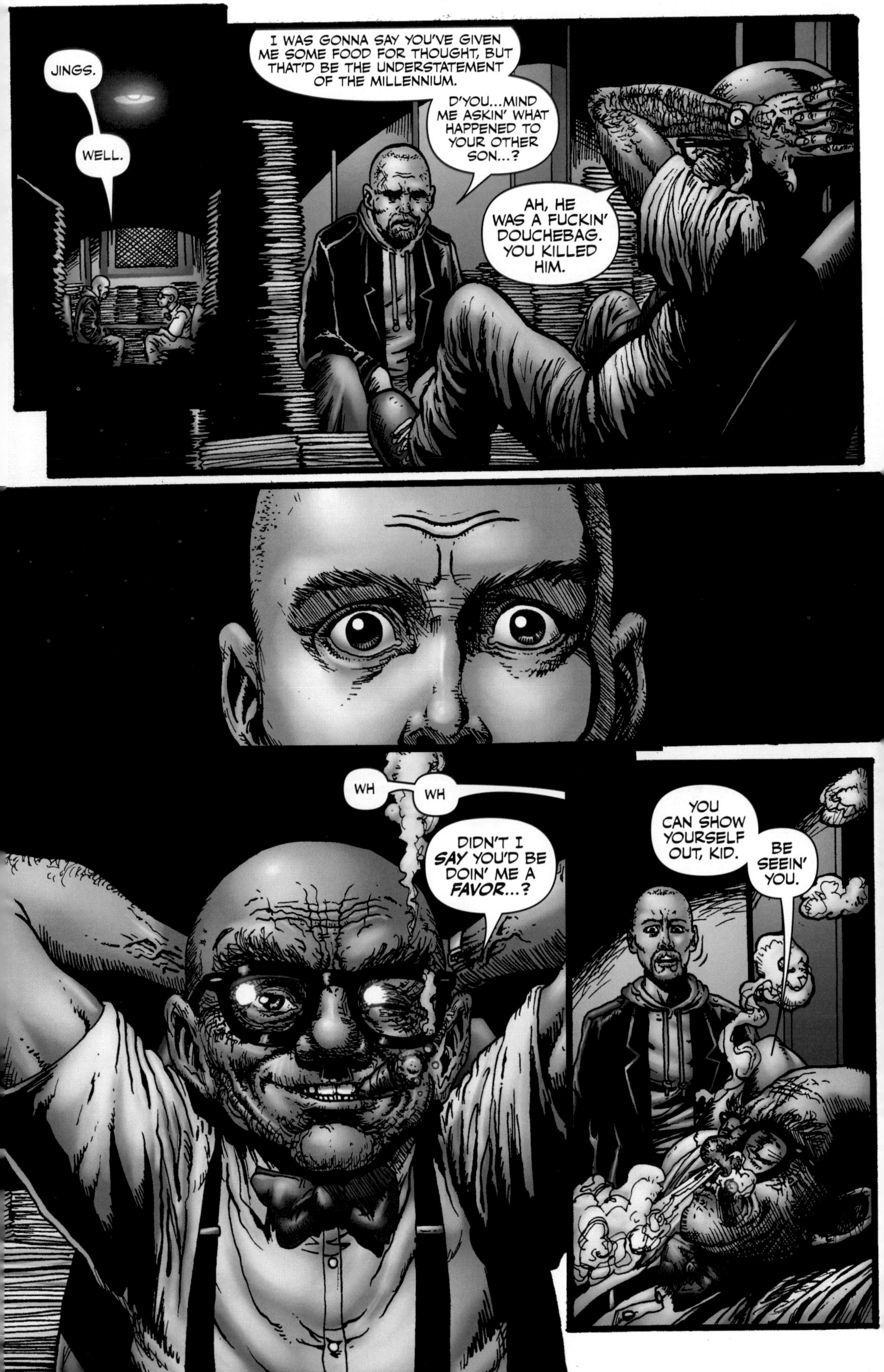
JINGS.
WELL.
I WAS GONNA SAY YOU'VE GIVEN ME SOME FOOD FOR THOUGHT, BUT THAT'D BE THE UNDERSTATEMENT OF THE MILLENNIUM.
D'YOU...MIND ME ASKIN' WHAT HAPPENED TO YOUR OTHER SON...?
AH, HE WAS A FUCKIN' DOUCHEBAG. YOU KILLED HIM.
WH
WH
DIDN'T I *SAY* YOU'D BE DOIN' ME A *FAVOR*...?
YOU CAN SHOW YOURSELF OUT, KID.
BE SEEIN' YOU.

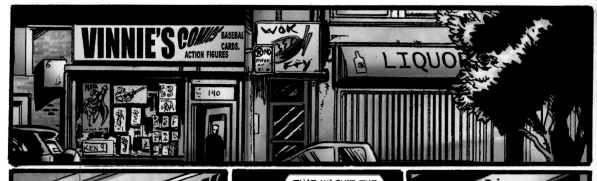

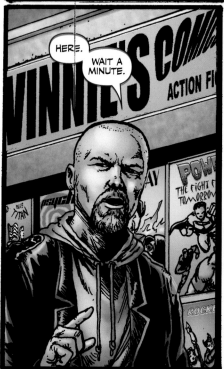

VINNIE'S COMICS BASEBALL CARDS. ACTION FIGURES
WOK FRY
LIQUOR
140
HERE.
WAIT A MINUTE.
THAT WASN'T THE BOYS' STORY, THAT WAS VOUGHT-AMERICAN'S...!
VINNIE'S
CLOSED
Hours Mon-Sat 9-6
THE WHOLE THING, FROM START TO--AW, C'MON TO FUCK!
HHHH.
I'M NO WISER THAN I EVER WAS.
WHAT A SWIZZ.

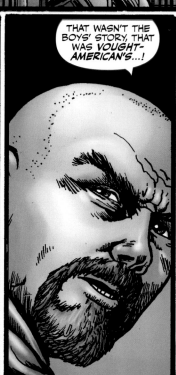

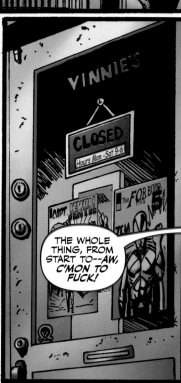

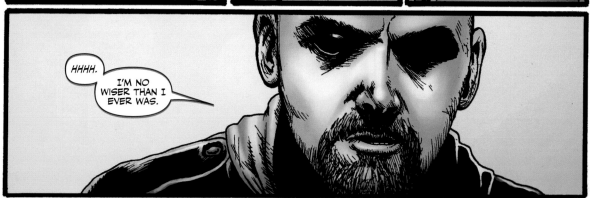

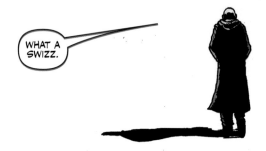

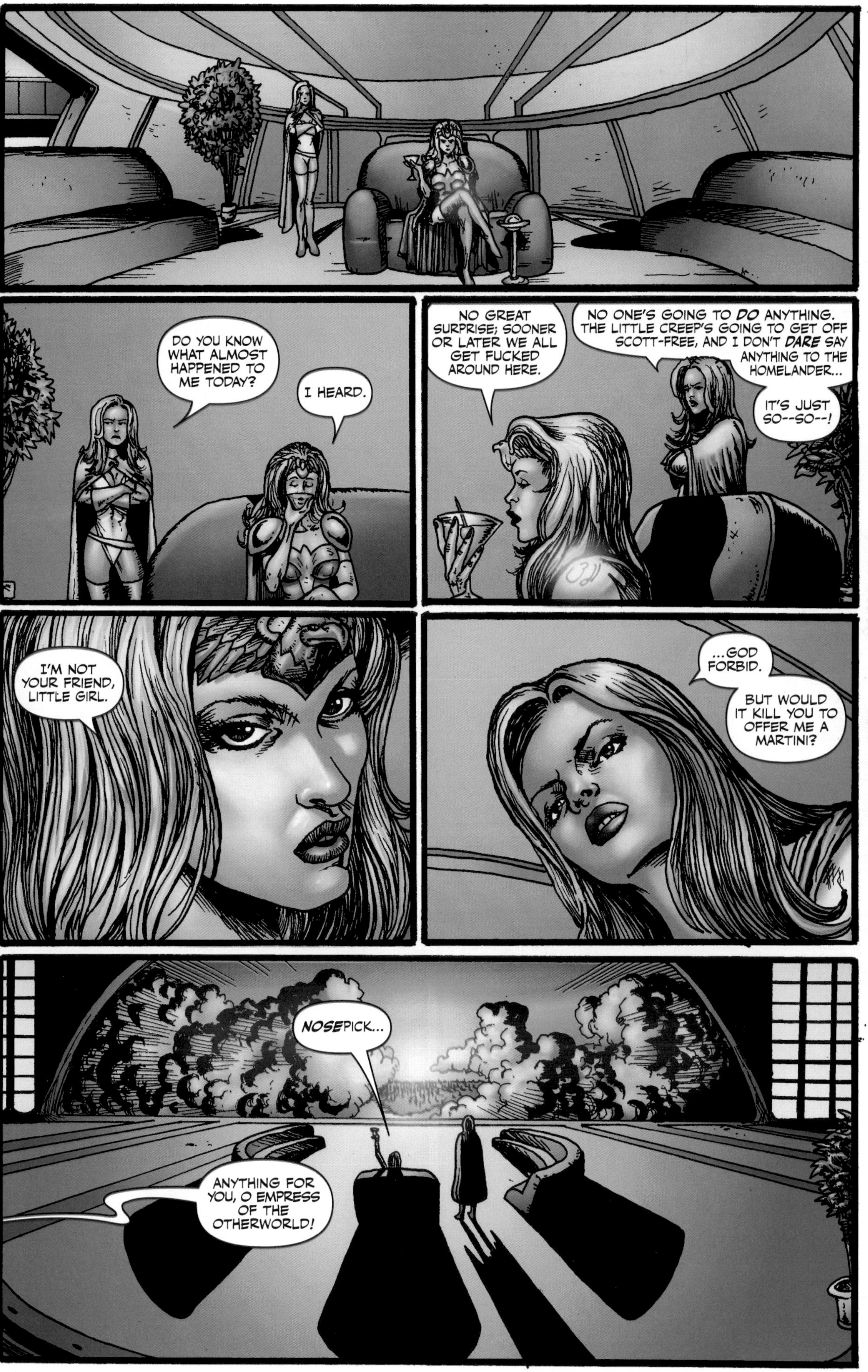
DO YOU KNOW WHAT ALMOST HAPPENED TO ME TODAY?
I HEARD.
NO GREAT SURPRISE; SOONER OR LATER WE ALL GET FUCKED AROUND HERE.
NO ONE'S GOING TO *DO* ANYTHING. THE LITTLE CREEP'S GOING TO GET OFF SCOTT-FREE, AND I DON'T *DARE* SAY ANYTHING TO THE HOMELANDER...
IT'S JUST SO--SO--!
I'M NOT YOUR FRIEND, LITTLE GIRL.
...GOD FORBID.
BUT WOULD IT KILL YOU TO OFFER ME A MARTINI?
*NOSE*PICK...
ANYTHING FOR YOU, O EMPRESS OF THE OTHERWORLD!

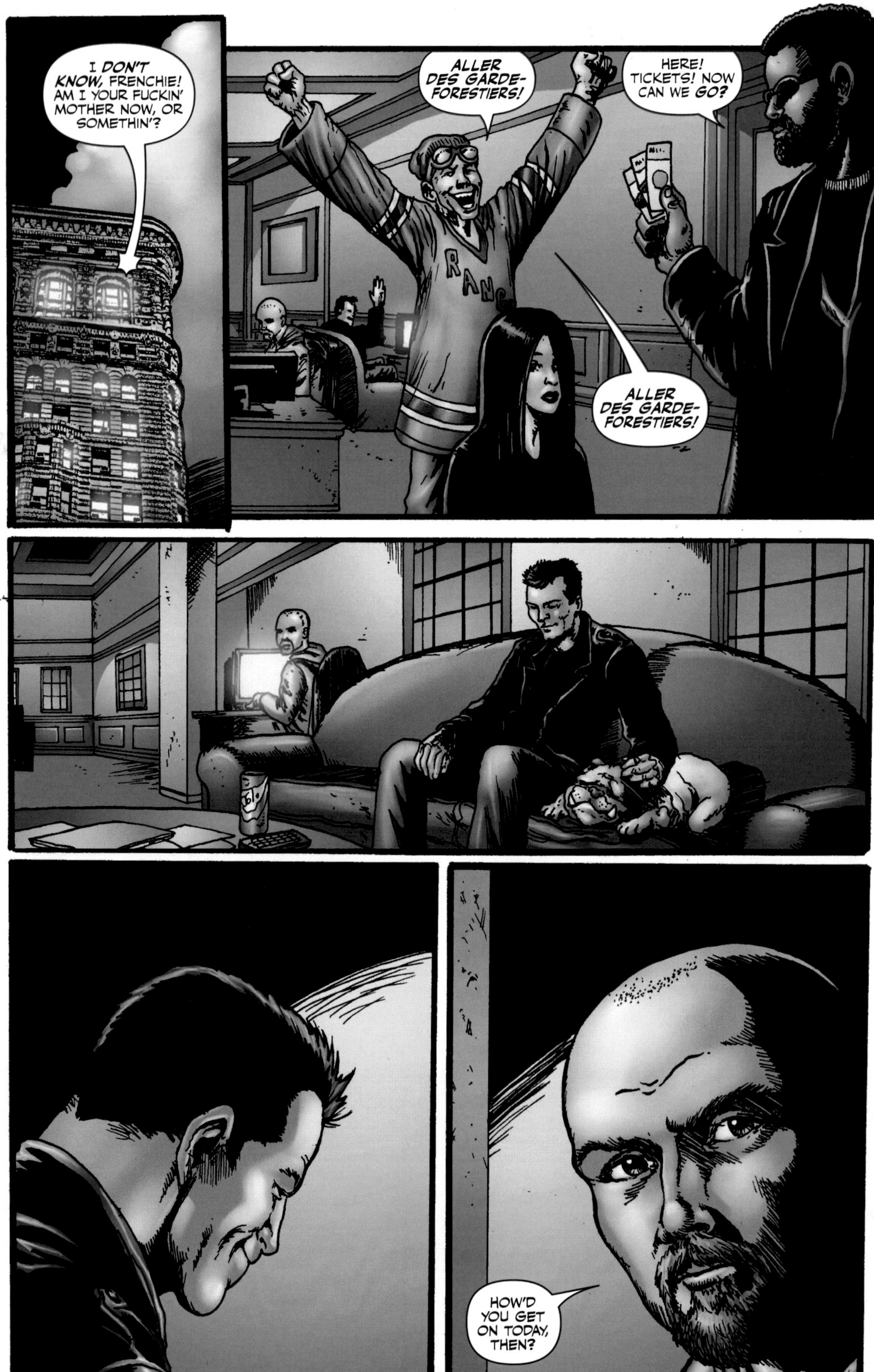
I DON'T KNOW, FRENCHIE! AM I YOUR FUCKIN' MOTHER NOW, OR SOMETHIN'?
ALLER DES GARDE-FORESTIERS!
HERE! TICKETS! NOW CAN WE GO?
ALLER DES GARDE-FORESTIERS!
HOW'D YOU GET ON TODAY, THEN?

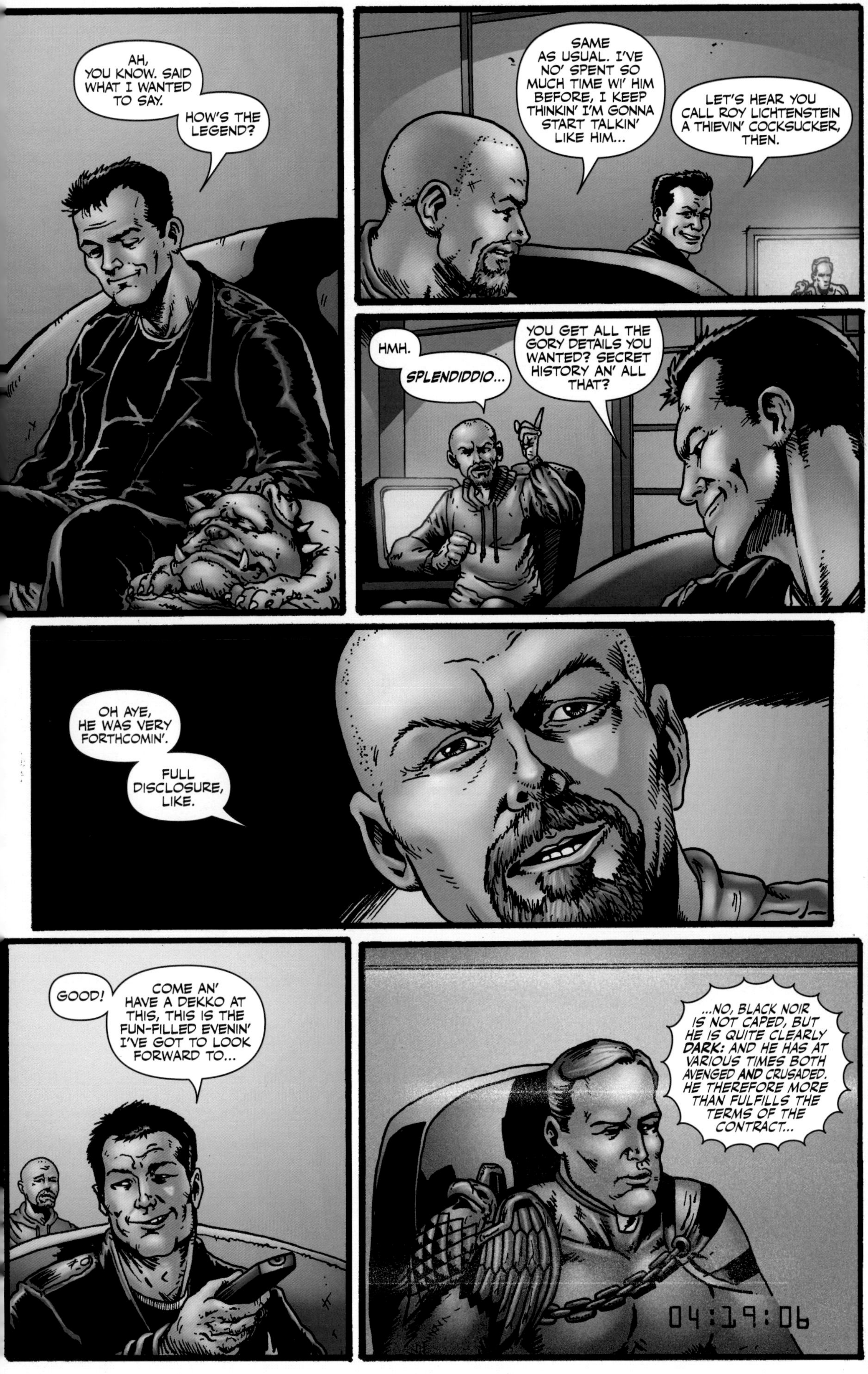
AH, YOU KNOW. SAID WHAT I WANTED TO SAY.
HOW'S THE LEGEND?
SAME AS USUAL. I'VE NO' SPENT SO MUCH TIME WI' HIM BEFORE, I KEEP THINKIN' I'M GONNA START TALKIN' LIKE HIM...
LET'S HEAR YOU CALL ROY LICHTENSTEIN A THIEVIN' COCKSUCKER, THEN.
HMH.
SPLENDIDDIO...
YOU GET ALL THE GORY DETAILS YOU WANTED? SECRET HISTORY AN' ALL THAT?
OH AYE, HE WAS VERY FORTHCOMIN'.
FULL DISCLOSURE, LIKE.
GOOD!
COME AN' HAVE A DEKKO AT THIS, THIS IS THE FUN-FILLED EVENIN' I'VE GOT TO LOOK FORWARD TO...
...NO, BLACK NOIR IS NOT CAPED, BUT HE IS QUITE CLEARLY DARK: AND HE HAS AT VARIOUS TIMES BOTH AVENGED AND CRUSADED. HE THEREFORE MORE THAN FULFILLS THE TERMS OF THE CONTRACT...
04:19:06

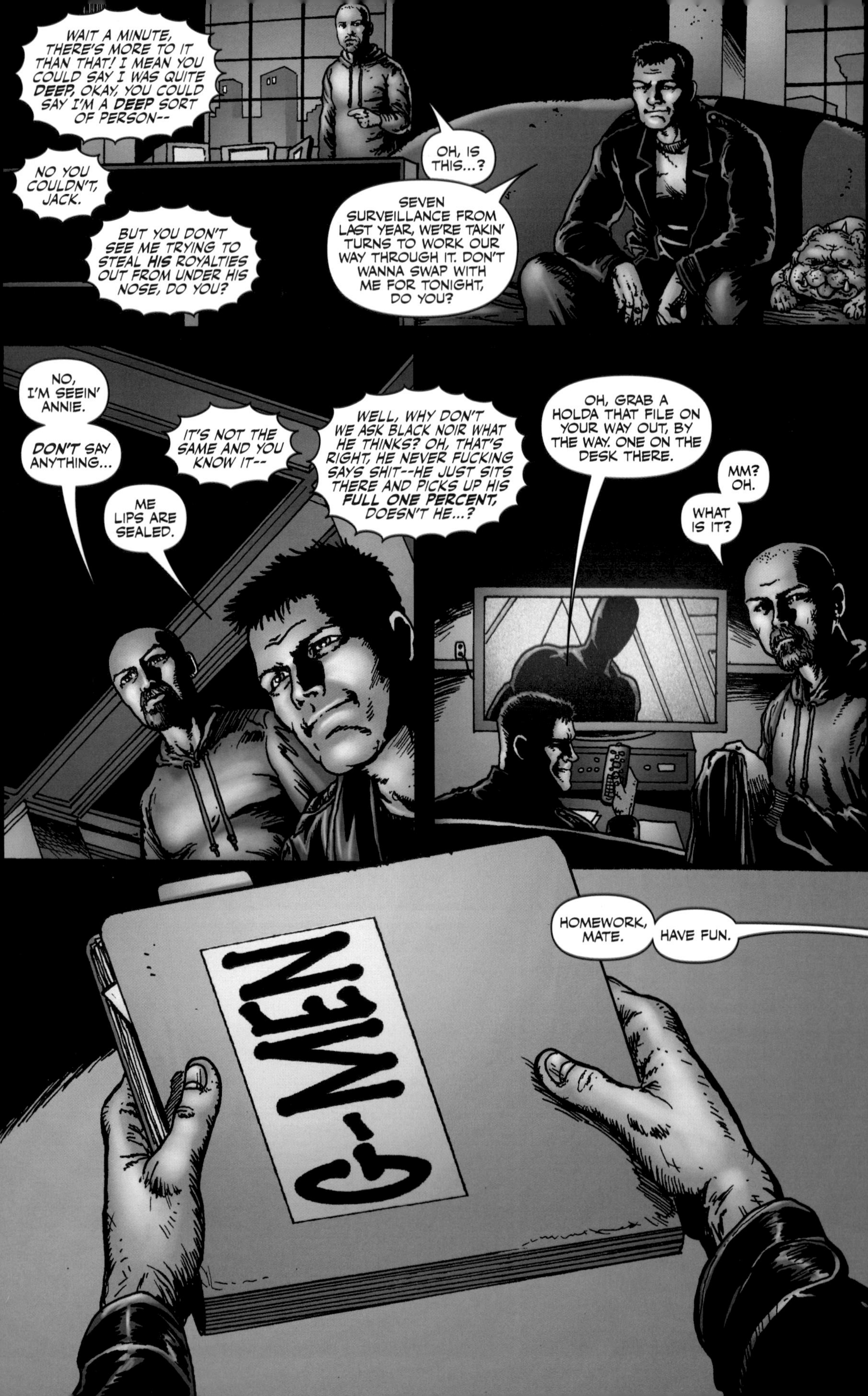
WAIT A MINUTE, THERE'S MORE TO IT THAN THAT! I MEAN YOU COULD SAY I WAS QUITE **DEEP**, OKAY, YOU COULD SAY I'M A **DEEP** SORT OF PERSON--
NO YOU COULDN'T, JACK.
BUT YOU DON'T SEE ME TRYING TO STEAL **HIS** ROYALTIES OUT FROM UNDER HIS NOSE, DO YOU?
OH, IS THIS...?
SEVEN SURVEILLANCE FROM LAST YEAR, WE'RE TAKIN' TURNS TO WORK OUR WAY THROUGH IT. DON'T WANNA SWAP WITH ME FOR TONIGHT, DO YOU?
NO, I'M SEEIN' ANNIE.
DON'T SAY ANYTHING...
ME LIPS ARE SEALED.
IT'S NOT THE SAME AND YOU KNOW IT--
WELL, WHY DON'T WE ASK BLACK NOIR WHAT HE THINKS? OH, THAT'S RIGHT, HE NEVER FUCKING SAYS SHIT--HE JUST SITS THERE AND PICKS UP HIS **FULL ONE PERCENT,** DOESN'T HE...?
OH, GRAB A HOLDA THAT FILE ON YOUR WAY OUT, BY THE WAY. ONE ON THE DESK THERE.
MM? OH.
WHAT IS IT?
G-MEN
HOMEWORK, MATE.
HAVE FUN.

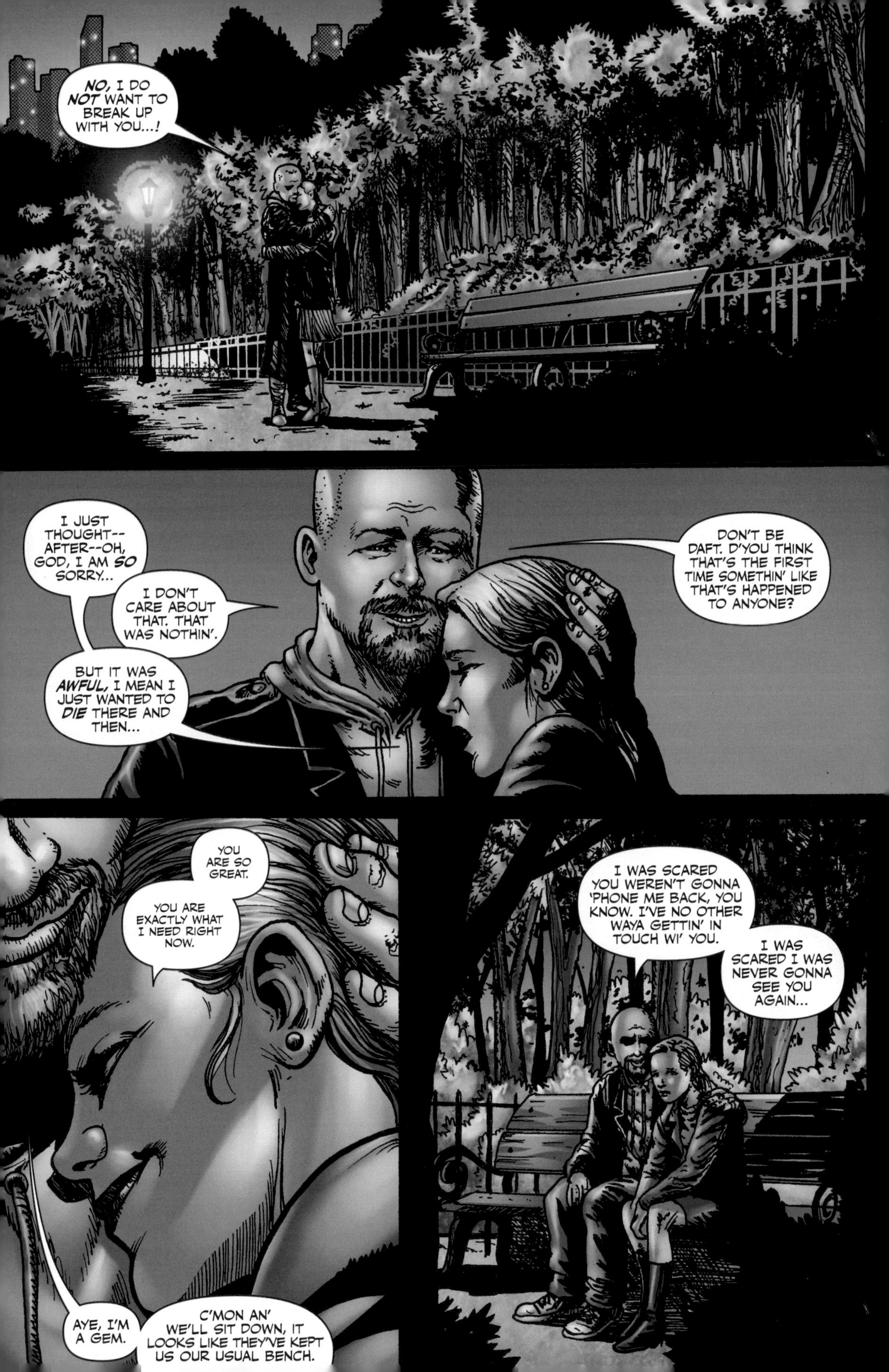
NO, I DO NOT WANT TO BREAK UP WITH YOU...!
I JUST THOUGHT--AFTER--OH, GOD, I AM SO SORRY...
I DON'T CARE ABOUT THAT. THAT WAS NOTHIN'.
DON'T BE DAFT. D'YOU THINK THAT'S THE FIRST TIME SOMETHIN' LIKE THAT'S HAPPENED TO ANYONE?
BUT IT WAS AWFUL, I MEAN I JUST WANTED TO DIE THERE AND THEN...
YOU ARE SO GREAT.
YOU ARE EXACTLY WHAT I NEED RIGHT NOW.
AYE, I'M A GEM.
C'MON AN' WE'LL SIT DOWN, IT LOOKS LIKE THEY'VE KEPT US OUR USUAL BENCH.
I WAS SCARED YOU WEREN'T GONNA 'PHONE ME BACK, YOU KNOW. I'VE NO OTHER WAYA GETTIN' IN TOUCH WI' YOU.
I WAS SCARED I WAS NEVER GONNA SEE YOU AGAIN...

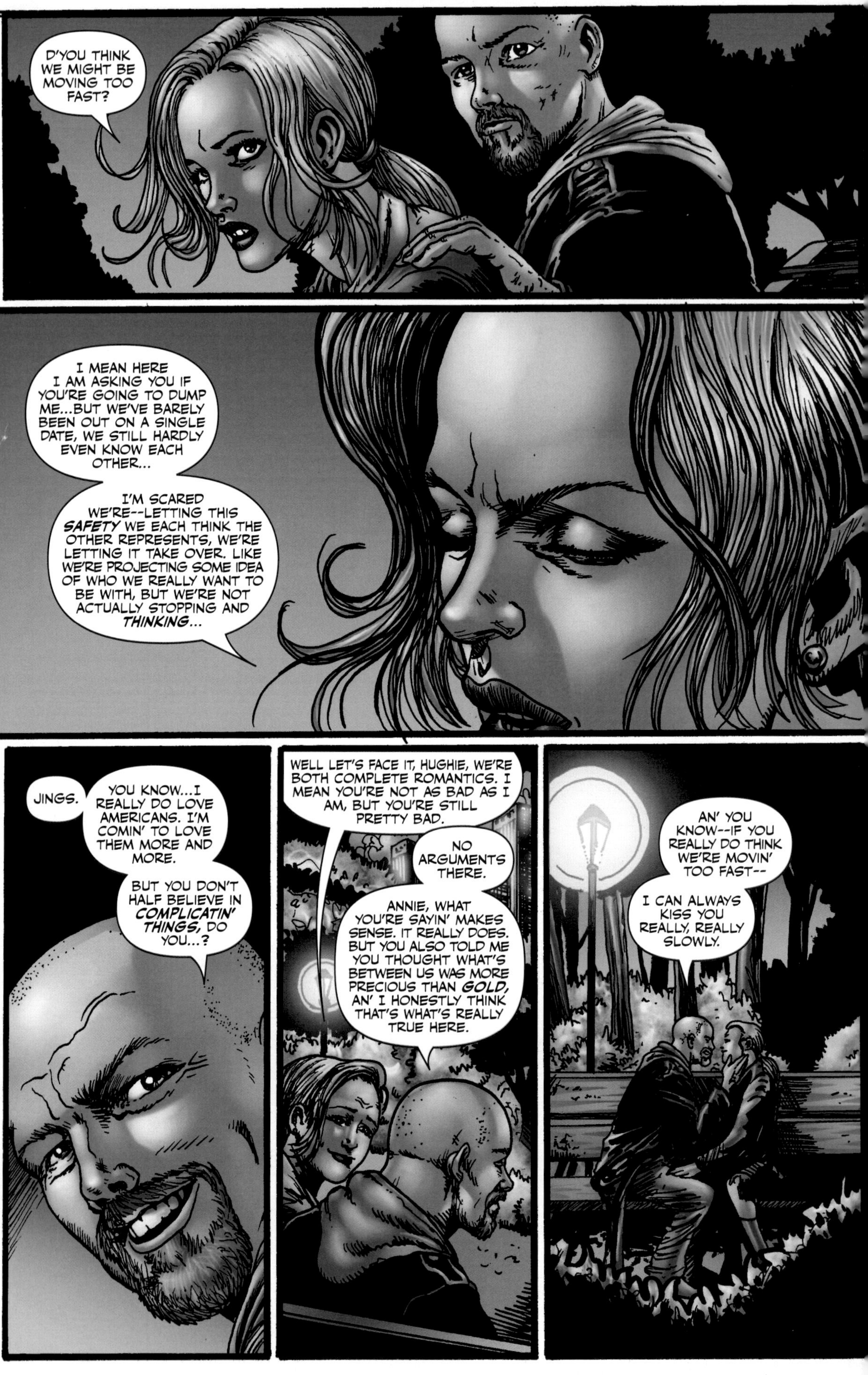
D'YOU THINK WE MIGHT BE MOVING TOO FAST?
I MEAN HERE I AM ASKING YOU IF YOU'RE GOING TO DUMP ME...BUT WE'VE BARELY BEEN OUT ON A SINGLE DATE, WE STILL HARDLY EVEN KNOW EACH OTHER...
I'M SCARED WE'RE--LETTING THIS *SAFETY* WE EACH THINK THE OTHER REPRESENTS, WE'RE LETTING IT TAKE OVER. LIKE WE'RE PROJECTING SOME IDEA OF WHO WE REALLY WANT TO BE WITH, BUT WE'RE NOT ACTUALLY STOPPING AND *THINKING*...
JINGS.
YOU KNOW...I REALLY DO LOVE AMERICANS. I'M COMIN' TO LOVE THEM MORE AND MORE.
BUT YOU DON'T HALF BELIEVE IN *COMPLICATIN' THINGS,* DO YOU...?
WELL LET'S FACE IT, HUGHIE, WE'RE BOTH COMPLETE ROMANTICS. I MEAN YOU'RE NOT AS BAD AS I AM, BUT YOU'RE STILL PRETTY BAD.
NO ARGUMENTS THERE.
ANNIE, WHAT YOU'RE SAYIN' MAKES SENSE. IT REALLY DOES. BUT YOU ALSO TOLD ME YOU THOUGHT WHAT'S BETWEEN US WAS MORE PRECIOUS THAN *GOLD,* AN' I HONESTLY THINK THAT'S WHAT'S REALLY TRUE HERE.
AN' YOU KNOW--IF YOU REALLY DO THINK WE'RE MOVIN' TOO FAST--
I CAN ALWAYS KISS YOU REALLY, REALLY SLOWLY.

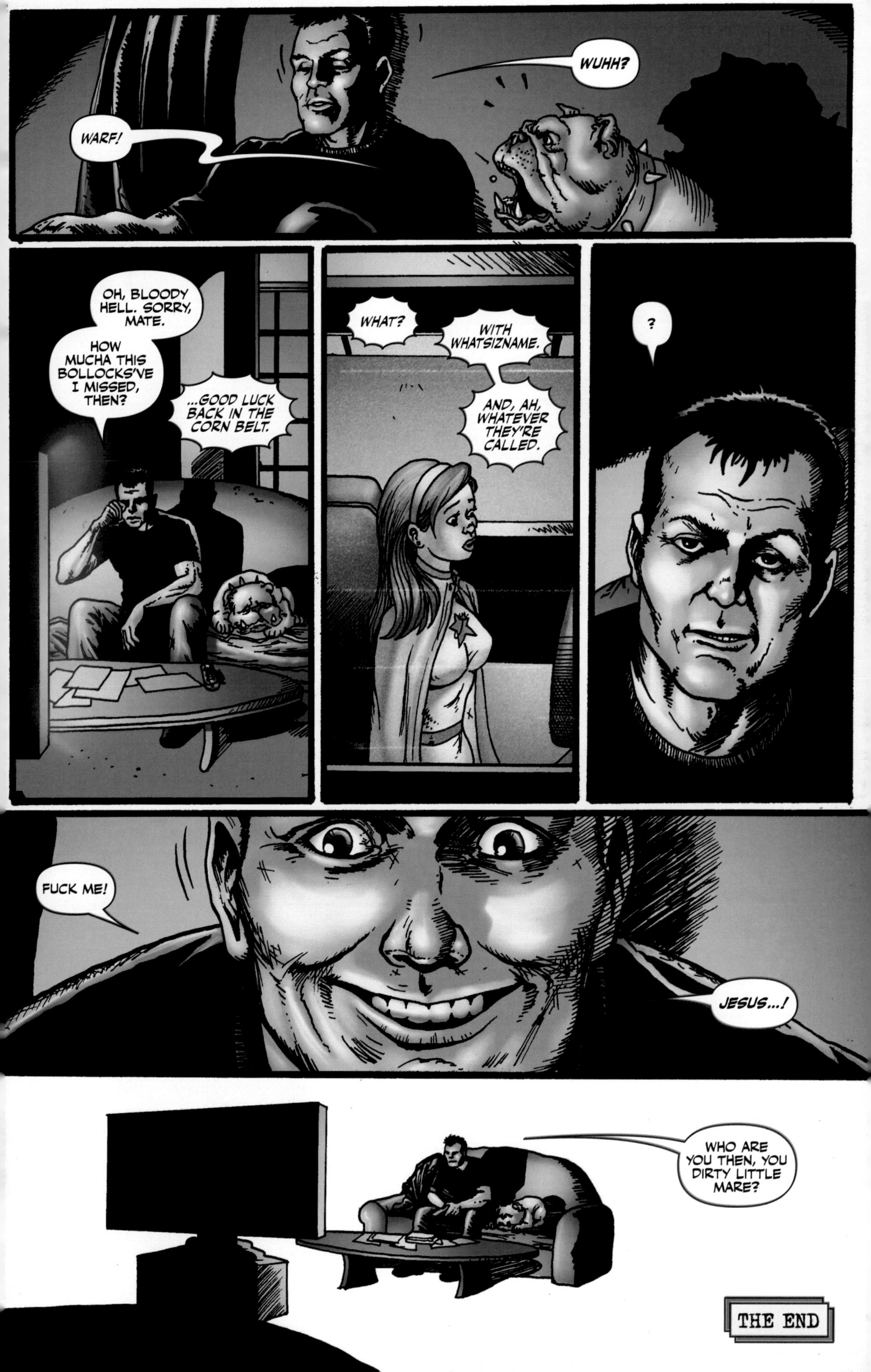
WUHH?
WARF!
OH, BLOODY HELL. SORRY, MATE.
HOW MUCHA THIS BOLLOCKS'VE I MISSED, THEN?
...GOOD LUCK BACK IN THE CORN BELT.
WHAT?
WITH WHATSIZNAME.
AND, AH, WHATEVER THEY'RE CALLED.
?
FUCK ME!
JESUS...!
WHO ARE YOU THEN, YOU DIRTY LITTLE MARE?
THE END

Emerald City Con '08 Exclusive cover to issue #18

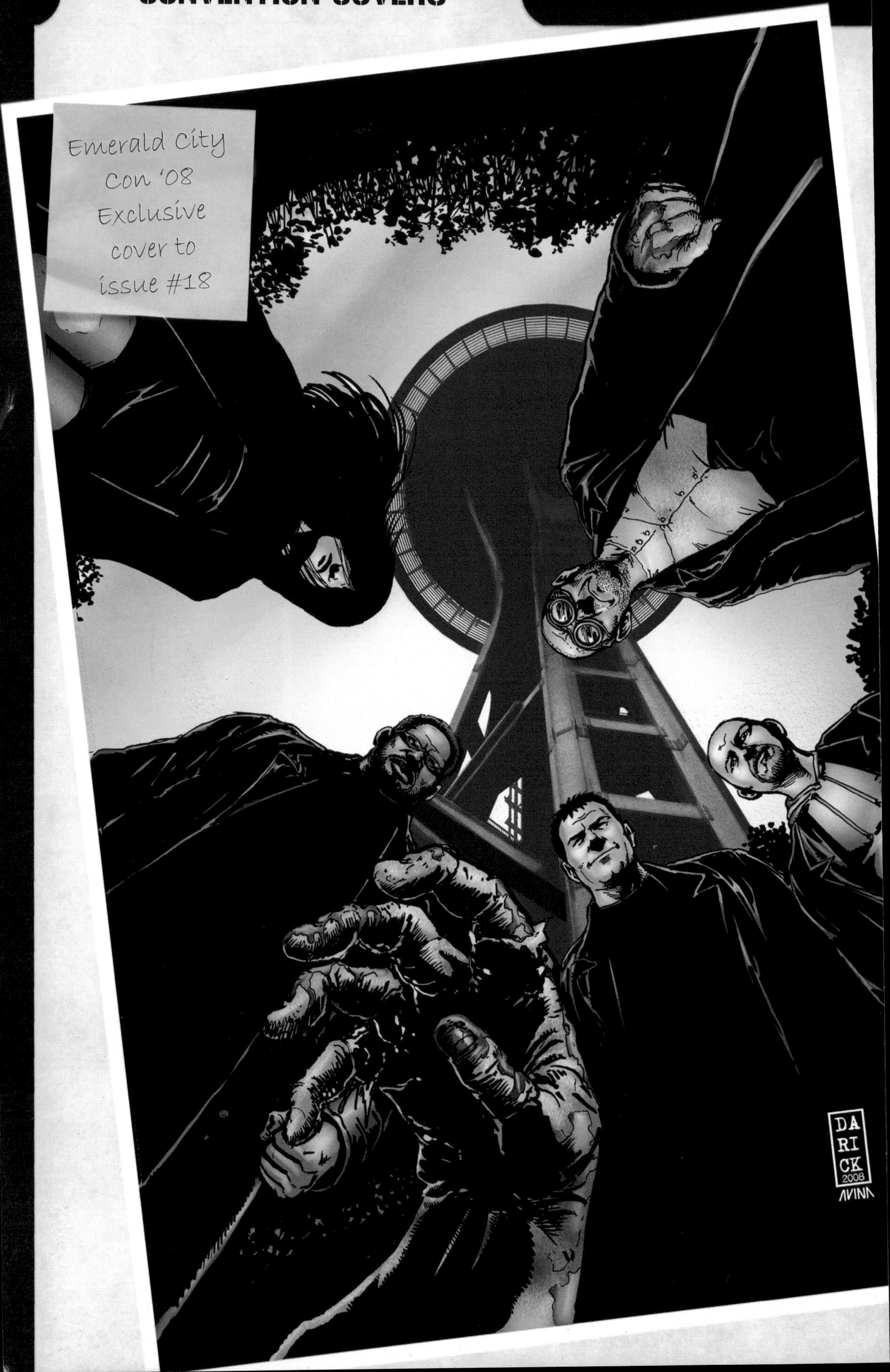
DA
RI
CK
2008
AVINA

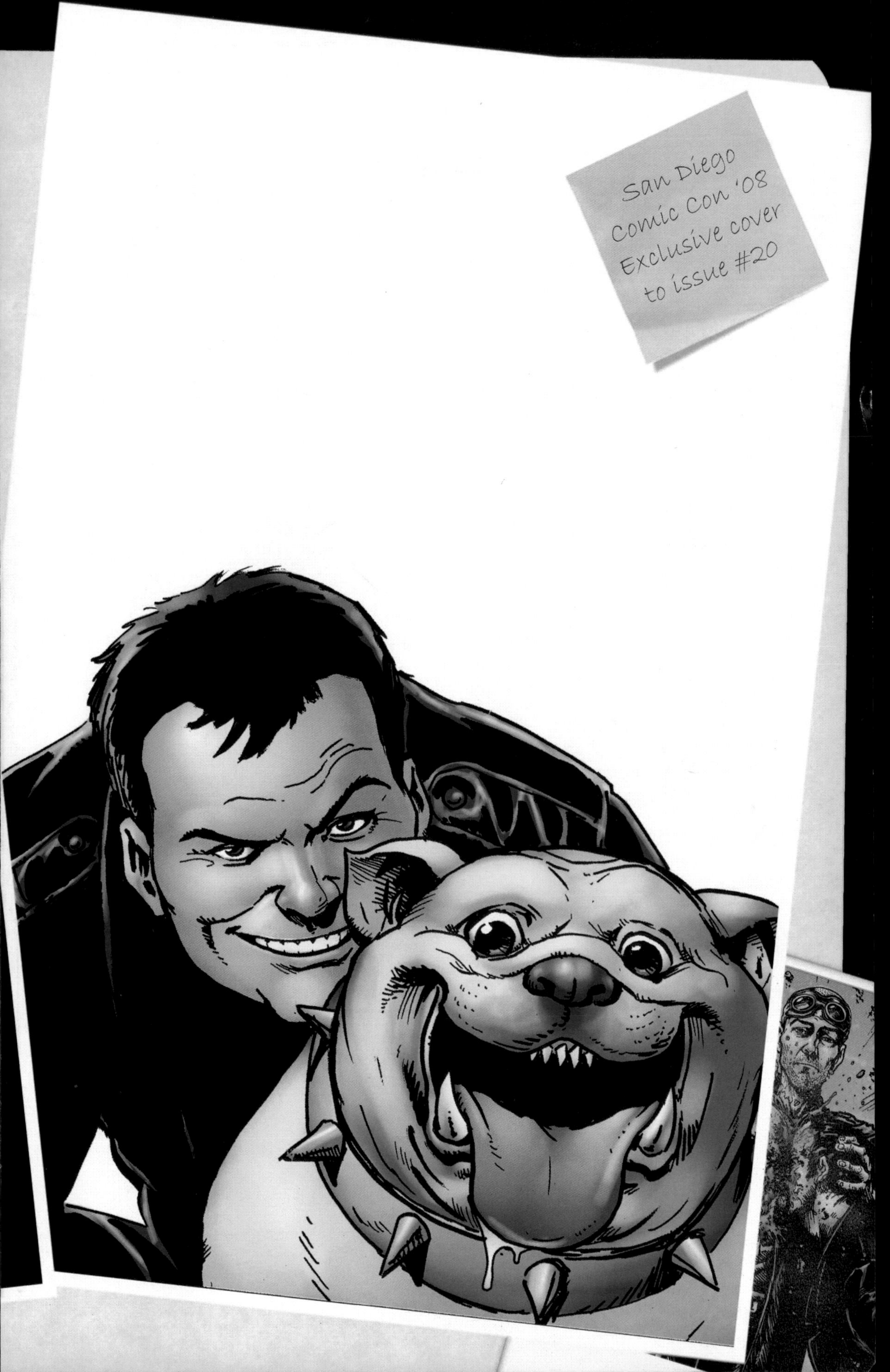
San Diego
Comic Con '08
Exclusive cover
to issue #20

COMPLETE YOUR COLLECTION TODAY!

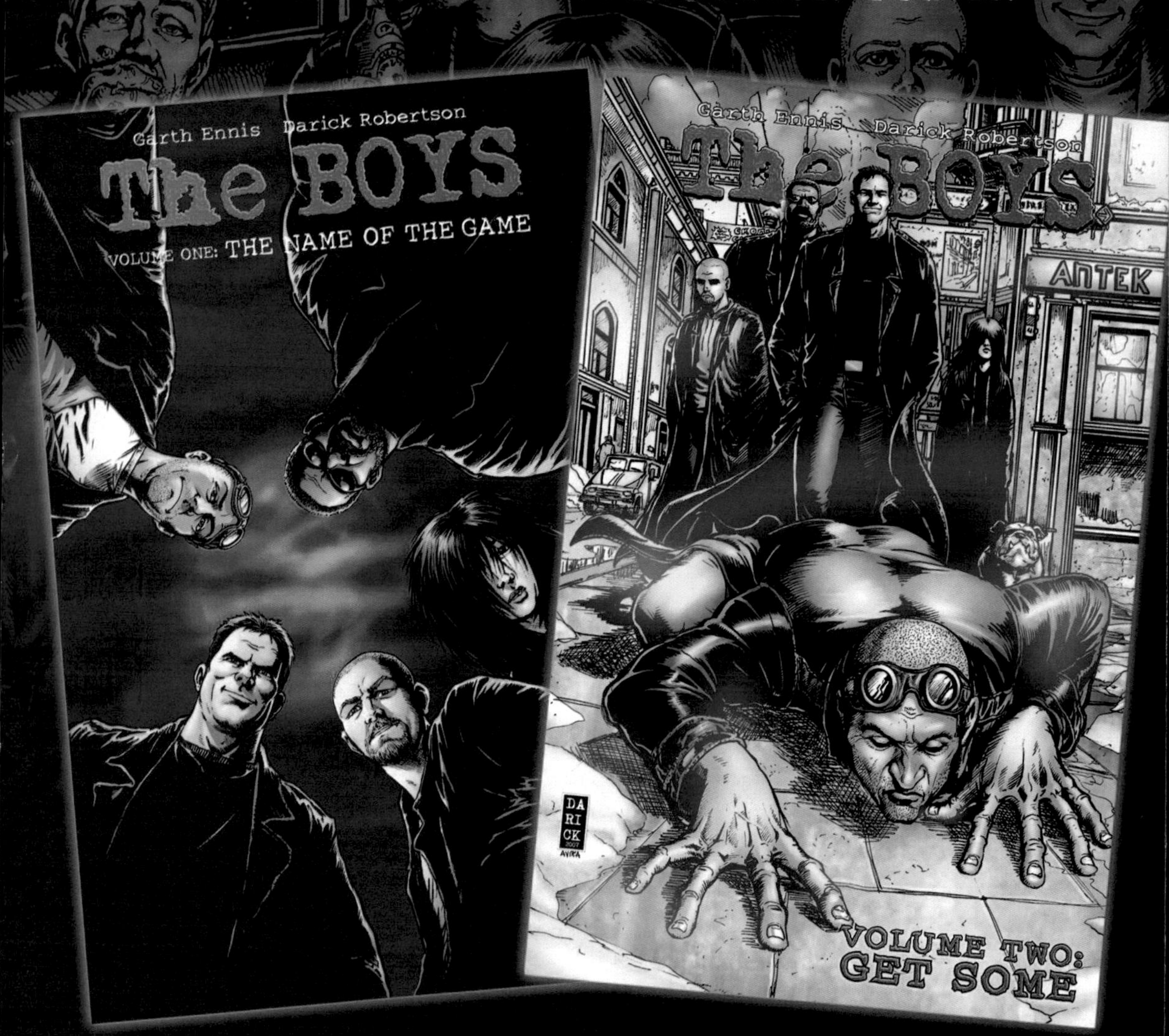
Garth Ennis Darick Robertson
The BOYS
VOLUME ONE: THE NAME OF THE GAME
Garth Ennis Darick Robertson
The BOYS
ANTEK
DA RI CK 2007
VOLUME TWO: GET SOME

IN STORES NOW:

The Boys Vol. 1: The Name Of The Game

ISBN: 9781845764944

- By Ennis and Robertson
- Collecting issues 1-6
- See how it all began!
- Introduction by Simon Pegg (Hot Fuzz)
- Sketchbook by Darick Robertson
- In stores now!

The Boys Vol. 2: Get Some

ISBN: 9781845769246

- By Ennis, Robertson and Peter Snejbjerg
- Collecting issues 7-14
- Featuring the introduction of The Tek Knight and the man named Love Sausage!
- In stores now!

www.titanbooks.com

ALSO AVAILABLE FROM TITAN BOOKS

OTHER COLLECTIONS FEATURING GARTH ENNIS AND DARICK ROBERTSON

The Authority: Kev
Garth Ennis & Glenn Fabry
ISBN: 9781845760403

The Authority: The Magnificent Kevin
Garth Ennis & Carlos Ezquerra
ISBN: 9781845762834

A Man Called Kev
Garth Ennis & Carlos Ezquerra
ISBN: 9781845765965

The Authority: Prime
Christos Gage & Darick Robertson
ISBN: 9781845768614

Battler Britton
Garth Ennis & Colin Wilson
ISBN: 9781845765606

Bloody Mary
Garth Ennis & Carlos Ezquerra
ISBN: 9781845761981

The Exterminators: Crossfire and Collateral
Simon Oliver & Darick Robertson
ISBN: 9781845767785

Goddess
Garth Ennis & Phil Winslade
ISBN: 9781840233278

Constantine: The Hellblazer Collection
Steven T. Seagle, Jamie Delano, Neil Gaiman, Garth Ennis, Ron Randall, John Ridgway, Dave McKean & Will Simpson
ISBN: 9781840239799

Hellblazer: Dangerous Habits
Garth Ennis, Will Simpson, Mark Pennington, Tom Sutton & Malcolm Jones III
ISBN: 9781845761059

Hellblazer: Rare Cuts
Jamie Delano, Grant Morrison, Garth Ennis, Richard Piers Rayner, Mark Buckingham, David Lloyd & Sean Phillips
ISBN: 9781840239743

Hellblazer: Bloodlines
Garth Ennis, Steve Dillon, Will Simpson & Mike Hoffmann
ISBN: 9781845766504

Hellblazer: Fear and Loathing
Garth Ennis & Steve Dillon
ISBN: 9781852868192

Hellblazer: Tainted Love
Garth Ennis & Steve Dillon
ISBN: 9781852869946

Hellblazer: Damnation's Flame
Garth Ennis & Steve Dillon
ISBN: 9781840230963

Hellblazer: Rake at the Gates of Hell
Garth Ennis & Steve Dillon
ISBN: 9781840236736

Hellblazer: Son of Man
Garth Ennis & John Higgins
ISBN: 9781840238303

Just a Pilgrim
Garth Ennis & Carlos Ezquerra
ISBN: 9781840233773

Just a Pilgrim: Garden of Eden
Garth Ennis & Carlos Ezquerra
ISBN: 9781840235906

Midnighter: Killing Machine
Garth Ennis & Chris Sprouse
ISBN: 9781845766337

Midnighter: Anthem
Keith Giffen, Chris Sprouse, Darick Robertson & Karl Story
ISBN: 97818457667358

Preacher: Gone to Texas
Garth Ennis & Steve Dillon
ISBN: 9781852867133

Preacher: Until the End of the World
Garth Ennis & Steve Dillon
ISBN: 9781852867867

Preacher: Proud Americans
Garth Ennis & Steve Dillon
ISBN: 9781852868505

Preacher: Ancient History
Garth Ennis, Steve Pugh, Carlos Ezquerra & Richard Case
ISBN: 9781852869144

Preacher: Dixie Fried
Garth Ennis & Steve Dillon
ISBN: 9781852869830

Preacher: War in the Sun
Garth Ennis & Steve Dillon
ISBN: 9781840230741

Preacher: Salvation
Garth Ennis & Steve Dillon
ISBN: 9781840231045

Preacher: All Hell's A-Coming
Garth Ennis & Steve Dillon
ISBN: 9781840231489

Preacher: Alamo
Garth Ennis & Steve Dillon
ISBN: 9781840232691

Preacher: Dead or Alive — The Collected Covers
Garth Ennis & Steve Dillon
ISBN: 9781840232899

Pride & Joy
Garth Ennis & John Higgins
ISBN: 9781840238037

Transmetropolitan: Back on the Street
Warren Ellis & Darick Robertson
ISBN: 9781840232585

Transmetropolitan: Lust For Life
Warren Ellis & Darick Robertson
ISBN: 9781840233124

Transmetropolitan: Year of the Bastard
Warren Ellis & Darick Robertson
ISBN: 9781840232936

Transmetropolitan: The New Scum
Warren Ellis & Darick Robertson
ISBN: 9781840232172

Transmetropolitan: Lonely City
Warren Ellis & Darick Robertson
ISBN: 9781840232967

Transmetropolitan: Gouge Away
Warren Ellis & Darick Robertson
ISBN: 9781840233940

Transmetropolitan: Spider's Thrash
Warren Ellis & Darick Robertson
ISBN: 9781840234572

Transmetropolitan: Dirge
Warren Ellis & Darick Robertson
ISBN: 9781840236309

Transmetropolitan: The Cure
Warren Ellis & Darick Robertson
ISBN: 9781840237122

Transmetropolitan: One More Time
Warren Ellis & Darick Robertson
ISBN: 9781840238259

War Stories Vol. 1
Garth Ennis, Chris Weston, Gary Erskine, John Higgins, Dave Gibbons & David Lloyd
ISBN: 9781840239123

War Stories Vol. 2
Garth Ennis, David Lloyd, Cam Kennedy, Carlos Ezquerra & Gary Erskine
ISBN: 9781845763068

To find more collected editions from Titan Books, please visit our website:

WWW.TITANBOOKS.COM

Poor bastard...